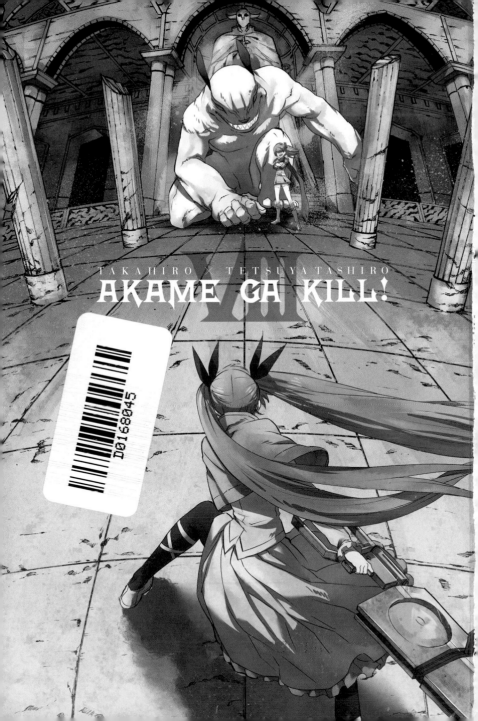

TAKAHIRO × TETSUYA TASHIRO

# AKAME GA KILL!

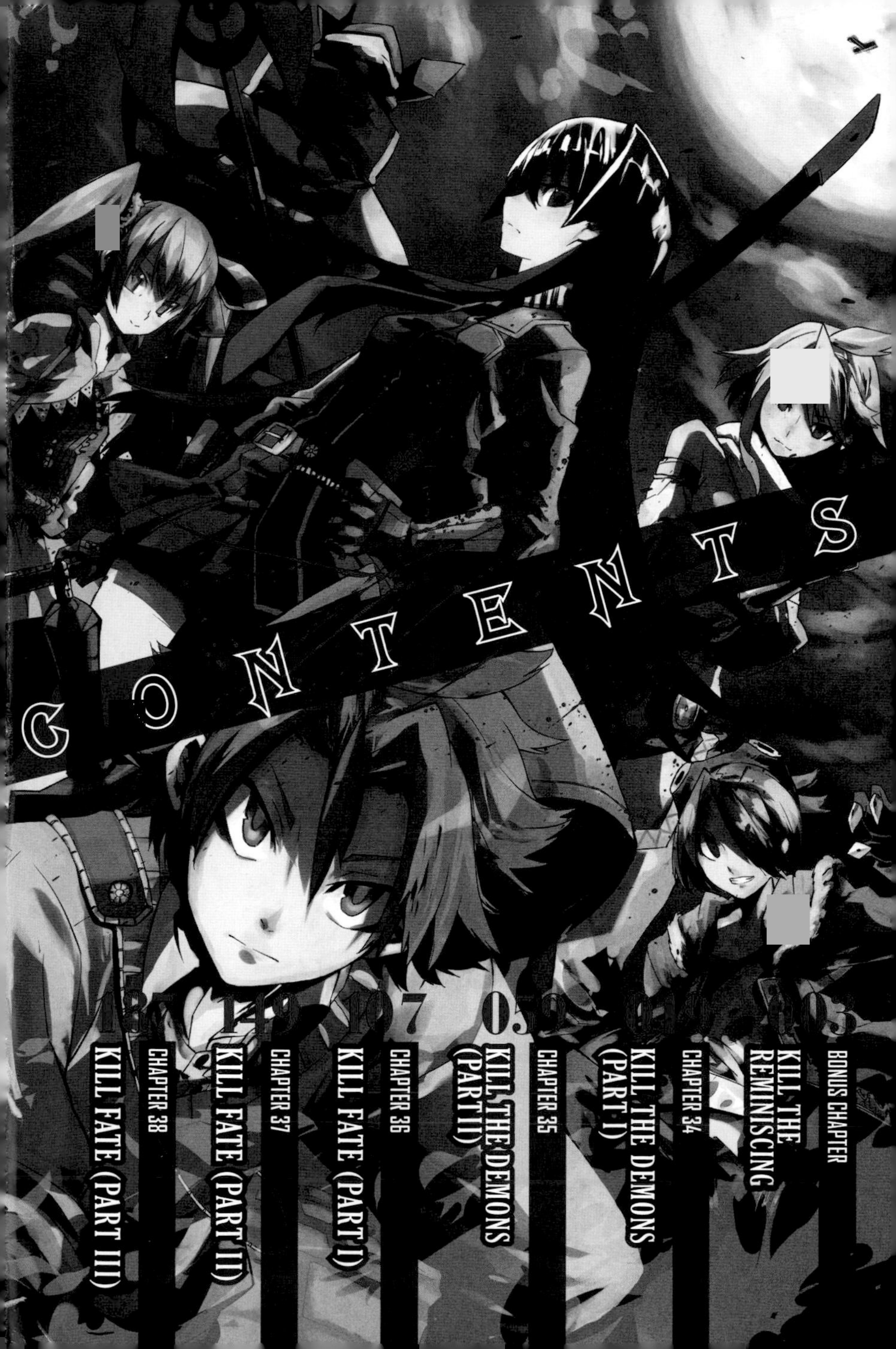

# CONTENTS

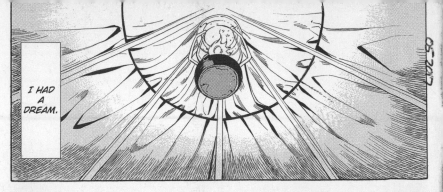

I HAD A DREAM.

...MEM-ORIES OF THE PAST.

THESE ARE...

BONUS CHAPTER –
KILL THE REMINISCING

# MEMORIES OF SHEELE

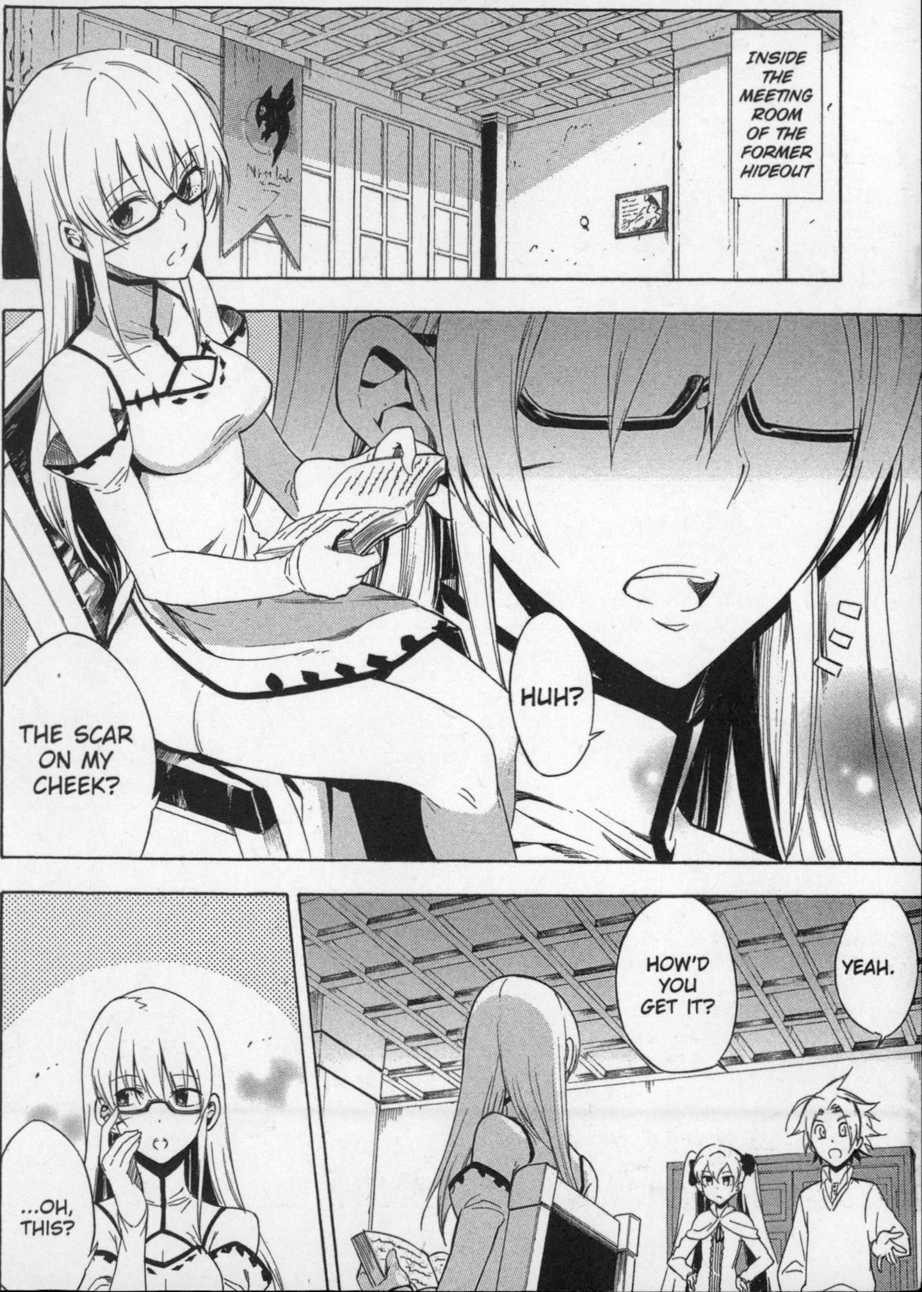
INSIDE THE MEETING ROOM OF THE FORMER HIDEOUT
HUH?
THE SCAR ON MY CHEEK?
YEAH.
HOW'D YOU GET IT?
...OH, THIS?

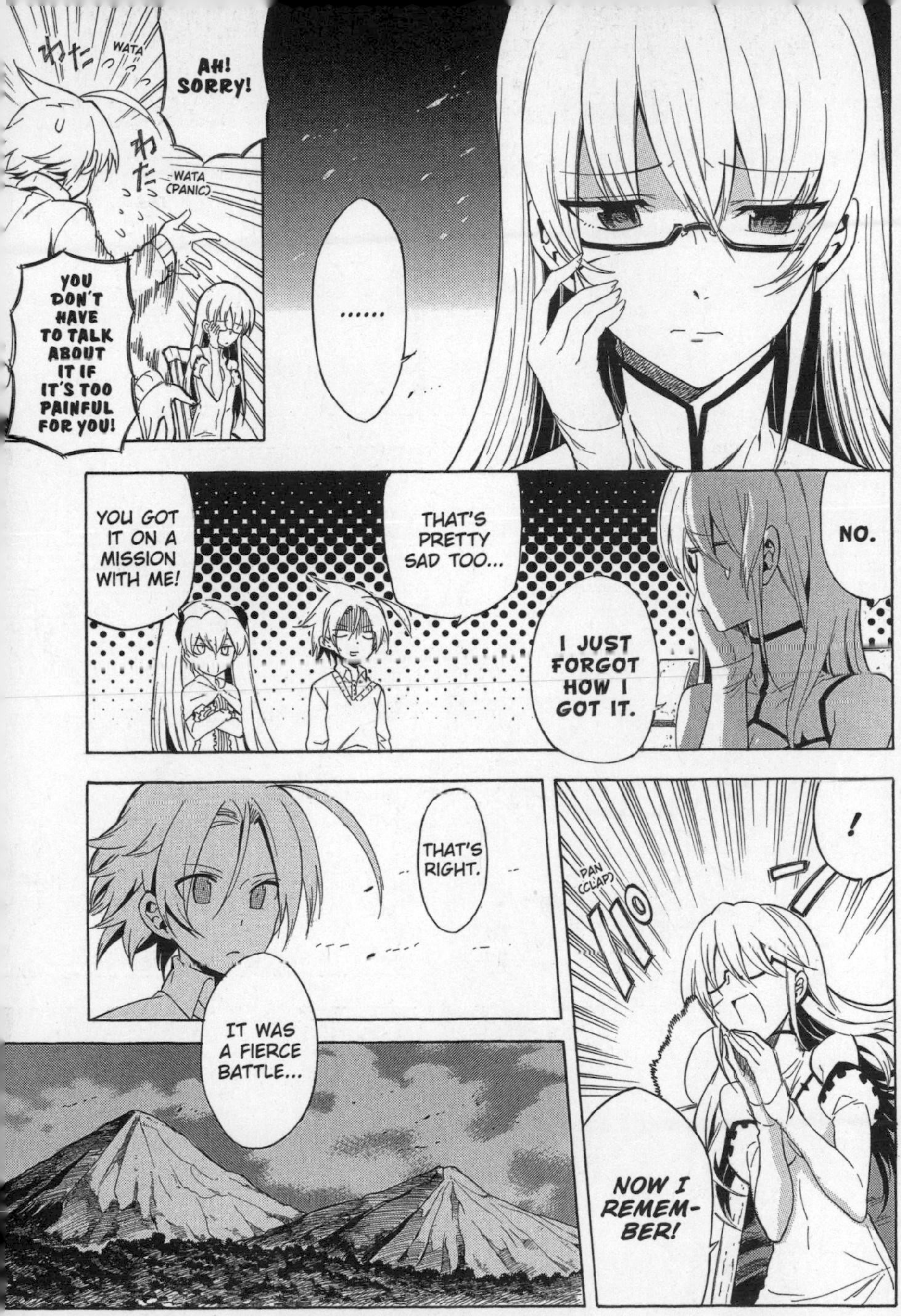
......
わた
WATA
AH! SORRY!
わた
WATA (PANIC)
YOU DON'T HAVE TO TALK ABOUT IT IF IT'S TOO PAINFUL FOR YOU!
NO.
I JUST FORGOT HOW I GOT IT.
THAT'S PRETTY SAD TOO...
YOU GOT IT ON A MISSION WITH ME!
!
PAN (CLAP)
NOW I REMEMBER!
THAT'S RIGHT.
IT WAS A FIERCE BATTLE...

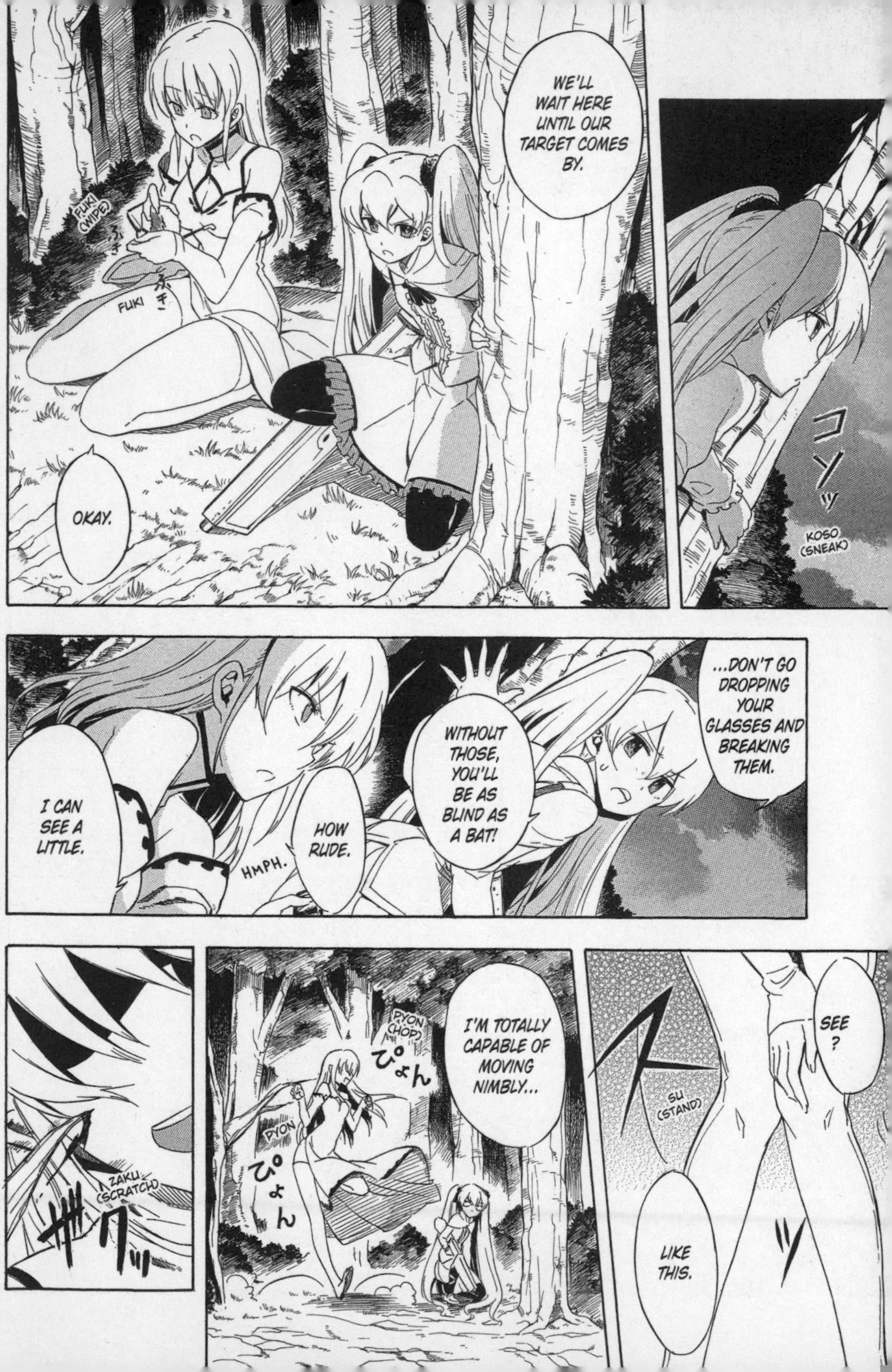
KOSO (SNEAK)
WE'LL WAIT HERE UNTIL OUR TARGET COMES BY.
FUKI (WIPE)
ふき
FUKI
ふき
OKAY.
...DON'T GO DROPPING YOUR GLASSES AND BREAKING THEM.
WITHOUT THOSE, YOU'LL BE AS BLIND AS A BAT!
HOW RUDE.
HMPH.
I CAN SEE A LITTLE.
SEE?
SU (STAND)
LIKE THIS.
I'M TOTALLY CAPABLE OF MOVING NIMBLY...
PYON (HOP)
ぴょん
PYON
ぴょん
ZAKU (SCRATCH)

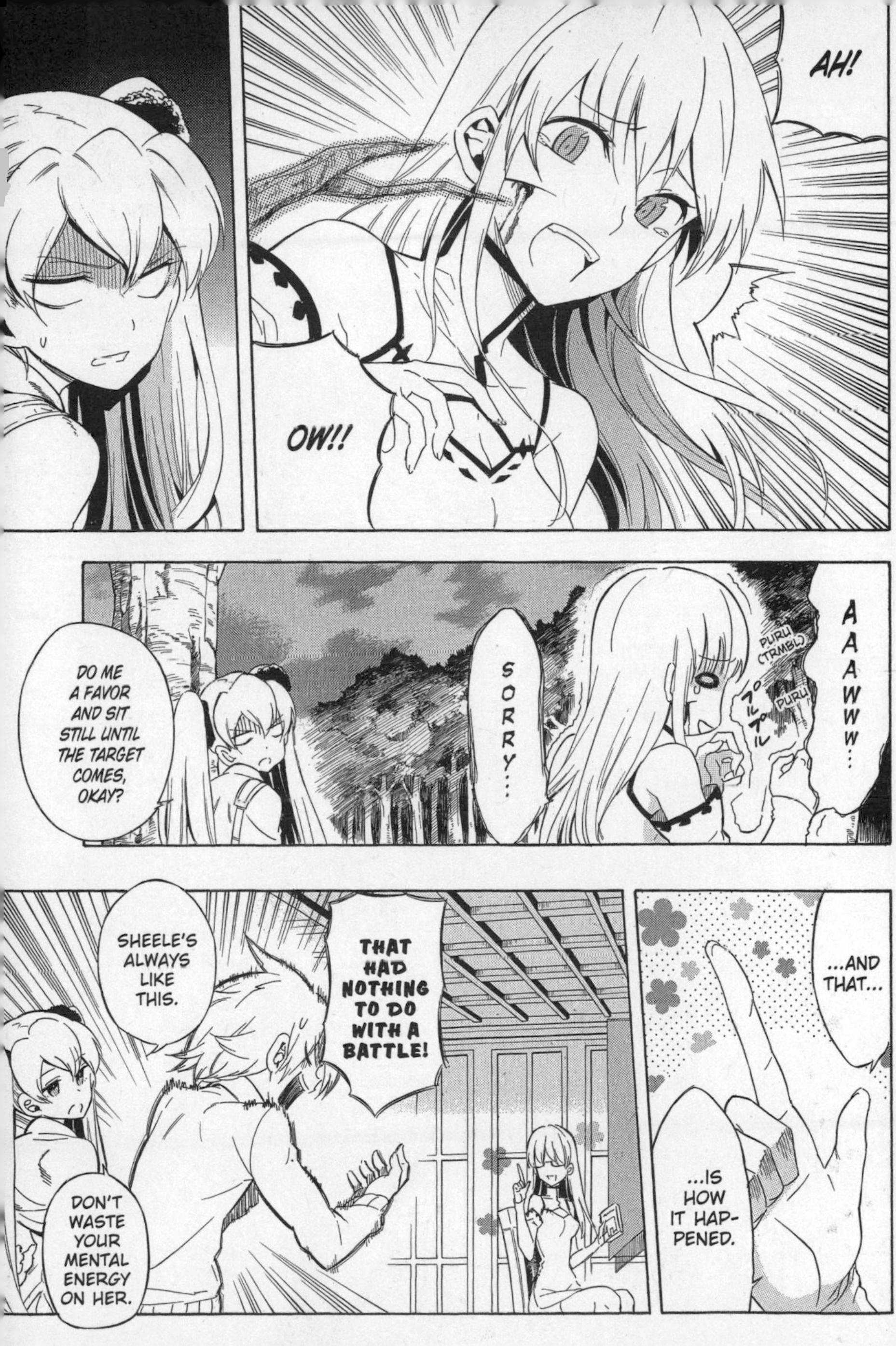
AH!
OW!!
AAAAWWW...
PURU (TRMBL)
プルプル
PURU
SORRY...
DO ME A FAVOR AND SIT STILL UNTIL THE TARGET COMES, OKAY?
...AND THAT...
...IS HOW IT HAPPENED.
THAT HAD NOTHING TO DO WITH A BATTLE!
SHEELE'S ALWAYS LIKE THIS.
DON'T WASTE YOUR MENTAL ENERGY ON HER.

# MEMORIES OF BULAT

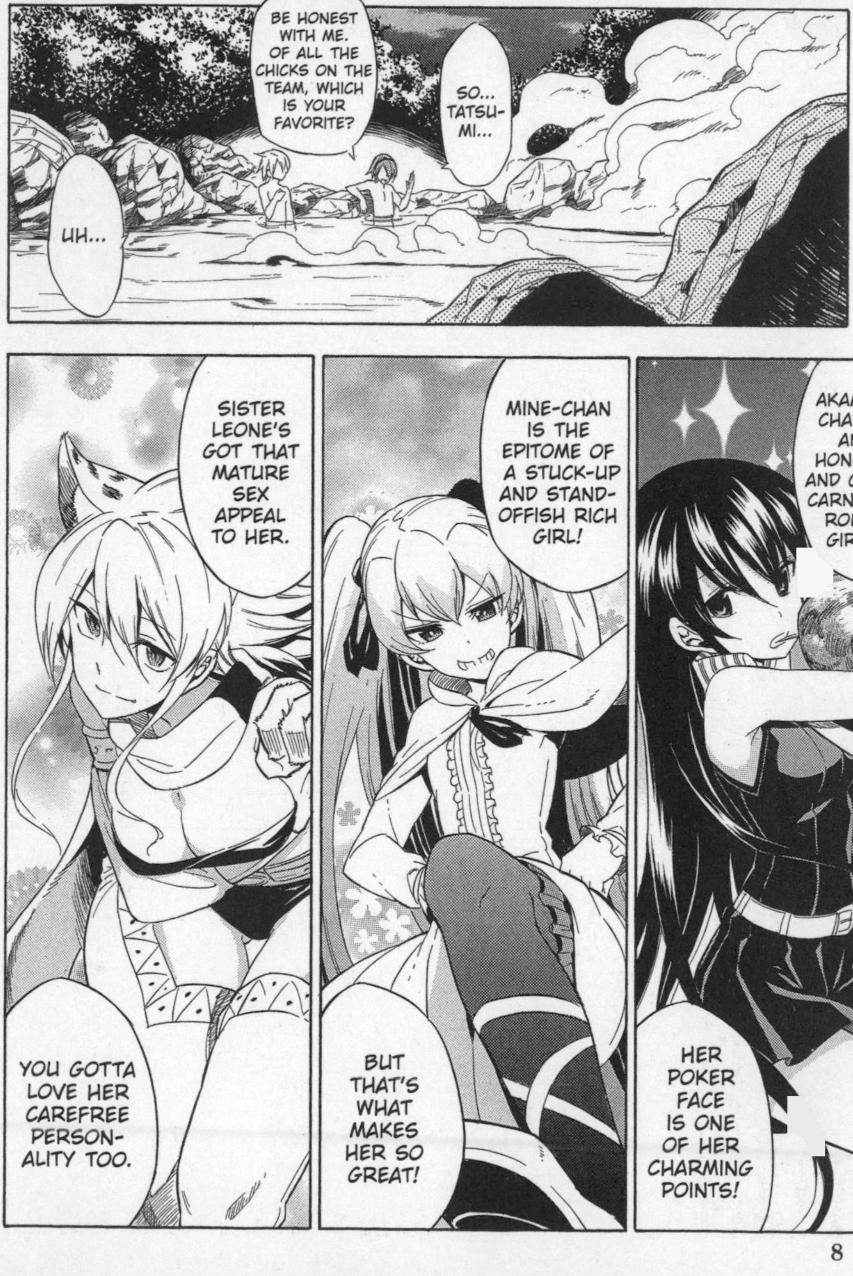

SO... TATSUMI...
BE HONEST WITH ME. OF ALL THE CHICKS ON THE TEAM, WHICH IS YOUR FAVORITE?
UH...
AKAME-CHAN'S AN HONEST AND COOL CARNIVO-ROUS GIRL.
HER POKER FACE IS ONE OF HER CHARMING POINTS!
MINE-CHAN IS THE EPITOME OF A STUCK-UP AND STAND-OFFISH RICH GIRL!
BUT THAT'S WHAT MAKES HER SO GREAT!
SISTER LEONE'S GOT THAT MATURE SEX APPEAL TO HER.
YOU GOTTA LOVE HER CAREFREE PERSON-ALITY TOO.

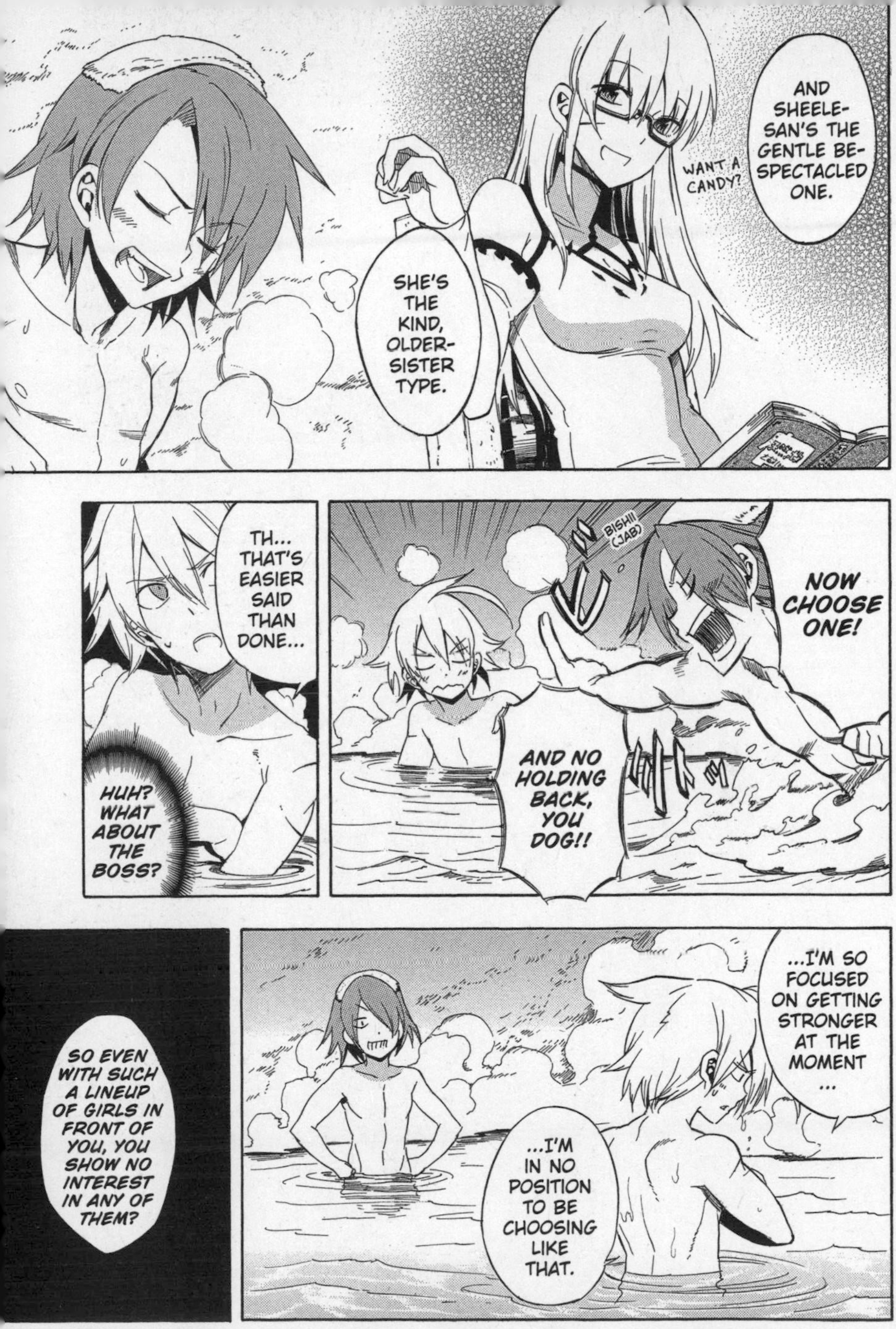
AND SHEELE-SAN'S THE GENTLE BE-SPECTACLED ONE.
WANT A CANDY?
SHE'S THE KIND, OLDER-SISTER TYPE.
NOW CHOOSE ONE!
BISHI (JAB)
AND NO HOLDING BACK, YOU DOG!!
TH... THAT'S EASIER SAID THAN DONE...
HUH? WHAT ABOUT THE BOSS?
...I'M SO FOCUSED ON GETTING STRONGER AT THE MOMENT ...
...I'M IN NO POSITION TO BE CHOOSING LIKE THAT.
SO EVEN WITH SUCH A LINEUP OF GIRLS IN FRONT OF YOU, YOU SHOW NO INTEREST IN ANY OF THEM?

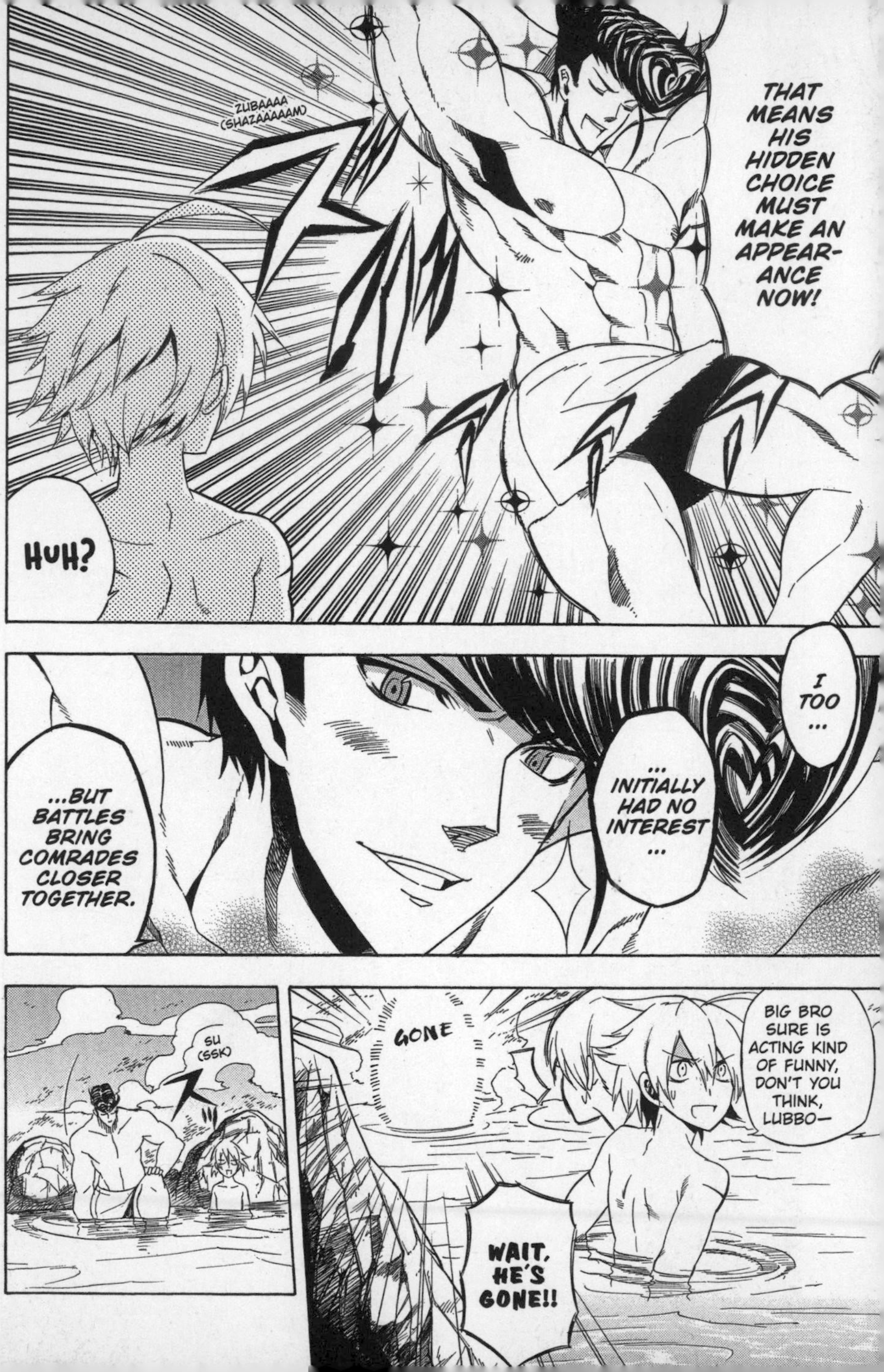
THAT MEANS HIS HIDDEN CHOICE MUST MAKE AN APPEARANCE NOW!
ZUBAAAA (SHAZAAAAAM)
HUH?
I TOO...
...INITIALLY HAD NO INTEREST...
...BUT BATTLES BRING COMRADES CLOSER TOGETHER.
BIG BRO SURE IS ACTING KIND OF FUNNY, DON'T YOU THINK, LUBBO—
GONE
WAIT, HE'S GONE!!
SU (SSK)

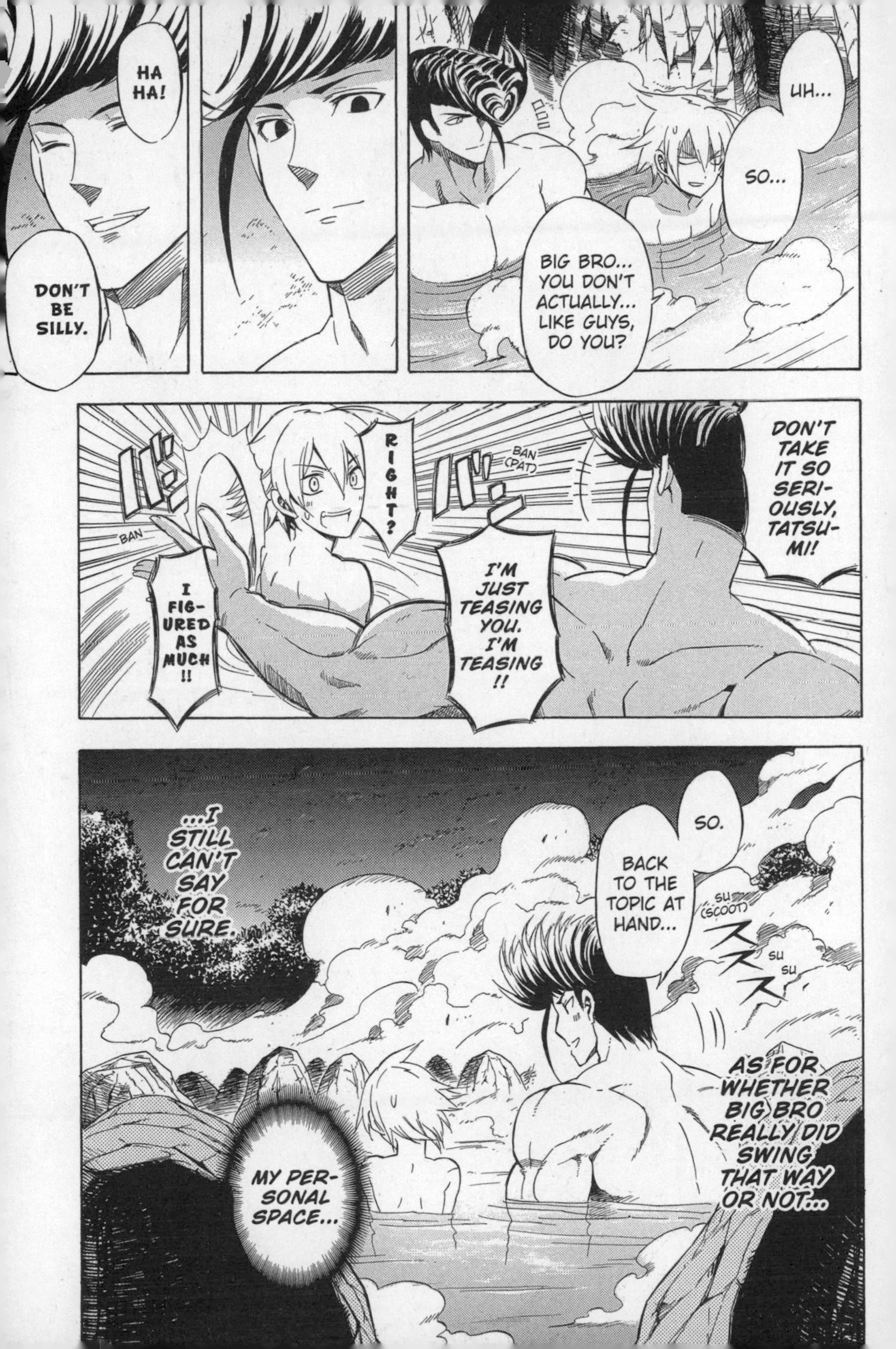
UH...
SO...
BIG BRO... YOU DON'T ACTUALLY... LIKE GUYS, DO YOU?
HA HA!
DON'T BE SILLY.
DON'T TAKE IT SO SERIOUSLY, TATSUMI!
BAN (PAT)
I'M JUST TEASING YOU. I'M TEASING!!
RIGHT?
BAN
I FIGURED AS MUCH!!
SO.
BACK TO THE TOPIC AT HAND...
SU (SCOOT)
SU
SU
AS FOR WHETHER BIG BRO REALLY DID SWING THAT WAY OR NOT...
...I STILL CAN'T SAY FOR SURE.
MY PERSONAL SPACE...

# MEMORIES OF CHELSEA

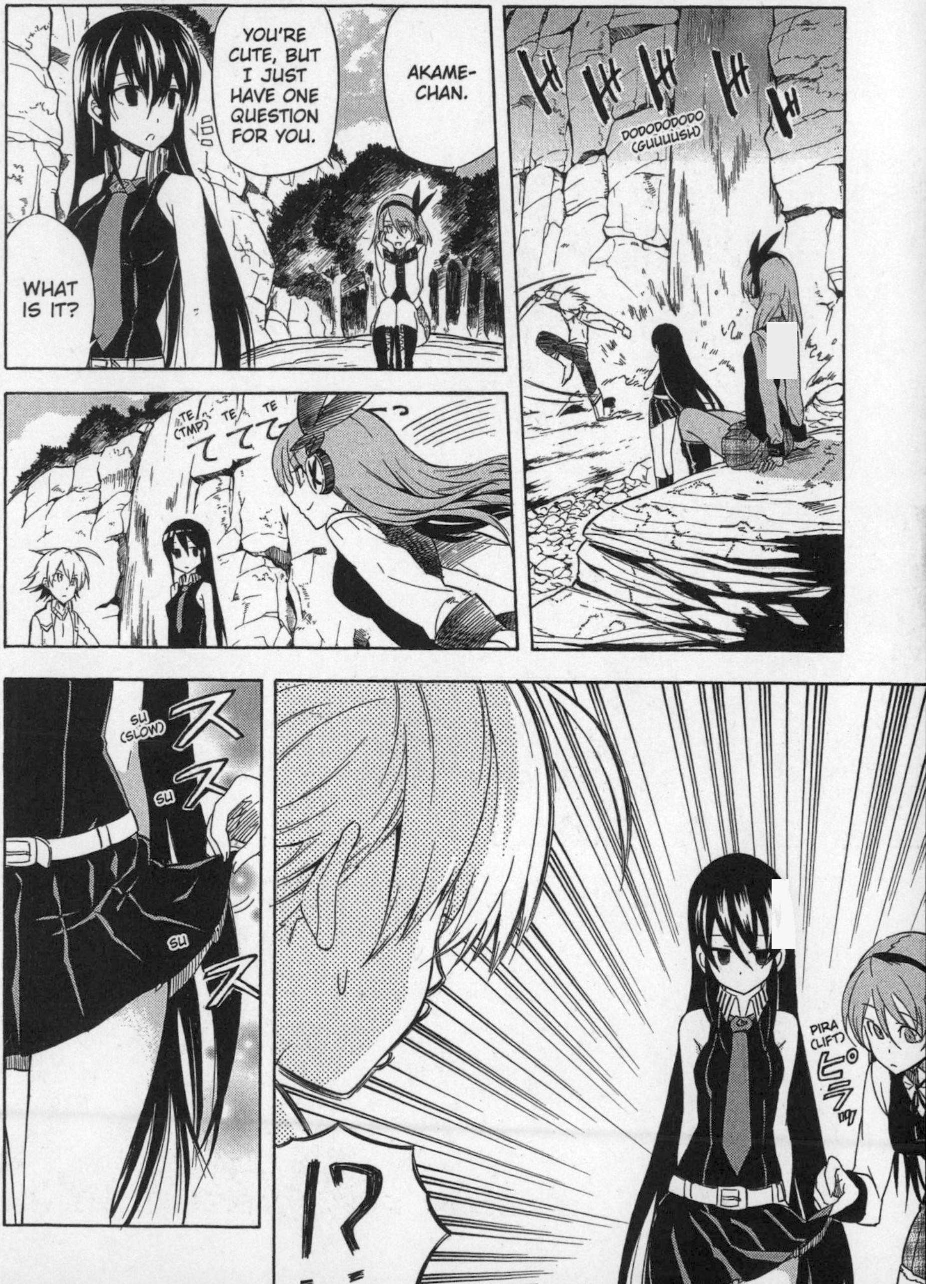
DODODODODO (GUUUUSH)
AKAME-CHAN.
YOU'RE CUTE, BUT I JUST HAVE ONE QUESTION FOR YOU.
WHAT IS IT?
TE (TMP) TE TE
てててー
PIRA (LIFT)
ピラ
!?
SU (SLOW)
ス
SU
ス
SU
ス

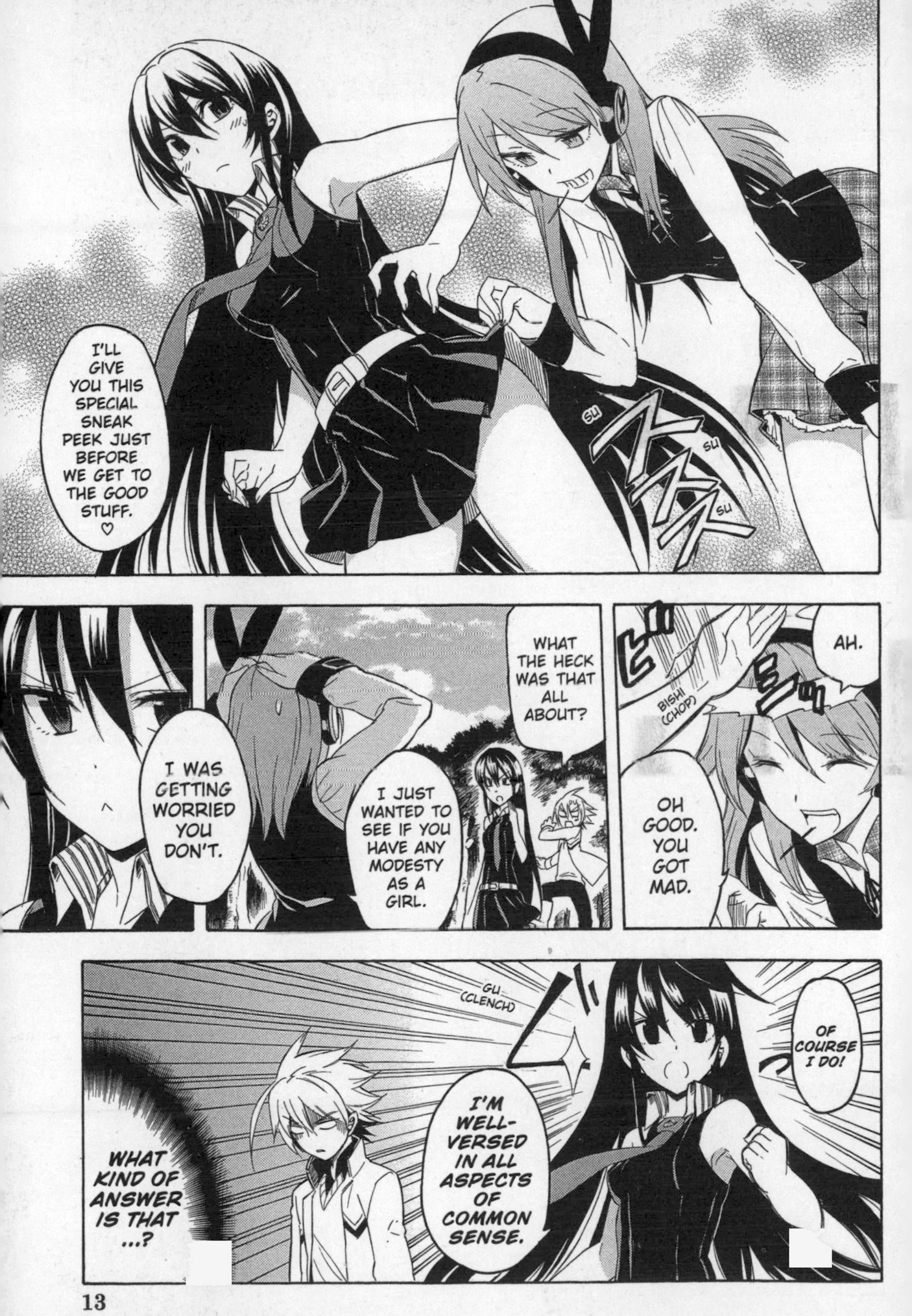
I'LL GIVE YOU THIS SPECIAL SNEAK PEEK JUST BEFORE WE GET TO THE GOOD STUFF. ♡
SU
SU
SU
AH.
BISHI (CHOP)
OH GOOD. YOU GOT MAD.
WHAT THE HECK WAS THAT ALL ABOUT?
I JUST WANTED TO SEE IF YOU HAVE ANY MODESTY AS A GIRL.
I WAS GETTING WORRIED YOU DON'T.
OF COURSE I DO!
GU (CLENCH)
I'M WELL-VERSED IN ALL ASPECTS OF COMMON SENSE.
WHAT KIND OF ANSWER IS THAT ...?

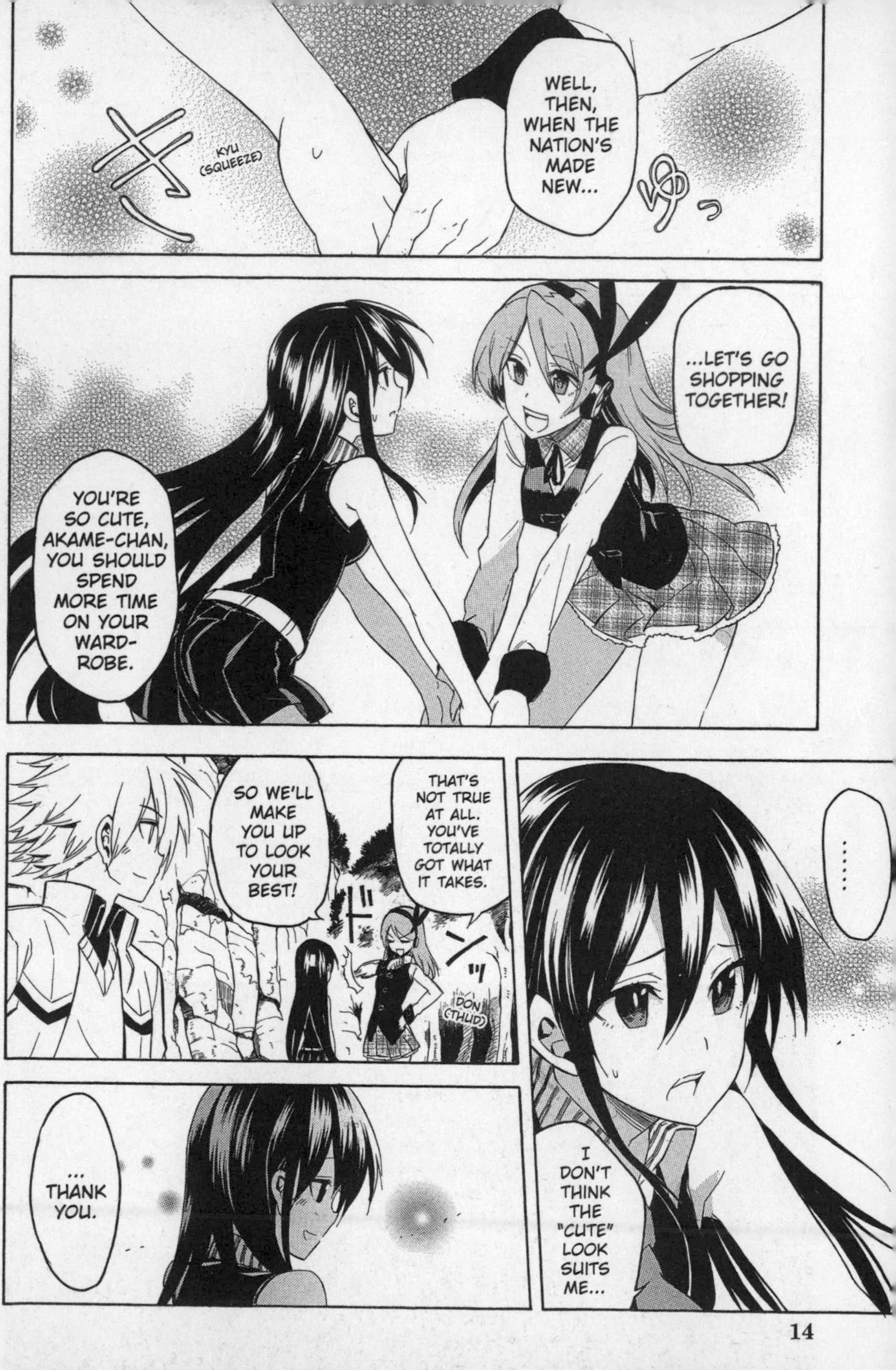
WELL, THEN, WHEN THE NATION'S MADE NEW...
KYU (SQUEEZE)
...LET'S GO SHOPPING TOGETHER!
YOU'RE SO CUTE, AKAME-CHAN, YOU SHOULD SPEND MORE TIME ON YOUR WARD-ROBE.
......
I DON'T THINK THE "CUTE" LOOK SUITS ME...
THAT'S NOT TRUE AT ALL. YOU'VE TOTALLY GOT WHAT IT TAKES.
SO WE'LL MAKE YOU UP TO LOOK YOUR BEST!
DON (THUD)
... THANK YOU.

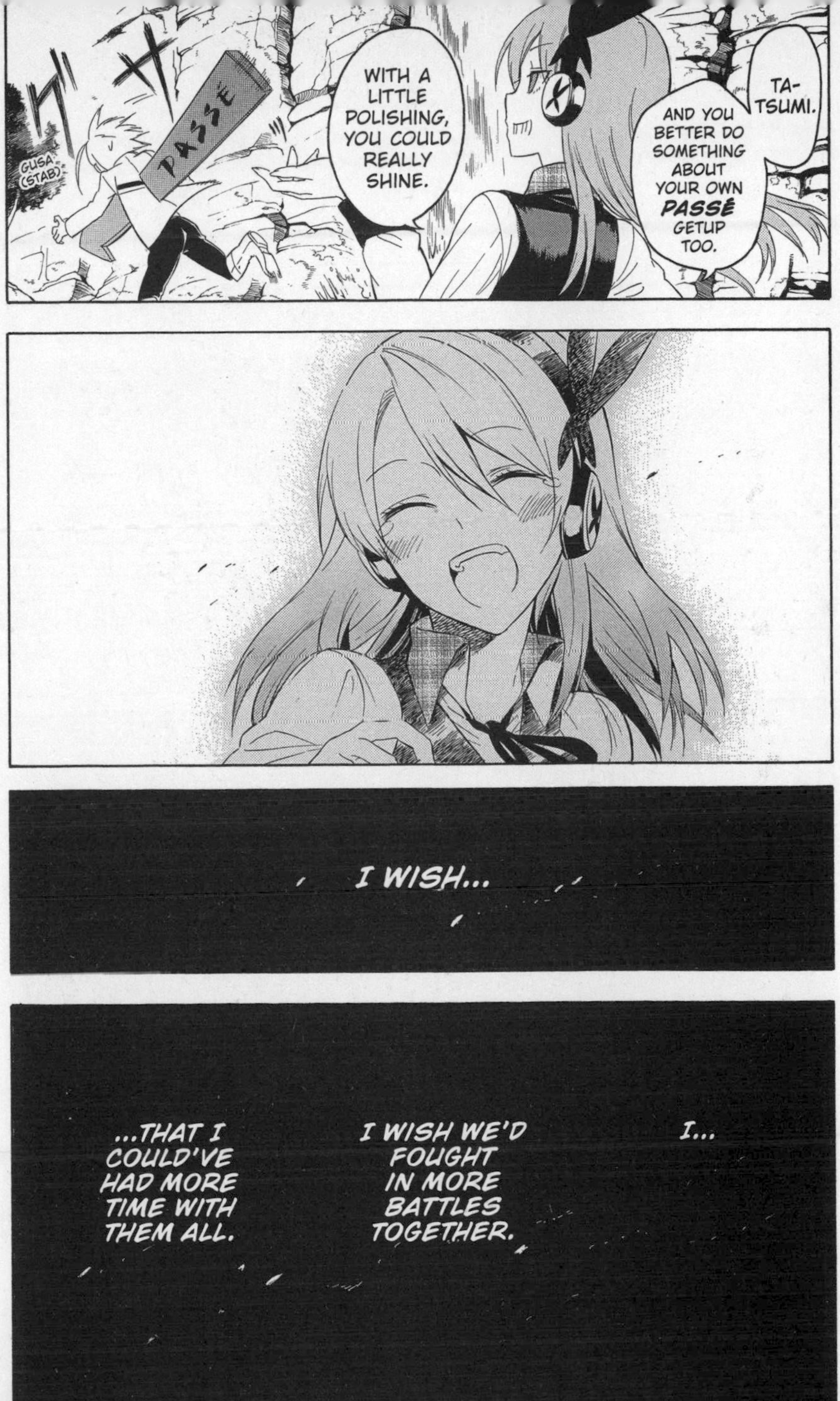
TA-TSUMI.
WITH A LITTLE POLISHING, YOU COULD REALLY SHINE.
AND YOU BETTER DO SOMETHING ABOUT YOUR OWN PASSÉ GETUP TOO.
PASSÉ
GUSA (STAB)
I WISH...
I...
I WISH WE'D FOUGHT IN MORE BATTLES TOGETHER.
...THAT I COULD'VE HAD MORE TIME WITH THEM ALL.

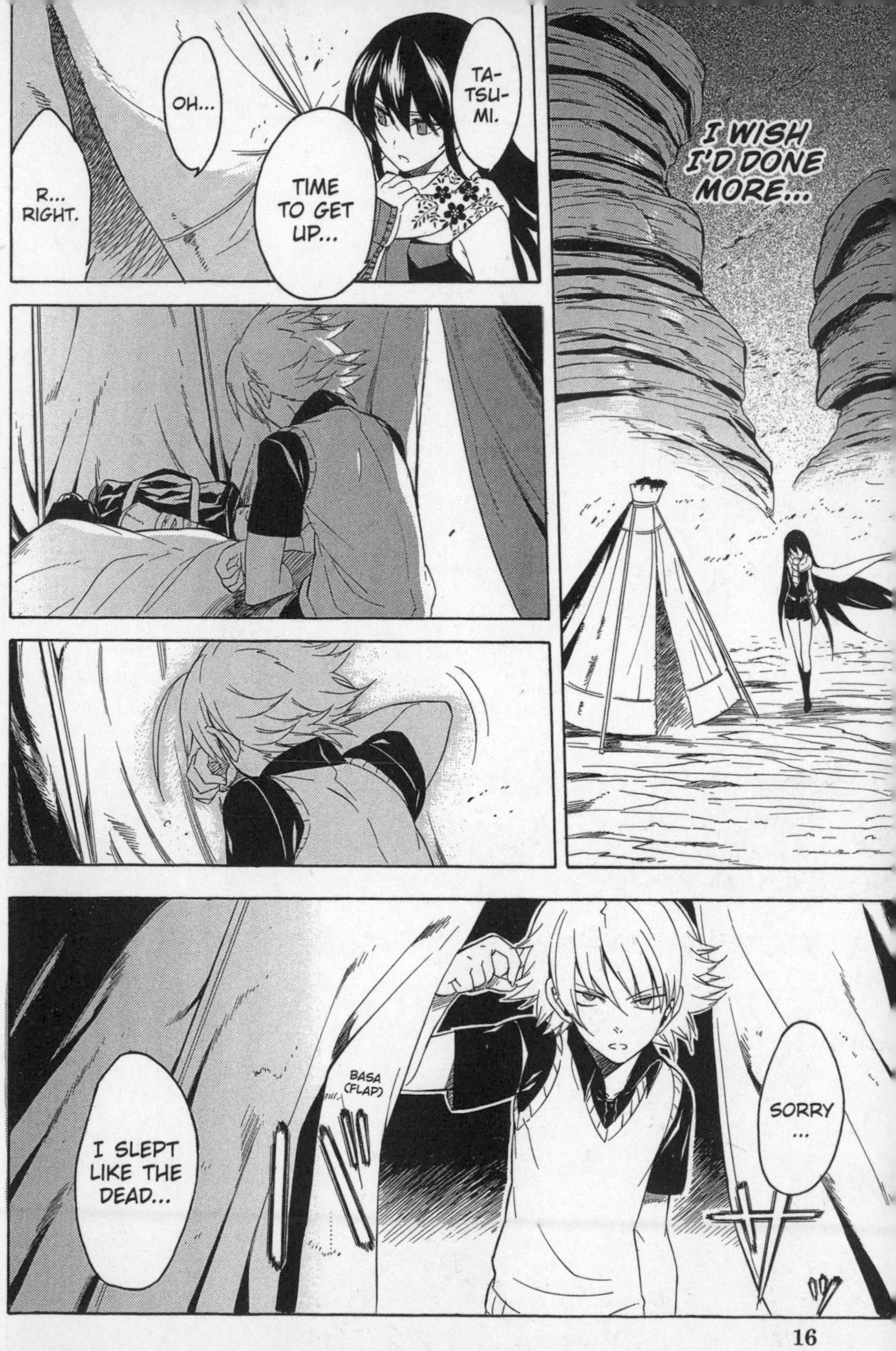

I WISH I'D DONE MORE...
TA-TSU-MI.
TIME TO GET UP...
OH...
R... RIGHT.
SORRY...
BASA (FLAP)
I SLEPT LIKE THE DEAD...

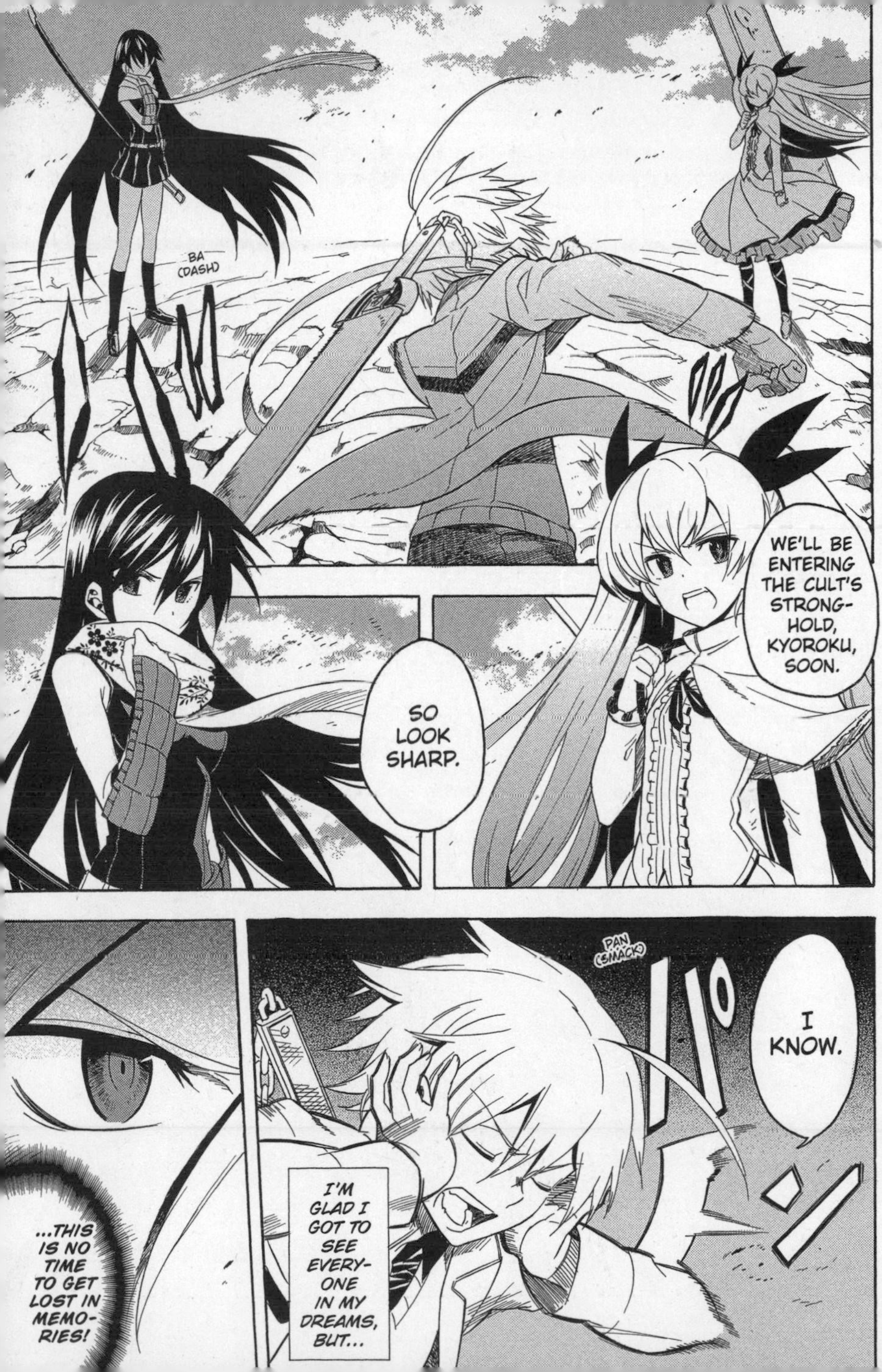
BA (DASH)
WE'LL BE ENTERING THE CULT'S STRONGHOLD, KYOROKU, SOON.
SO LOOK SHARP.
PAN (SMACK)
I KNOW.
I'M GLAD I GOT TO SEE EVERYONE IN MY DREAMS, BUT...
...THIS IS NO TIME TO GET LOST IN MEMORIES!

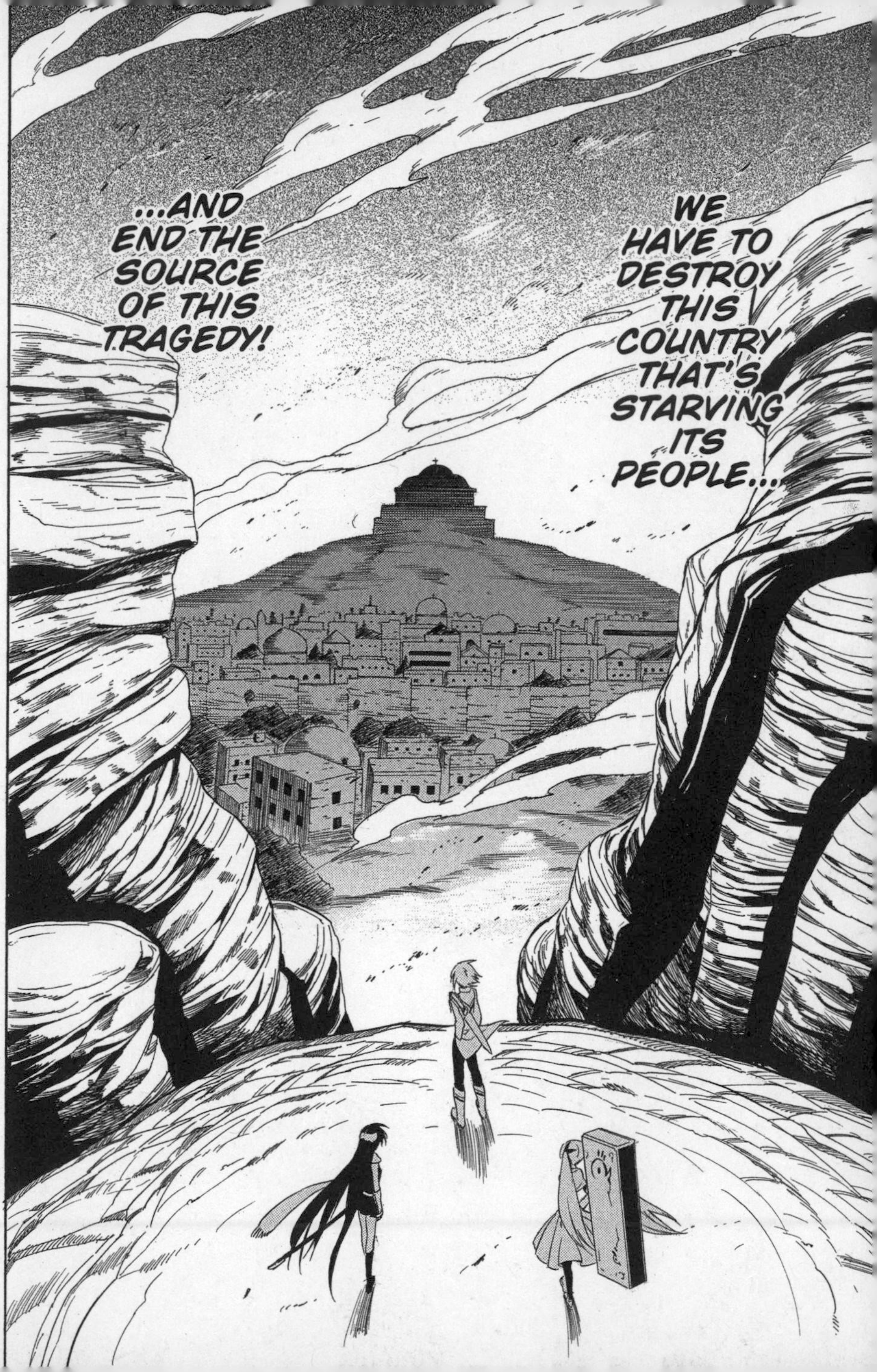
WE HAVE TO DESTROY THIS COUNTRY THAT'S STARVING ITS PEOPLE...
...AND END THE SOURCE OF THIS TRAGEDY!

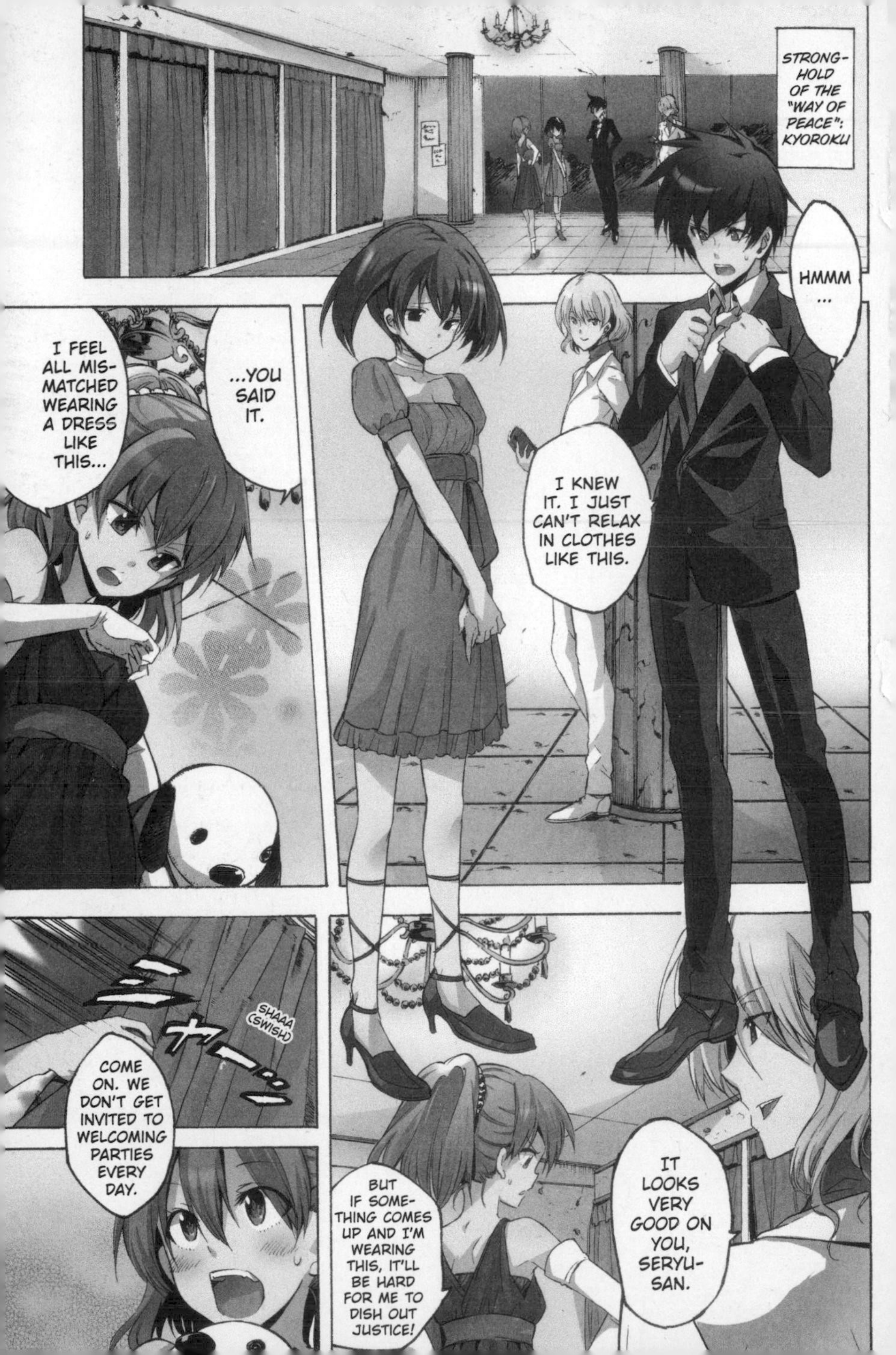

STRONGHOLD OF THE "WAY OF PEACE": KYOROKU
HMMM...
I KNEW IT. I JUST CAN'T RELAX IN CLOTHES LIKE THIS.
...YOU SAID IT.
I FEEL ALL MISMATCHED WEARING A DRESS LIKE THIS...
IT LOOKS VERY GOOD ON YOU, SERYU-SAN.
BUT IF SOMETHING COMES UP AND I'M WEARING THIS, IT'LL BE HARD FOR ME TO DISH OUT JUSTICE!
SHAAA (SWISH)
COME ON. WE DON'T GET INVITED TO WELCOMING PARTIES EVERY DAY.

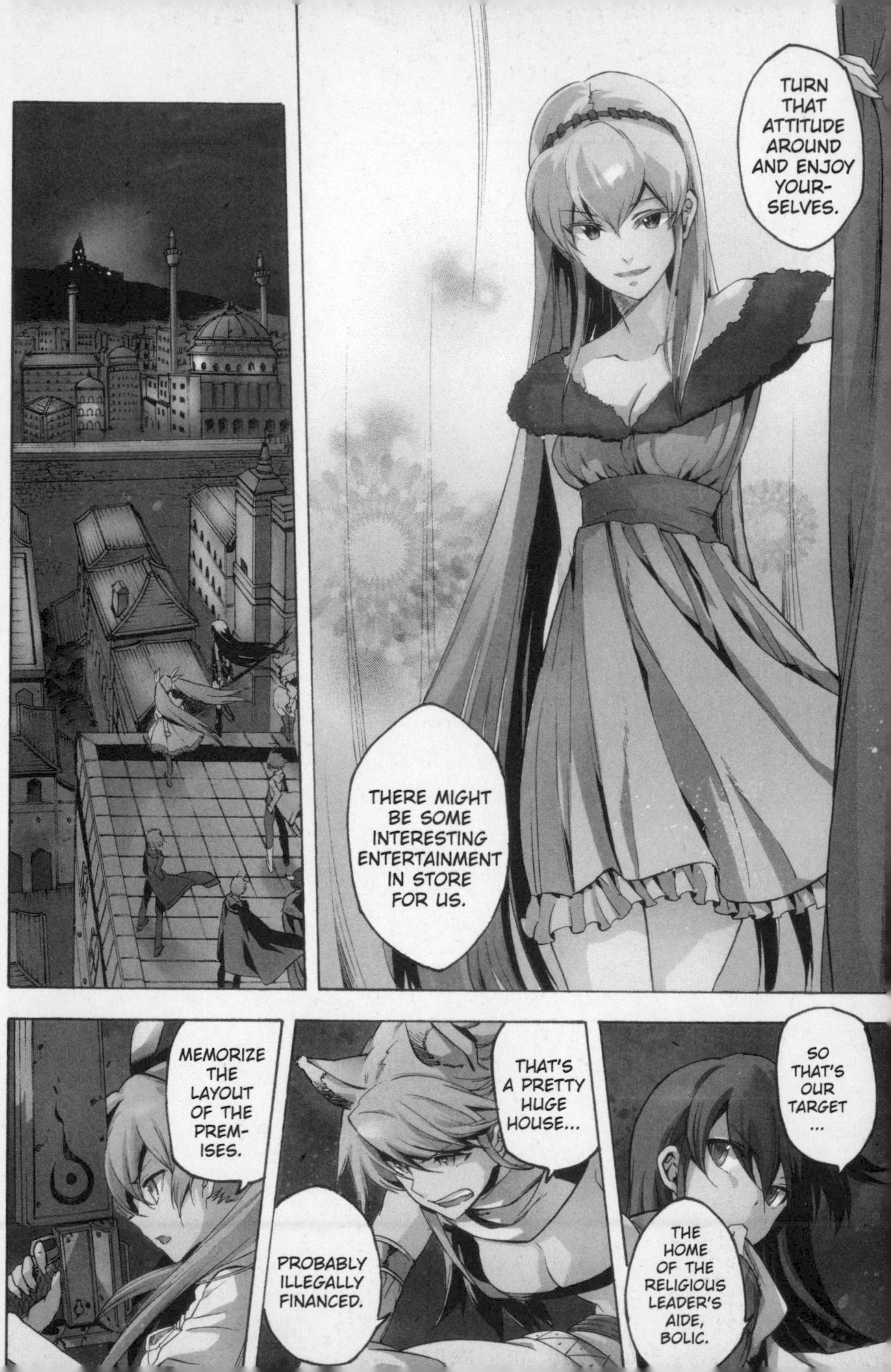
TURN THAT ATTITUDE AROUND AND ENJOY YOURSELVES.
THERE MIGHT BE SOME INTERESTING ENTERTAINMENT IN STORE FOR US.
SO THAT'S OUR TARGET ...
THE HOME OF THE RELIGIOUS LEADER'S AIDE, BOLIC.
THAT'S A PRETTY HUGE HOUSE...
PROBABLY ILLEGALLY FINANCED.
MEMORIZE THE LAYOUT OF THE PREMISES.

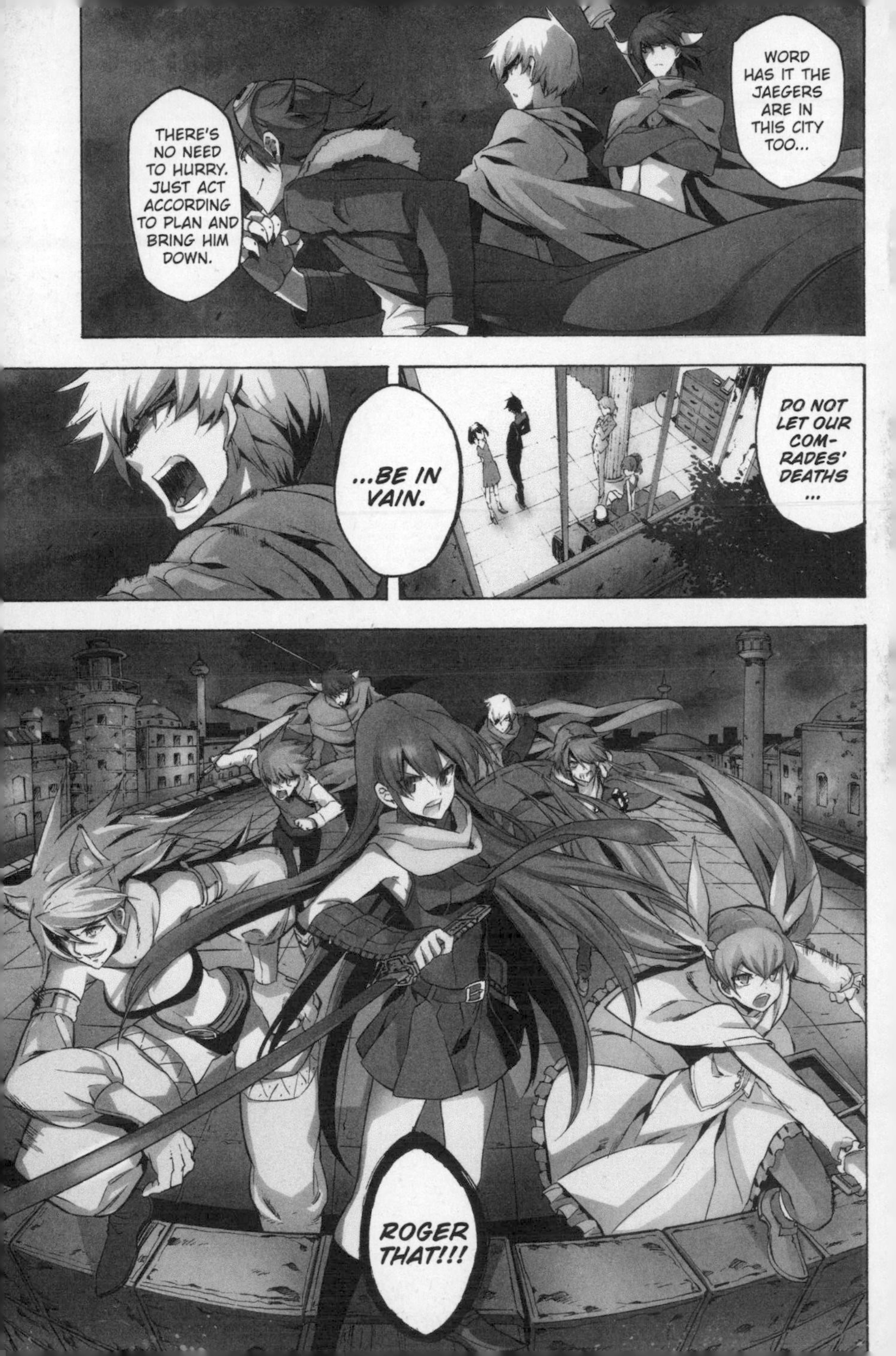
WORD HAS IT THE JAEGERS ARE IN THIS CITY TOO...
THERE'S NO NEED TO HURRY. JUST ACT ACCORDING TO PLAN AND BRING HIM DOWN.
DO NOT LET OUR COM-RADES' DEATHS ...
...BE IN VAIN.
ROGER THAT!!!

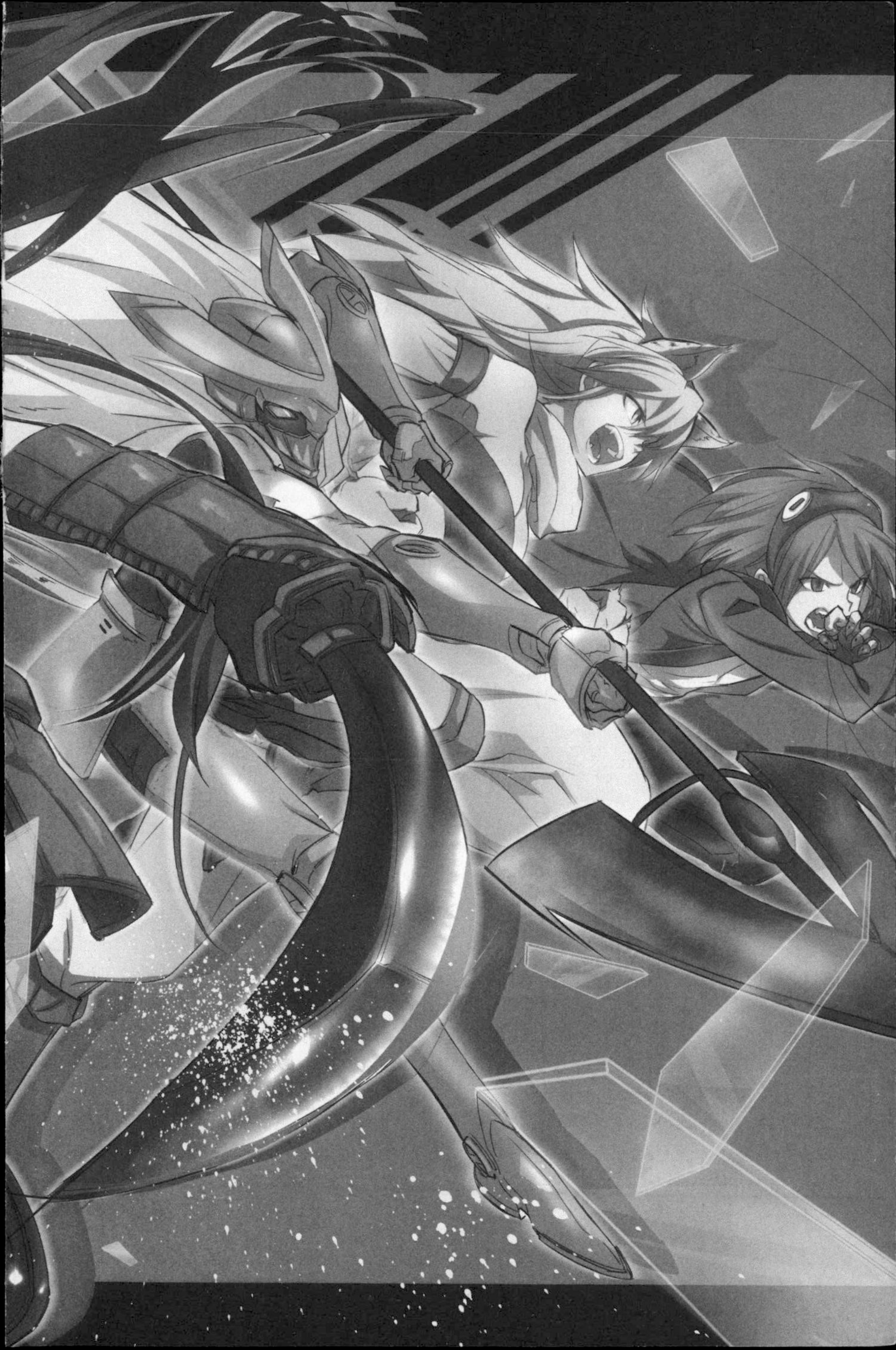

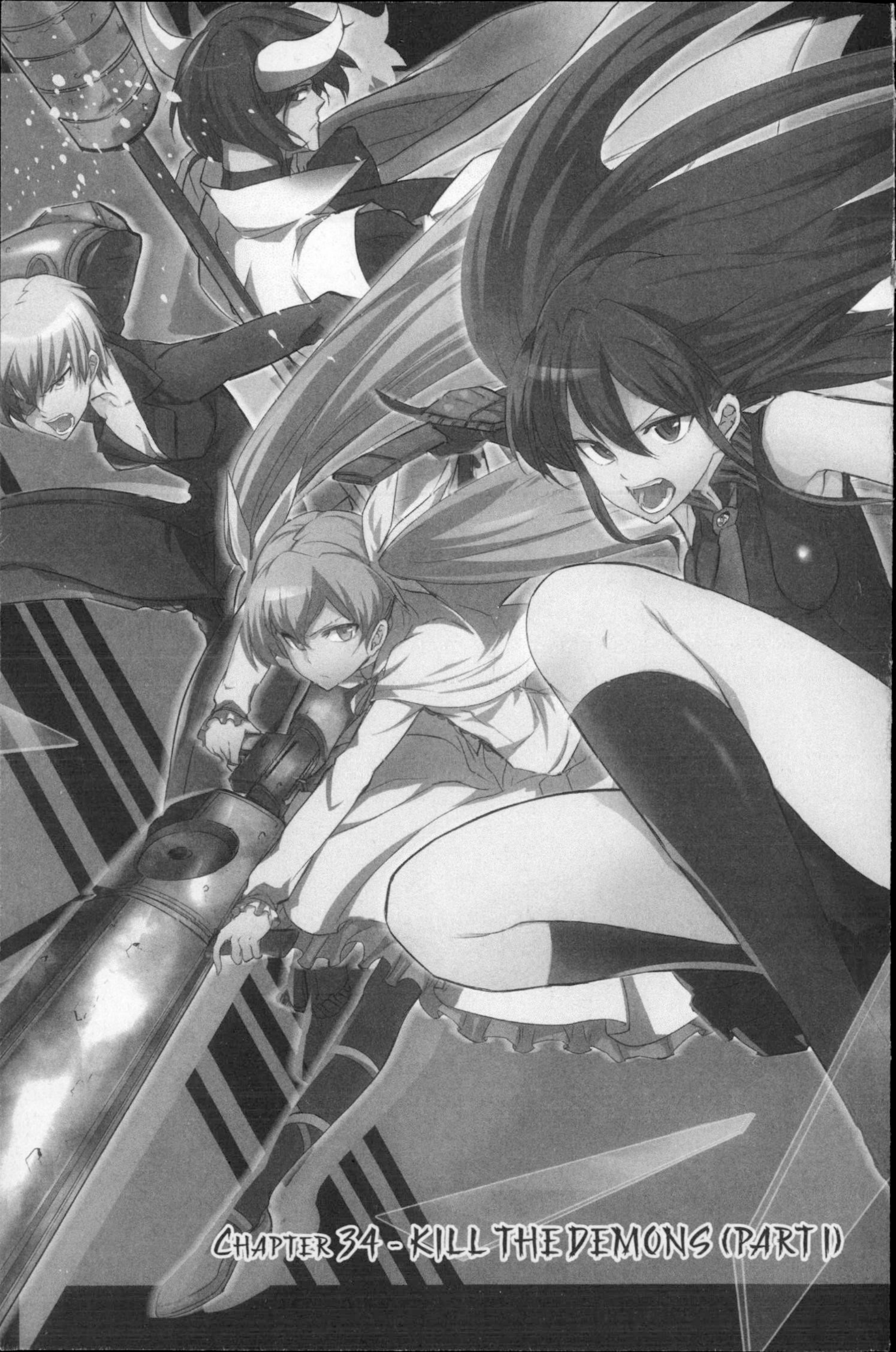
Chapter 34 - Kill the Demons (Part 1)

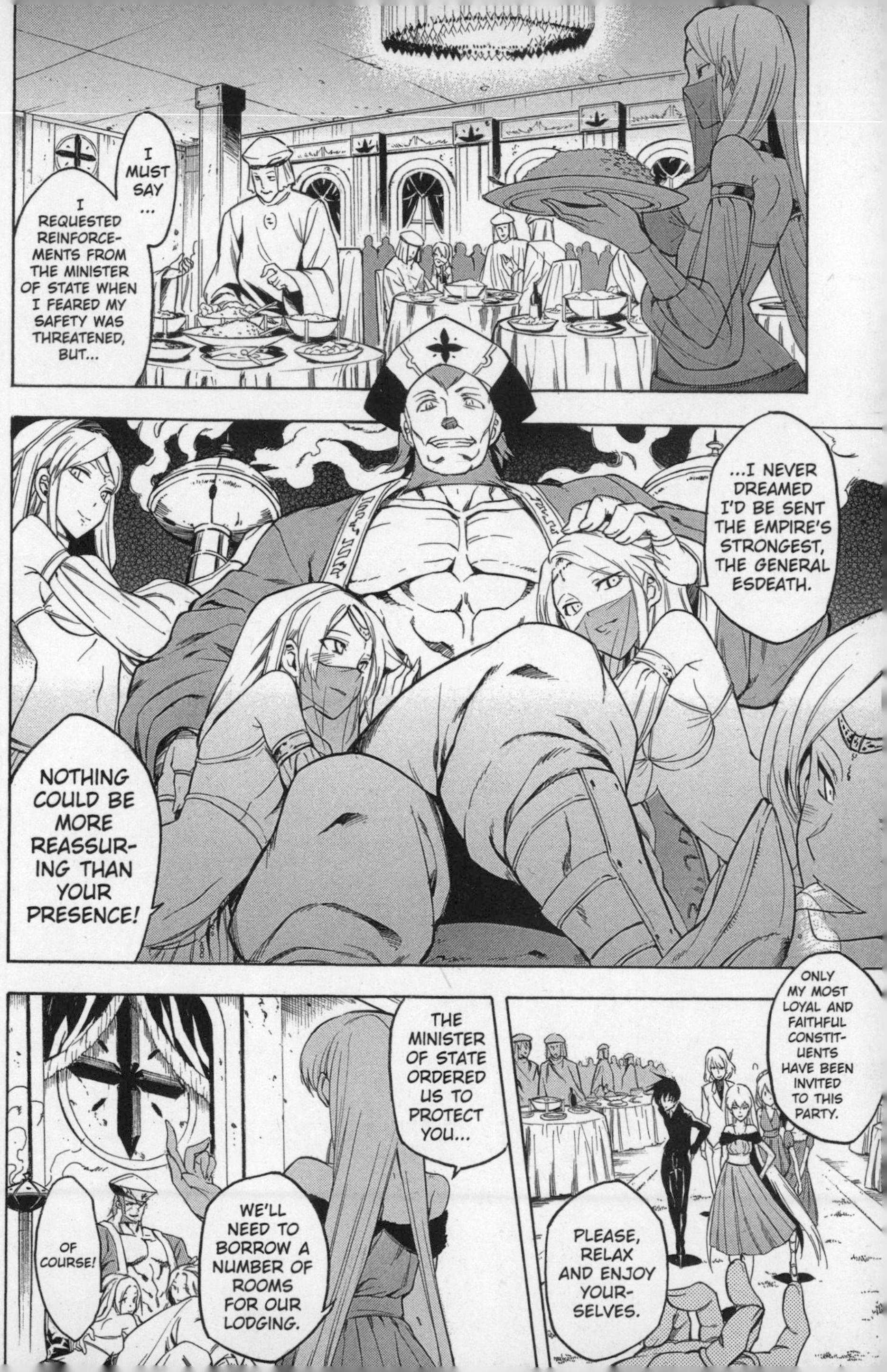
I MUST SAY...
I REQUESTED REINFORCEMENTS FROM THE MINISTER OF STATE WHEN I FEARED MY SAFETY WAS THREATENED, BUT...
...I NEVER DREAMED I'D BE SENT THE EMPIRE'S STRONGEST, THE GENERAL ESDEATH.
NOTHING COULD BE MORE REASSURING THAN YOUR PRESENCE!
ONLY MY MOST LOYAL AND FAITHFUL CONSTITUENTS HAVE BEEN INVITED TO THIS PARTY.
PLEASE, RELAX AND ENJOY YOURSELVES.
THE MINISTER OF STATE ORDERED US TO PROTECT YOU...
WE'LL NEED TO BORROW A NUMBER OF ROOMS FOR OUR LODGING.
OF COURSE!

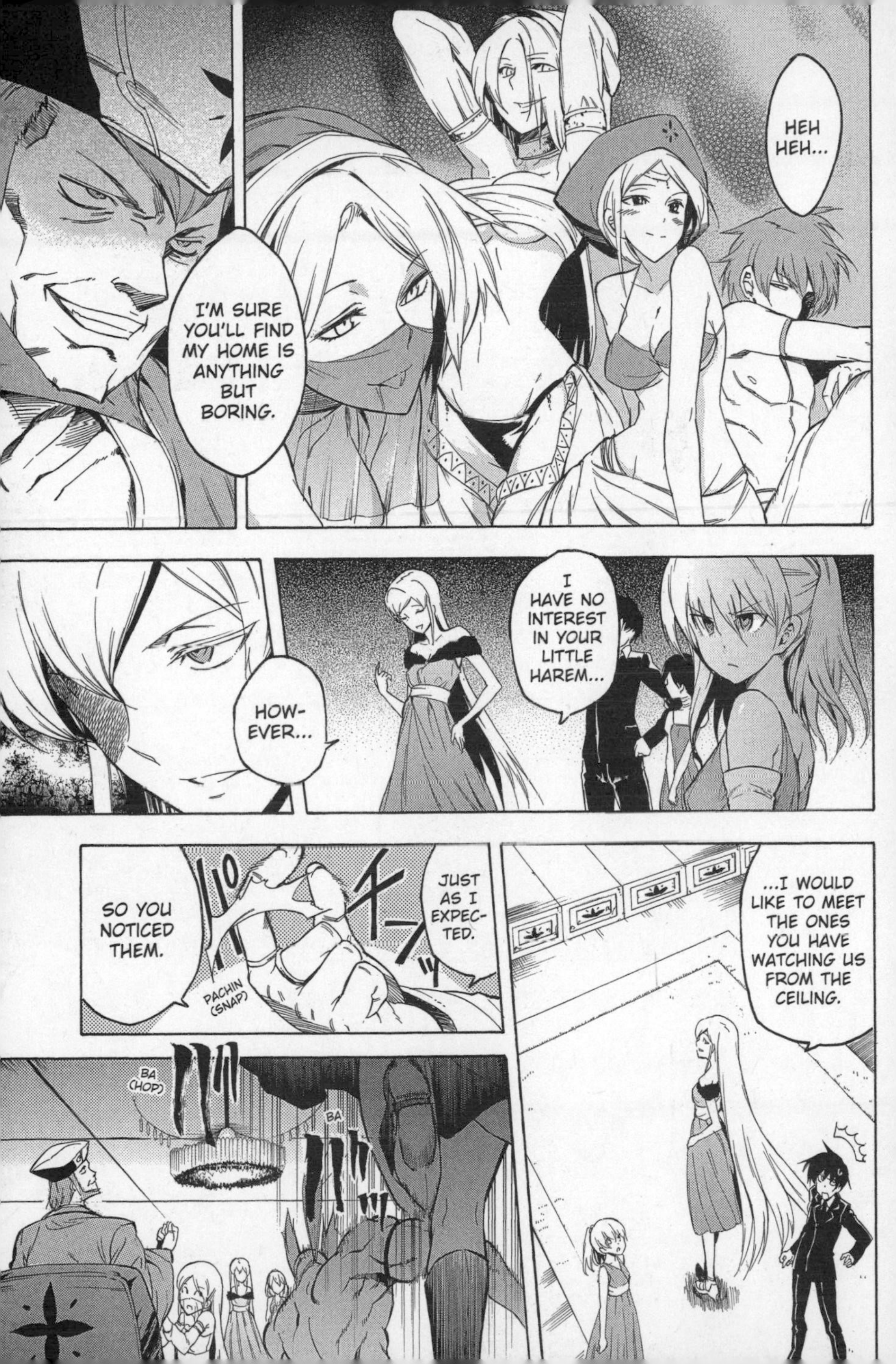
HEH HEH...
I'M SURE YOU'LL FIND MY HOME IS ANYTHING BUT BORING.
I HAVE NO INTEREST IN YOUR LITTLE HAREM...
HOW-EVER...
...I WOULD LIKE TO MEET THE ONES YOU HAVE WATCHING US FROM THE CEILING.
JUST AS I EXPECTED.
PACHIN (SNAP)
SO YOU NOTICED THEM.
BA (HOP)
BA

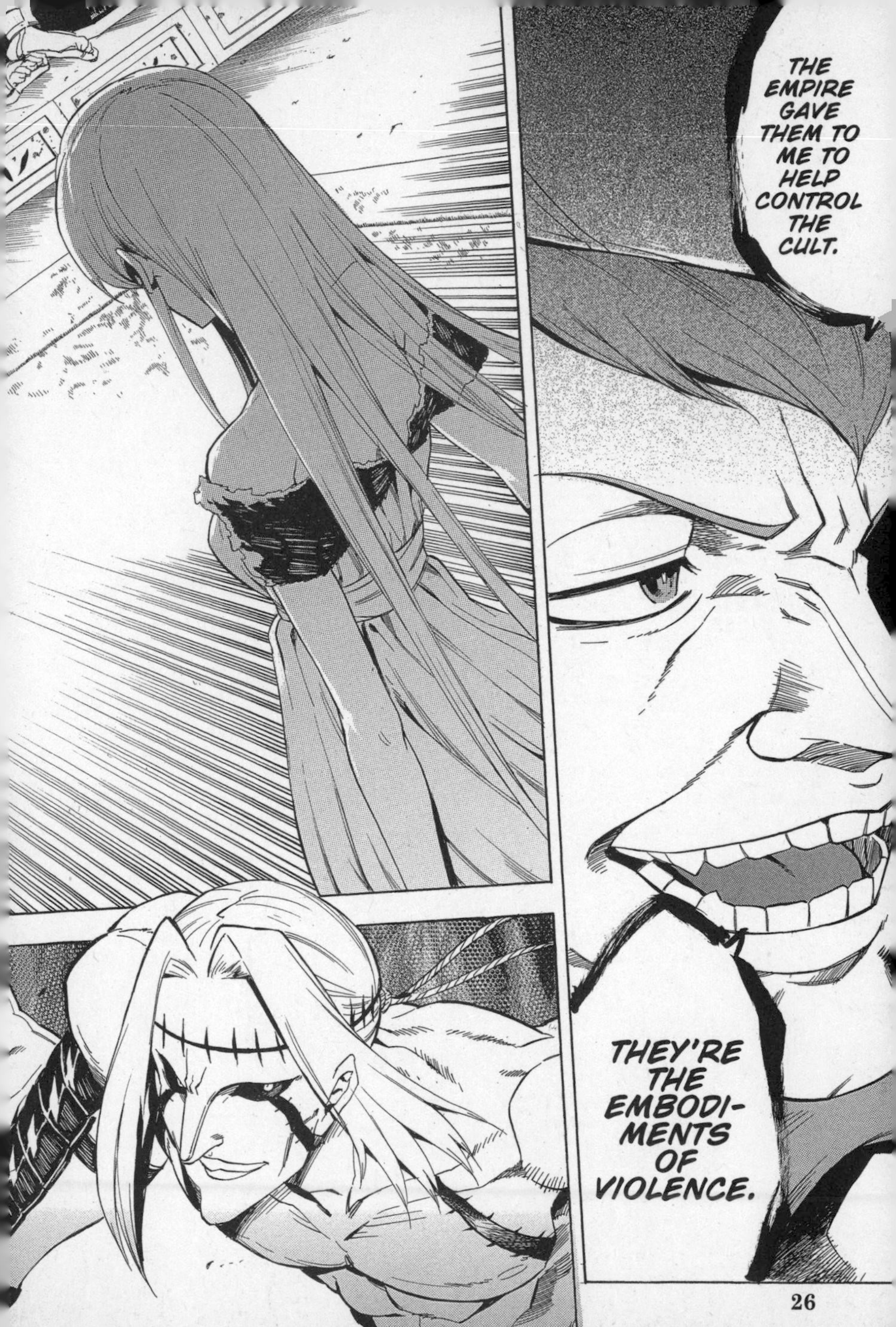
THE EMPIRE GAVE THEM TO ME TO HELP CONTROL THE CULT.
THEY'RE THE EMBODIMENTS OF VIOLENCE.

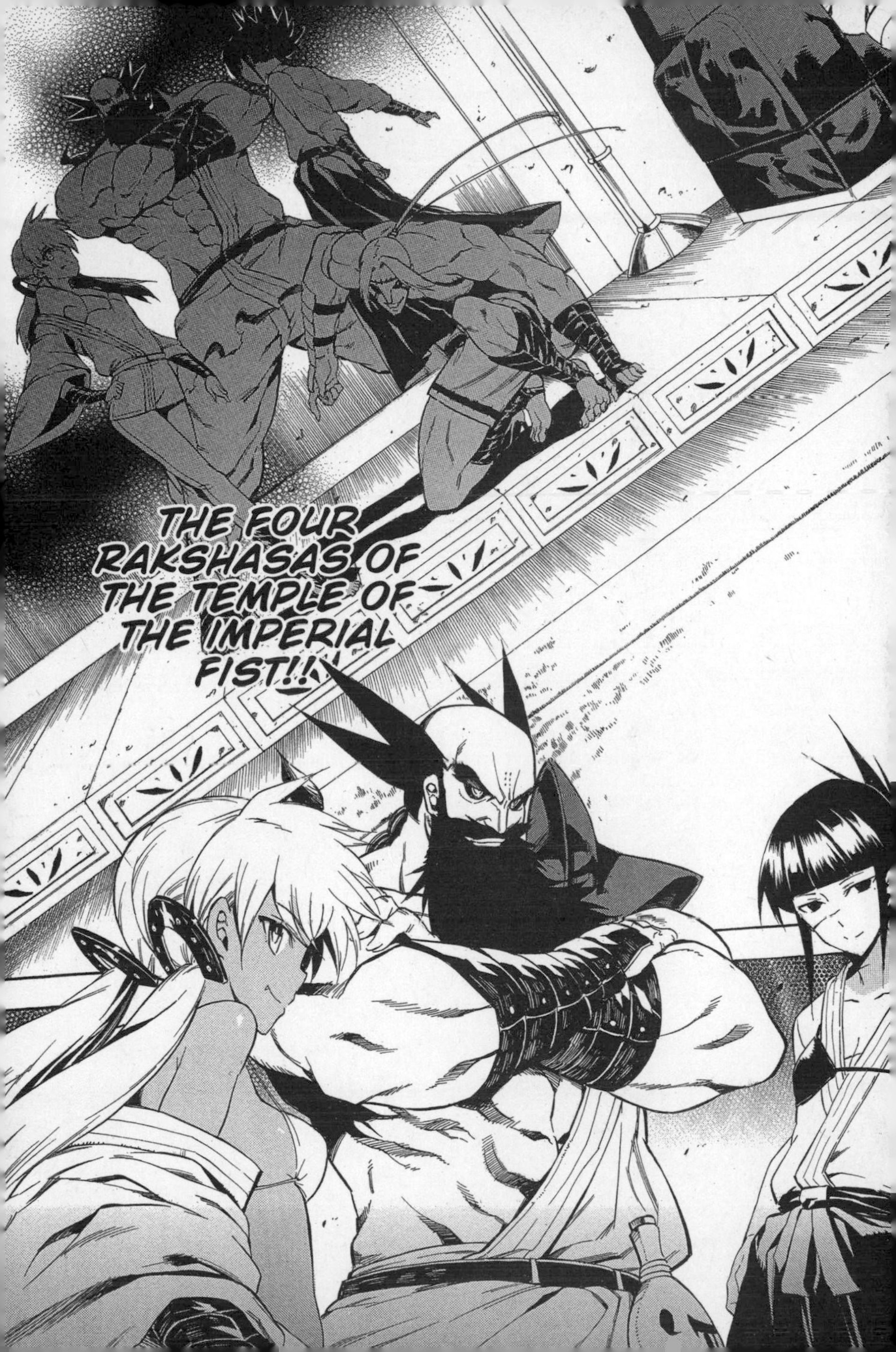
THE FOUR RAKSHASAS OF THE TEMPLE OF THE IMPERIAL FIST!!

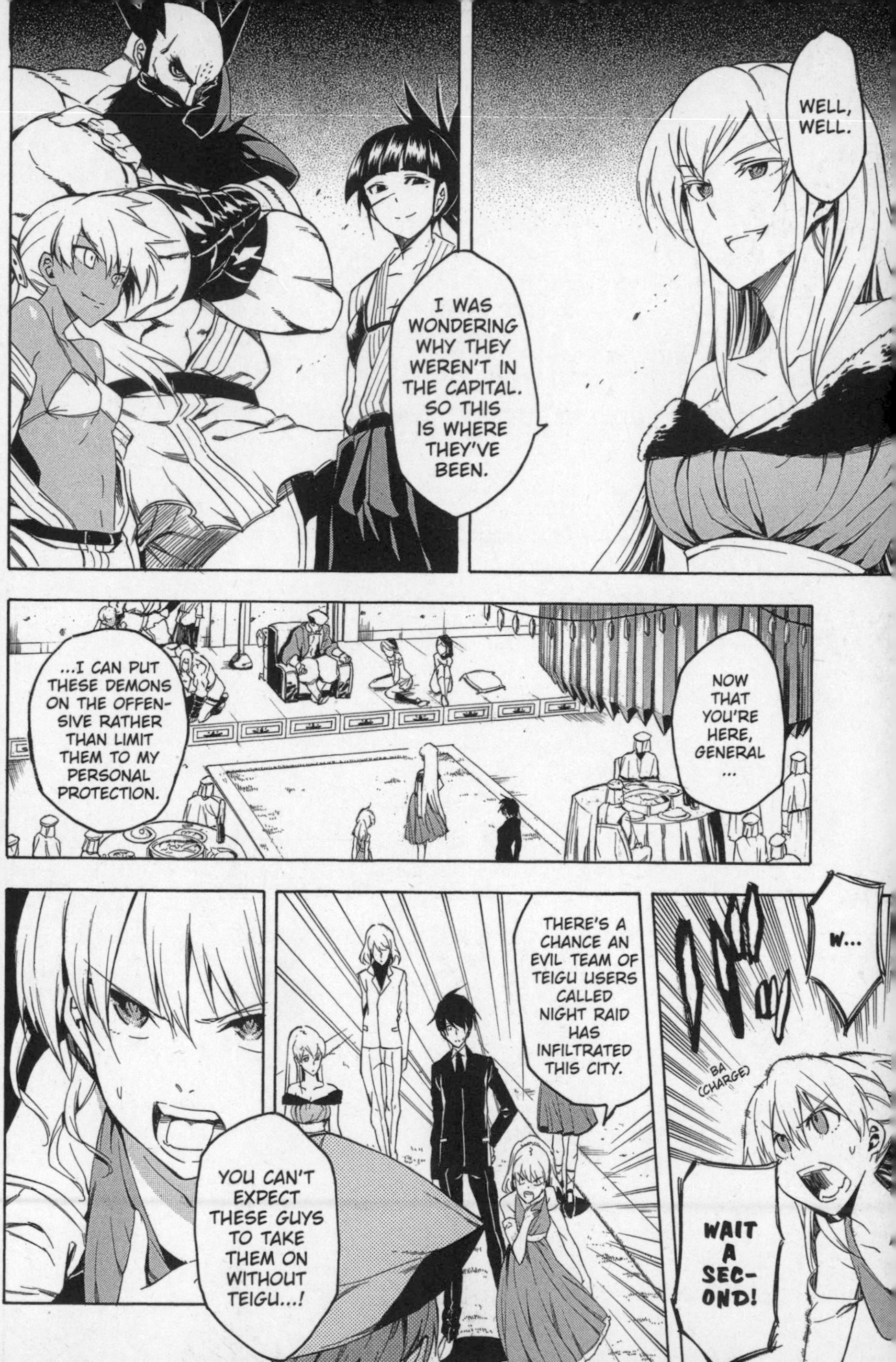
WELL, WELL.
I WAS WONDERING WHY THEY WEREN'T IN THE CAPITAL. SO THIS IS WHERE THEY'VE BEEN.
NOW THAT YOU'RE HERE, GENERAL ...
...I CAN PUT THESE DEMONS ON THE OFFEN-SIVE RATHER THAN LIMIT THEM TO MY PERSONAL PROTECTION.
W...
BA (CHARGE)
WAIT A SEC-OND!
THERE'S A CHANCE AN EVIL TEAM OF TEIGU USERS CALLED NIGHT RAID HAS INFILTRATED THIS CITY.
YOU CAN'T EXPECT THESE GUYS TO TAKE THEM ON WITHOUT TEIGU...!

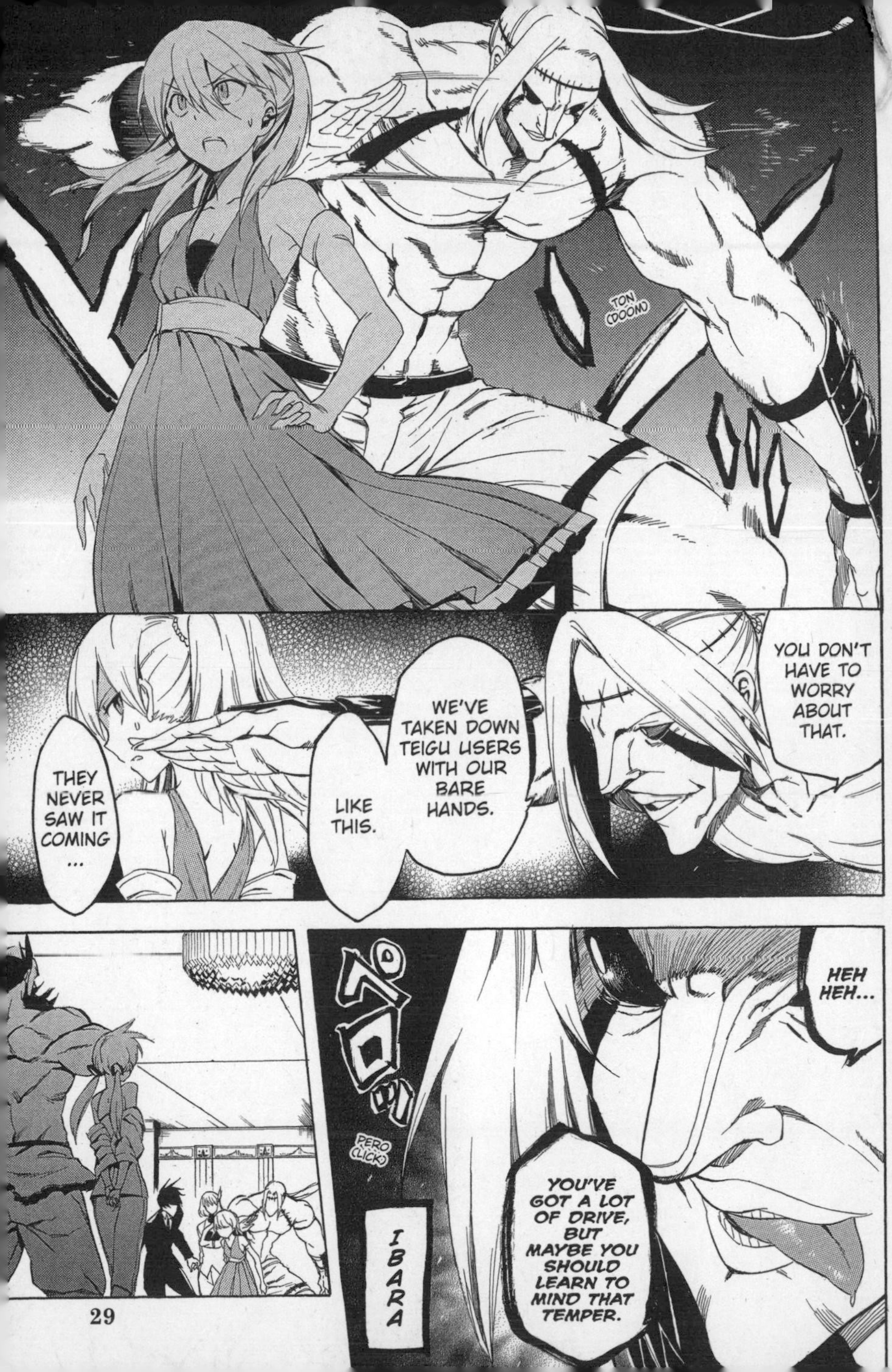
TON (DOOM)
YOU DON'T HAVE TO WORRY ABOUT THAT.
WE'VE TAKEN DOWN TEIGU USERS WITH OUR BARE HANDS.
LIKE THIS.
THEY NEVER SAW IT COMING ...
HEH HEH...
YOU'VE GOT A LOT OF DRIVE, BUT MAYBE YOU SHOULD LEARN TO MIND THAT TEMPER.
PERO (LICK)
IBARA

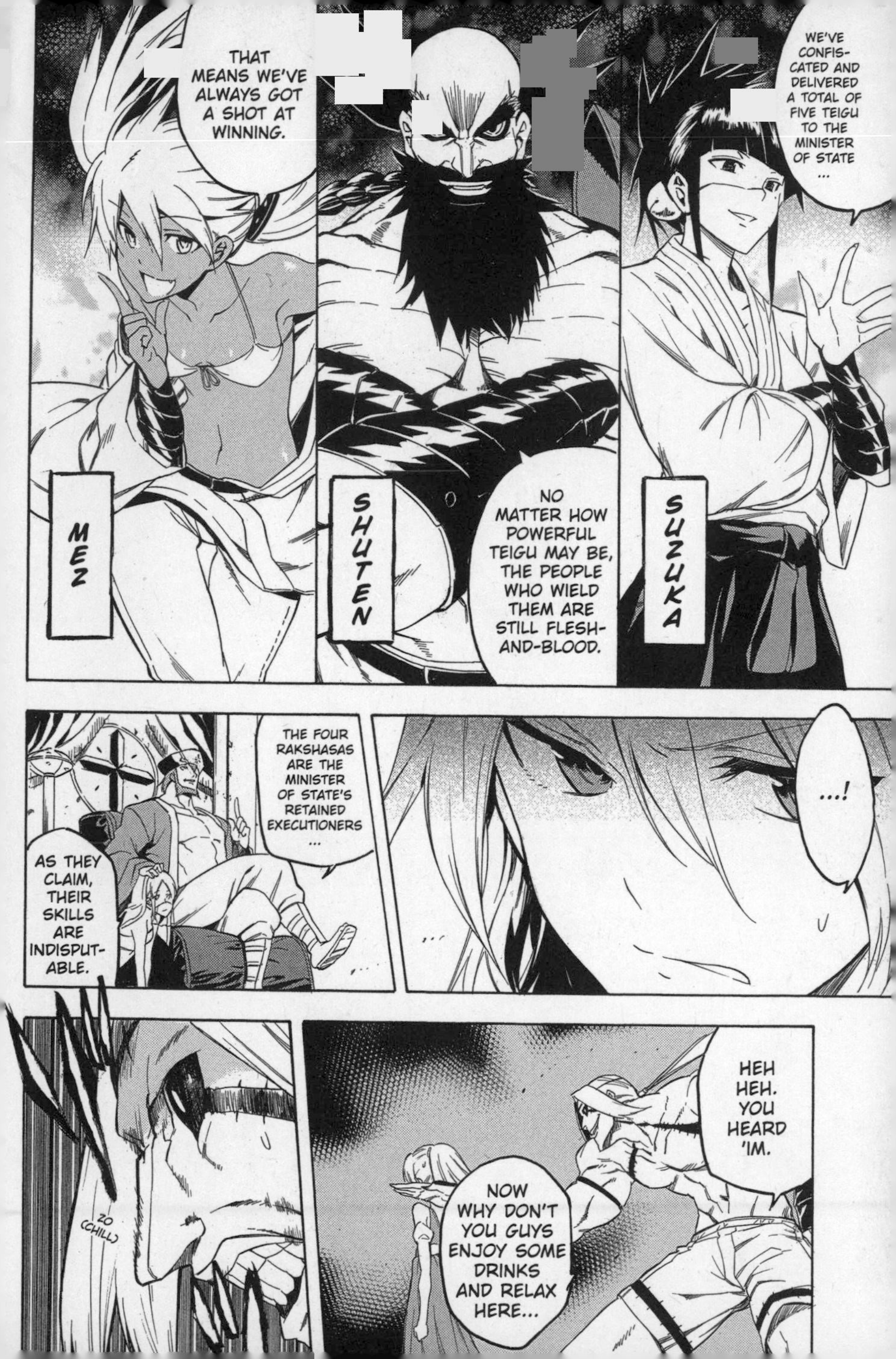
WE'VE CONFIS-CATED AND DELIVERED A TOTAL OF FIVE TEIGU TO THE MINISTER OF STATE ...
SUZUKA
NO MATTER HOW POWERFUL TEIGU MAY BE, THE PEOPLE WHO WIELD THEM ARE STILL FLESH-AND-BLOOD.
SHUTEN
THAT MEANS WE'VE ALWAYS GOT A SHOT AT WINNING.
MEZ
...!
...
THE FOUR RAKSHASAS ARE THE MINISTER OF STATE'S RETAINED EXECUTIONERS ...
AS THEY CLAIM, THEIR SKILLS ARE INDISPUT-ABLE.
...
HEH HEH. YOU HEARD 'IM.
NOW WHY DON'T YOU GUYS ENJOY SOME DRINKS AND RELAX HERE...
ZO (CHILL)

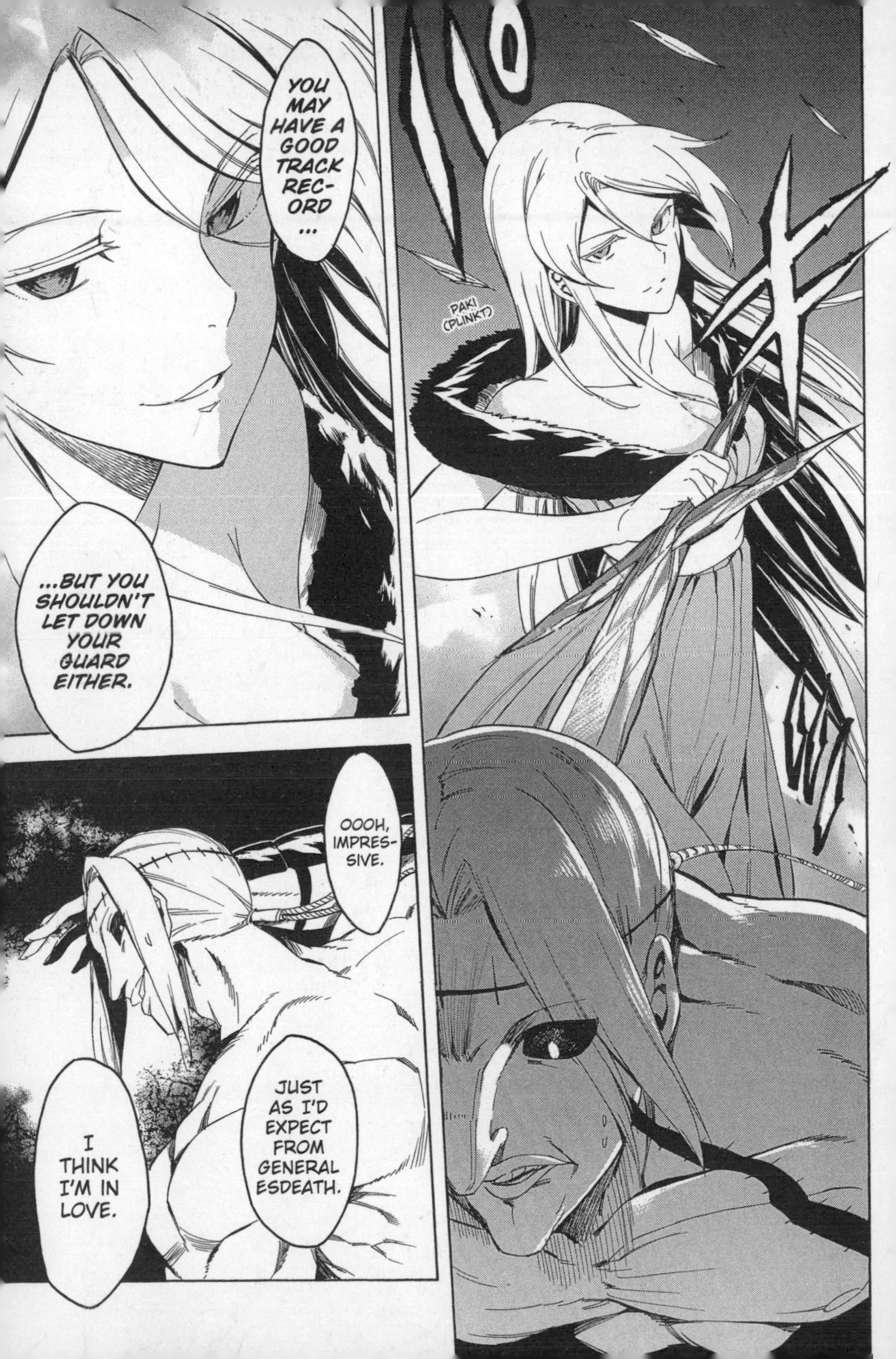
PAKI (PLINKT)
YOU MAY HAVE A GOOD TRACK RECORD ...
...BUT YOU SHOULDN'T LET DOWN YOUR GUARD EITHER.
OOOH, IMPRESSIVE.
JUST AS I'D EXPECT FROM GENERAL ESDEATH.
I THINK I'M IN LOVE.

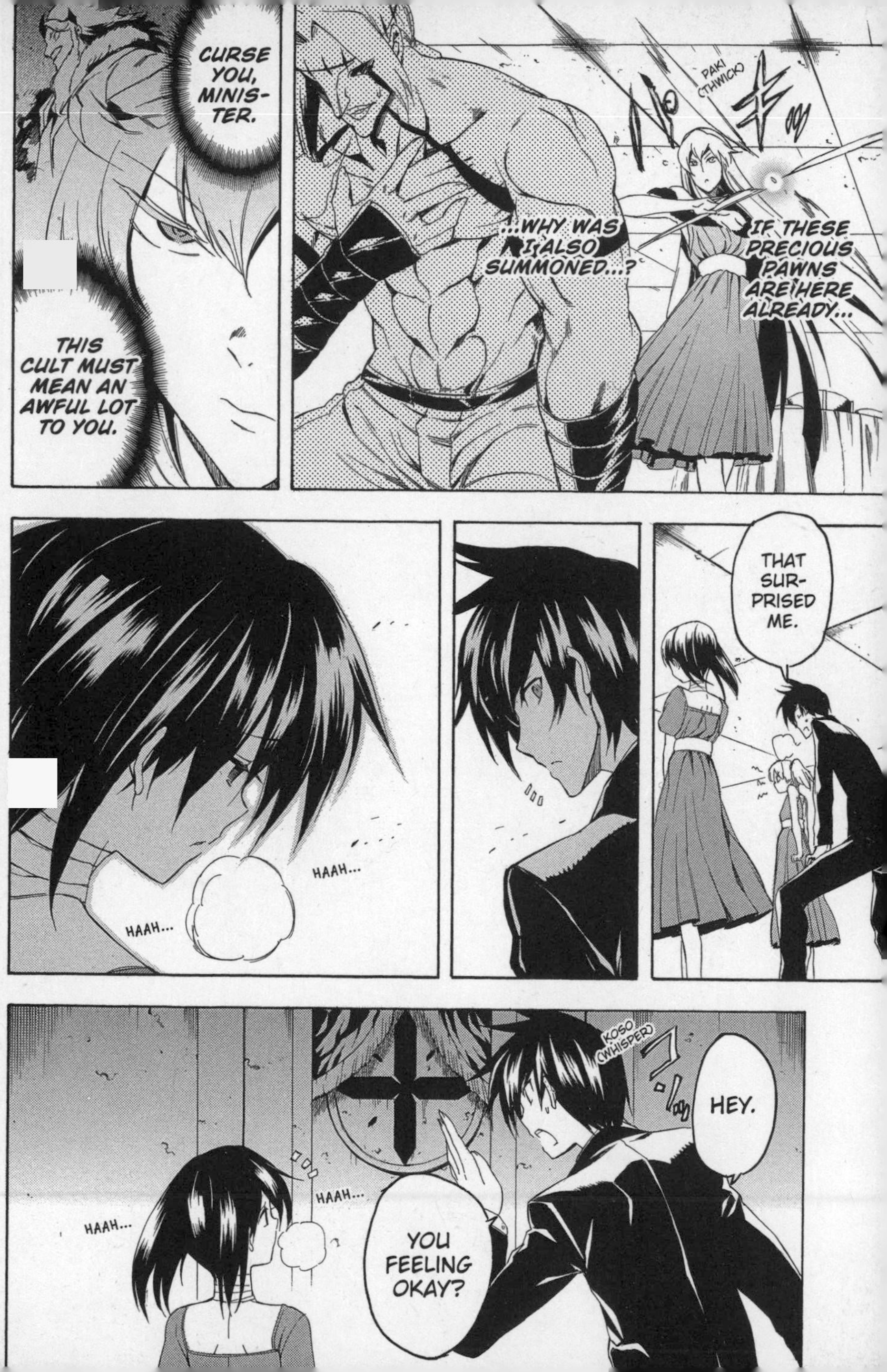
PAKI (THWICK)
IF THESE PRECIOUS PAWNS ARE HERE ALREADY...
...WHY WAS I ALSO SUMMONED...?
CURSE YOU, MINISTER.
THIS CULT MUST MEAN AN AWFUL LOT TO YOU.
THAT SURPRISED ME.
HAAH...
HAAH...
KOSO (WHISPER)
HEY.
YOU FEELING OKAY?
HAAH...
HAAH...

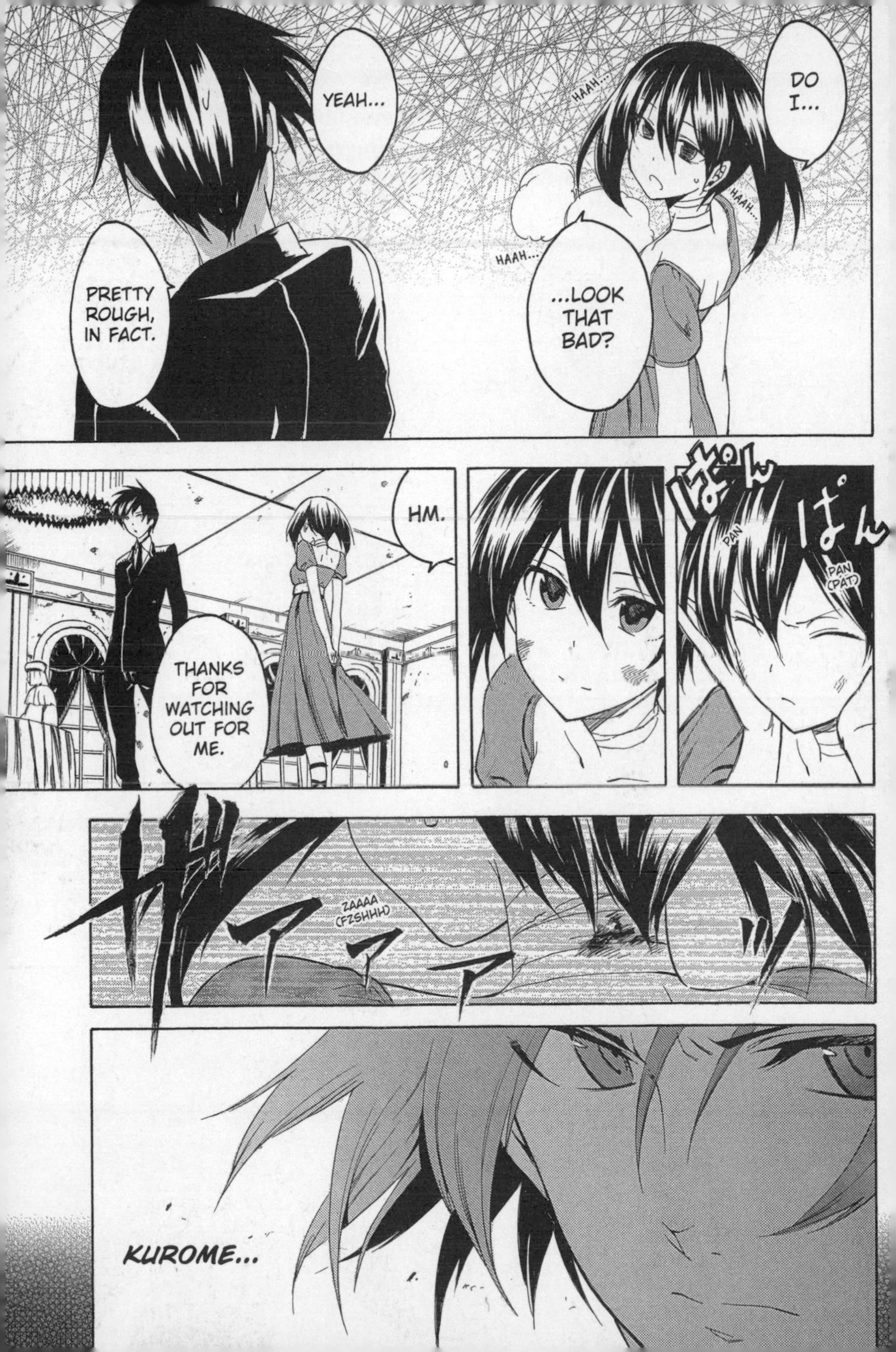

HAAH...
DO I...
HAAH...
HAAH...
...LOOK THAT BAD?
YEAH...
PRETTY ROUGH, IN FACT.
PAN
PAN (PAT)
HM.
THANKS FOR WATCHING OUT FOR ME.
ZAAAA (FZSHHH)
KUROME...

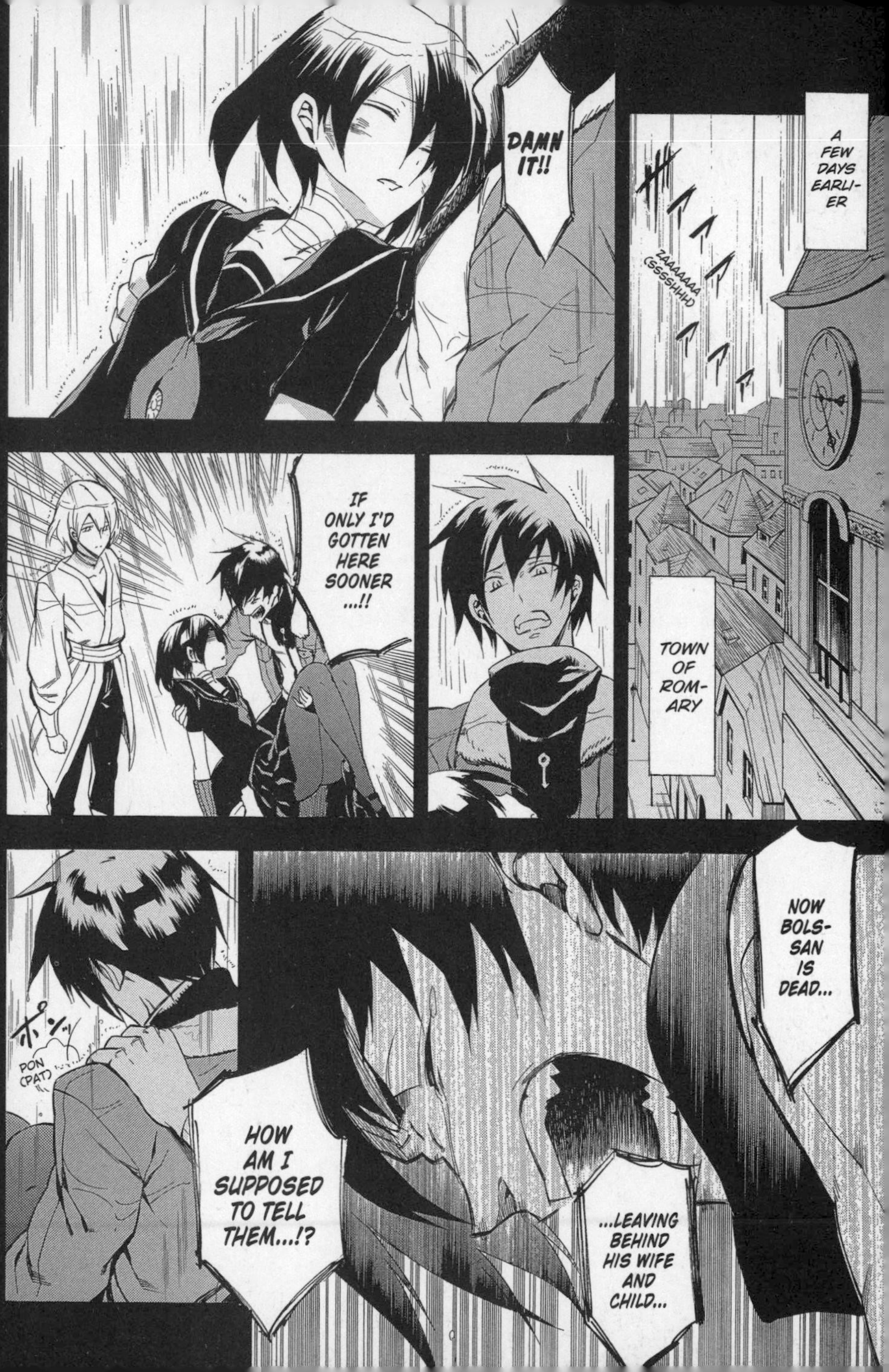
A FEW DAYS EARLIER
ZAAAAAAA (SSSSHHH)
TOWN OF ROMARY
DAMN IT!!
IF ONLY I'D GOTTEN HERE SOONER ...!!
NOW BOLS-SAN IS DEAD...
...LEAVING BEHIND HIS WIFE AND CHILD...
HOW AM I SUPPOSED TO TELL THEM...!?
PON (PAT)

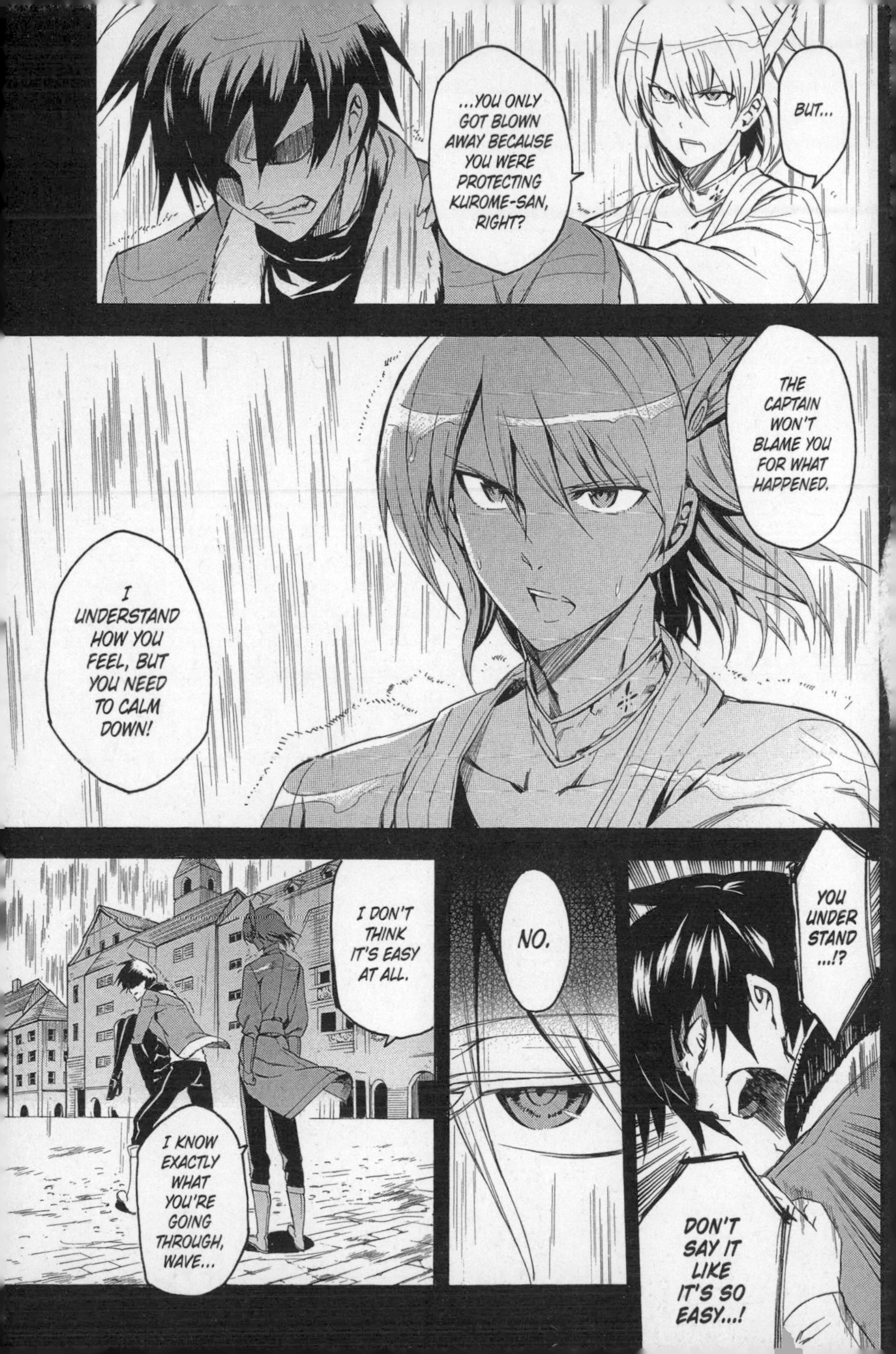
BUT...
...YOU ONLY GOT BLOWN AWAY BECAUSE YOU WERE PROTECTING KUROME-SAN, RIGHT?
THE CAPTAIN WON'T BLAME YOU FOR WHAT HAPPENED.
I UNDERSTAND HOW YOU FEEL, BUT YOU NEED TO CALM DOWN!
YOU UNDER STAND ...!?
DON'T SAY IT LIKE IT'S SO EASY...!
NO.
I DON'T THINK IT'S EASY AT ALL.
I KNOW EXACTLY WHAT YOU'RE GOING THROUGH, WAVE...

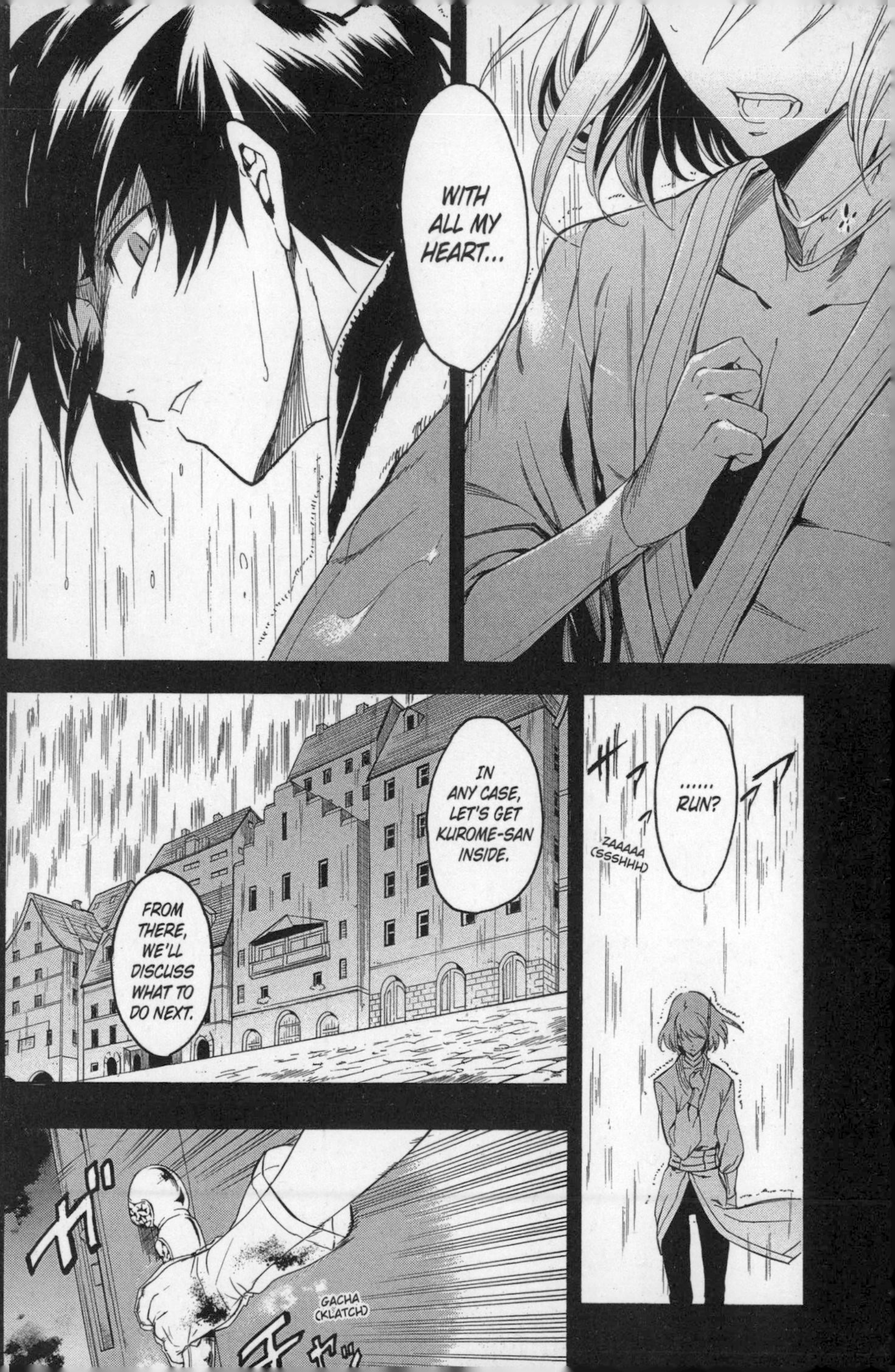
WITH ALL MY HEART...
......RUN?
ZAAAAA (SSSHHH)
IN ANY CASE, LET'S GET KUROME-SAN INSIDE.
FROM THERE, WE'LL DISCUSS WHAT TO DO NEXT.
GACHA (KLATCH)

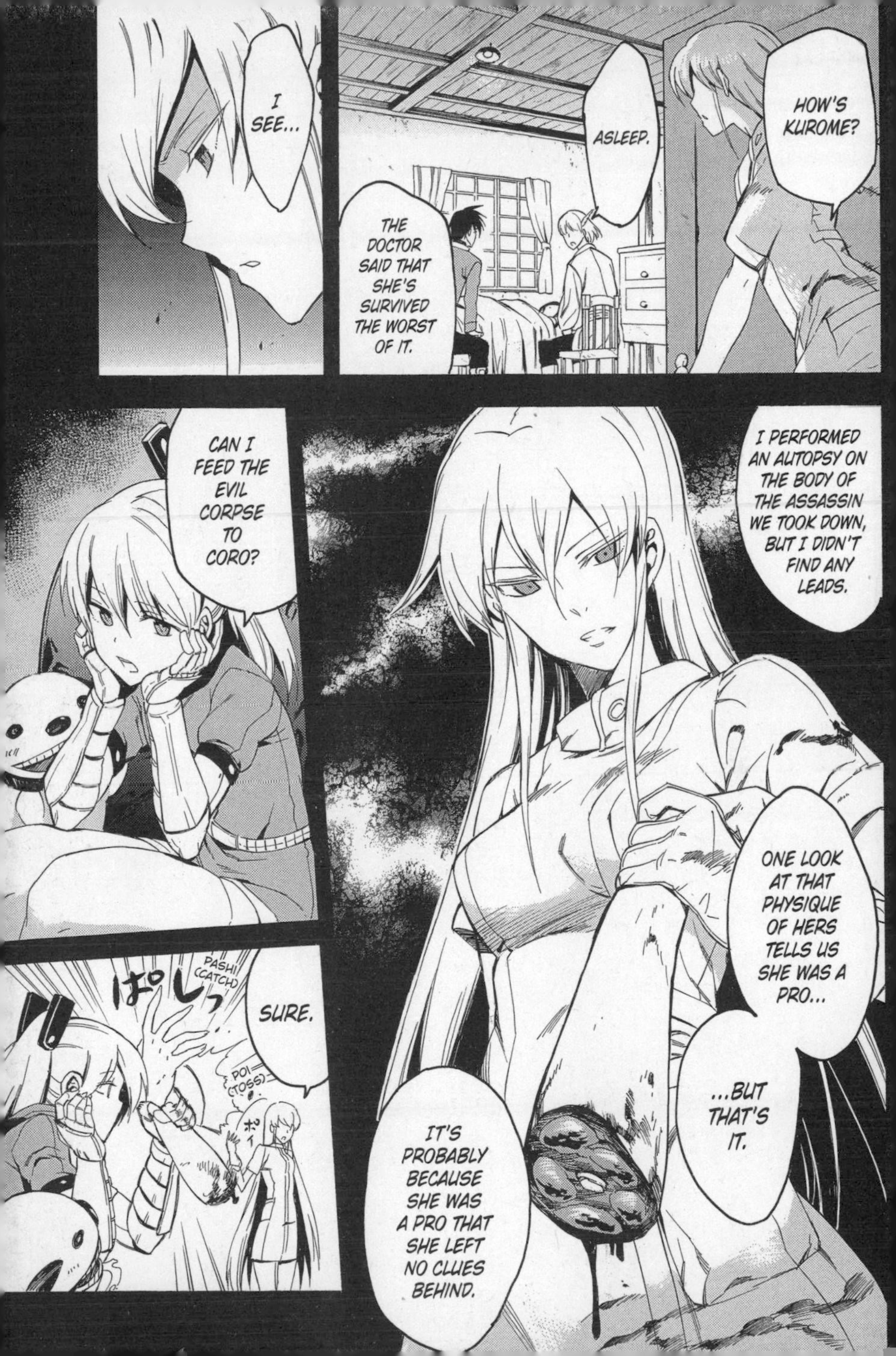
HOW'S KUROME?
ASLEEP.
THE DOCTOR SAID THAT SHE'S SURVIVED THE WORST OF IT.
I SEE...
I PERFORMED AN AUTOPSY ON THE BODY OF THE ASSASSIN WE TOOK DOWN, BUT I DIDN'T FIND ANY LEADS.
ONE LOOK AT THAT PHYSIQUE OF HERS TELLS US SHE WAS A PRO...
...BUT THAT'S IT.
IT'S PROBABLY BECAUSE SHE WAS A PRO THAT SHE LEFT NO CLUES BEHIND.
CAN I FEED THE EVIL CORPSE TO CORO?
SURE.
ぱしっ
PASHI (CATCH)
POI (TOSS)

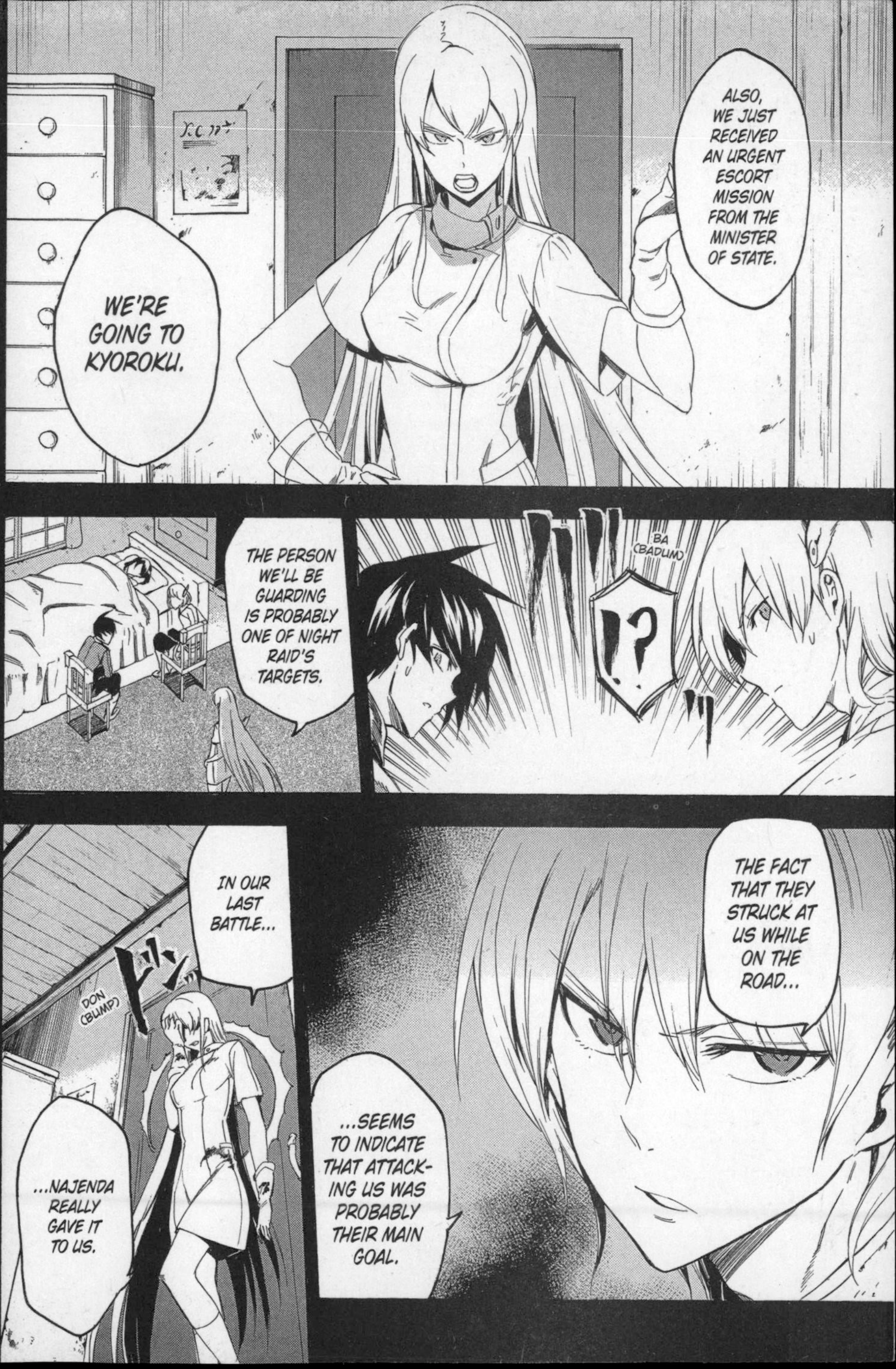
ALSO, WE JUST RECEIVED AN URGENT ESCORT MISSION FROM THE MINISTER OF STATE.
WE'RE GOING TO KYOROKU.
THE PERSON WE'LL BE GUARDING IS PROBABLY ONE OF NIGHT RAID'S TARGETS.
BA (BADUM)
!?
THE FACT THAT THEY STRUCK AT US WHILE ON THE ROAD...
...SEEMS TO INDICATE THAT ATTACK-ING US WAS PROBABLY THEIR MAIN GOAL.
IN OUR LAST BATTLE...
DON (BUMP)
...NAJENDA REALLY GAVE IT TO US.

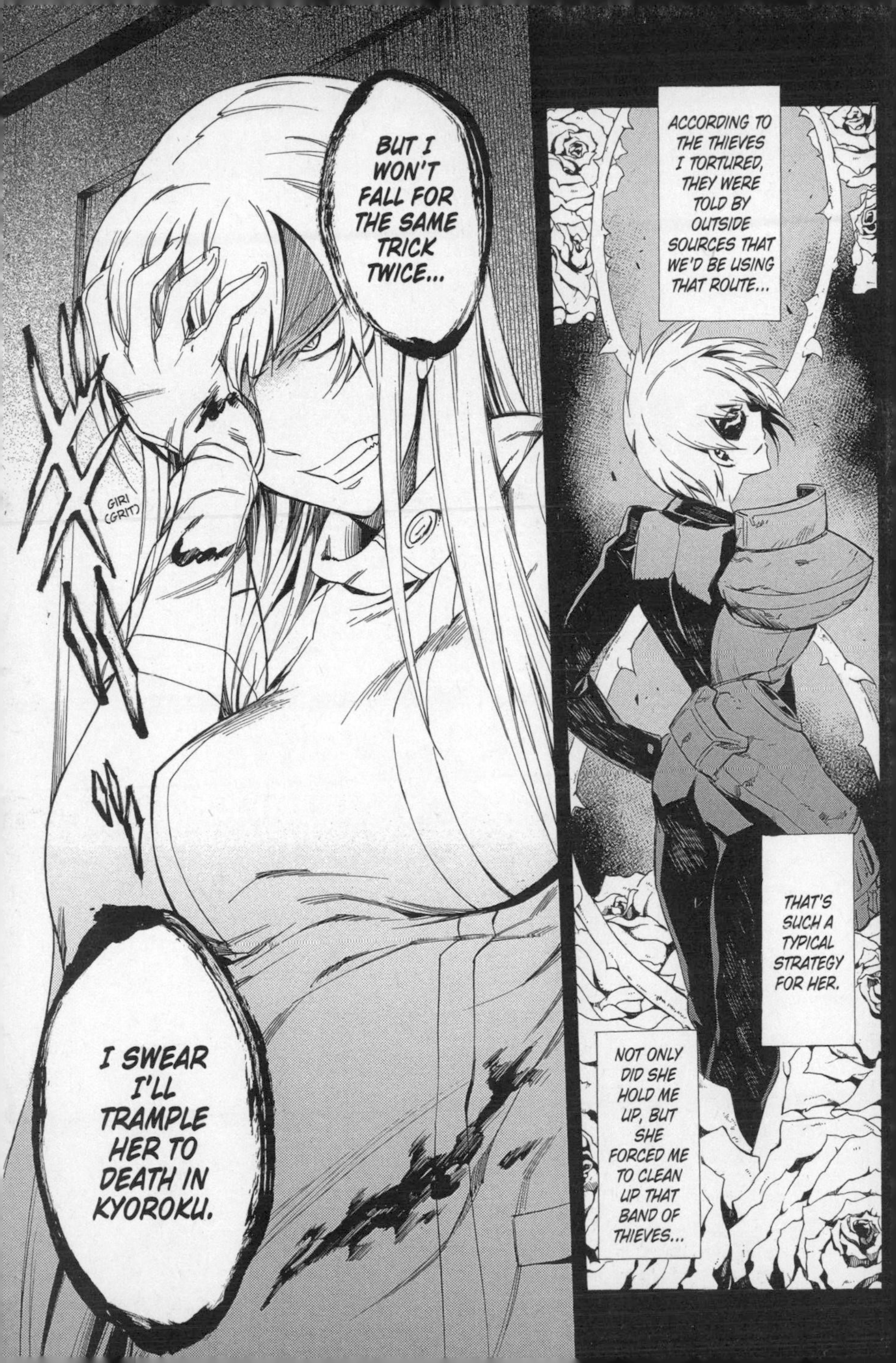
ACCORDING TO THE THIEVES I TORTURED, THEY WERE TOLD BY OUTSIDE SOURCES THAT WE'D BE USING THAT ROUTE...
THAT'S SUCH A TYPICAL STRATEGY FOR HER.
NOT ONLY DID SHE HOLD ME UP, BUT SHE FORCED ME TO CLEAN UP THAT BAND OF THIEVES...
BUT I WON'T FALL FOR THE SAME TRICK TWICE...
GIRI (GRIT)
I SWEAR I'LL TRAMPLE HER TO DEATH IN KYOROKU.

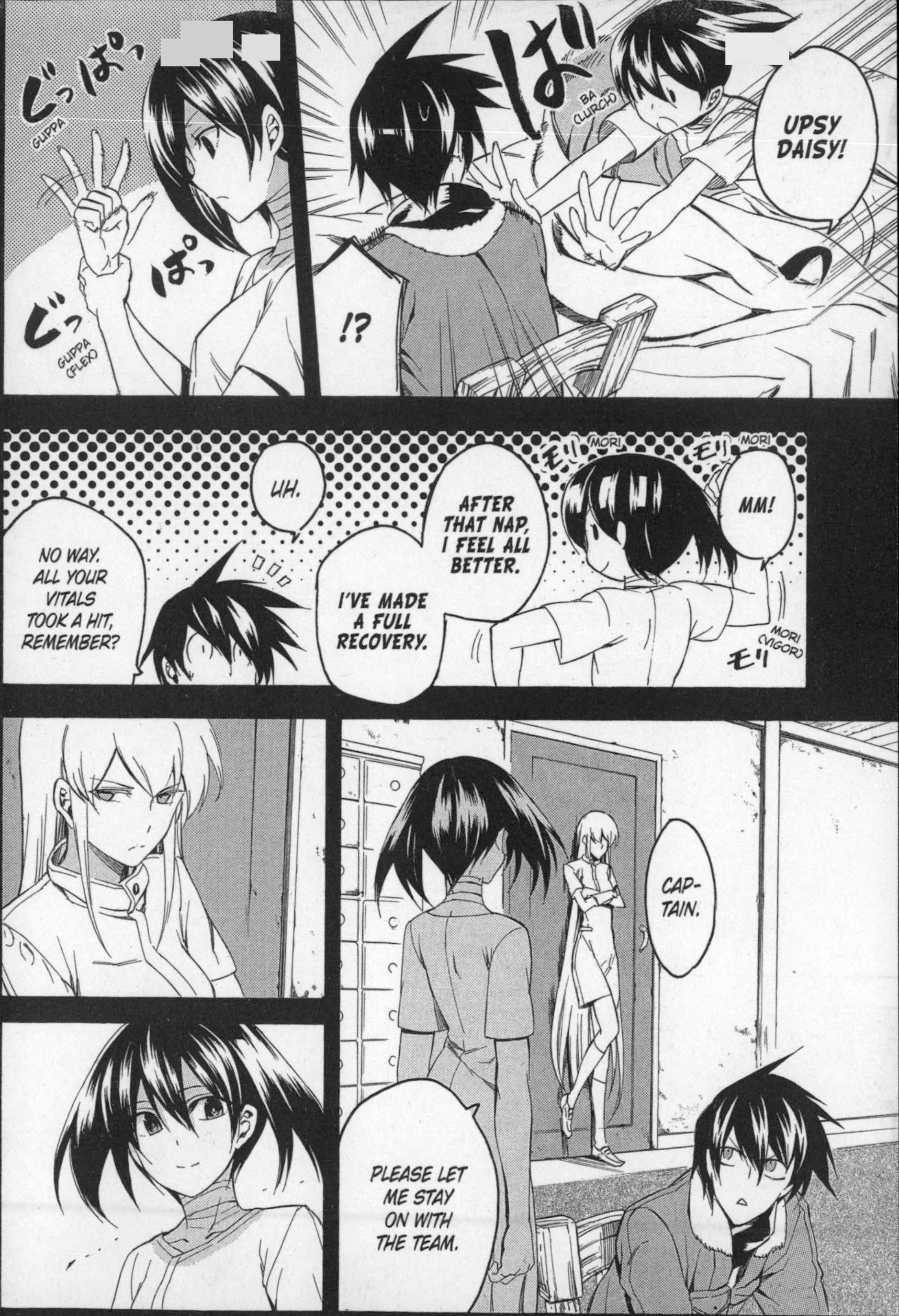

BA (LURCH)
UPSY DAISY!
!?
ぐっぱっ
GUPPA
ぐっ ぱっ
GUPPA (FLEX)
モリ MORI
モリ MORI
MM!
AFTER THAT NAP, I FEEL ALL BETTER.
I'VE MADE A FULL RECOVERY.
モリ MORI (VIGOR)
UH.
NO WAY. ALL YOUR VITALS TOOK A HIT, REMEMBER?
CAP-TAIN.
PLEASE LET ME STAY ON WITH THE TEAM.

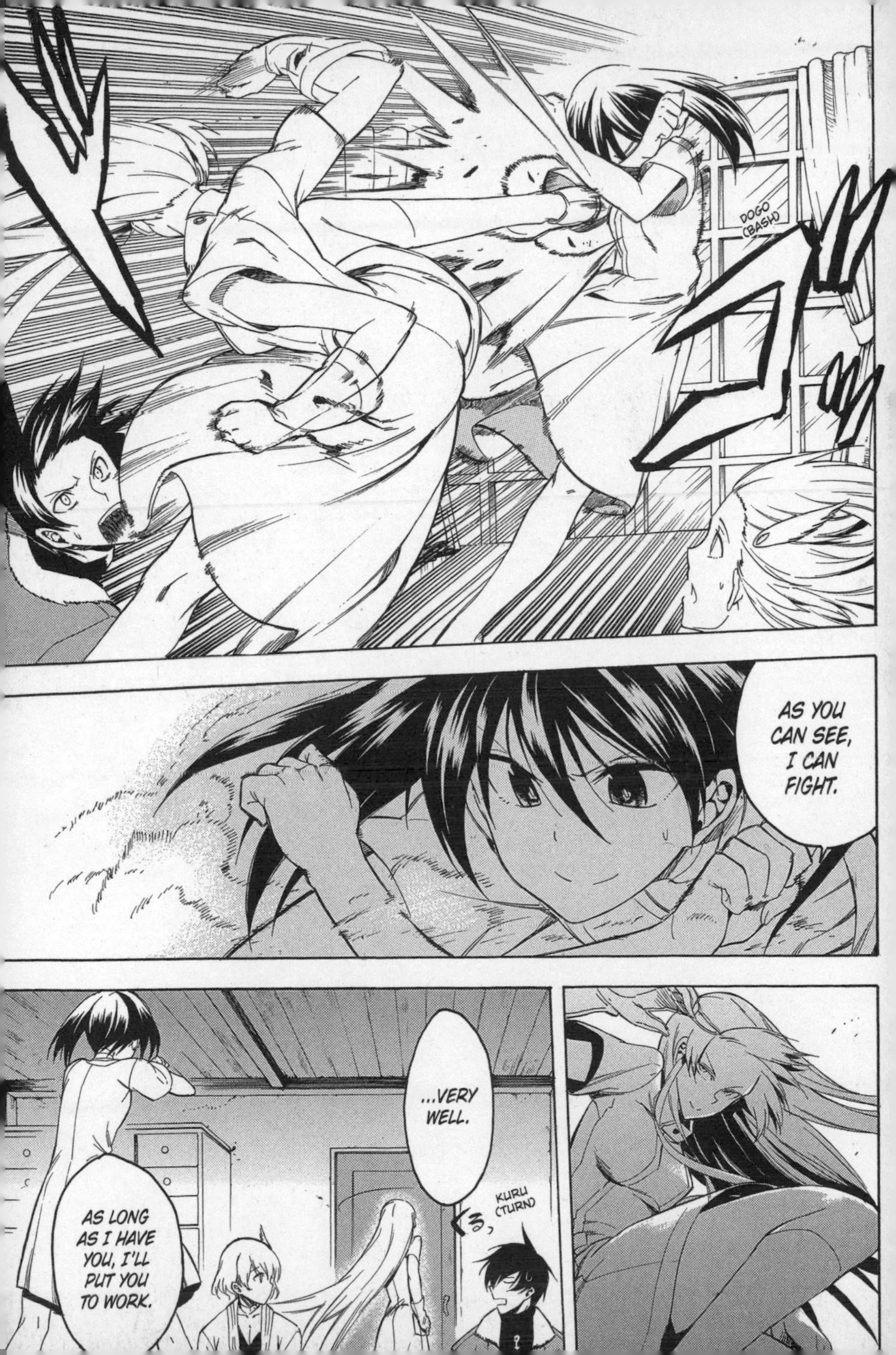
DOGO (BASH)
AS YOU CAN SEE, I CAN FIGHT.
...VERY WELL.
くる
KURU (TURN)
AS LONG AS I HAVE YOU, I'LL PUT YOU TO WORK.

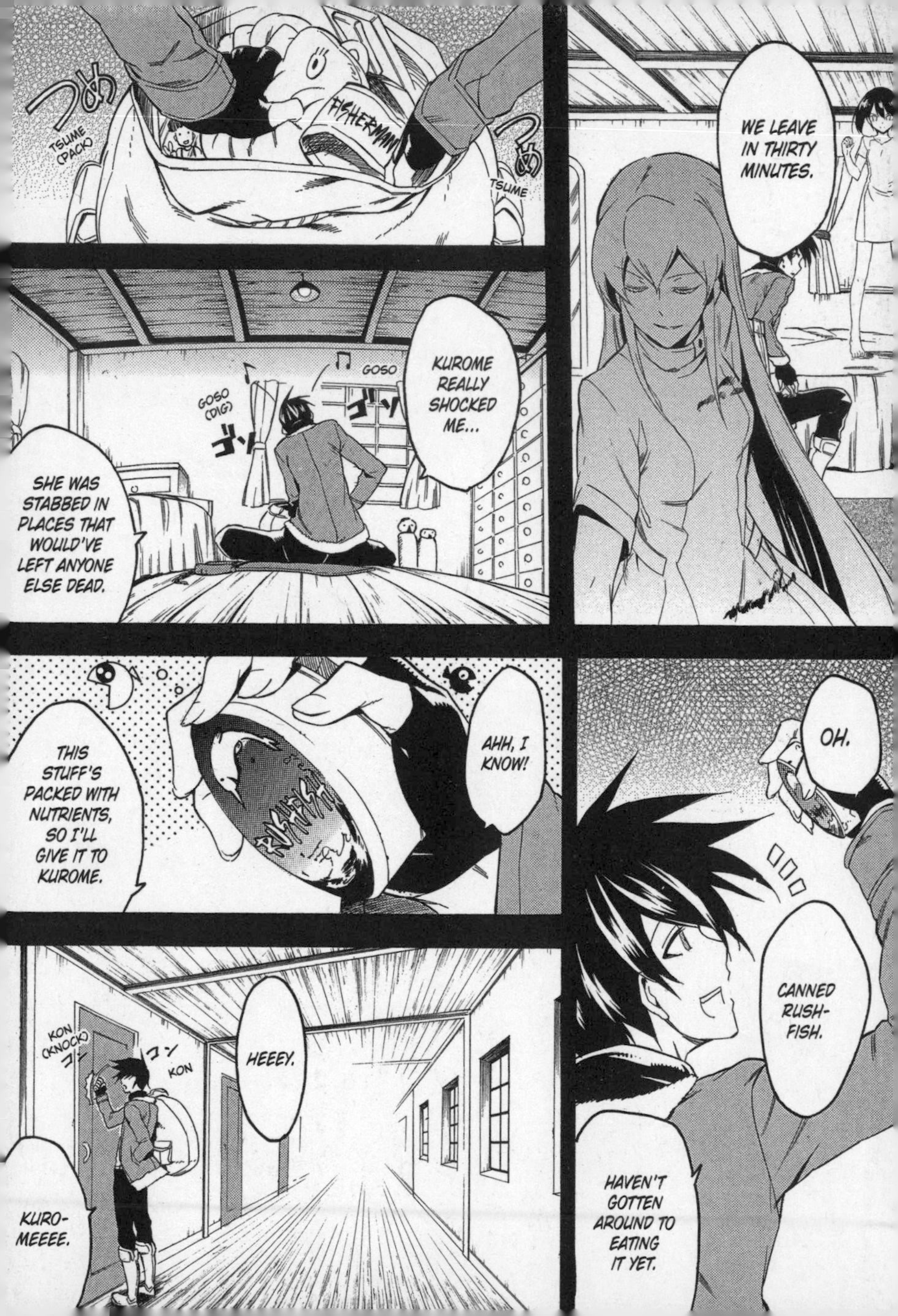

WE LEAVE IN THIRTY MINUTES.
つめ TSUME (PACK)
FISHERMAN
つめ TSUME
GOSO (DIG)
GOSO
KUROME REALLY SHOCKED ME...
SHE WAS STABBED IN PLACES THAT WOULD'VE LEFT ANYONE ELSE DEAD.
OH.
CANNED RUSH-FISH.
HAVEN'T GOTTEN AROUND TO EATING IT YET.
AHH, I KNOW!
THIS STUFF'S PACKED WITH NUTRIENTS, SO I'LL GIVE IT TO KUROME.
HEEEY.
KON (KNOCK)
KON
KURO-MEEEE.

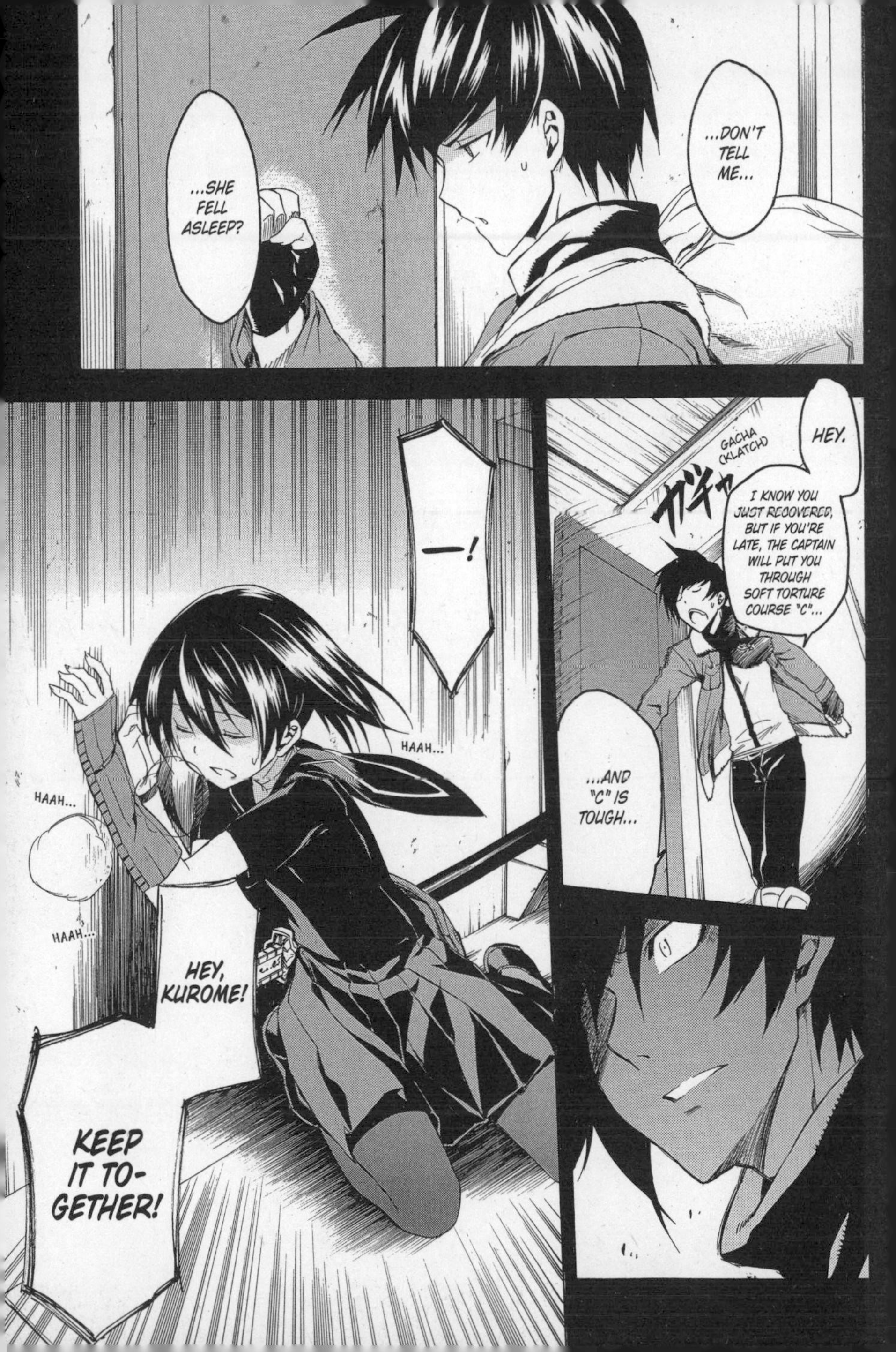
...DON'T TELL ME...
...SHE FELL ASLEEP?
GACHA (KLATCH)
HEY.
I KNOW YOU JUST RECOVERED, BUT IF YOU'RE LATE, THE CAPTAIN WILL PUT YOU THROUGH SOFT TORTURE COURSE "C"...
...AND "C" IS TOUGH...
—!
HAAH...
HAAH...
HAAH...
HEY, KUROME!
KEEP IT TO-GETHER!

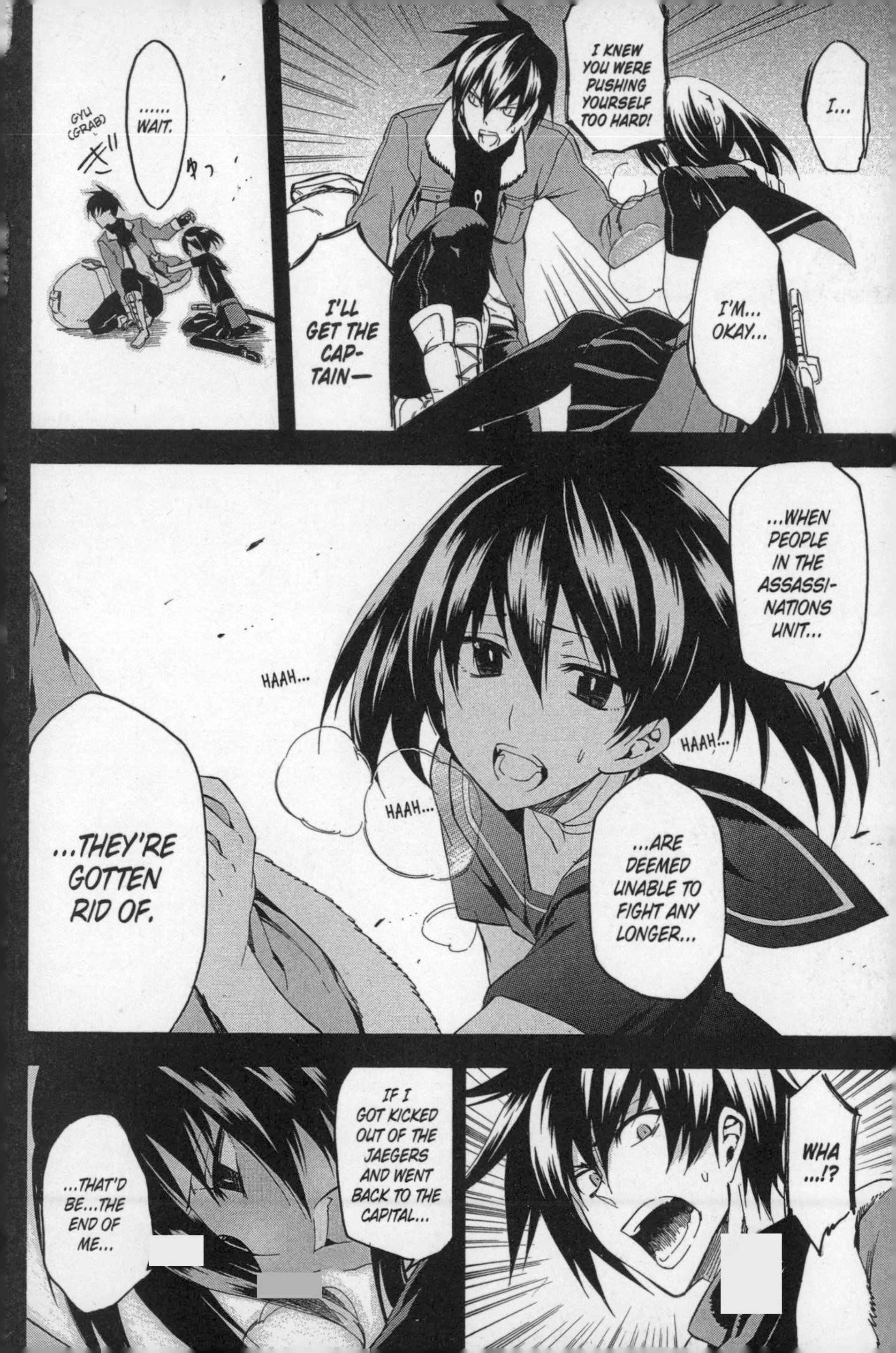
I...
I KNEW YOU WERE PUSHING YOURSELF TOO HARD!
I'M... OKAY...
I'LL GET THE CAP-TAIN—
GYU (GRAB)
...... WAIT.
...WHEN PEOPLE IN THE ASSASSI-NATIONS UNIT...
HAAH...
HAAH...
HAAH...
...ARE DEEMED UNABLE TO FIGHT ANY LONGER...
...THEY'RE GOTTEN RID OF.
WHA ...!?
IF I GOT KICKED OUT OF THE JAEGERS AND WENT BACK TO THE CAPITAL...
...THAT'D BE...THE END OF ME...

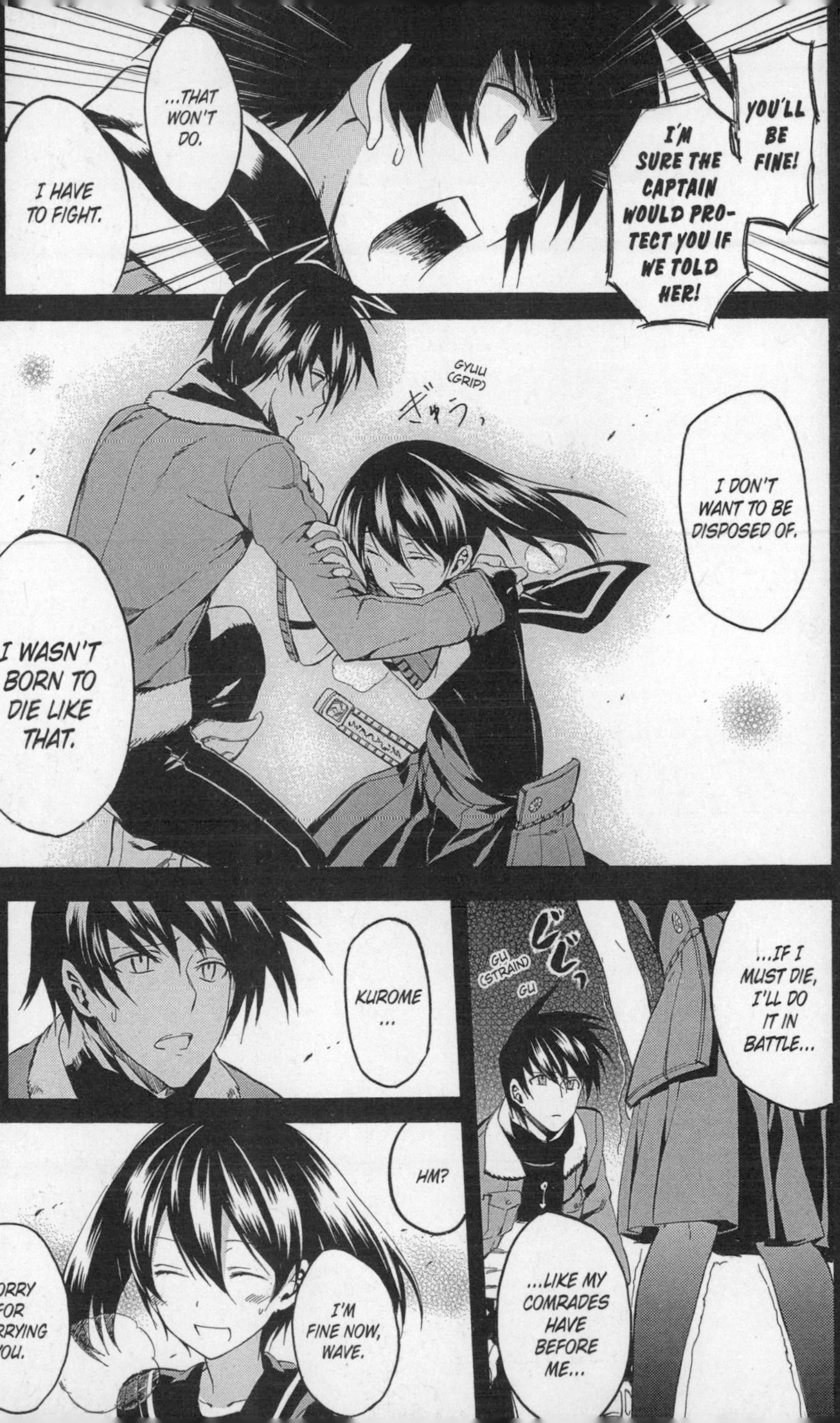
YOU'LL BE FINE!
I'M SURE THE CAPTAIN WOULD PROTECT YOU IF WE TOLD HER!
...THAT WON'T DO.
I HAVE TO FIGHT.
GYUU (GRIP)
I DON'T WANT TO BE DISPOSED OF.
I WASN'T BORN TO DIE LIKE THAT.
GU (STRAIN) GU
...IF I MUST DIE, I'LL DO IT IN BATTLE...
...LIKE MY COMRADES HAVE BEFORE ME...
KUROME...
HM?
I'M FINE NOW, WAVE.
SORRY FOR WORRYING YOU.

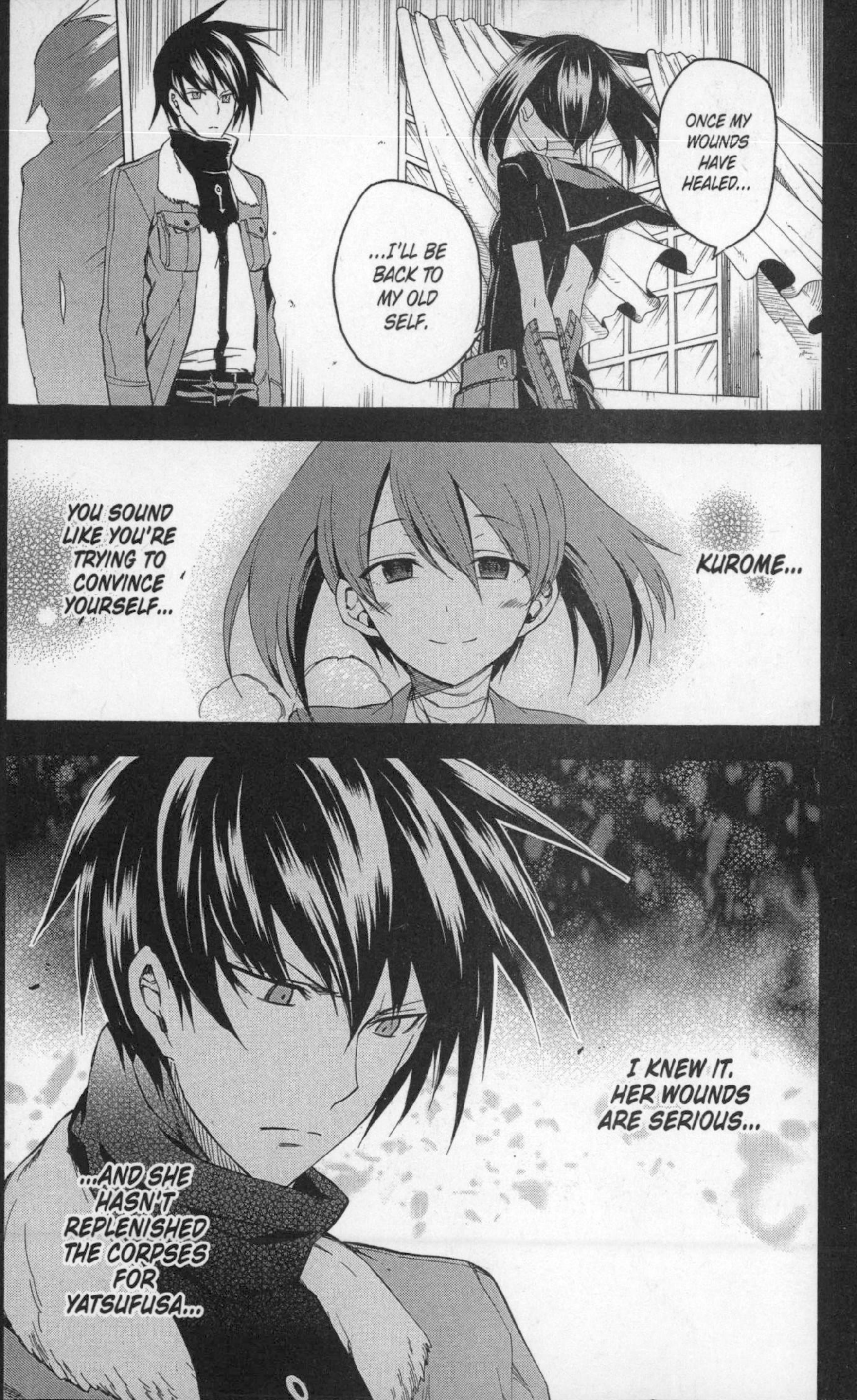
ONCE MY WOUNDS HAVE HEALED...
...I'LL BE BACK TO MY OLD SELF.
KUROME...
YOU SOUND LIKE YOU'RE TRYING TO CONVINCE YOURSELF...
I KNEW IT. HER WOUNDS ARE SERIOUS...
...AND SHE HASN'T REPLENISHED THE CORPSES FOR YATSUFUSA...

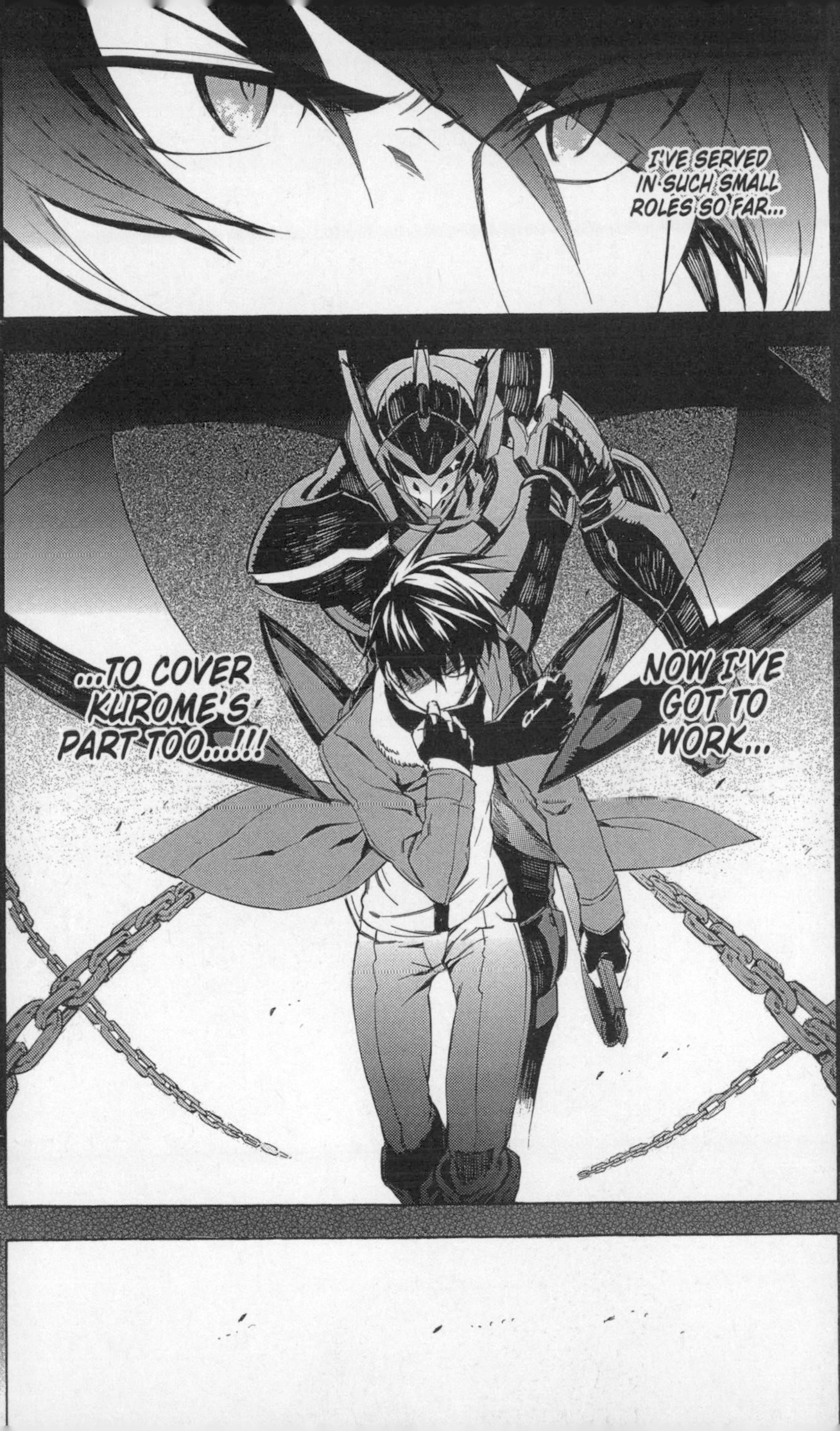
I'VE SERVED IN SUCH SMALL ROLES SO FAR...
NOW I'VE GOT TO WORK...
...TO COVER KUROME'S PART TOO...!!!

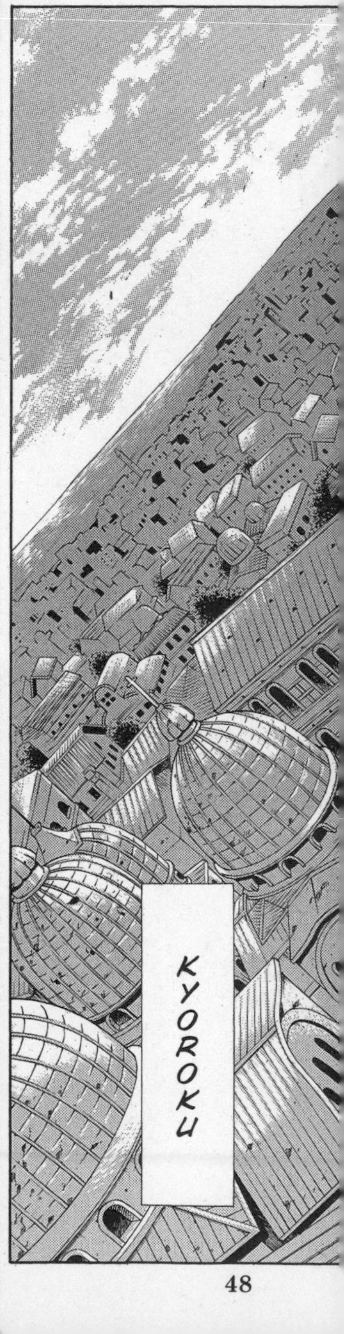
KYOROKU

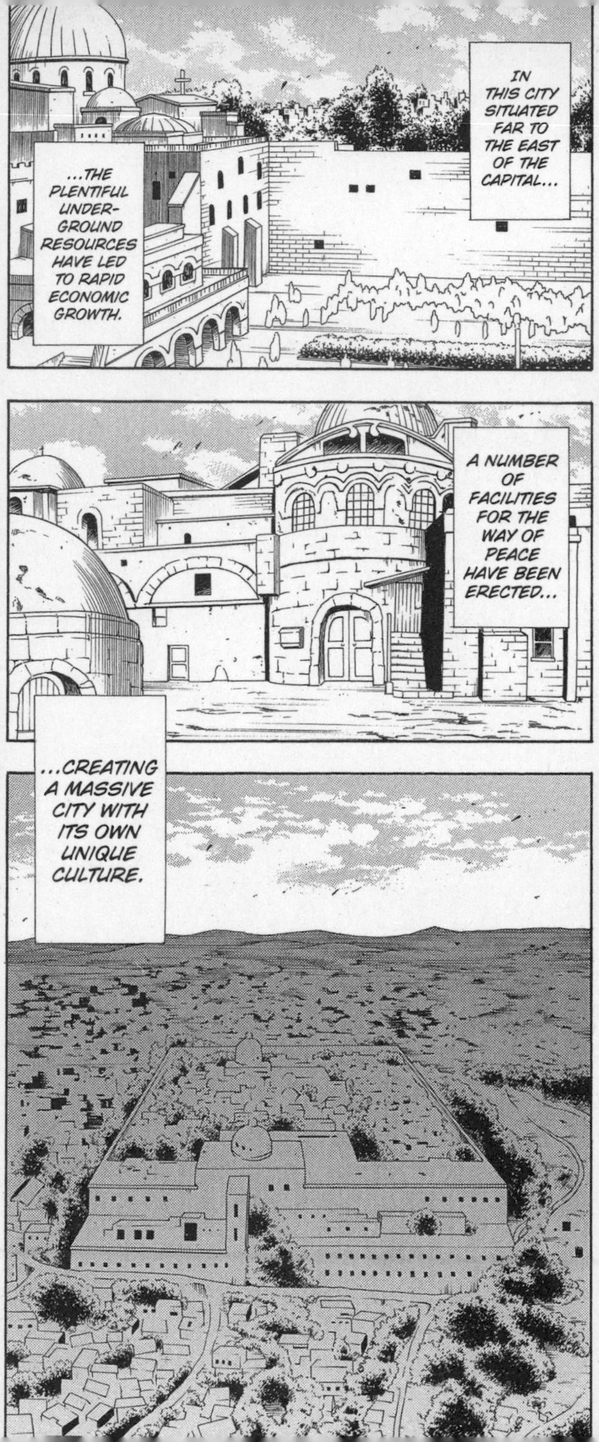
IN THIS CITY SITUATED FAR TO THE EAST OF THE CAPITAL...
...THE PLENTIFUL UNDER-GROUND RESOURCES HAVE LED TO RAPID ECONOMIC GROWTH.
A NUMBER OF FACILITIES FOR THE WAY OF PEACE HAVE BEEN ERECTED...
...CREATING A MASSIVE CITY WITH ITS OWN UNIQUE CULTURE.

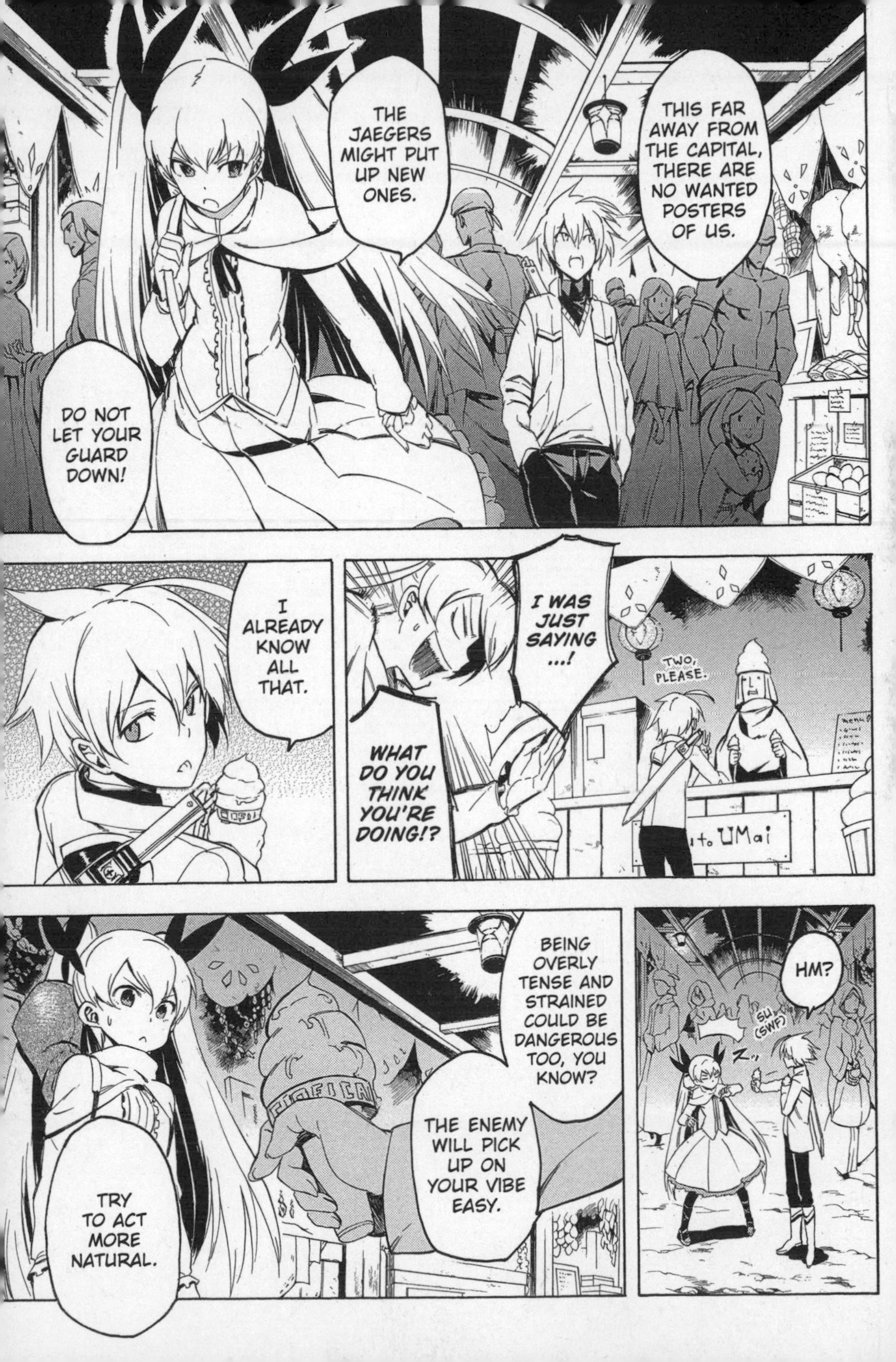
THIS FAR AWAY FROM THE CAPITAL, THERE ARE NO WANTED POSTERS OF US.
THE JAEGERS MIGHT PUT UP NEW ONES.
DO NOT LET YOUR GUARD DOWN!
TWO, PLEASE.
I WAS JUST SAYING ...!
WHAT DO YOU THINK YOU'RE DOING!?
I ALREADY KNOW ALL THAT.
HM?
SU (SWF)
BEING OVERLY TENSE AND STRAINED COULD BE DANGEROUS TOO, YOU KNOW?
THE ENEMY WILL PICK UP ON YOUR VIBE EASY.
TRY TO ACT MORE NATURAL.

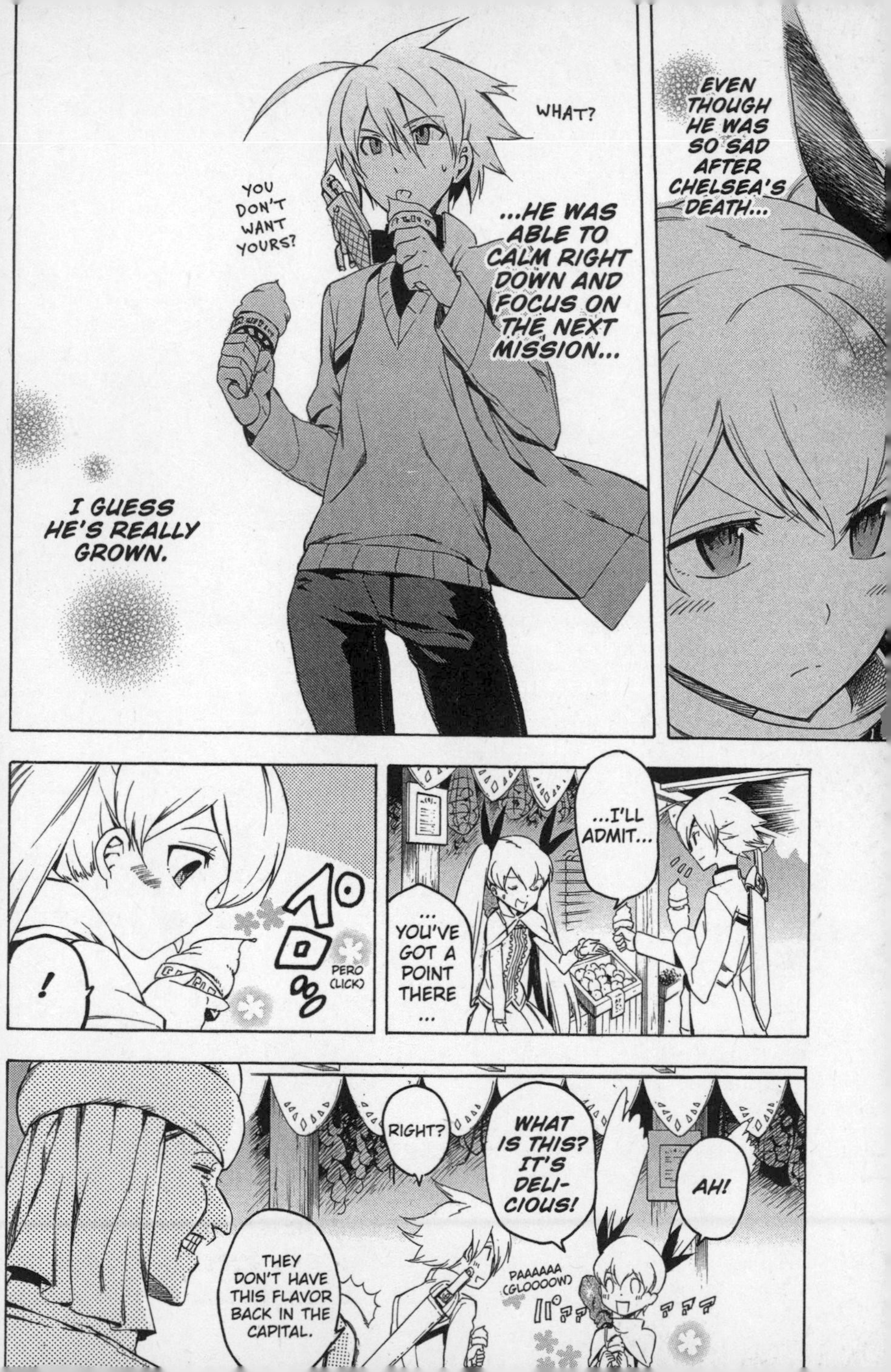
EVEN THOUGH HE WAS SO SAD AFTER CHELSEA'S DEATH...
...HE WAS ABLE TO CALM RIGHT DOWN AND FOCUS ON THE NEXT MISSION...
WHAT?
YOU DON'T WANT YOURS?
I GUESS HE'S REALLY GROWN.
...I'LL ADMIT...
...YOU'VE GOT A POINT THERE...
PERO (LICK)
!
AH!
WHAT IS THIS? IT'S DELICIOUS!
RIGHT?
THEY DON'T HAVE THIS FLAVOR BACK IN THE CAPITAL.
PAAAAAA (GLOOOOW)

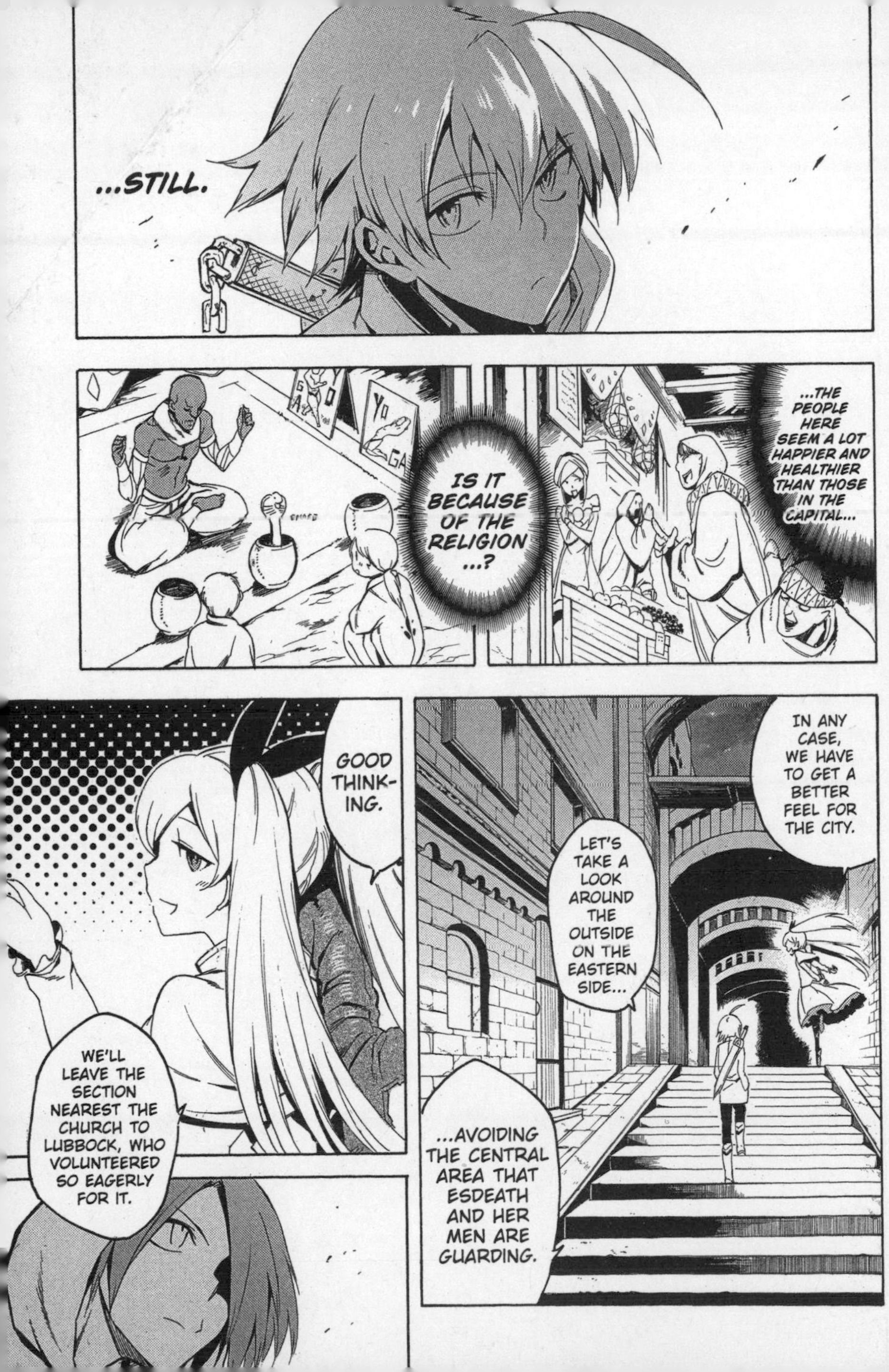
...STILL.
...THE PEOPLE HERE SEEM A LOT HAPPIER AND HEALTHIER THAN THOSE IN THE CAPITAL...
IS IT BECAUSE OF THE RELIGION ...?
IN ANY CASE, WE HAVE TO GET A BETTER FEEL FOR THE CITY.
LET'S TAKE A LOOK AROUND THE OUTSIDE ON THE EASTERN SIDE...
...AVOIDING THE CENTRAL AREA THAT ESDEATH AND HER MEN ARE GUARDING.
GOOD THINKING.
WE'LL LEAVE THE SECTION NEAREST THE CHURCH TO LUBBOCK, WHO VOLUNTEERED SO EAGERLY FOR IT.

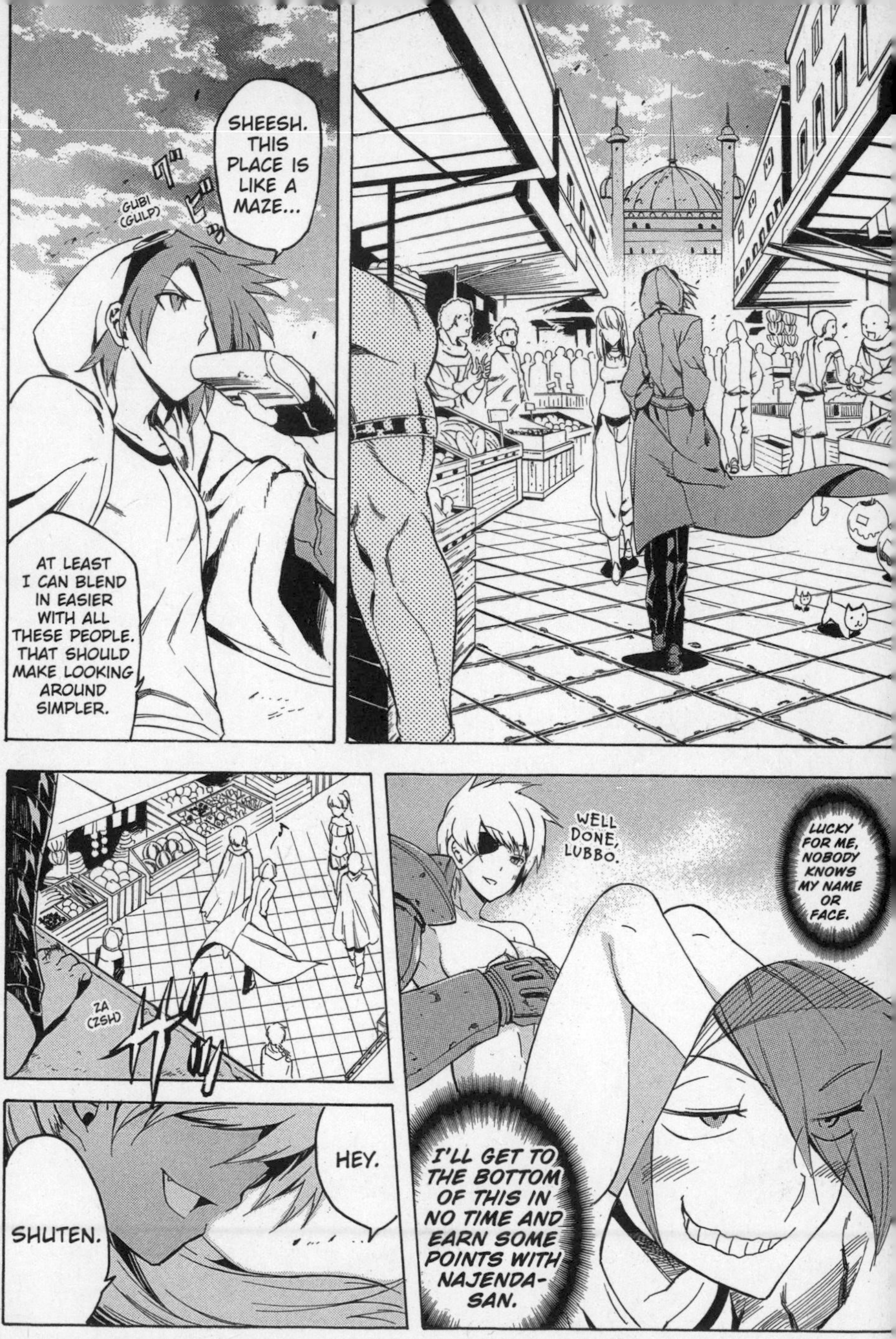
SHEESH. THIS PLACE IS LIKE A MAZE...
GUBI (GULP)
AT LEAST I CAN BLEND IN EASIER WITH ALL THESE PEOPLE. THAT SHOULD MAKE LOOKING AROUND SIMPLER.
WELL DONE, LUBBO.
LUCKY FOR ME, NOBODY KNOWS MY NAME OR FACE.
I'LL GET TO THE BOTTOM OF THIS IN NO TIME AND EARN SOME POINTS WITH NAJENDA-SAN.
ZA (ZSH)
HEY.
SHUTEN.

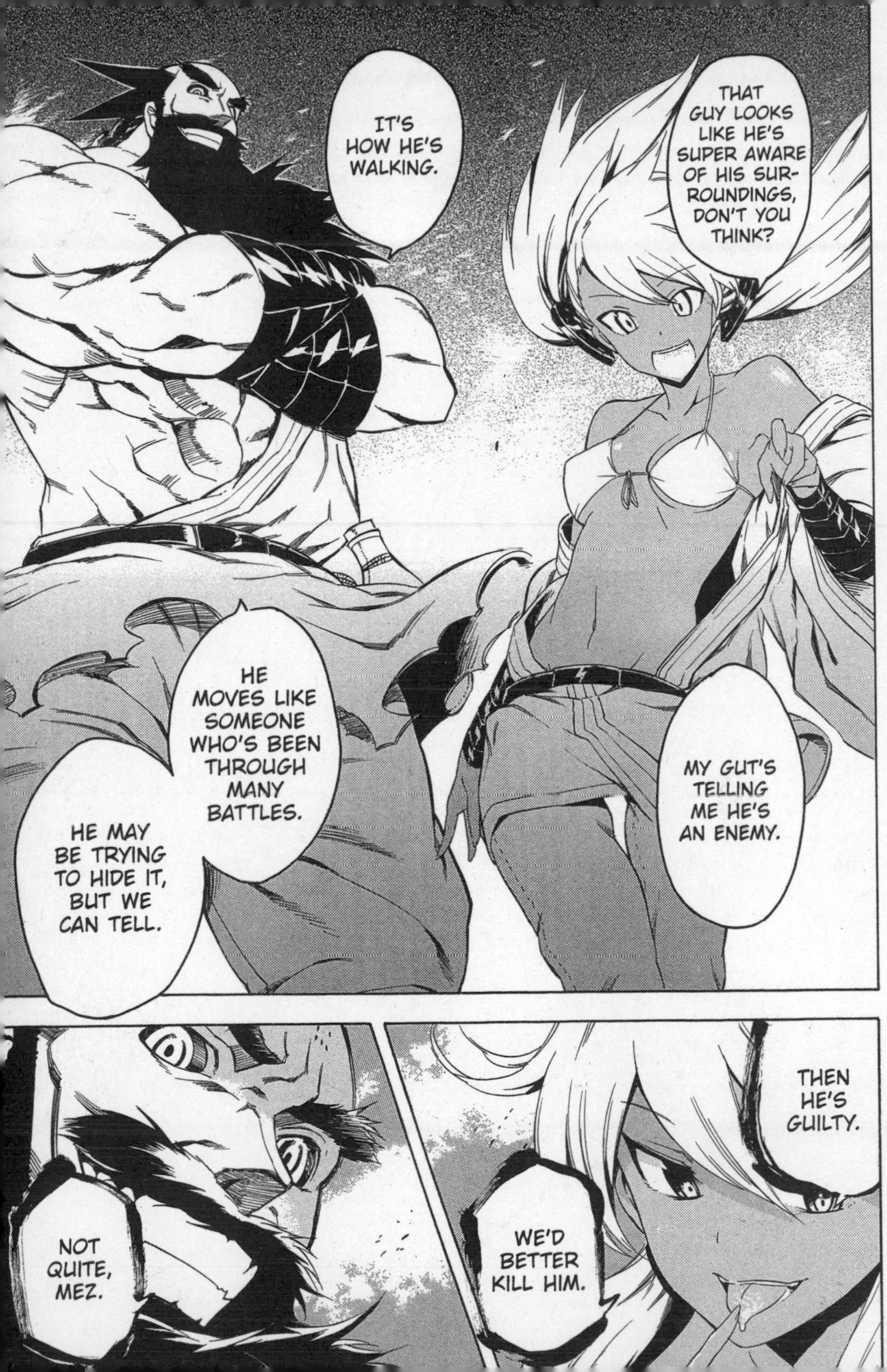
THAT GUY LOOKS LIKE HE'S SUPER AWARE OF HIS SUR-ROUNDINGS, DON'T YOU THINK?
IT'S HOW HE'S WALKING.
HE MOVES LIKE SOMEONE WHO'S BEEN THROUGH MANY BATTLES.
HE MAY BE TRYING TO HIDE IT, BUT WE CAN TELL.
MY GUT'S TELLING ME HE'S AN ENEMY.
THEN HE'S GUILTY.
WE'D BETTER KILL HIM.
NOT QUITE, MEZ.

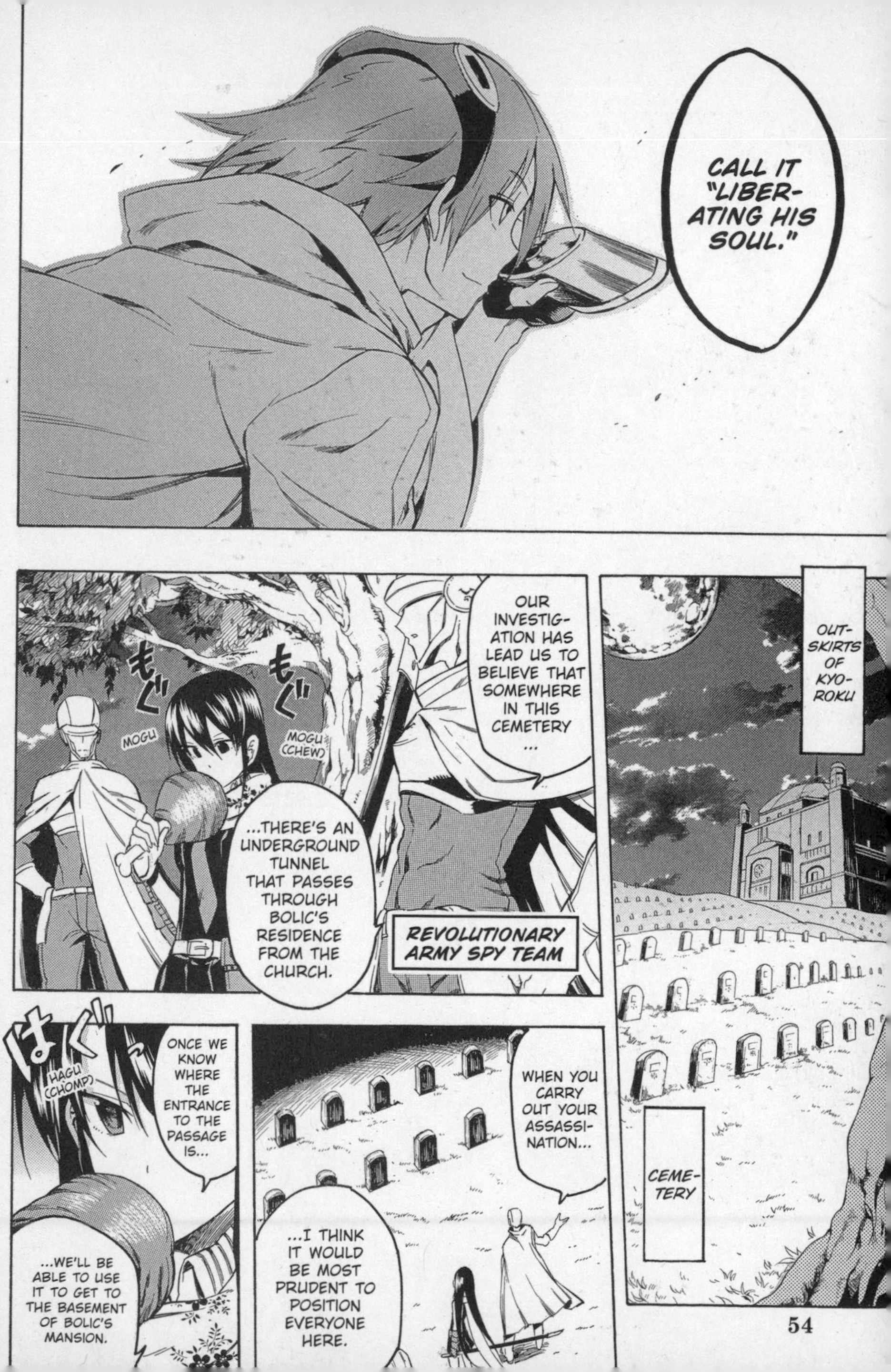
CALL IT "LIBERATING HIS SOUL."
OUTSKIRTS OF KYOROKU
CEMETERY
OUR INVESTIGATION HAS LEAD US TO BELIEVE THAT SOMEWHERE IN THIS CEMETERY ...
もぐ
MOGU (CHEW)
もぐ
MOGU
...THERE'S AN UNDERGROUND TUNNEL THAT PASSES THROUGH BOLIC'S RESIDENCE FROM THE CHURCH.
REVOLUTIONARY ARMY SPY TEAM
WHEN YOU CARRY OUT YOUR ASSASSINATION...
...I THINK IT WOULD BE MOST PRUDENT TO POSITION EVERYONE HERE.
はぐっ
HAGU (CHOMP)
ONCE WE KNOW WHERE THE ENTRANCE TO THE PASSAGE IS...
...WE'LL BE ABLE TO USE IT TO GET TO THE BASEMENT OF BOLIC'S MANSION.

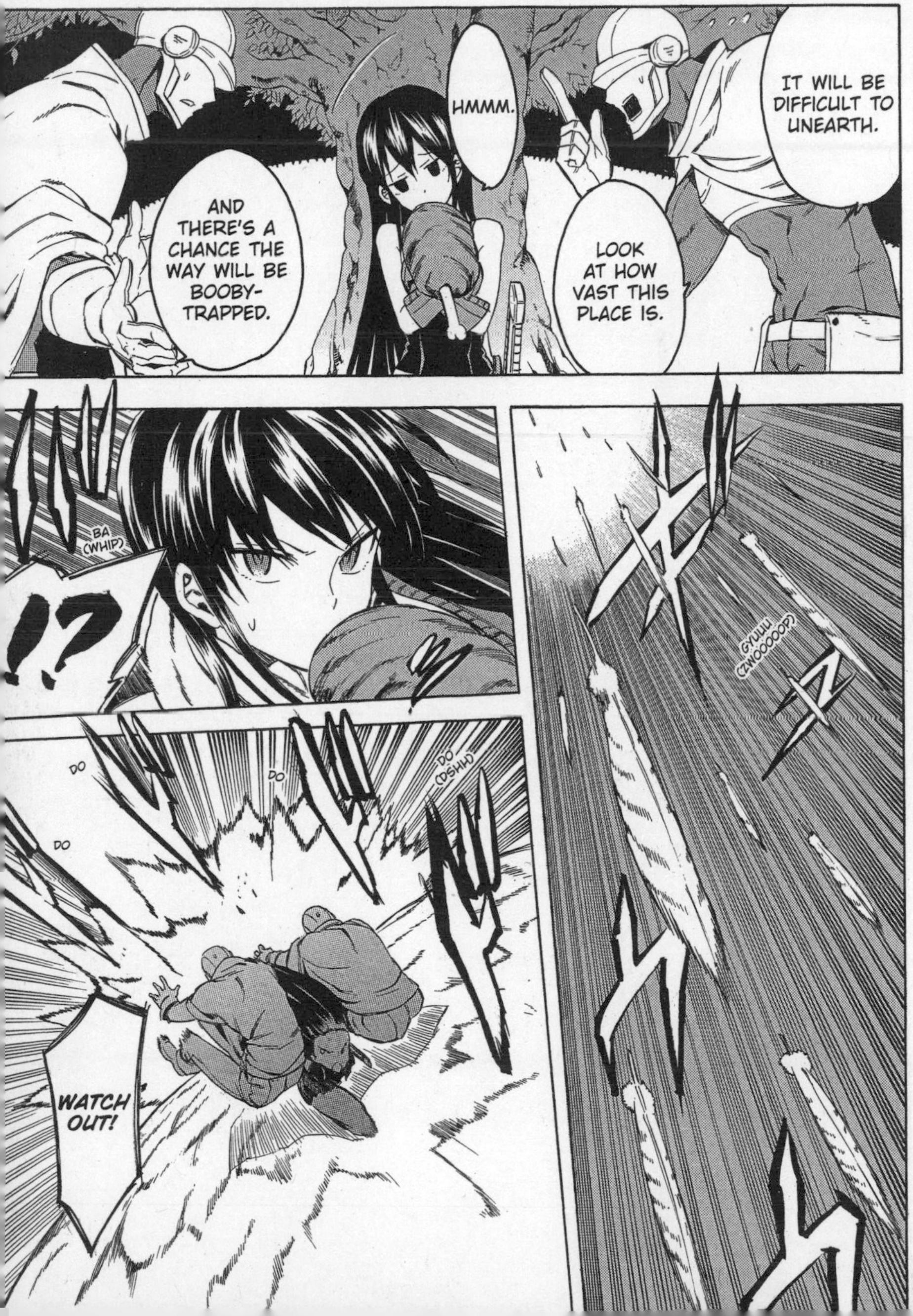
IT WILL BE DIFFICULT TO UNEARTH.
LOOK AT HOW VAST THIS PLACE IS.
HMMM.
AND THERE'S A CHANCE THE WAY WILL BE BOOBY-TRAPPED.
GYULLL (ZWOOOOOP)
BA (WHIP)
!?
DO (DSHH)
DO
DO
DO
WATCH OUT!

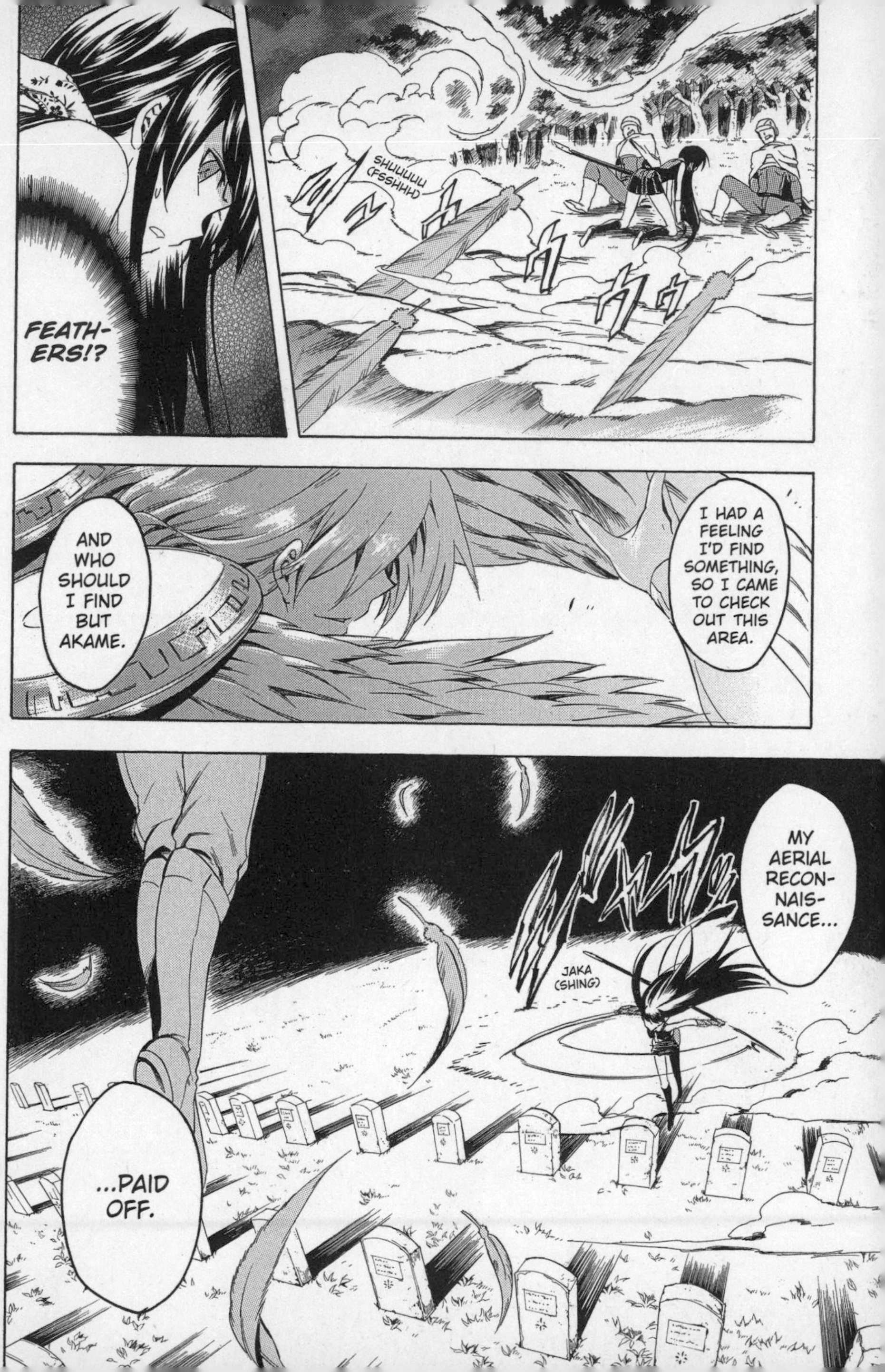
FEATH-
ERS!?
SHUUUUU
(FSSHHH)
I HAD A FEELING I'D FIND SOMETHING, SO I CAME TO CHECK OUT THIS AREA.
AND WHO SHOULD I FIND BUT AKAME.
MY AERIAL RECON- NAIS- SANCE...
JAKA
(SHING)
...PAID OFF.

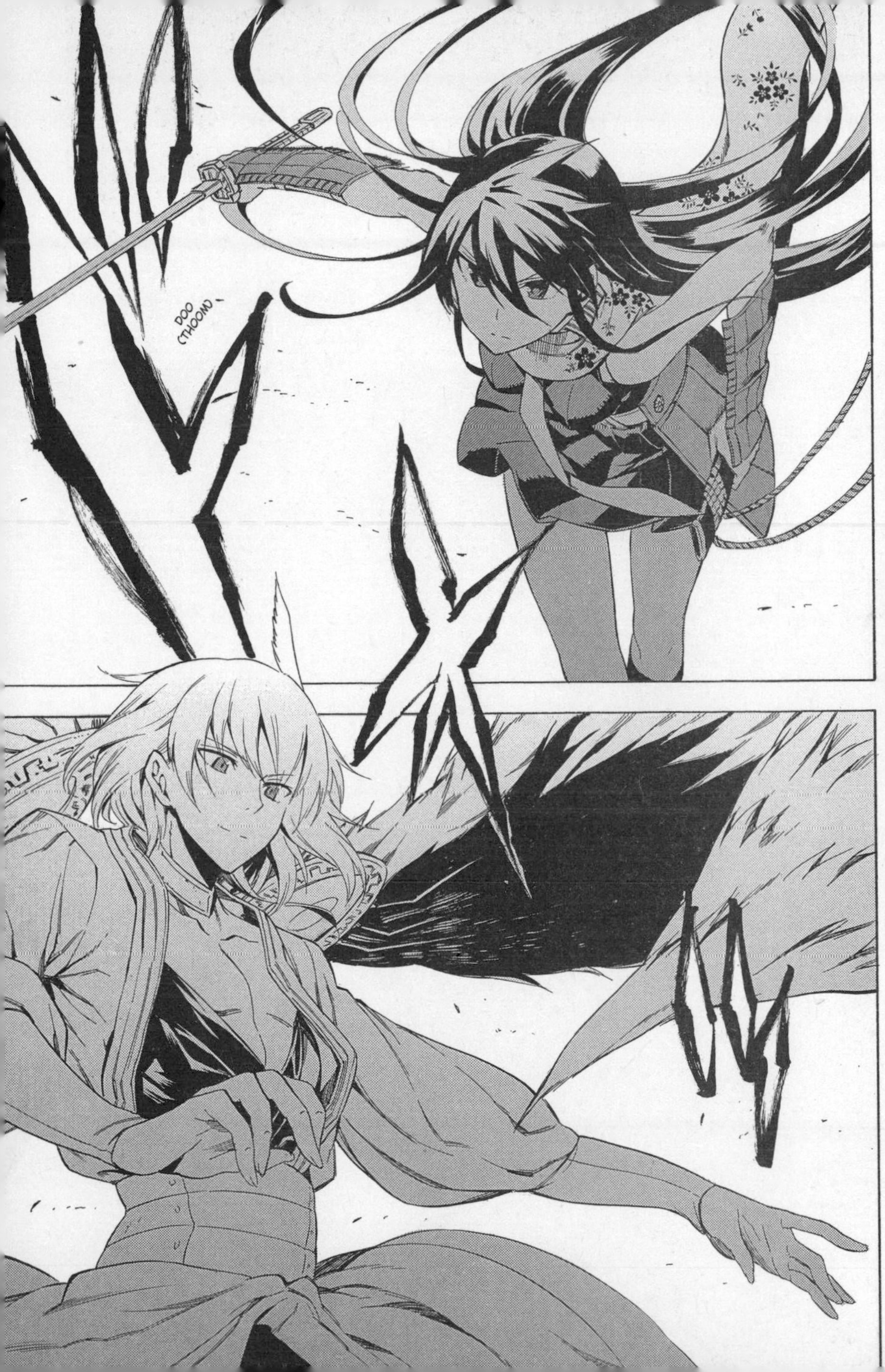
DOO
(THOOM)

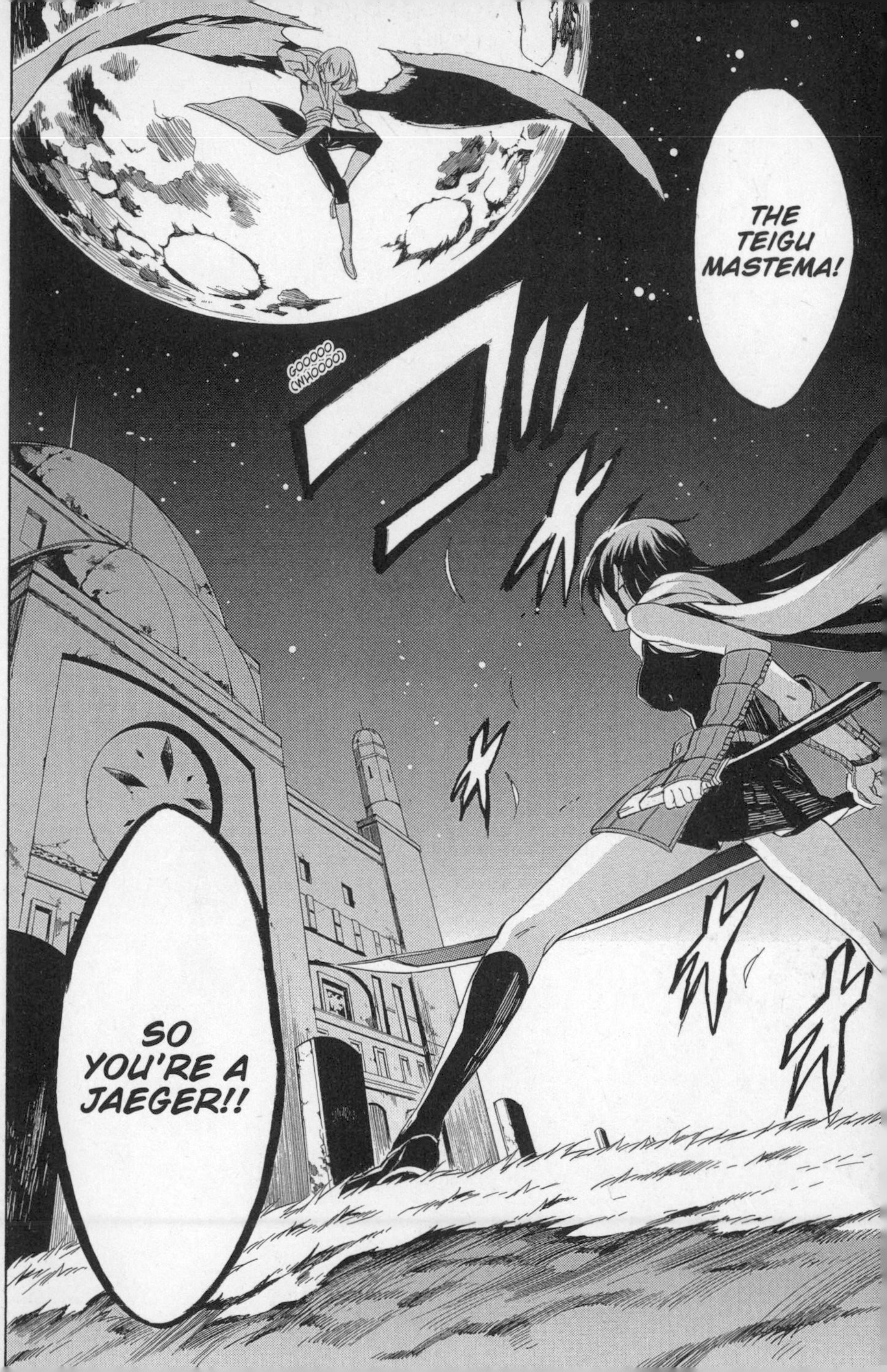
THE TEIGU MASTEMA!
GOOOOO (WHOOOOO)
SO YOU'RE A JAEGER!!

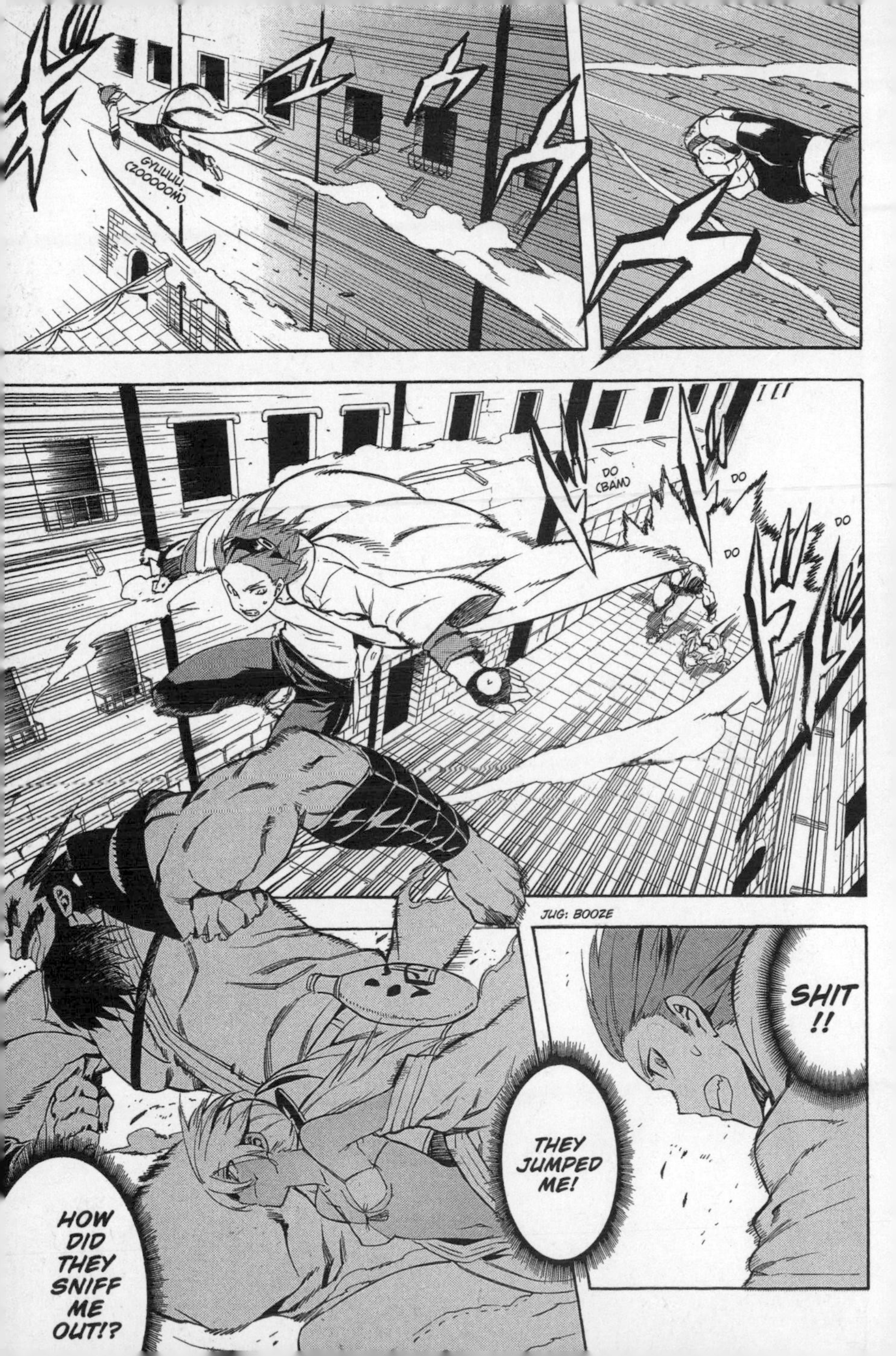

GYUUUN (ZOOOOOM)
DO (BAM)
DO
DO
DO
JUG: BOOZE
SHIT!!
THEY JUMPED ME!
HOW DID THEY SNIFF ME OUT!?

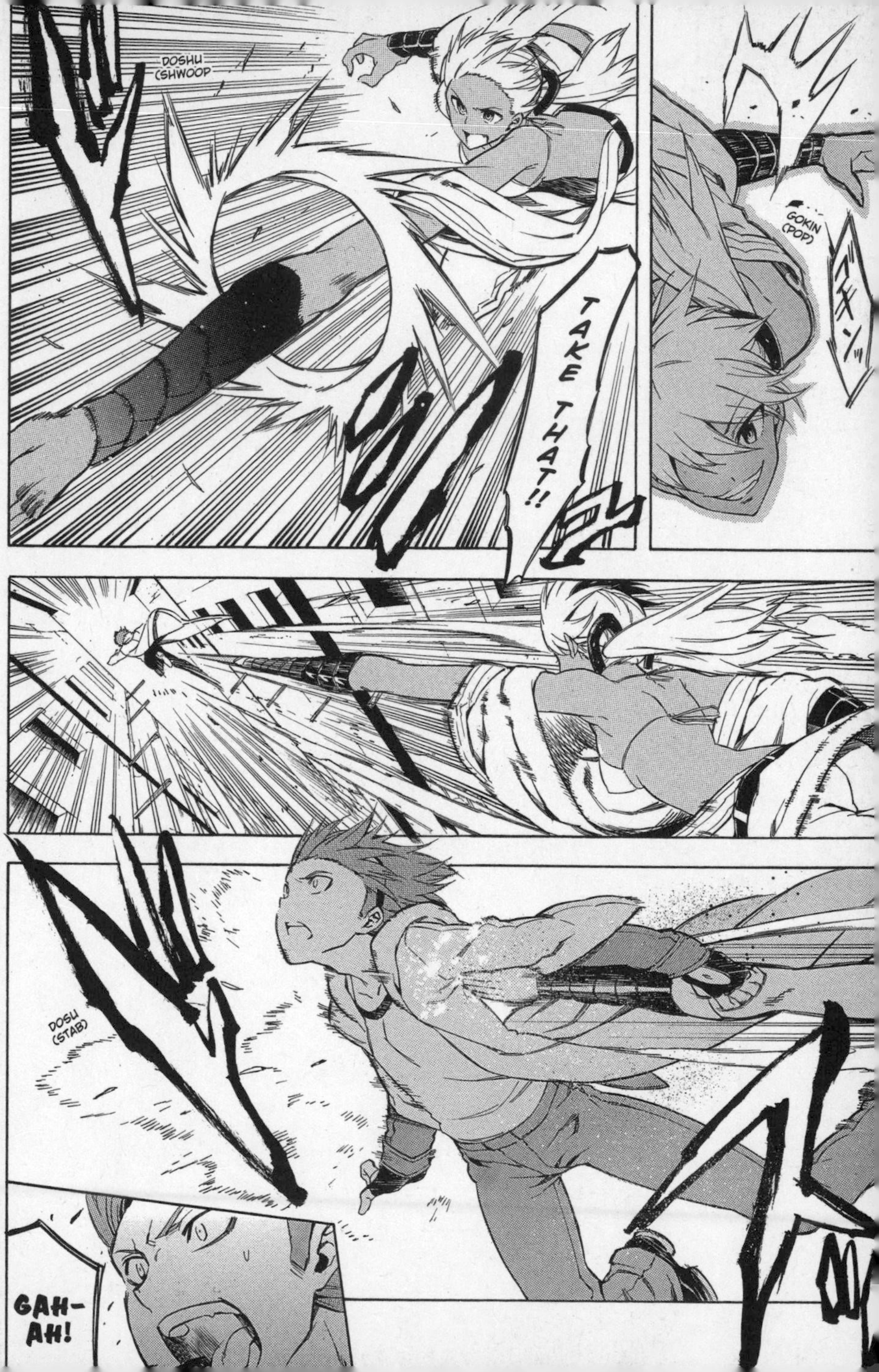
DOSHU
(SHWOOP
GOKIN
(POP)
TAKE THAT!!
DOSU
(STAB)
GAH-
AH!

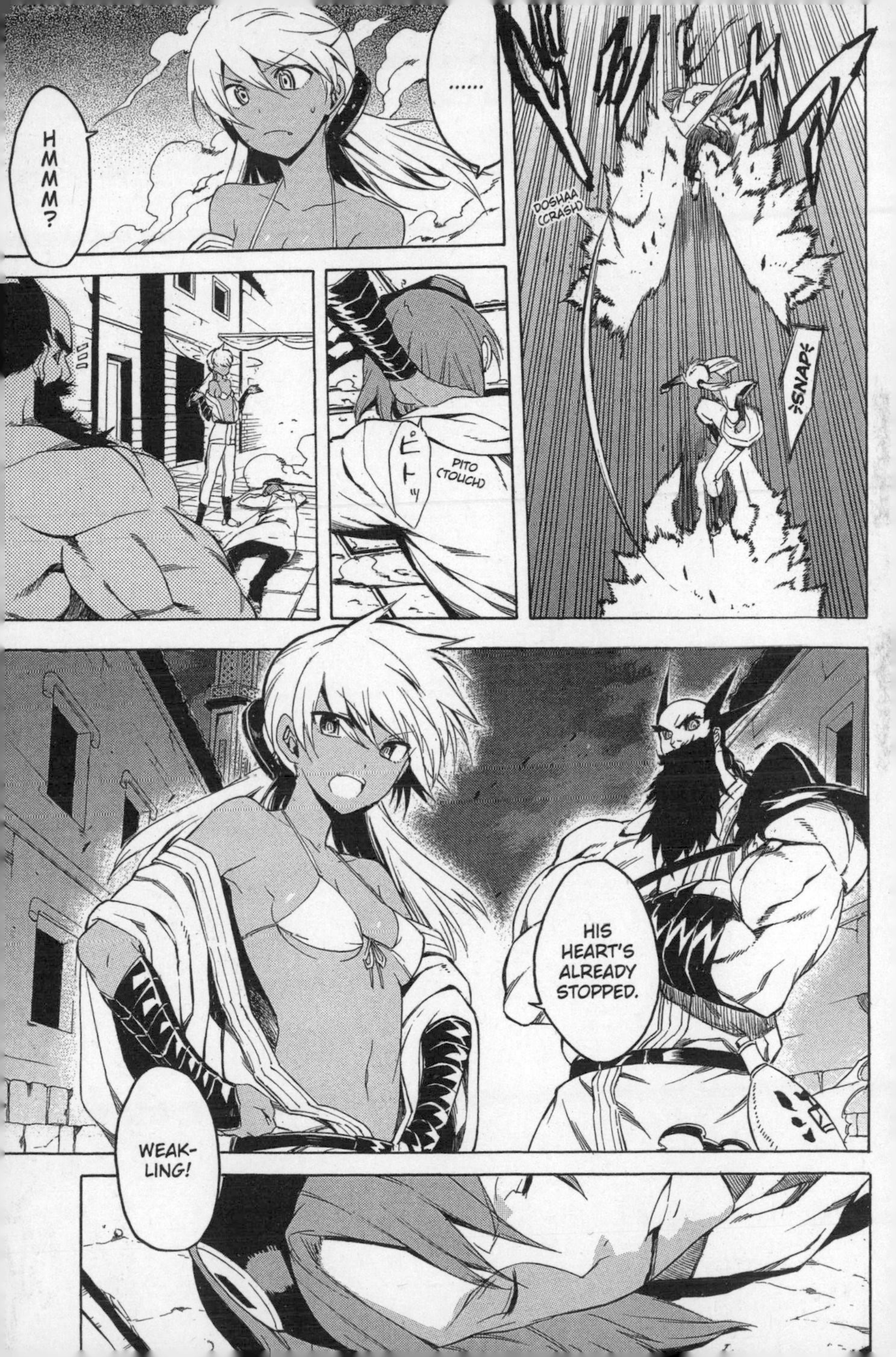
DOSHAA (CRASH)
SNAP
......
HMMMM?
ピトッ
PITO (TOUCH)
HIS HEART'S ALREADY STOPPED.
WEAK-LING!

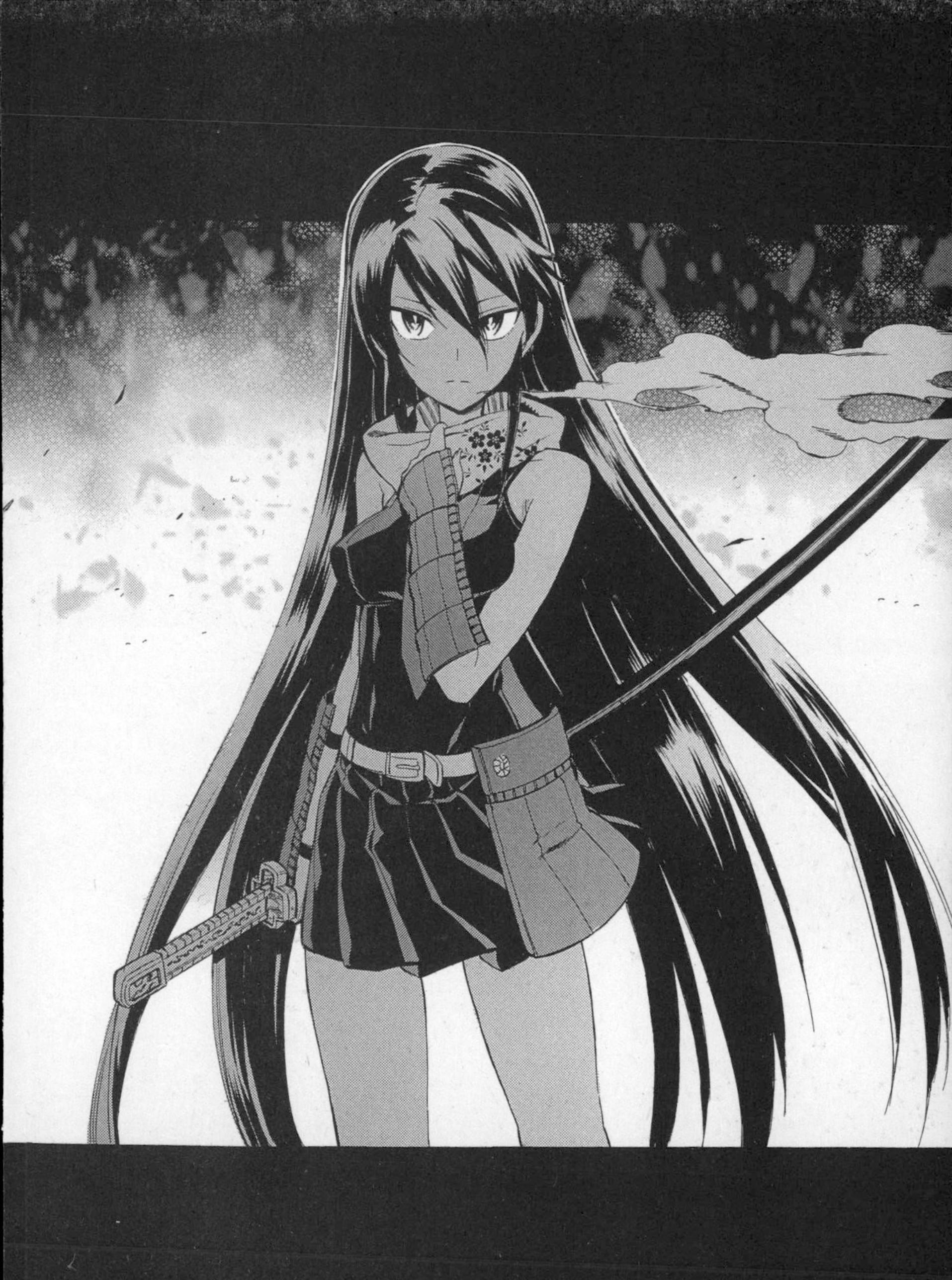

# Chapter 35 - Kill the Demons (Part II)

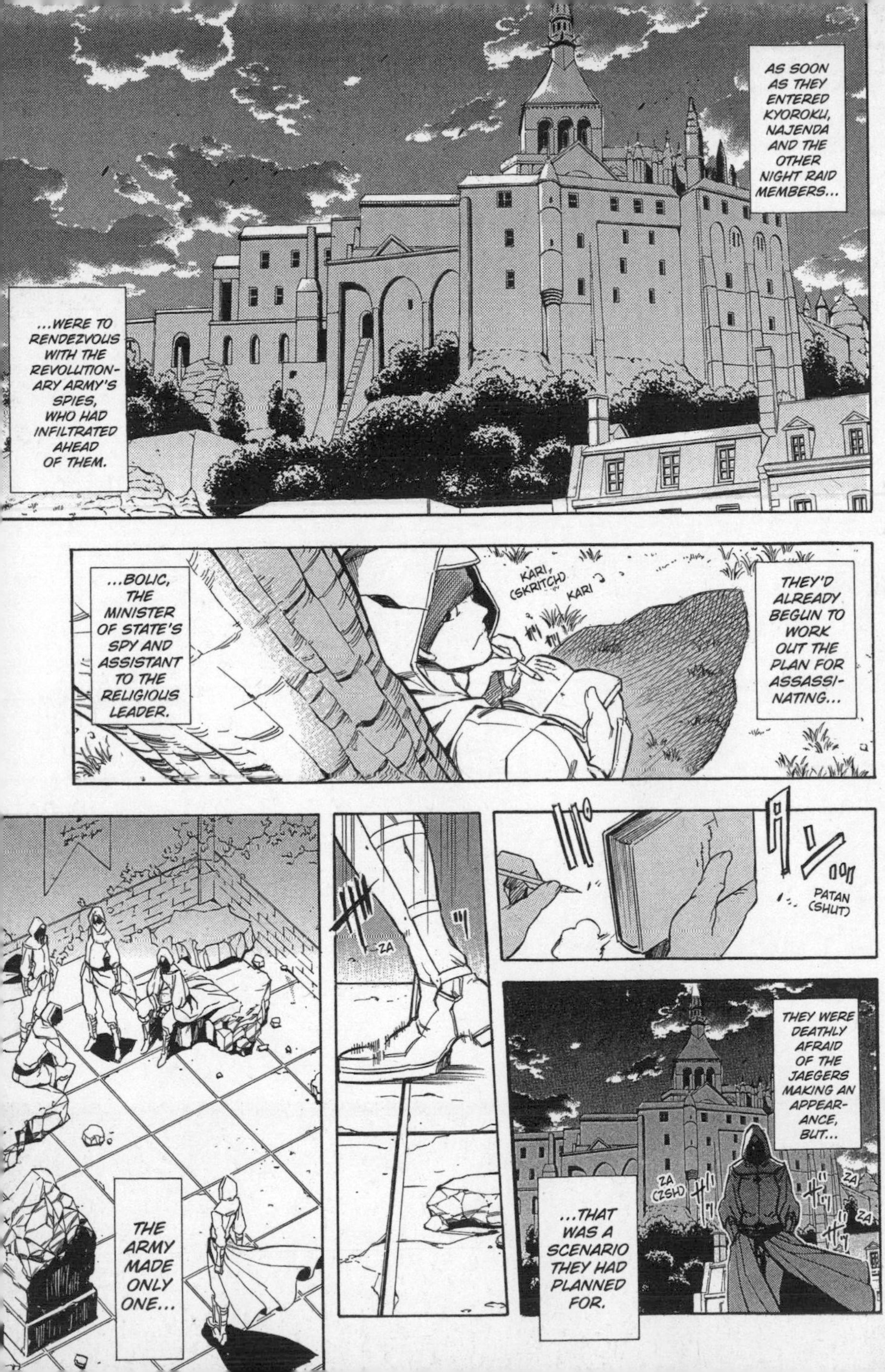

AS SOON AS THEY ENTERED KYOROKU, NAJENDA AND THE OTHER NIGHT RAID MEMBERS...
...WERE TO RENDEZVOUS WITH THE REVOLUTIONARY ARMY'S SPIES, WHO HAD INFILTRATED AHEAD OF THEM.
THEY'D ALREADY BEGUN TO WORK OUT THE PLAN FOR ASSASSINATING...
KARI (SKRITCH) KARI
...BOLIC, THE MINISTER OF STATE'S SPY AND ASSISTANT TO THE RELIGIOUS LEADER.
PATAN (SHUT)
ZA
THE ARMY MADE ONLY ONE...
THEY WERE DEATHLY AFRAID OF THE JAEGERS MAKING AN APPEARANCE, BUT...
ZA
ZA
ZA (ZSH)
...THAT WAS A SCENARIO THEY HAD PLANNED FOR.

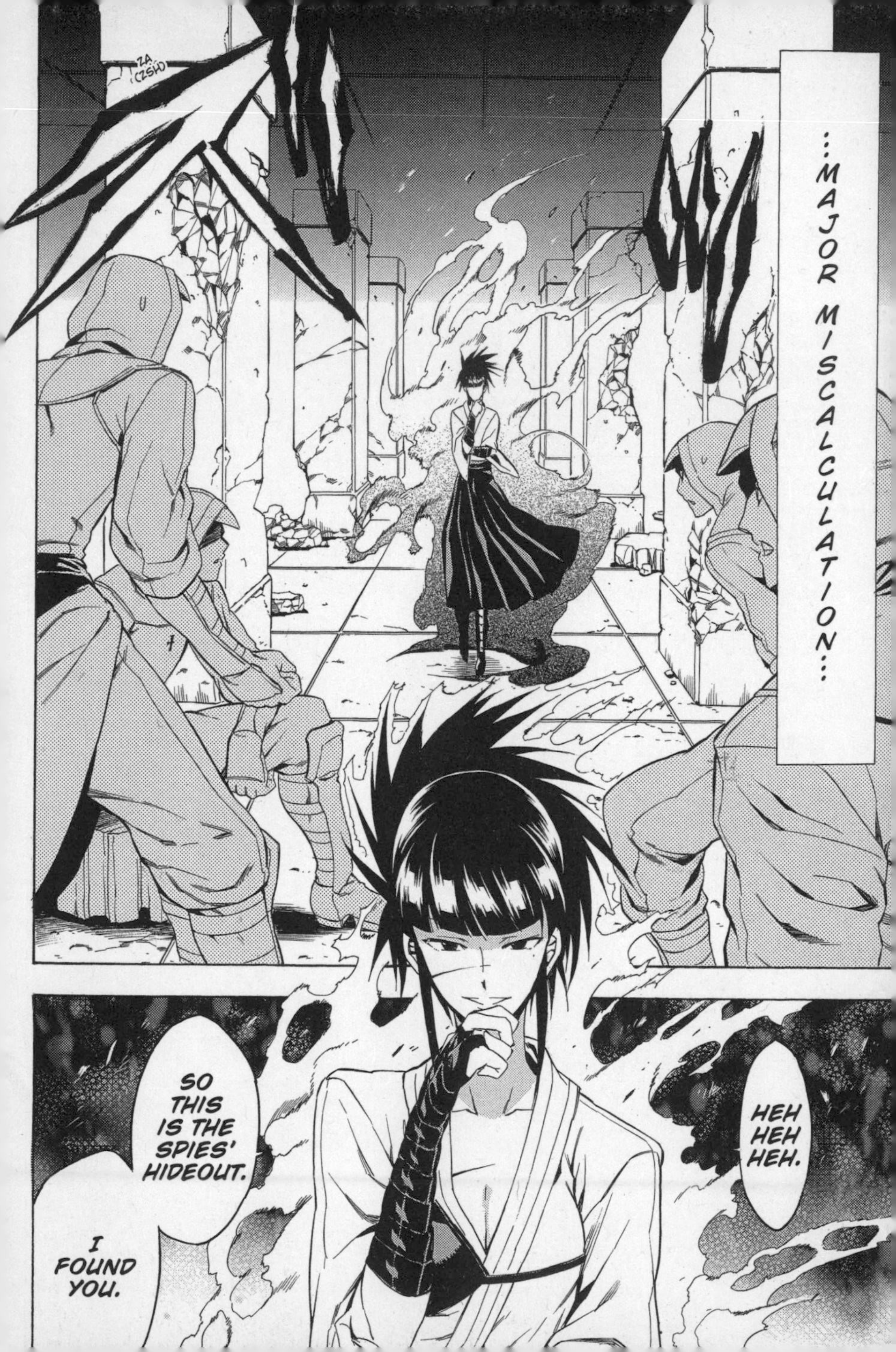
ZA (ZSH)
...MAJOR MISCALCULATION...
HEH HEH HEH.
SO THIS IS THE SPIES' HIDEOUT.
I FOUND YOU.

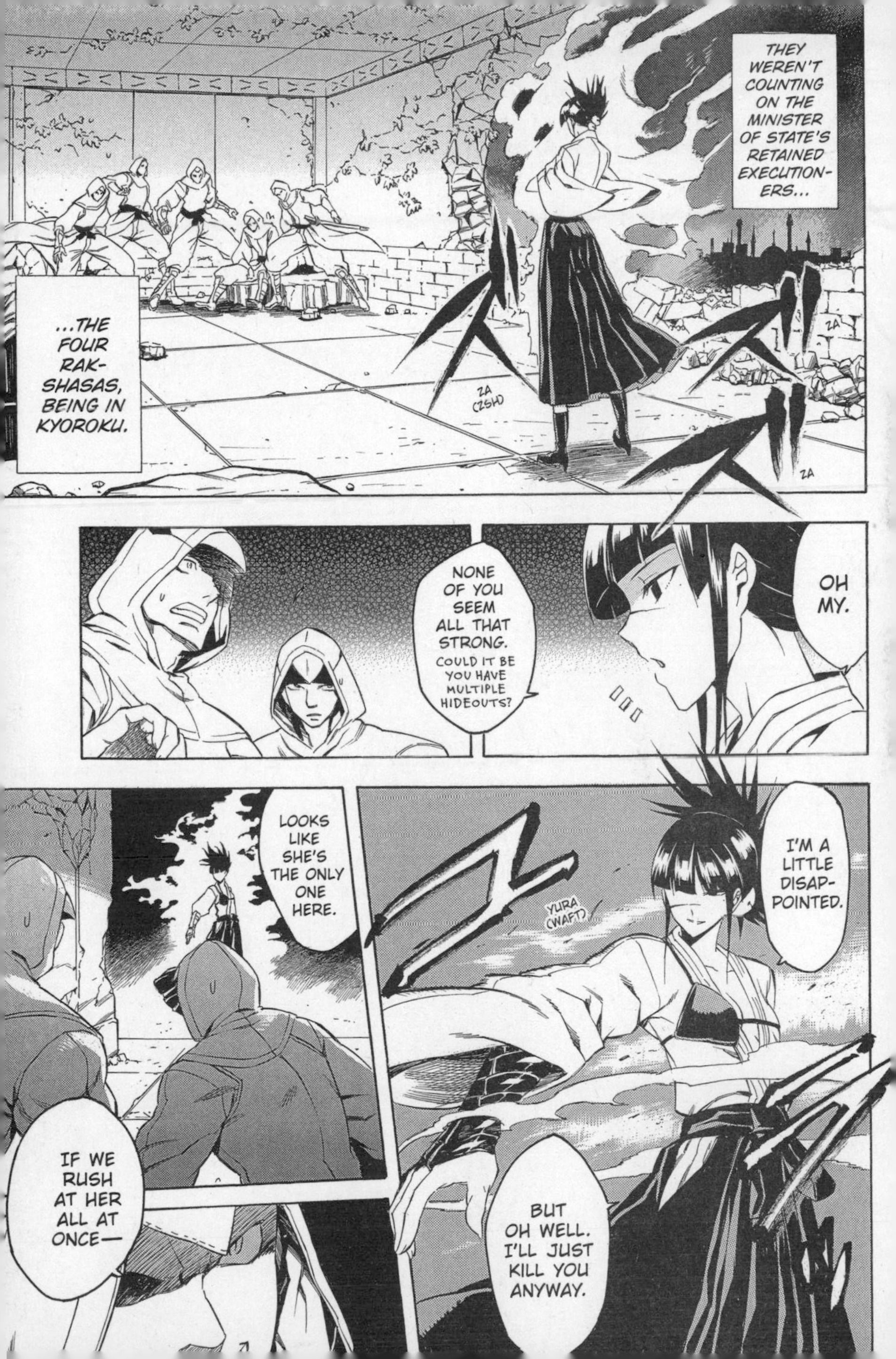
THEY WEREN'T COUNTING ON THE MINISTER OF STATE'S RETAINED EXECUTION-ERS...
...THE FOUR RAK-SHASAS, BEING IN KYOROKU.
ZA
ZA (ZSH)
ZA
OH MY.
NONE OF YOU SEEM ALL THAT STRONG. COULD IT BE YOU HAVE MULTIPLE HIDEOUTS?
I'M A LITTLE DISAP-POINTED.
YURA (WAFT)
LOOKS LIKE SHE'S THE ONLY ONE HERE.
BUT OH WELL. I'LL JUST KILL YOU ANYWAY.
IF WE RUSH AT HER ALL AT ONCE—

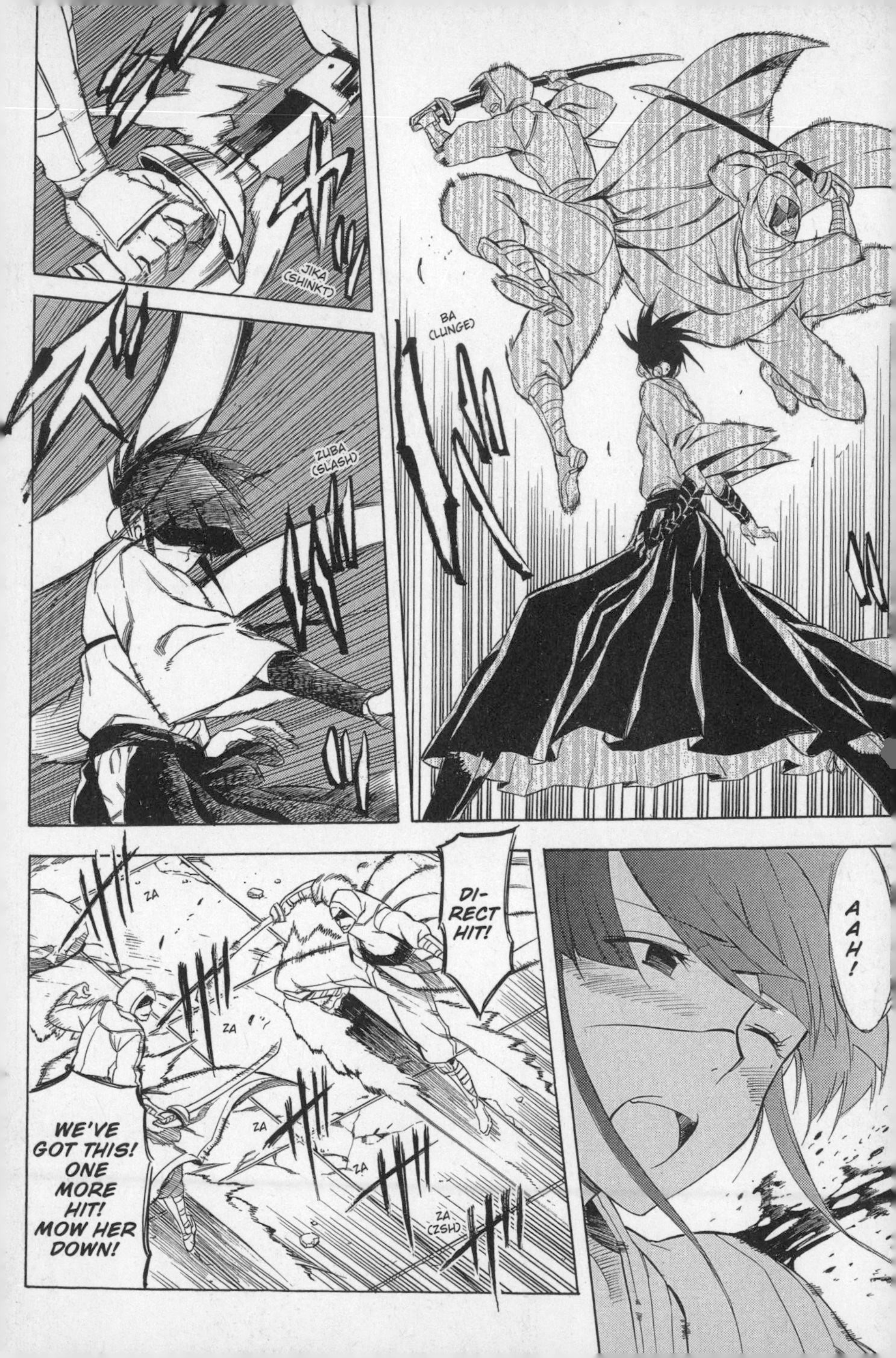
BA (LUNGE)
JIKA (SHINKT)
ZUBA (SLASH)
AAH!
DI-RECT HIT!
ZA
ZA
ZA
ZA
ZA (ZSH)
WE'VE GOT THIS! ONE MORE HIT! MOW HER DOWN!

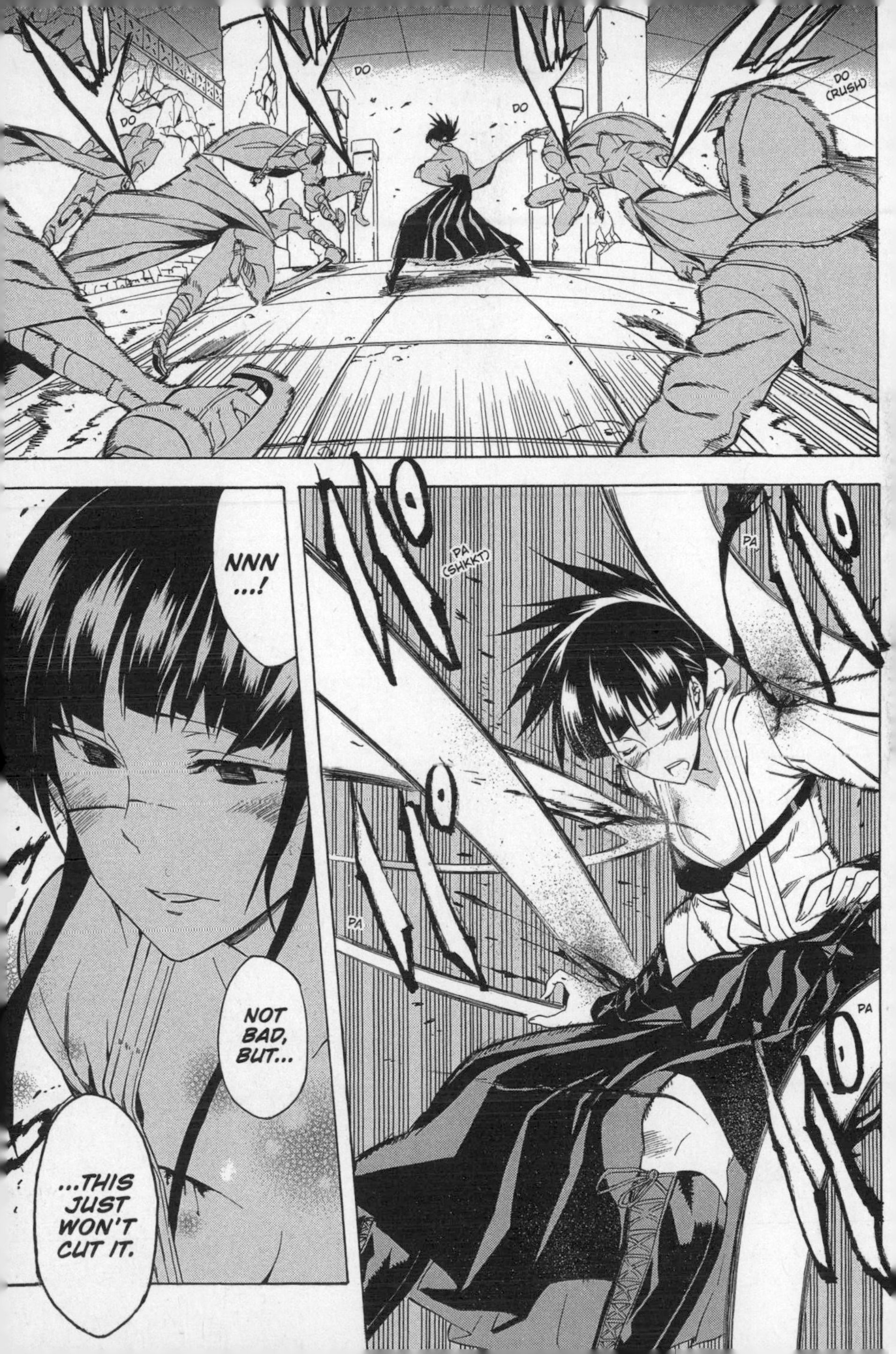
DO (RUSH)
DO
DO
DO
PA
PA (SHKKT)
PA
PA
NNN ...!
NOT BAD, BUT...
...THIS JUST WON'T CUT IT.

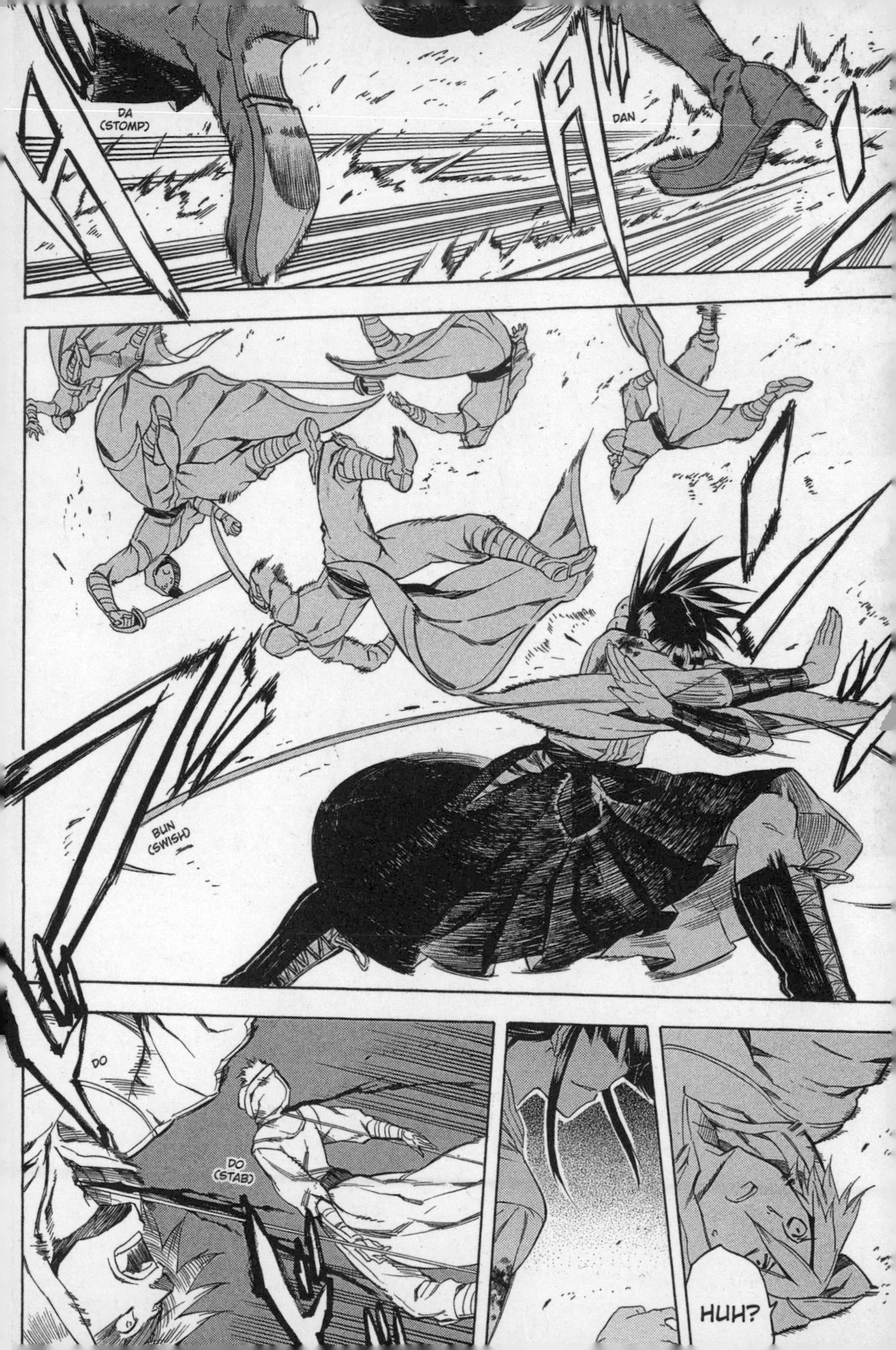
DAN
DA
(STOMP)
BUN
(SWISH)
HUH?
DO
DO
(STAB)

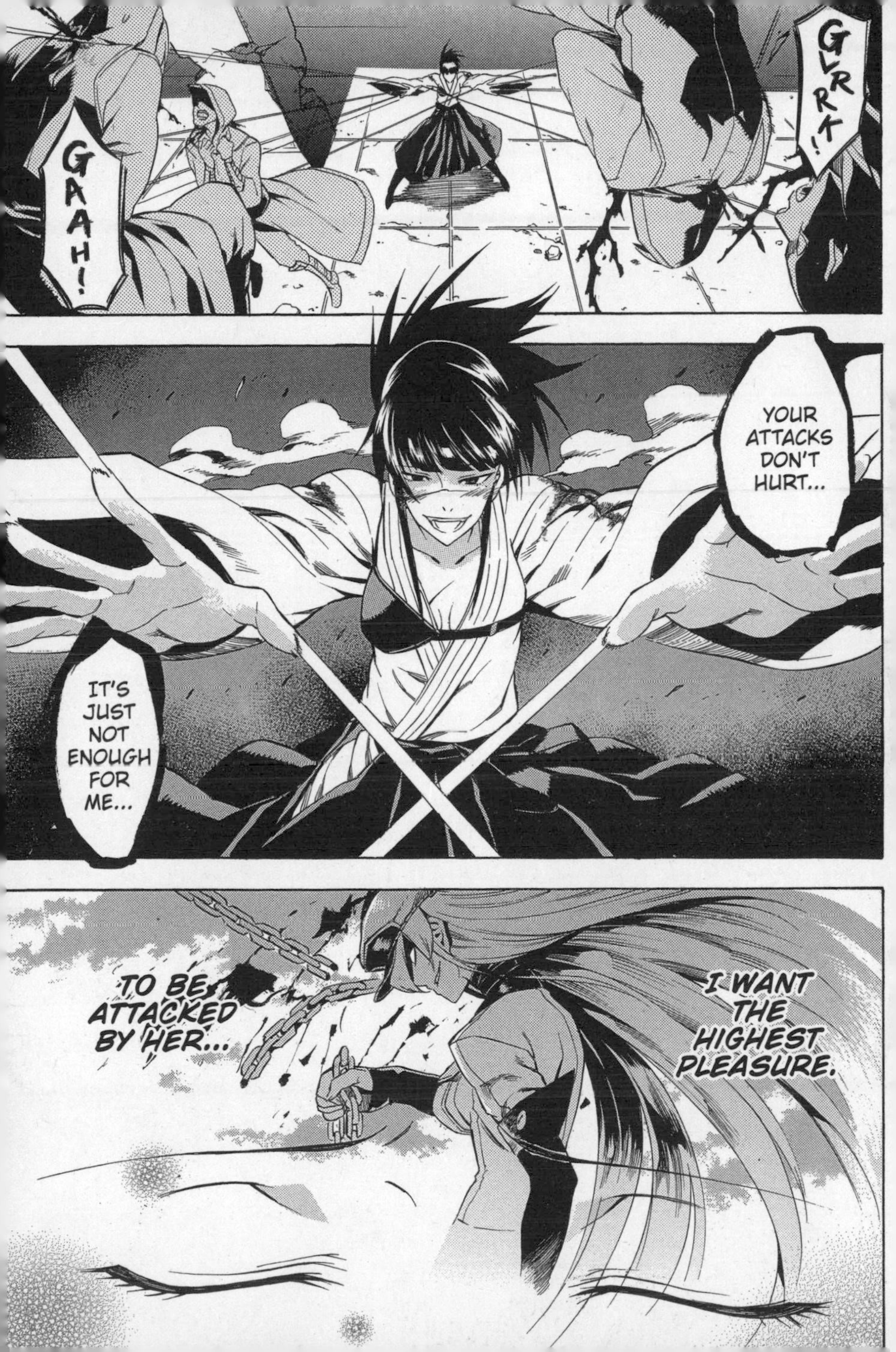
GLRRK!
GAAH!
YOUR ATTACKS DON'T HURT...
IT'S JUST NOT ENOUGH FOR ME...
I WANT THE HIGHEST PLEASURE.
TO BE ATTACKED BY HER...

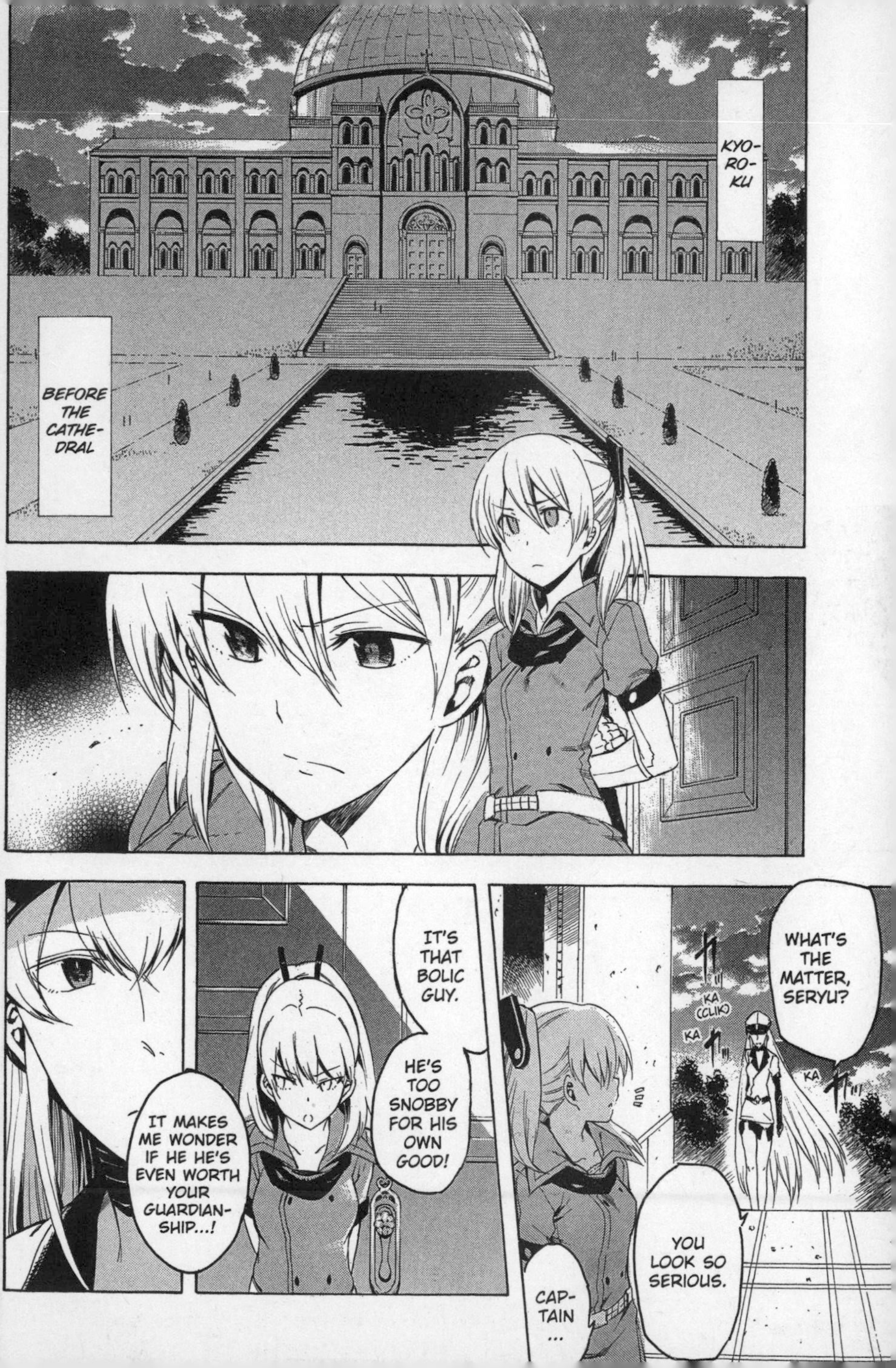
KYO-RO-KU
BEFORE THE CATHE-DRAL
WHAT'S THE MATTER, SERYU?
KA (CLIK)
KA
KA
YOU LOOK SO SERIOUS.
CAP-TAIN...
IT'S THAT BOLIC GUY.
HE'S TOO SNOBBY FOR HIS OWN GOOD!
IT MAKES ME WONDER IF HE HE'S EVEN WORTH YOUR GUARDIAN-SHIP...!

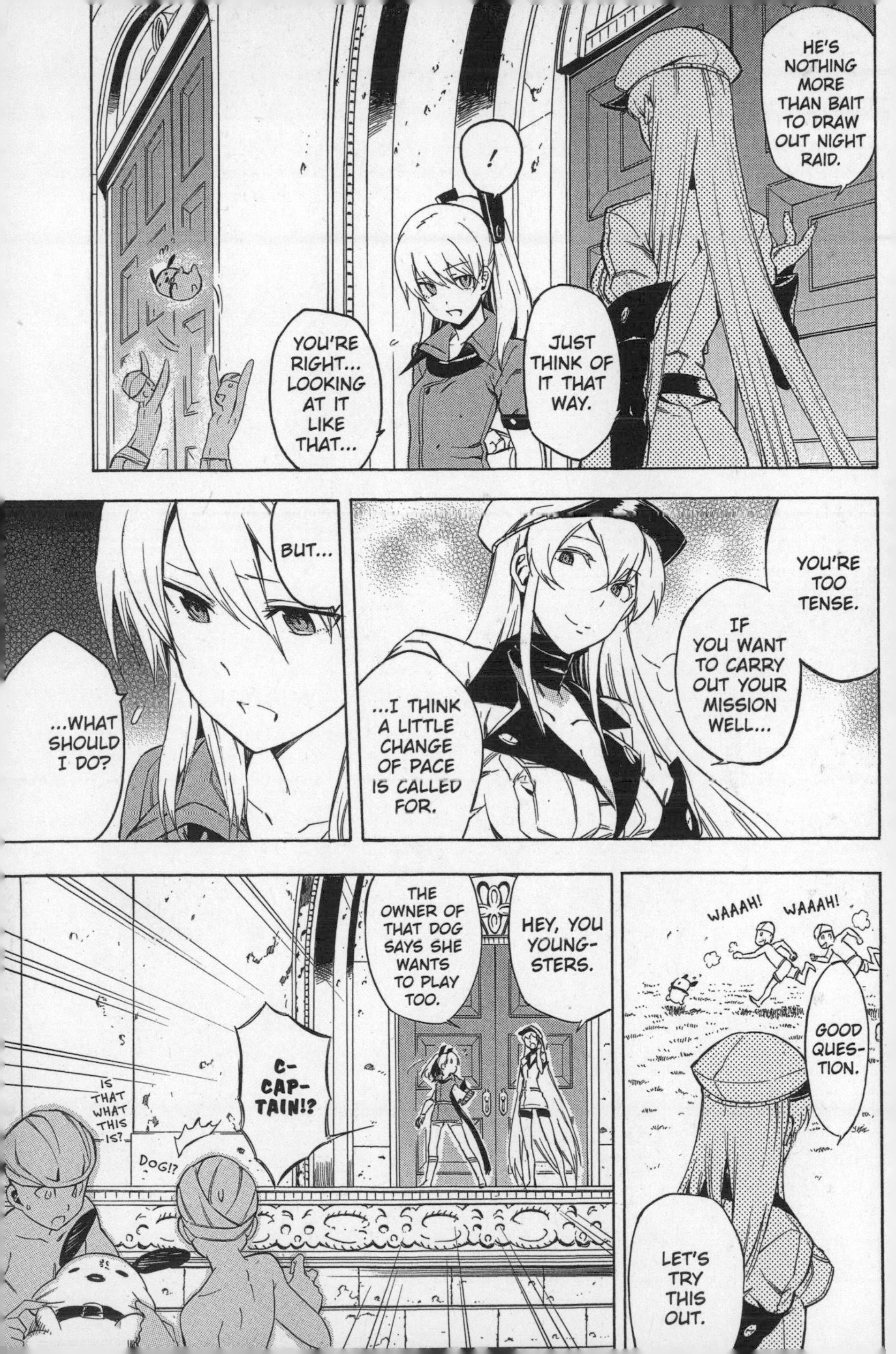
HE'S NOTHING MORE THAN BAIT TO DRAW OUT NIGHT RAID.
!
JUST THINK OF IT THAT WAY.
YOU'RE RIGHT... LOOKING AT IT LIKE THAT...
YOU'RE TOO TENSE.
IF YOU WANT TO CARRY OUT YOUR MISSION WELL...
...I THINK A LITTLE CHANGE OF PACE IS CALLED FOR.
BUT...
...WHAT SHOULD I DO?
WAAAH!
WAAAH!
GOOD QUESTION.
LET'S TRY THIS OUT.
HEY, YOU YOUNGSTERS.
THE OWNER OF THAT DOG SAYS SHE WANTS TO PLAY TOO.
C-CAPTAIN!?
DOG!?
IS THAT WHAT THIS IS?

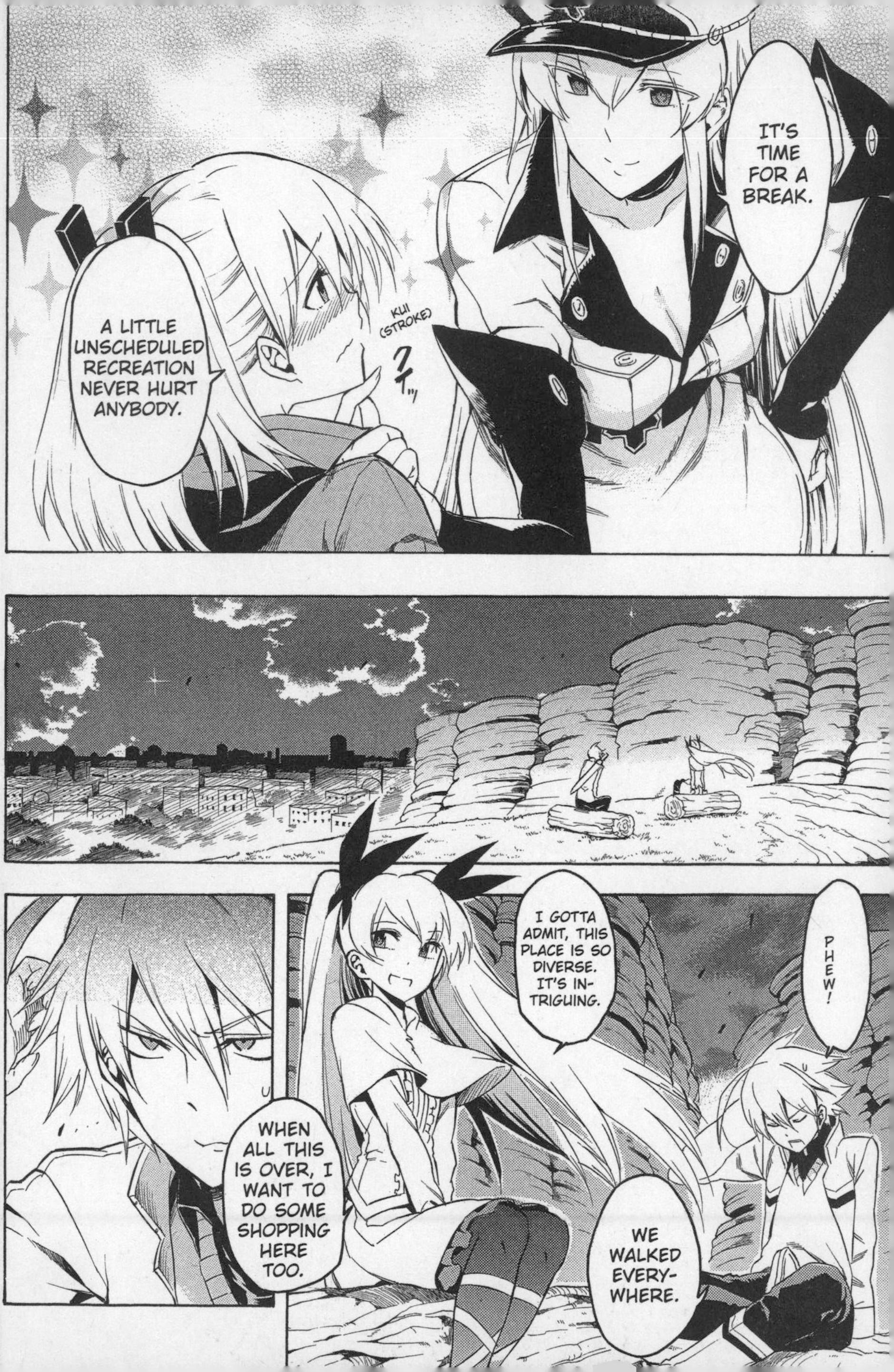

IT'S TIME FOR A BREAK.
KUI (STROKE)
A LITTLE UNSCHEDULED RECREATION NEVER HURT ANYBODY.
PHEW!
I GOTTA ADMIT, THIS PLACE IS SO DIVERSE. IT'S IN-TRIGUING.
WE WALKED EVERY-WHERE.
WHEN ALL THIS IS OVER, I WANT TO DO SOME SHOPPING HERE TOO.

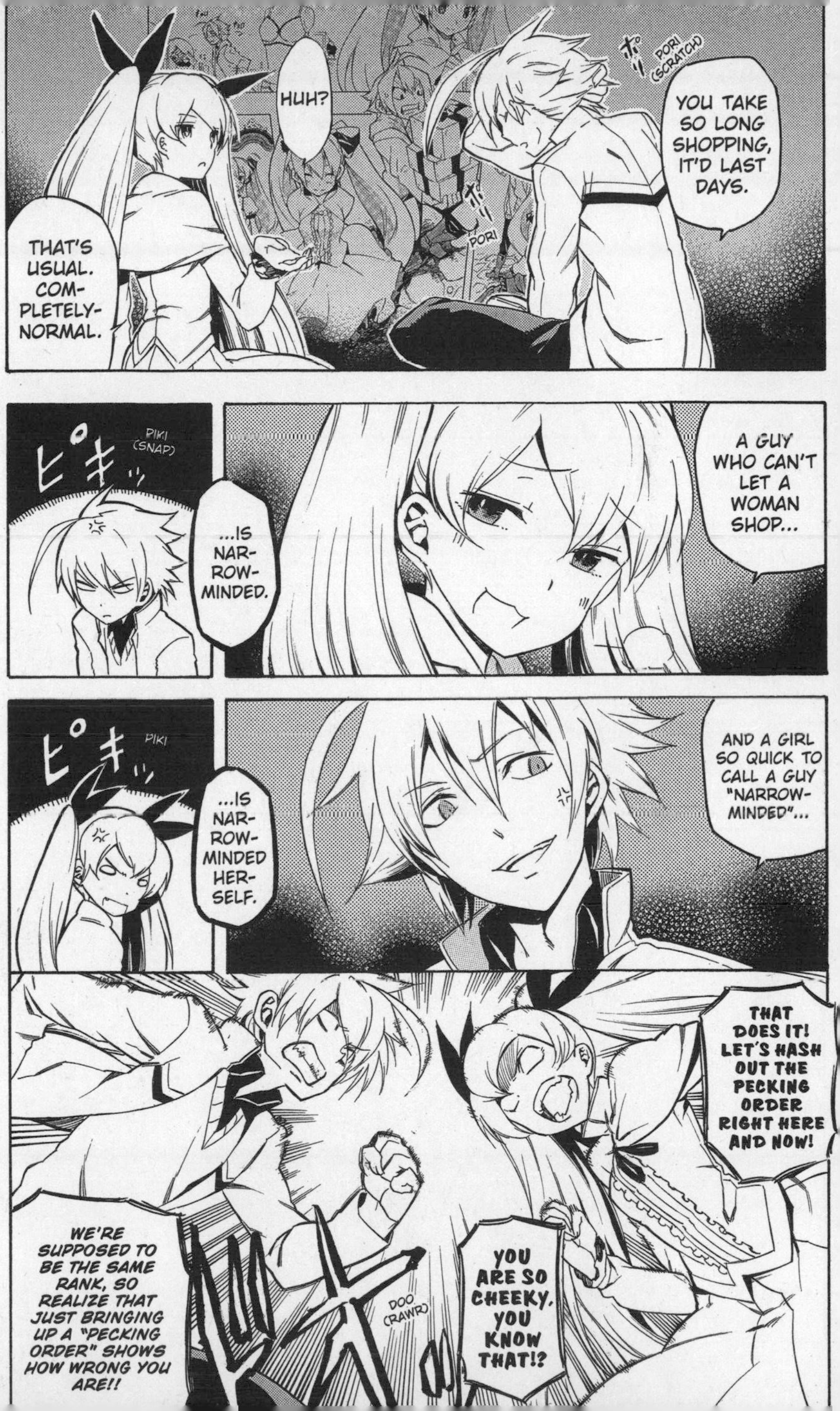

ポリ
PORI (SCRATCH)
YOU TAKE SO LONG SHOPPING, IT'D LAST DAYS.
ポリ
PORI
HUH?
THAT'S USUAL. COM-PLETELY-NORMAL.
A GUY WHO CAN'T LET A WOMAN SHOP...
ピキッ
PIKI (SNAP)
...IS NAR-ROW-MINDED.
AND A GIRL SO QUICK TO CALL A GUY "NARROW-MINDED"...
ピキッ
PIKI
...IS NAR-ROW-MINDED HER-SELF.
THAT DOES IT! LET'S HASH OUT THE PECKING ORDER RIGHT HERE AND NOW!
YOU ARE SO CHEEKY, YOU KNOW THAT!?
DOO (RAWR)
WE'RE SUPPOSED TO BE THE SAME RANK, SO REALIZE THAT JUST BRINGING UP A "PECKING ORDER" SHOWS HOW WRONG YOU ARE!!

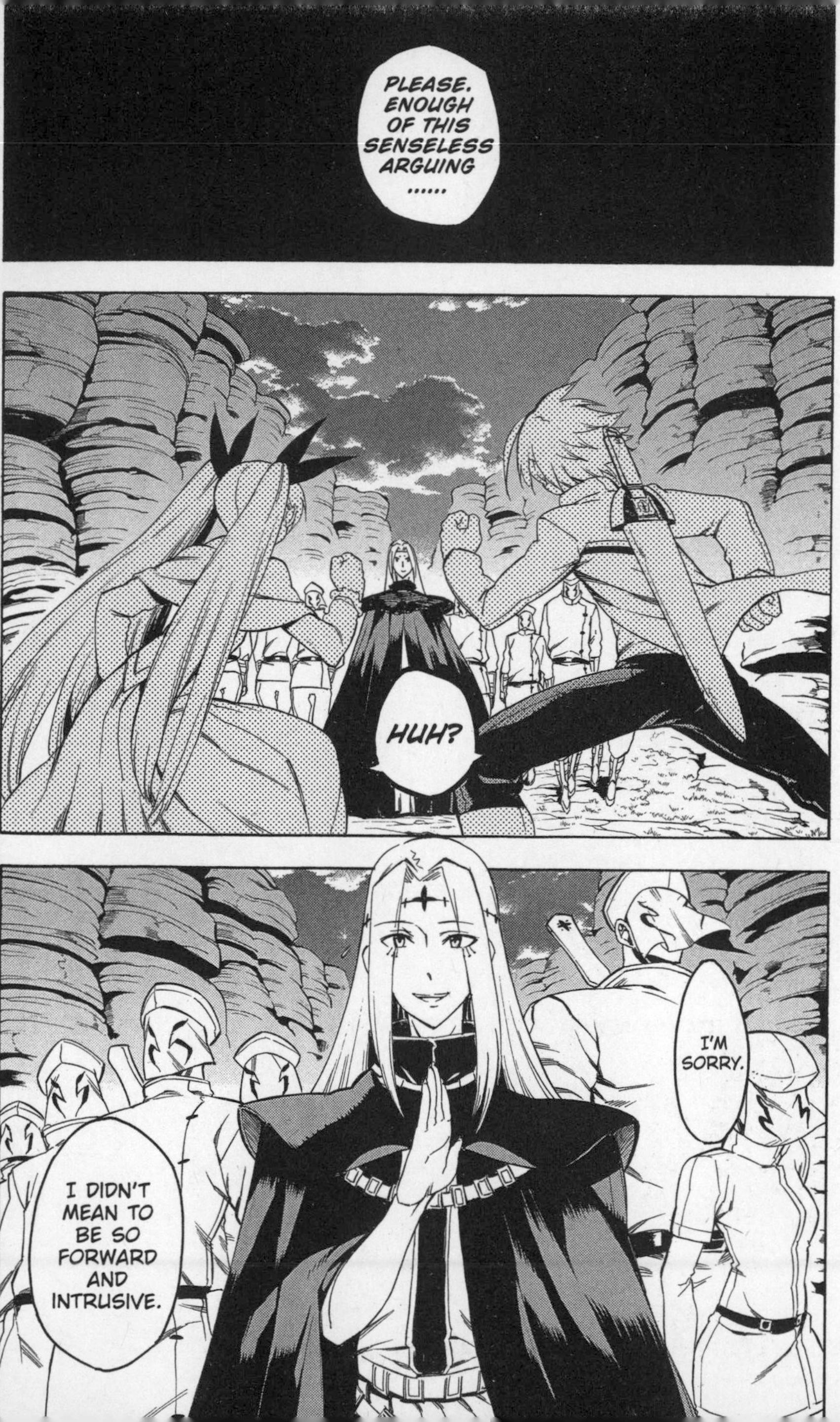
PLEASE. ENOUGH OF THIS SENSELESS ARGUING ......
HUH?
I'M SORRY.
I DIDN'T MEAN TO BE SO FORWARD AND INTRUSIVE.

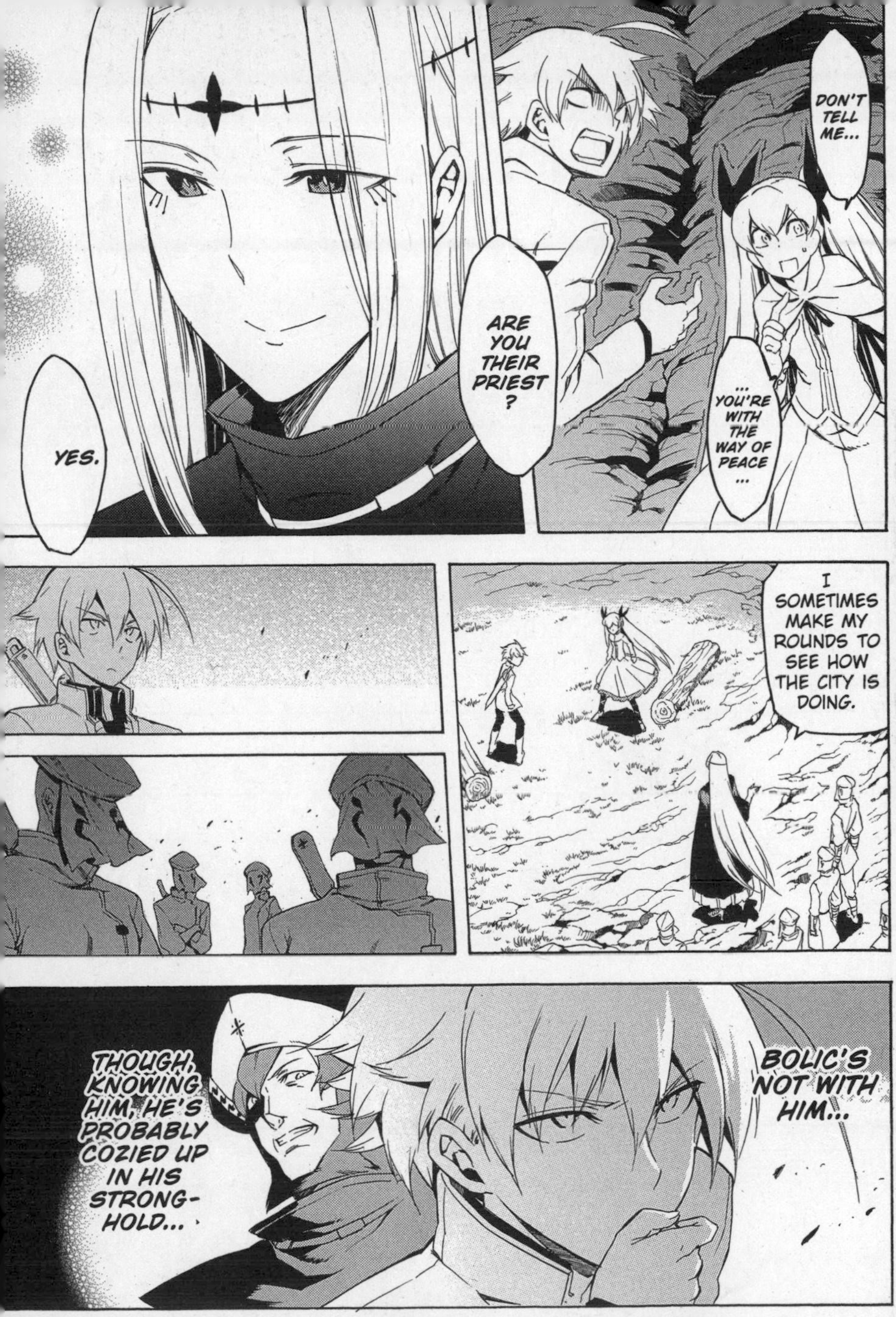
DON'T TELL ME...
...YOU'RE WITH THE WAY OF PEACE...
ARE YOU THEIR PRIEST?
YES.
I SOMETIMES MAKE MY ROUNDS TO SEE HOW THE CITY IS DOING.
BOLIC'S NOT WITH HIM...
THOUGH, KNOWING HIM, HE'S PROBABLY COZIED UP IN HIS STRONG-HOLD...

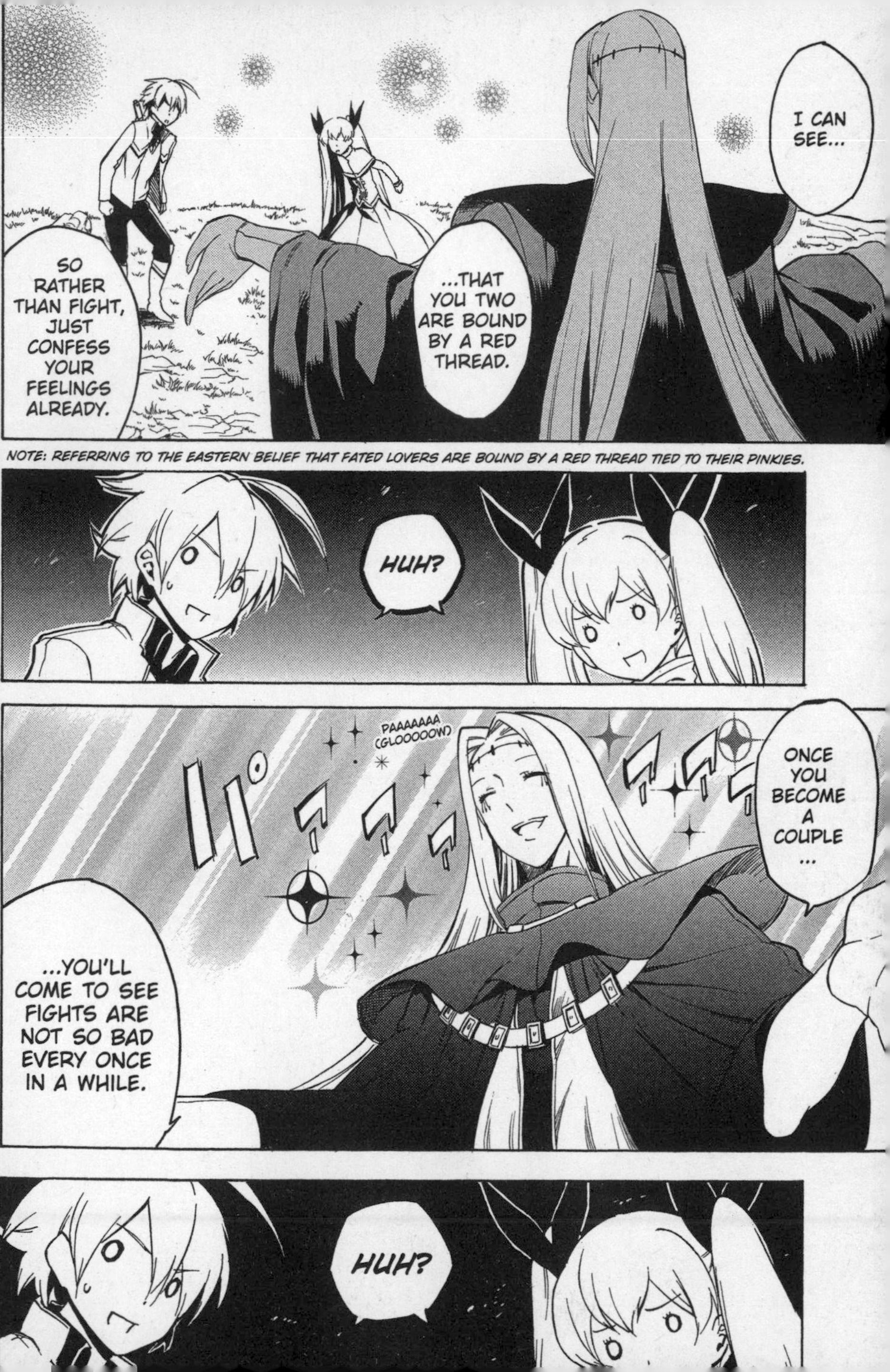

I CAN SEE...
...THAT YOU TWO ARE BOUND BY A RED THREAD.
SO RATHER THAN FIGHT, JUST CONFESS YOUR FEELINGS ALREADY.
HUH?
PAAAAAAA (GLOOOOOW)
ONCE YOU BECOME A COUPLE...
...YOU'LL COME TO SEE FIGHTS ARE NOT SO BAD EVERY ONCE IN A WHILE.
HUH?


*NOTE: REFERRING TO THE EASTERN BELIEF THAT FATED LOVERS ARE BOUND BY A RED THREAD TIED TO THEIR PINKIES.*

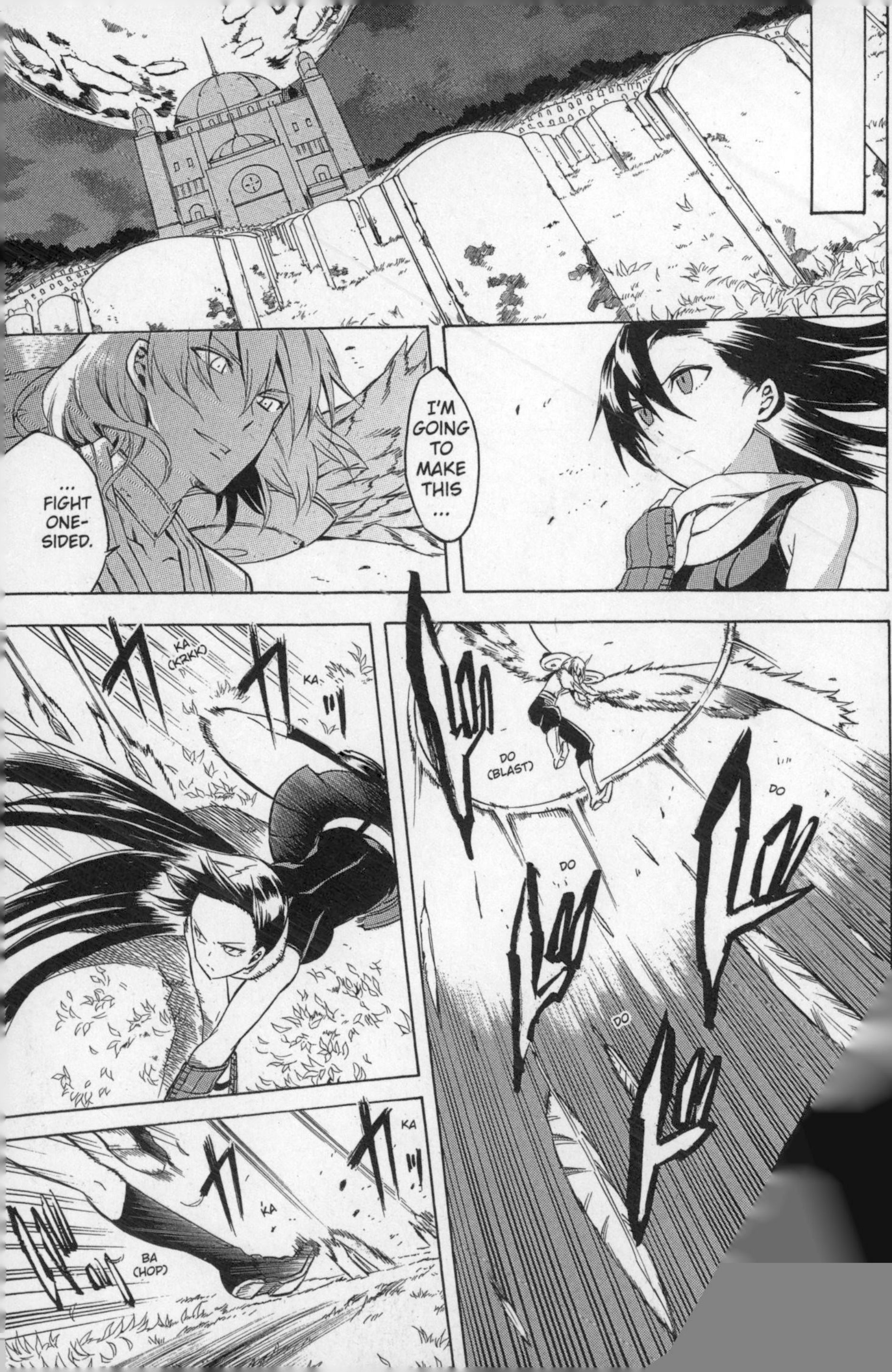

I'M GOING TO MAKE THIS ...
... FIGHT ONE-SIDED.
DO (BLAST)
DO
DO
DO
KA (KRKK)
KA
KA
KA
BA (HOP)

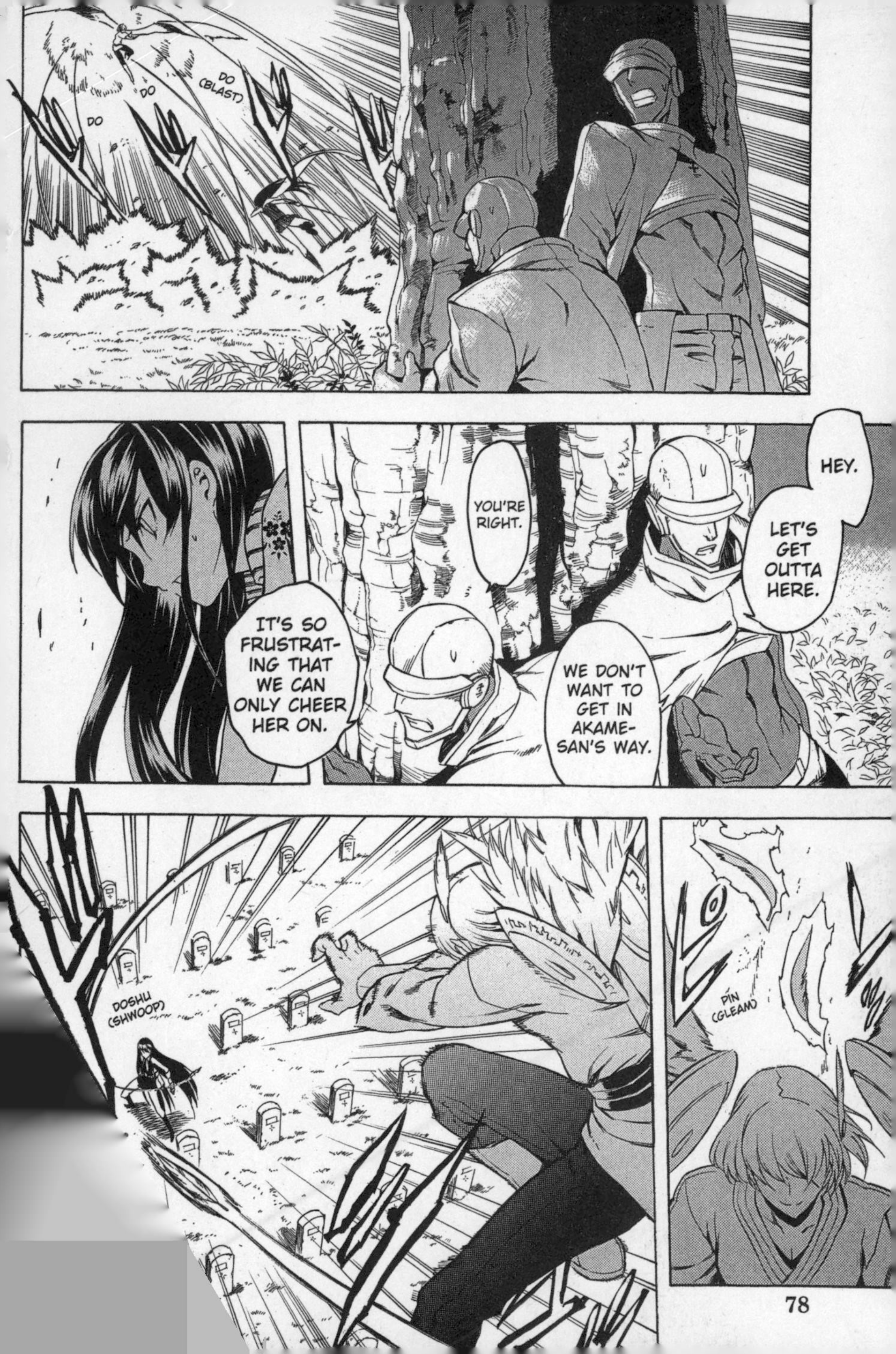
DO (BLAST)
DO
DO
HEY.
LET'S GET OUTTA HERE.
WE DON'T WANT TO GET IN AKAME-SAN'S WAY.
YOU'RE RIGHT.
IT'S SO FRUSTRATING THAT WE CAN ONLY CHEER HER ON.
PIN (GLEAM)
DOSHU (SHWOOP)

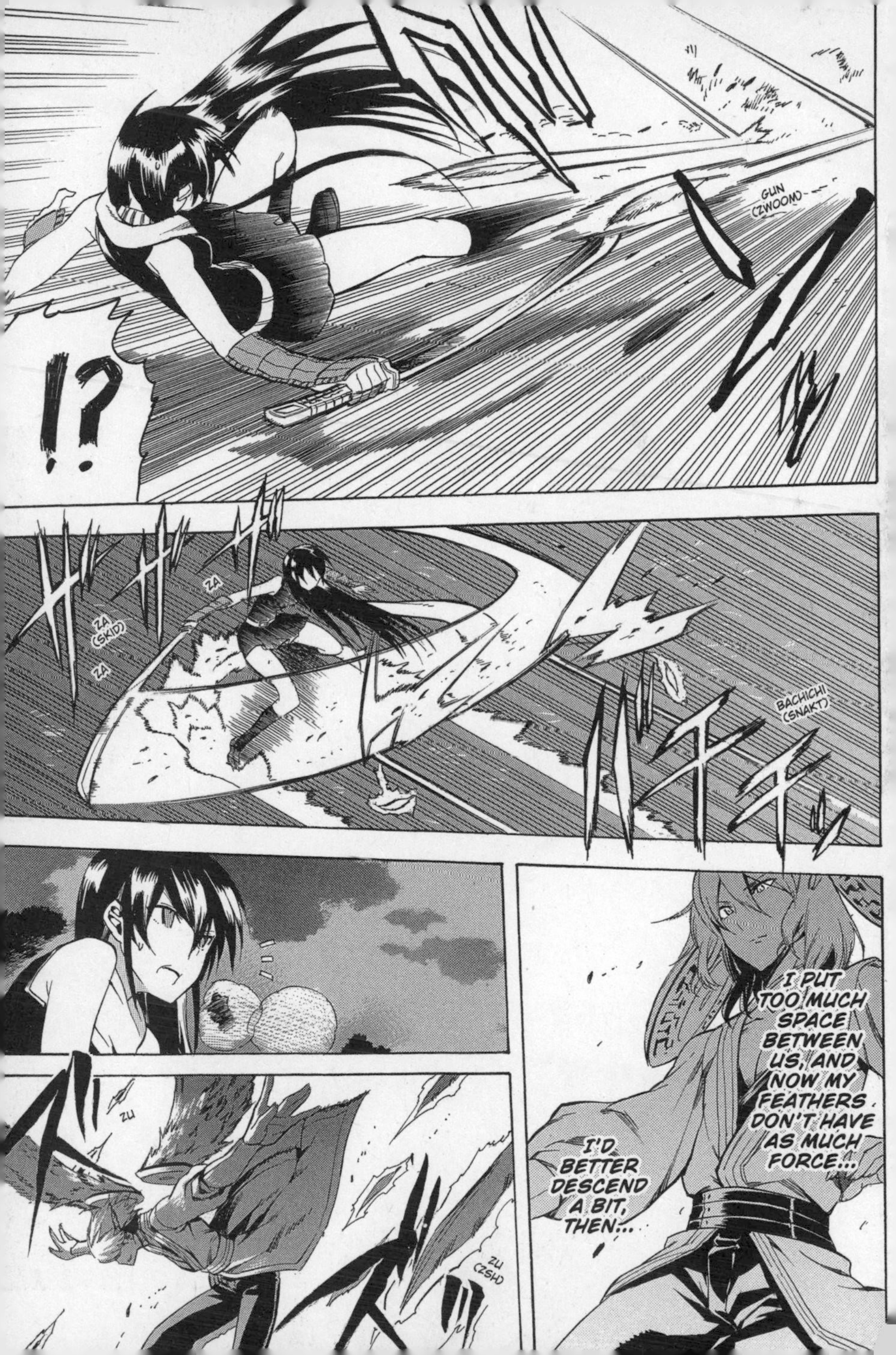
GUN
(ZWOOM)
!?
BACHICHI
(SNAKT)
ZA
ZA
(SKID)
ZA
I PUT TOO MUCH SPACE BETWEEN US, AND NOW MY FEATHERS DON'T HAVE AS MUCH FORCE...
I'D BETTER DESCEND A BIT, THEN...
ZU
ZU
(ZSH)

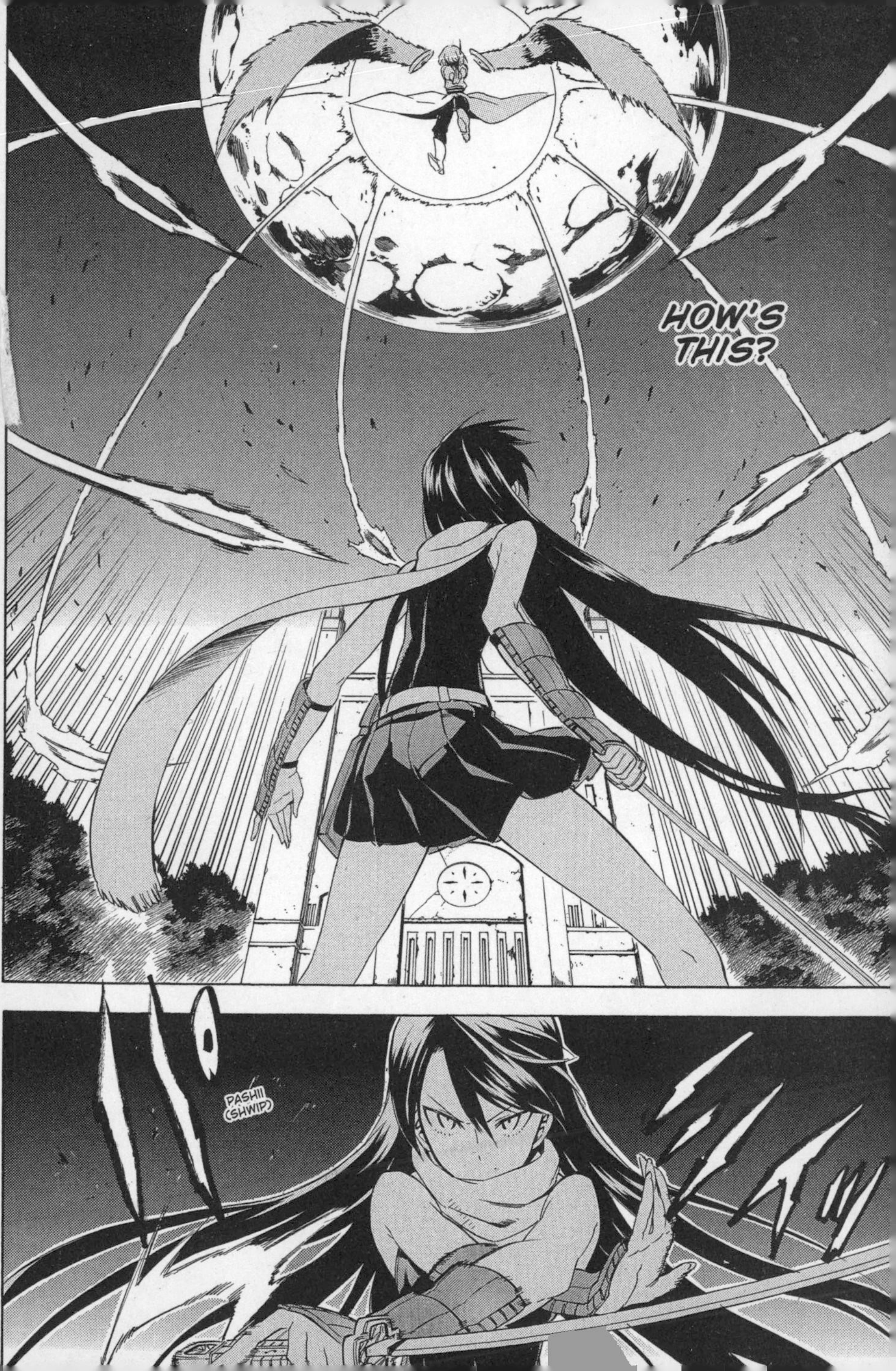
HOW'S THIS?
PASHII (SHWIP)

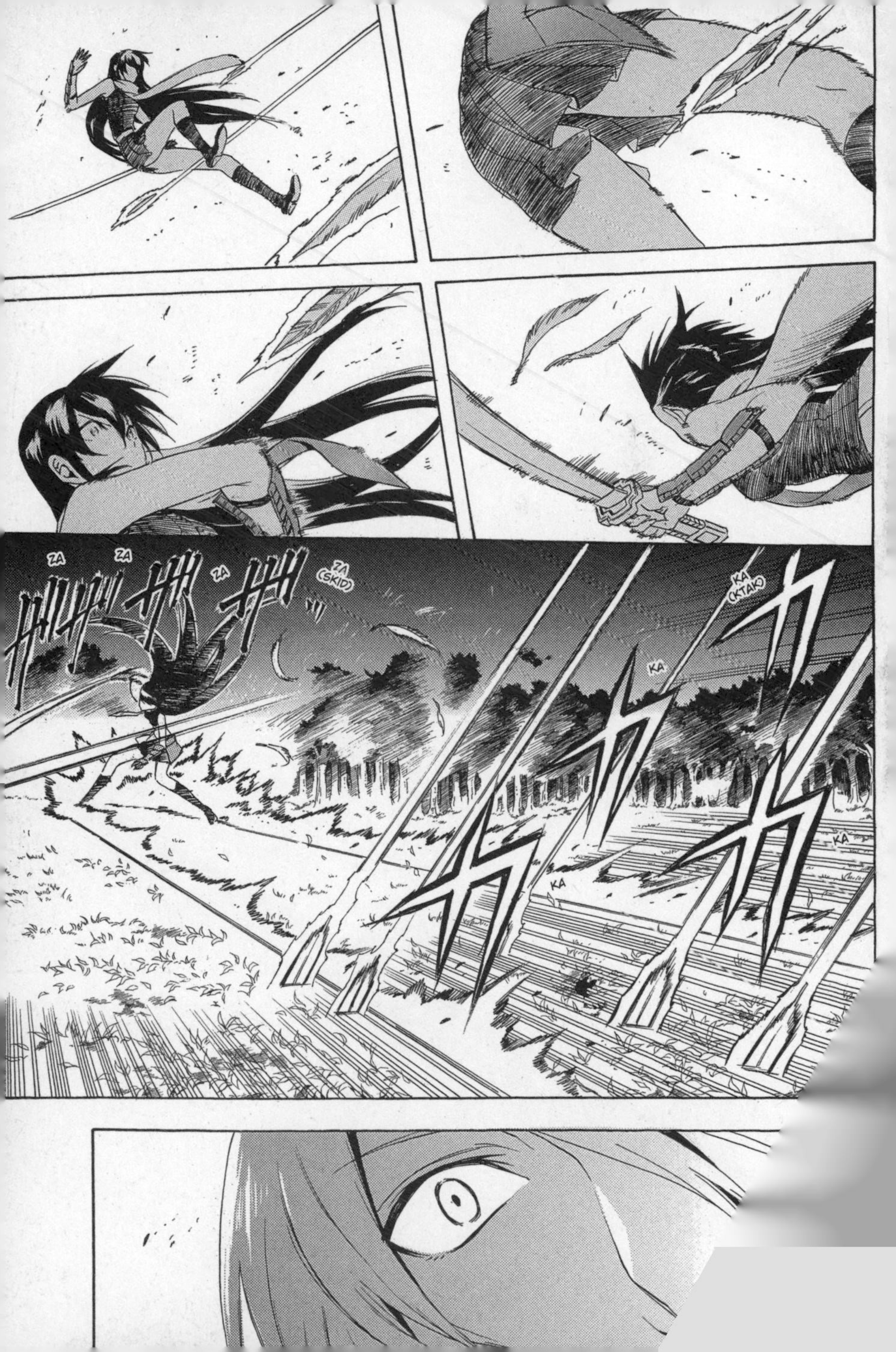
KA
(KTAK)
KA
KA
KA
ZA
(SKID)
ZA
ZA
ZA

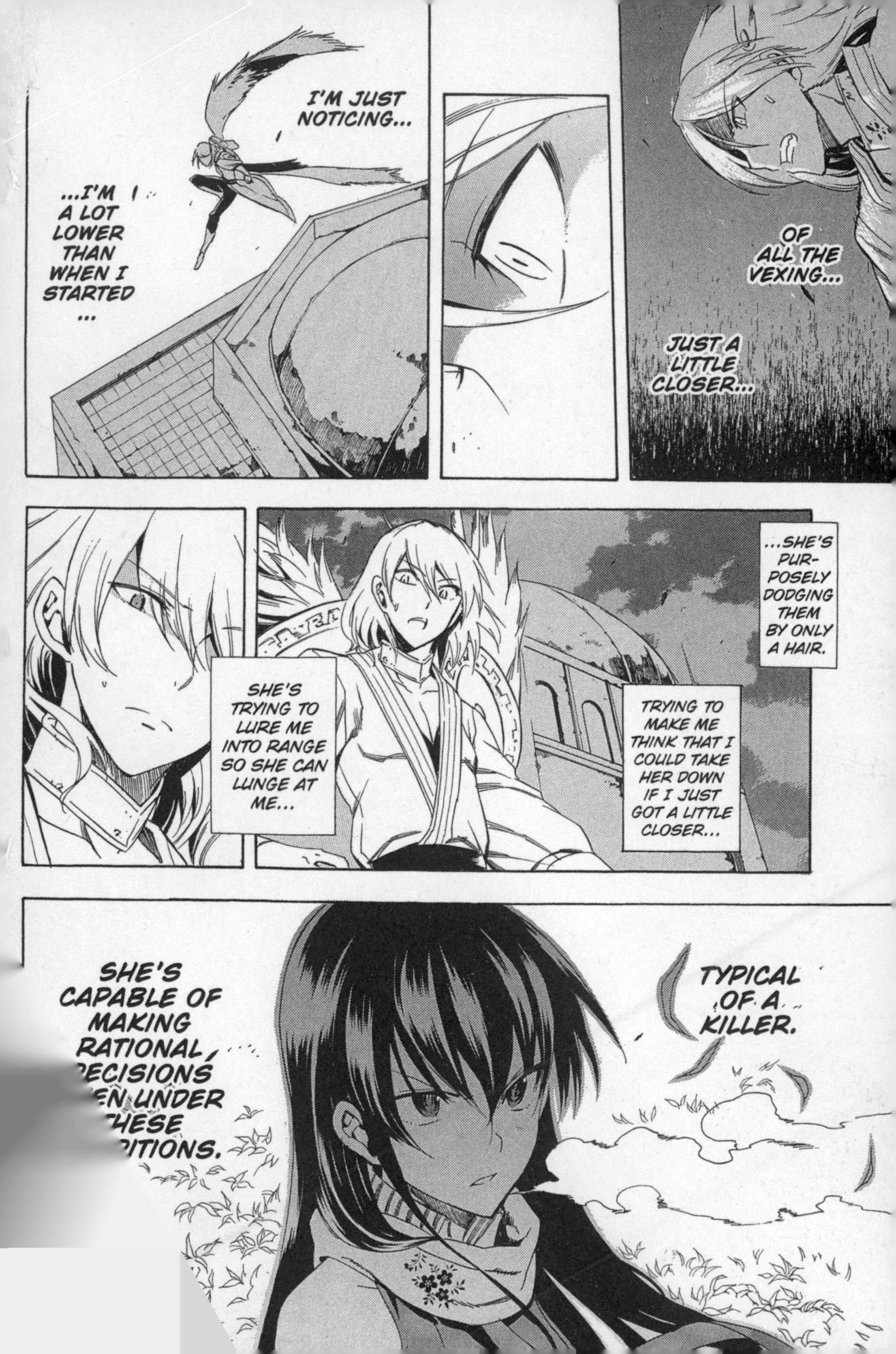
OF ALL THE VEXING...
JUST A LITTLE CLOSER...
I'M JUST NOTICING...
...I'M A LOT LOWER THAN WHEN I STARTED...
...SHE'S PURPOSELY DODGING THEM BY ONLY A HAIR.
TRYING TO MAKE ME THINK THAT I COULD TAKE HER DOWN IF I JUST GOT A LITTLE CLOSER...
SHE'S TRYING TO LURE ME INTO RANGE SO SHE CAN LUNGE AT ME...
TYPICAL OF A KILLER.
SHE'S CAPABLE OF MAKING RATIONAL ECISIONS EN UNDER HESE DITIONS.

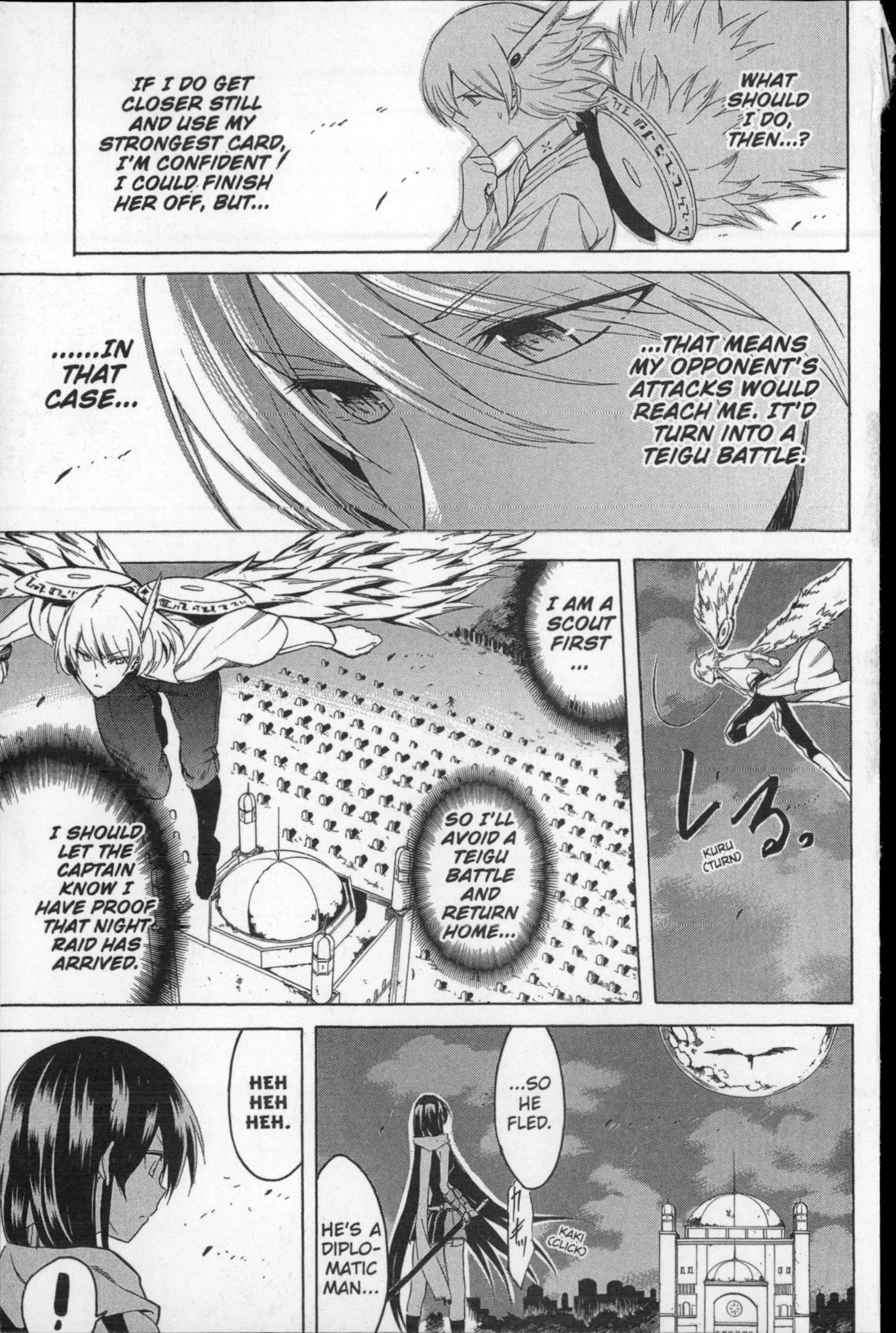
WHAT SHOULD I DO, THEN...?
IF I DO GET CLOSER STILL AND USE MY STRONGEST CARD, I'M CONFIDENT I COULD FINISH HER OFF, BUT...
...THAT MEANS MY OPPONENT'S ATTACKS WOULD REACH ME. IT'D TURN INTO A TEIGU BATTLE.
......IN THAT CASE...
KURU (TURN)
I AM A SCOUT FIRST ...
SO I'LL AVOID A TEIGU BATTLE AND RETURN HOME...
I SHOULD LET THE CAPTAIN KNOW I HAVE PROOF THAT NIGHT RAID HAS ARRIVED.
...SO HE FLED.
KAKI (CLICK)
HE'S A DIPLOMATIC MAN...
HEH HEH HEH.
!

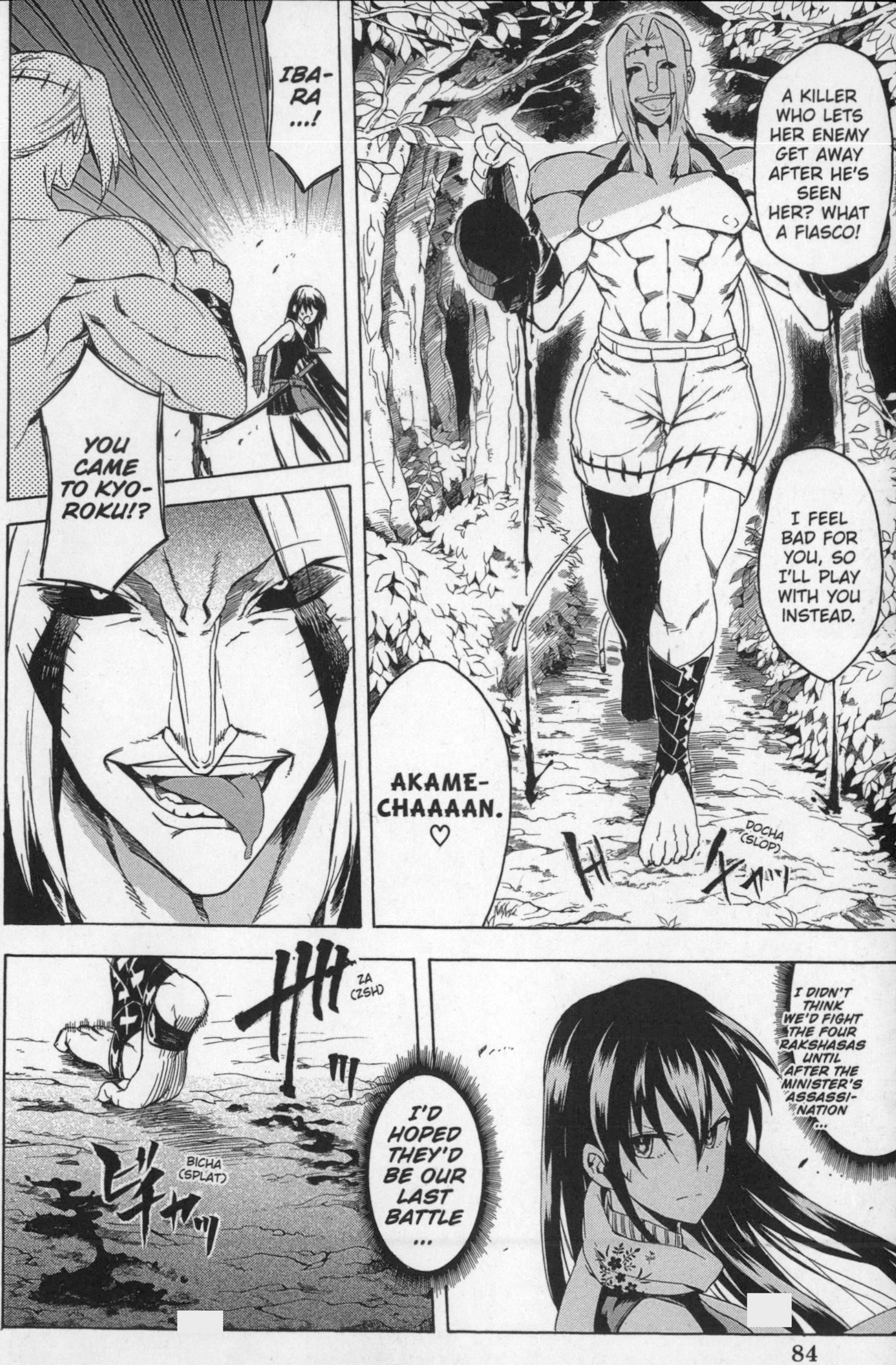
A KILLER WHO LETS HER ENEMY GET AWAY AFTER HE'S SEEN HER? WHAT A FIASCO!
I FEEL BAD FOR YOU, SO I'LL PLAY WITH YOU INSTEAD.
DOCHA (SLOP)
AKAME-CHAAAAN. ♡
IBA-RA ...!
YOU CAME TO KYO-ROKU!?
I DIDN'T THINK WE'D FIGHT THE FOUR RAKSHASAS UNTIL AFTER THE MINISTER'S ASSASSI-NATION ...
I'D HOPED THEY'D BE OUR LAST BATTLE ...
ZA (ZSH)
BICHA (SPLAT)

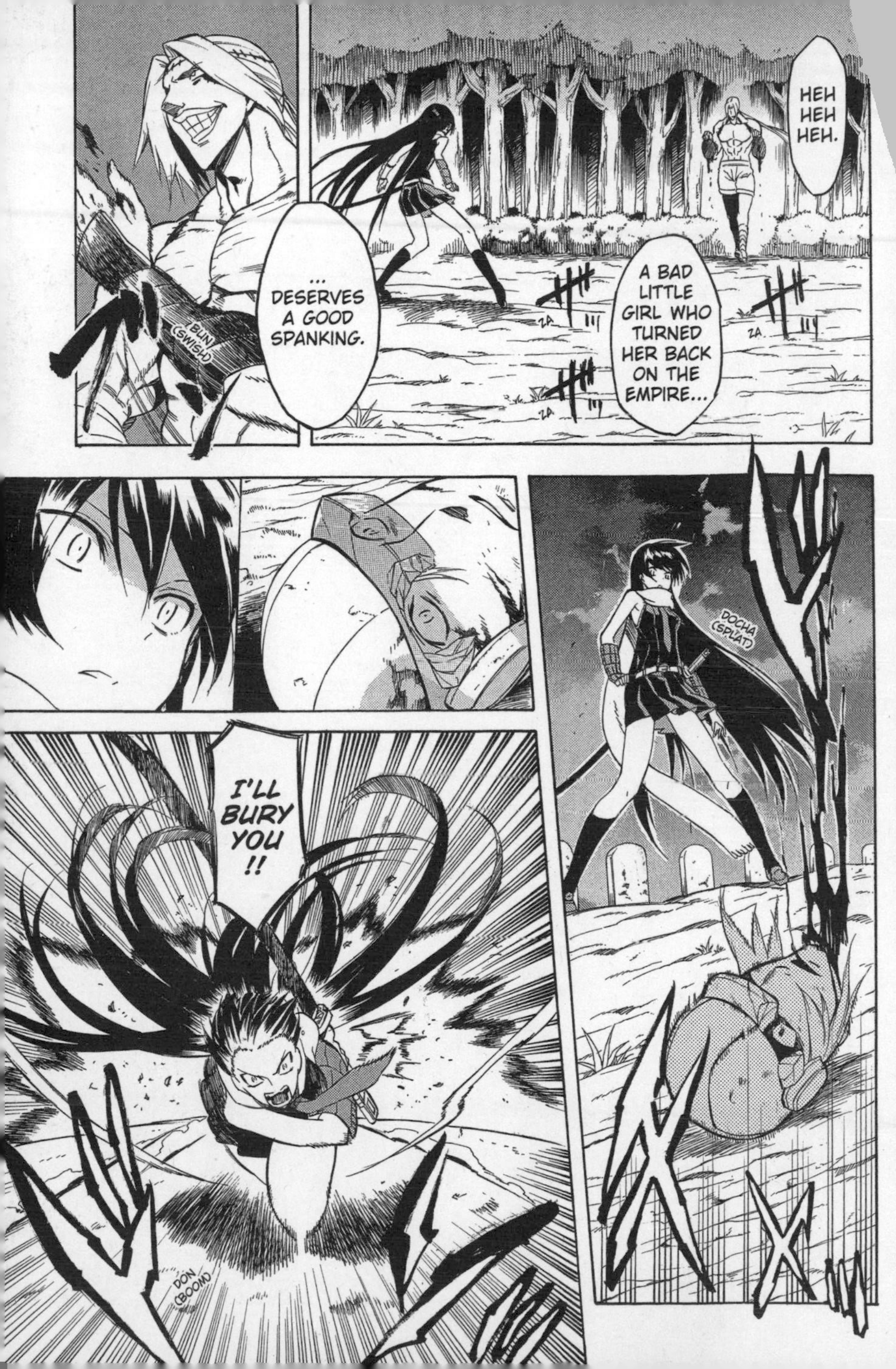
HEH HEH HEH.
A BAD LITTLE GIRL WHO TURNED HER BACK ON THE EMPIRE...
ZA
ZA
ZA
... DESERVES A GOOD SPANKING.
BUN (SWISH)
DOCHA (SPLAT)
I'LL BURY YOU !!
DON (BOOM)

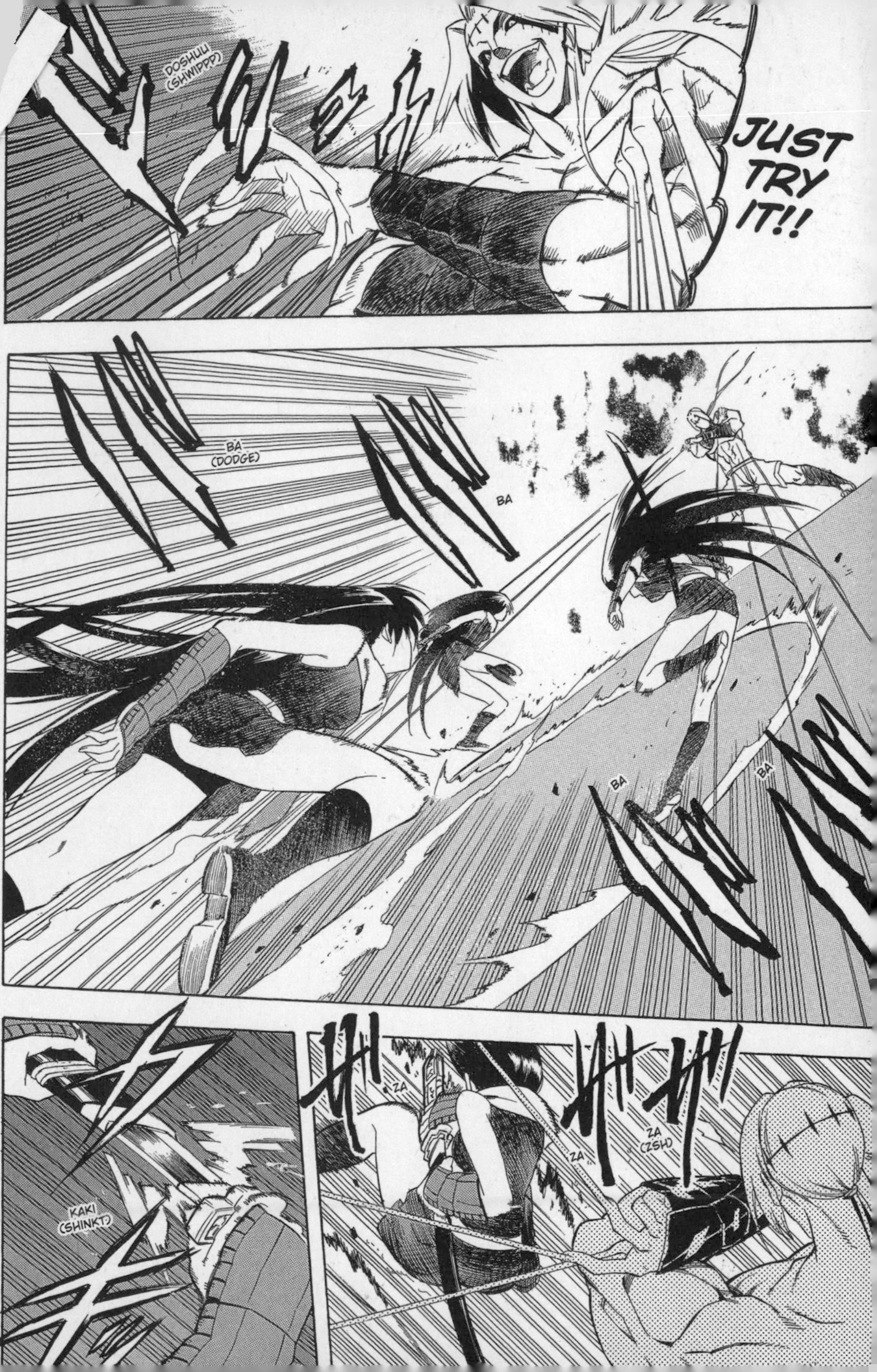
JUST TRY IT!!
DOSHUU (SHWIPPP)
BA
BA
BA
BA (DODGE)
ZA (ZSH)
ZA
ZA
KAKI (SHINKT)

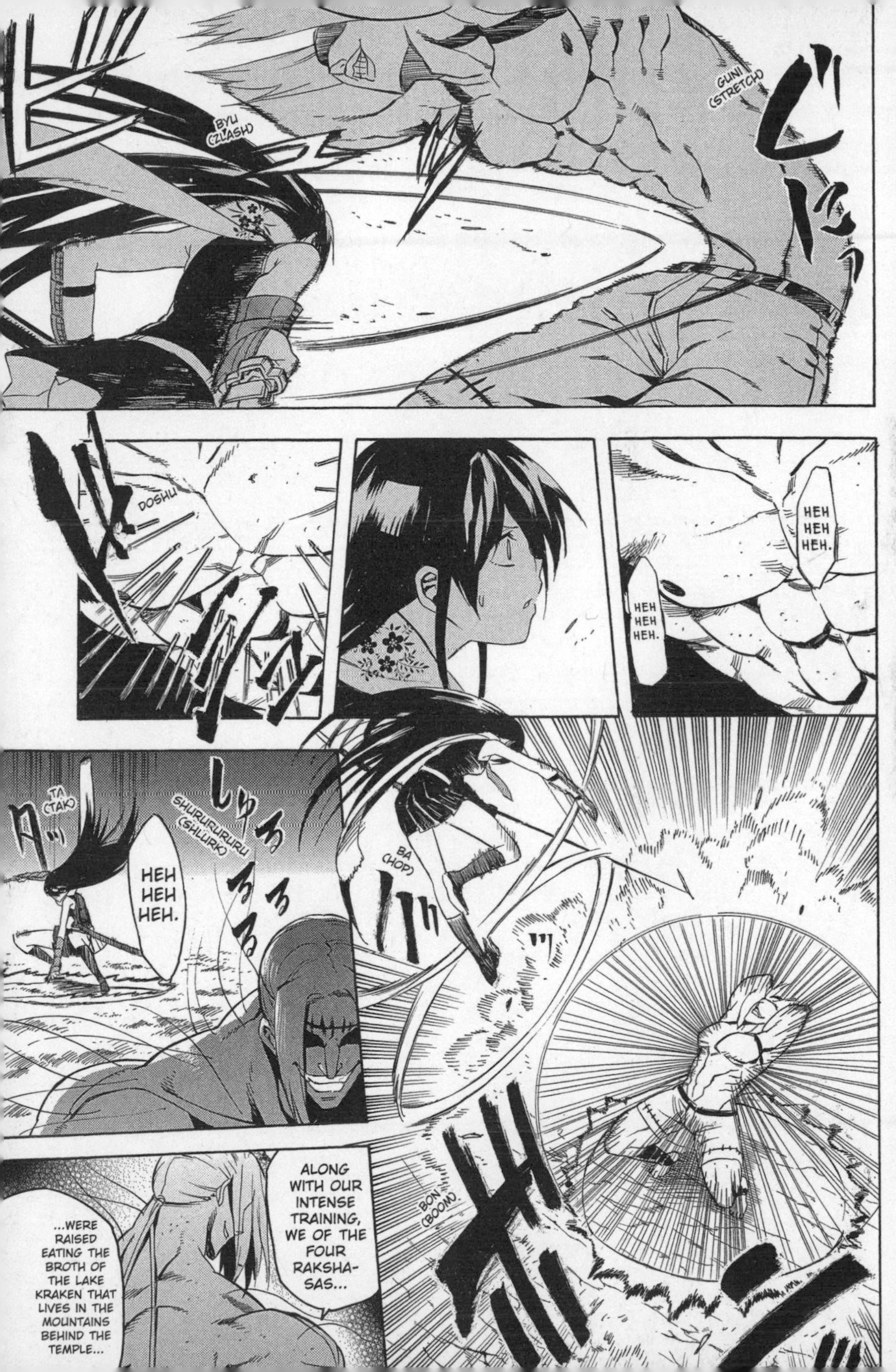
GUNI (STRETCH)
BYU (ZLASH)
HEH HEH HEH.
HEH HEH HEH.
DOSHU
BA (HOP)
SHURURURURU (SHLURK)
TA (TAK)
HEH HEH HEH.
BON (BOOM)
ALONG WITH OUR INTENSE TRAINING, WE OF THE FOUR RAKSHASAS...
...WERE RAISED EATING THE BROTH OF THE LAKE KRAKEN THAT LIVES IN THE MOUNTAINS BEHIND THE TEMPLE...

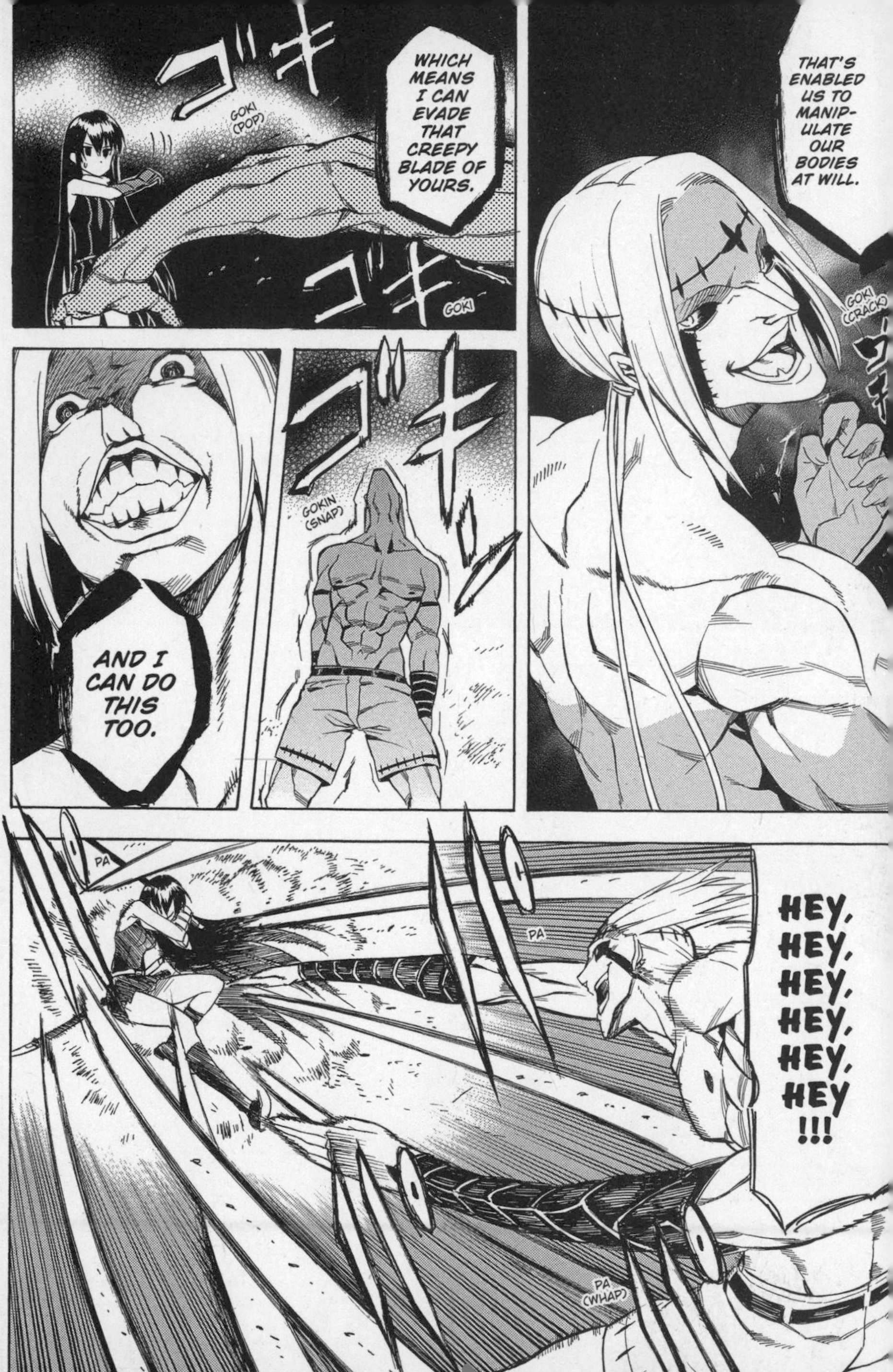
THAT'S ENABLED US TO MANIPULATE OUR BODIES AT WILL.
GOKI (CRACK)
WHICH MEANS I CAN EVADE THAT CREEPY BLADE OF YOURS.
GOKI (POP)
GOKI
GOKIN (SNAP)
AND I CAN DO THIS TOO.
HEY, HEY, HEY, HEY, HEY, HEY!!!
PA
PA
PA (WHAP)

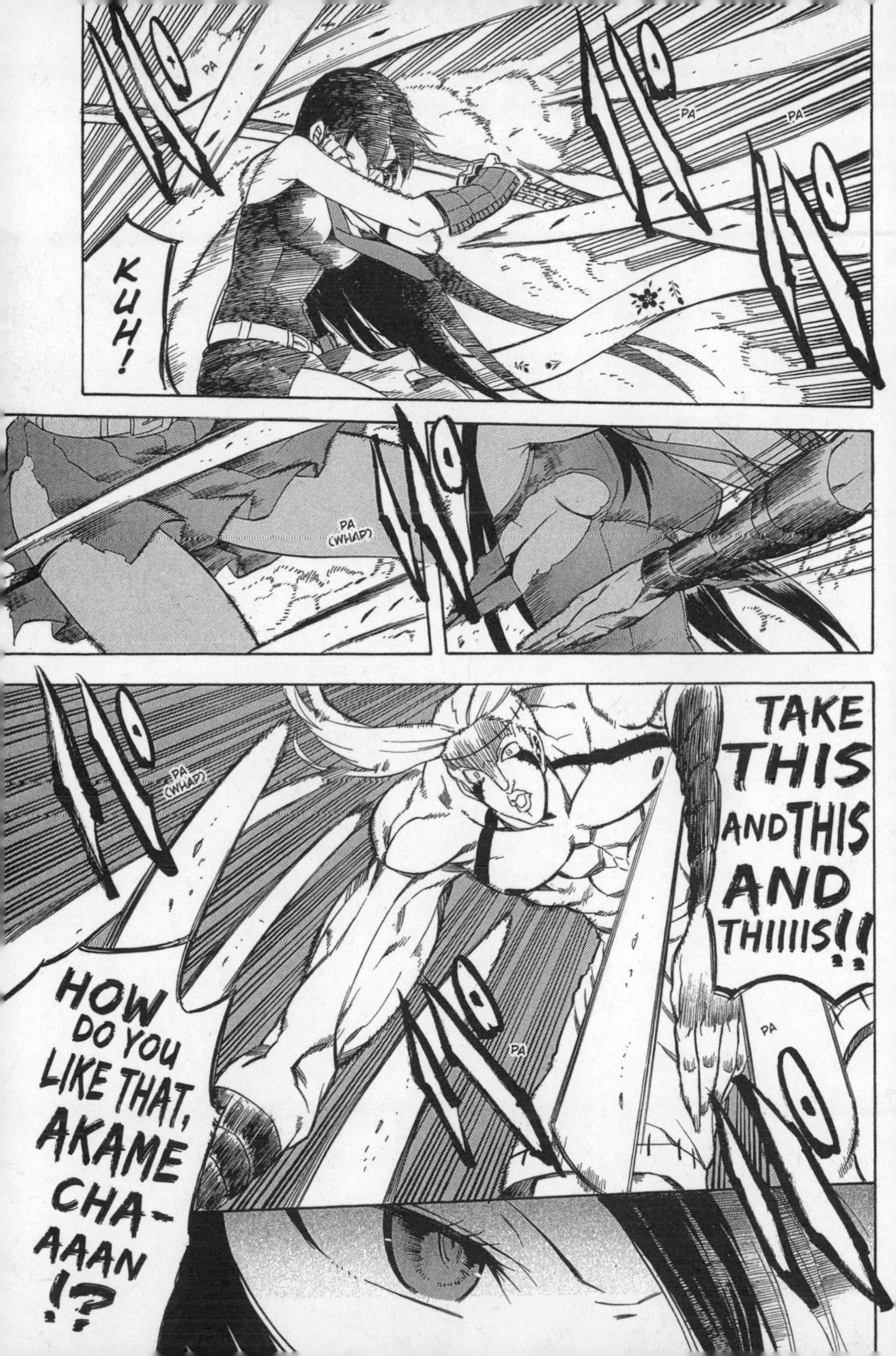
PA
PA
PA
KUH!
PA (WHAP)
TAKE THIS AND THIS AND THIIIIS!!
PA (WHAP)
PA
PA
HOW DO YOU LIKE THAT, AKAME CHA-AAAN!?

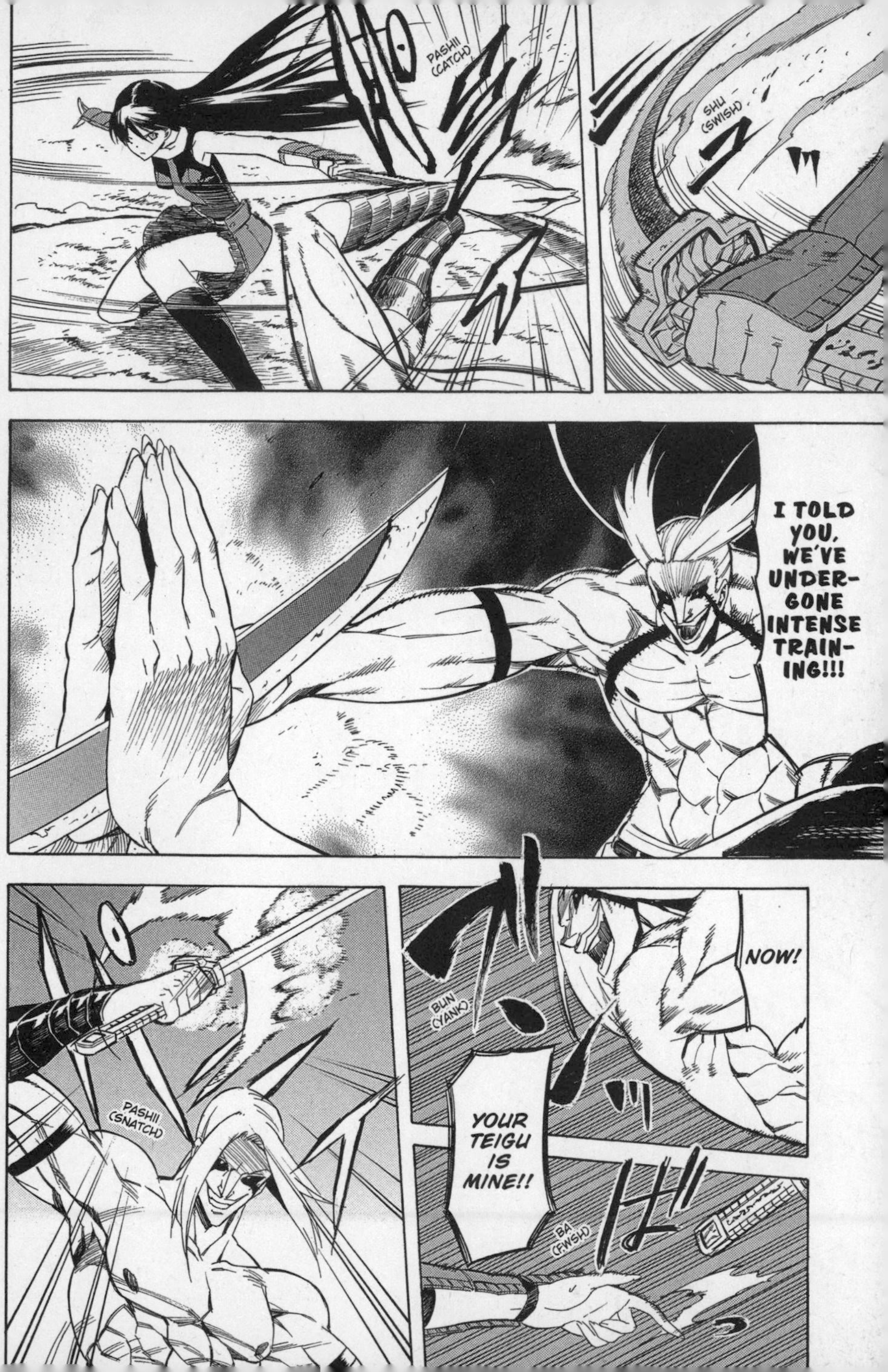
SHU (SWISH)
PASHII (CATCH)
I TOLD YOU, WE'VE UNDERGONE INTENSE TRAINING!!!
NOW!
BUN (YANK)
YOUR TEIGU IS MINE!!
BA (FWSH)
PASHII (SNATCH)

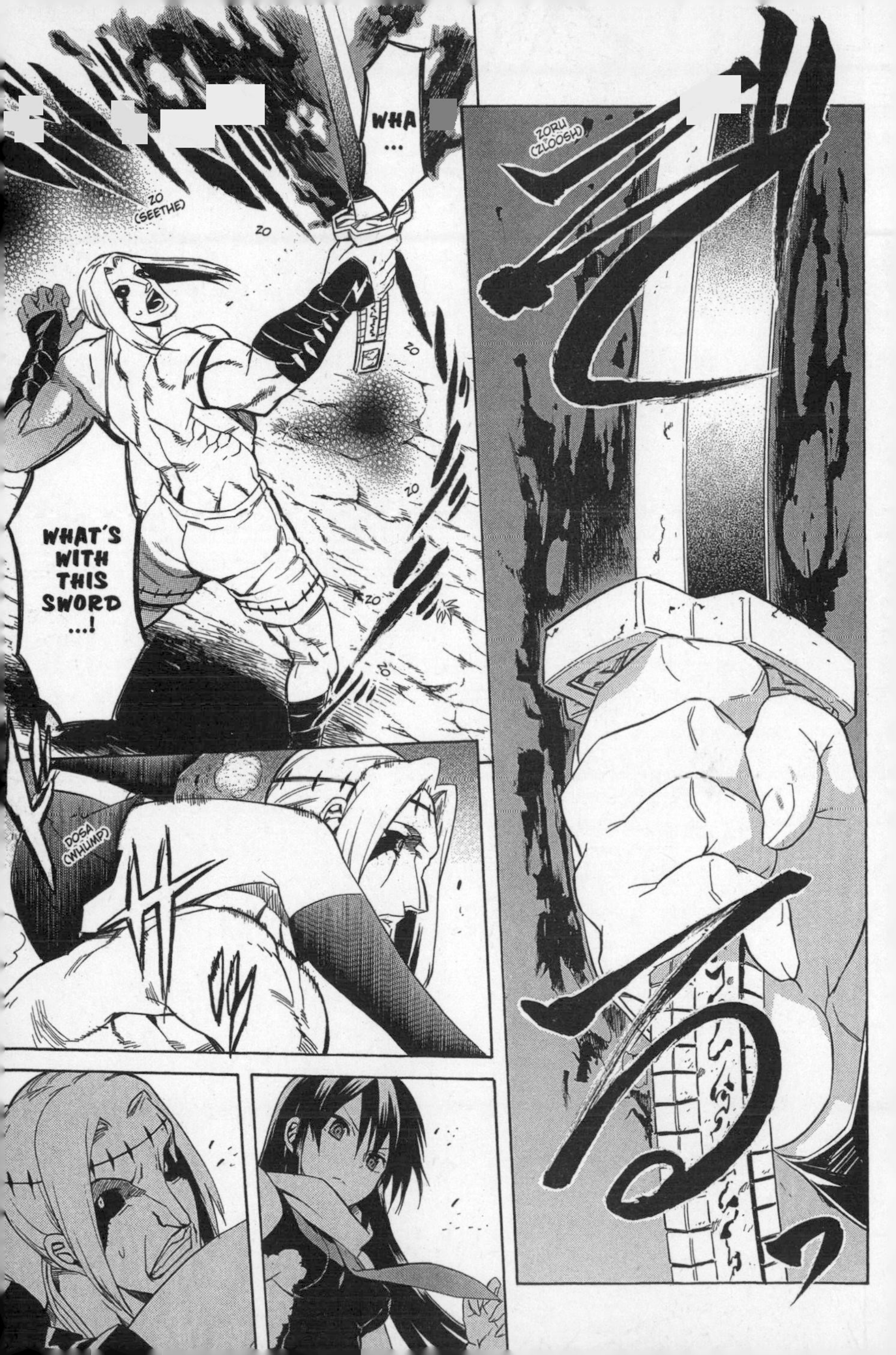
ZORU
(ZLOOSH)
WHA
...
ZO
(SEETHE)
ZO
ZO
ZO
ZO
ZO
WHAT'S WITH THIS SWORD ...!
DOSA
(WHUMP)

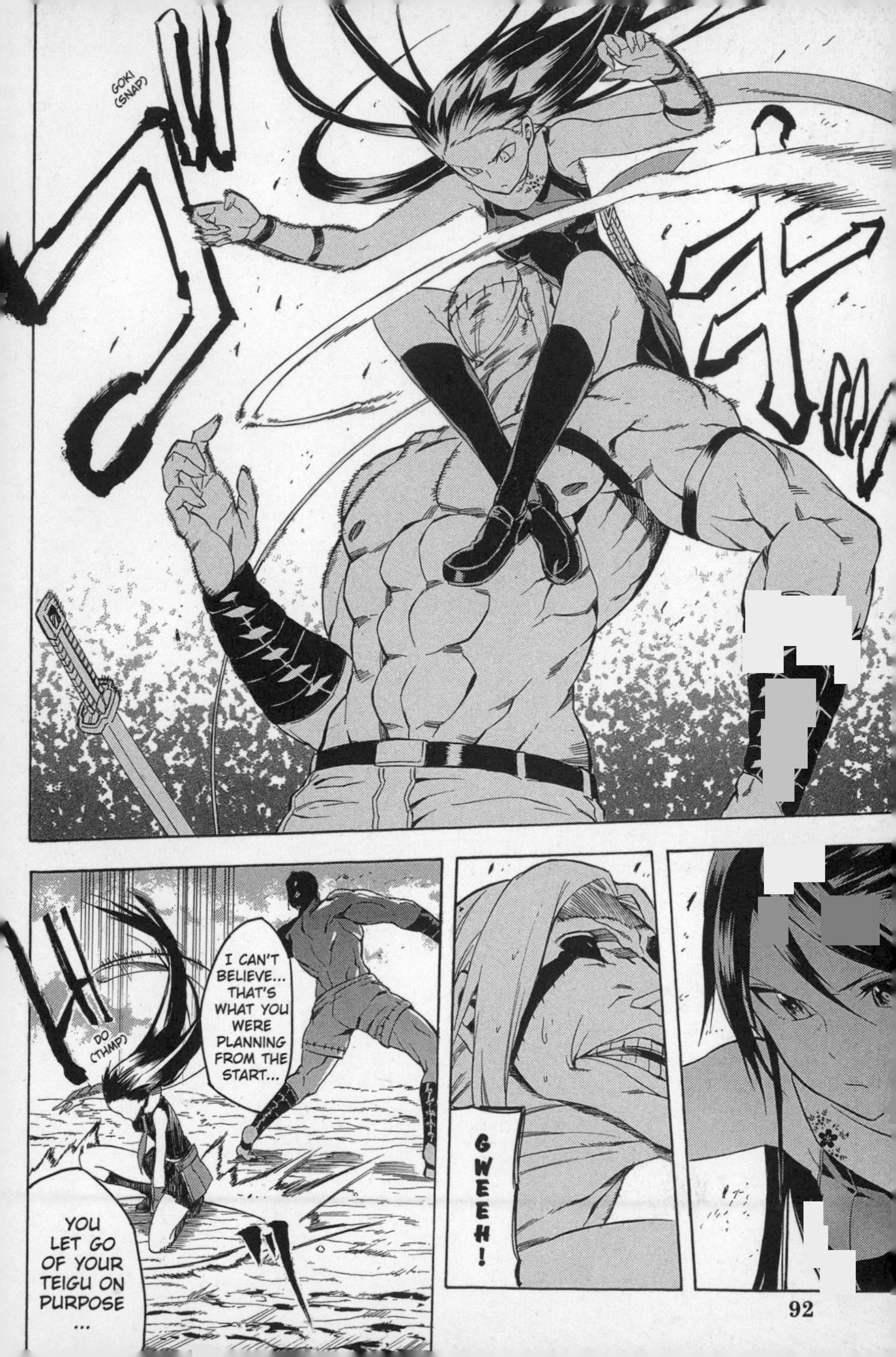
GOKI (SNAP)
GWEEH!
I CAN'T BELIEVE... THAT'S WHAT YOU WERE PLANNING FROM THE START...
DO (THMP)
YOU LET GO OF YOUR TEIGU ON PURPOSE ...

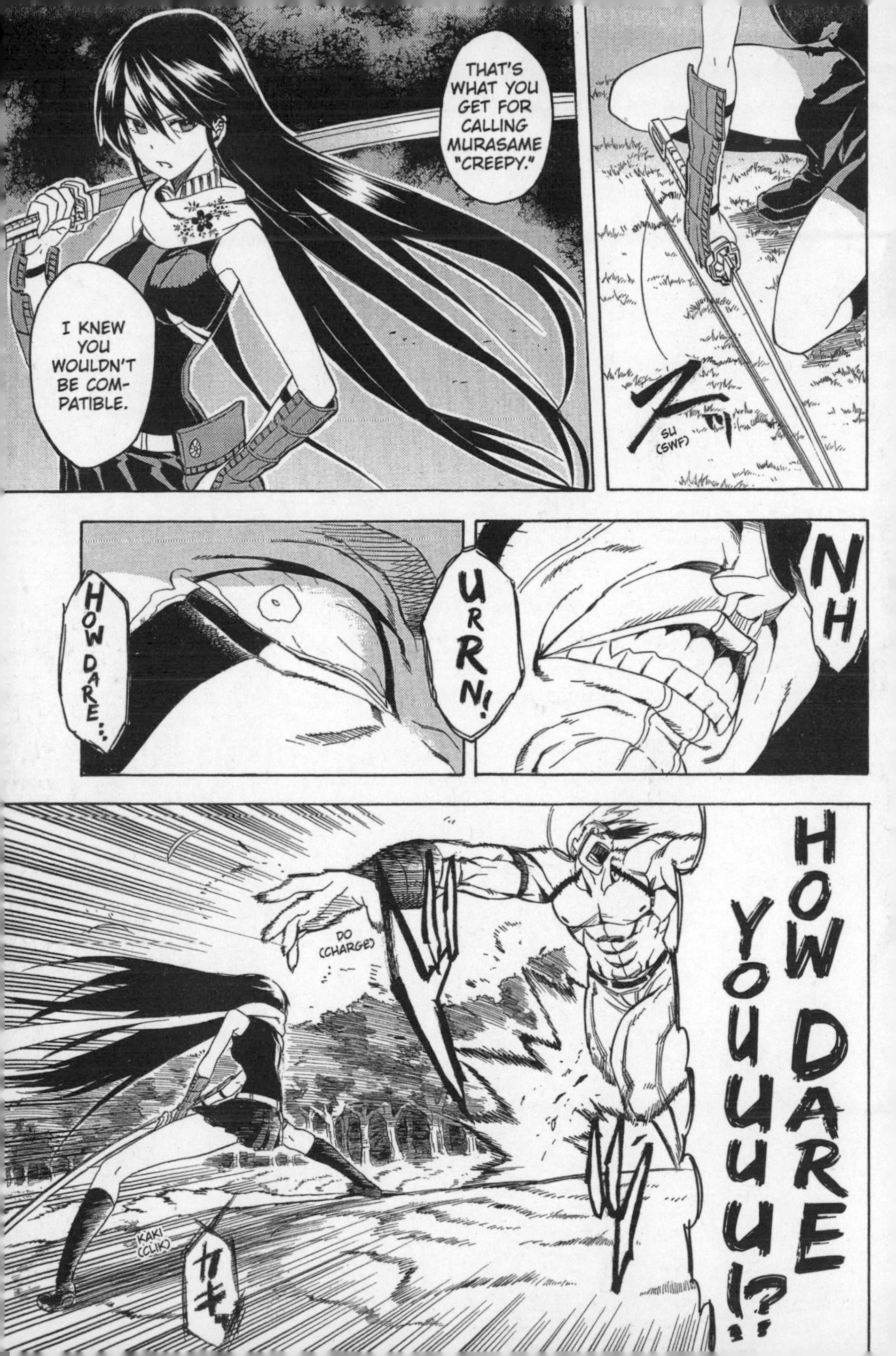
SU (SWF)
THAT'S WHAT YOU GET FOR CALLING MURASAME "CREEPY."
I KNEW YOU WOULDN'T BE COM-PATIBLE.
NH
URRN!
HOW DARE...
HOW DARE YOUUUUU!?
DO (CHARGE)
KAKI (CLIK)

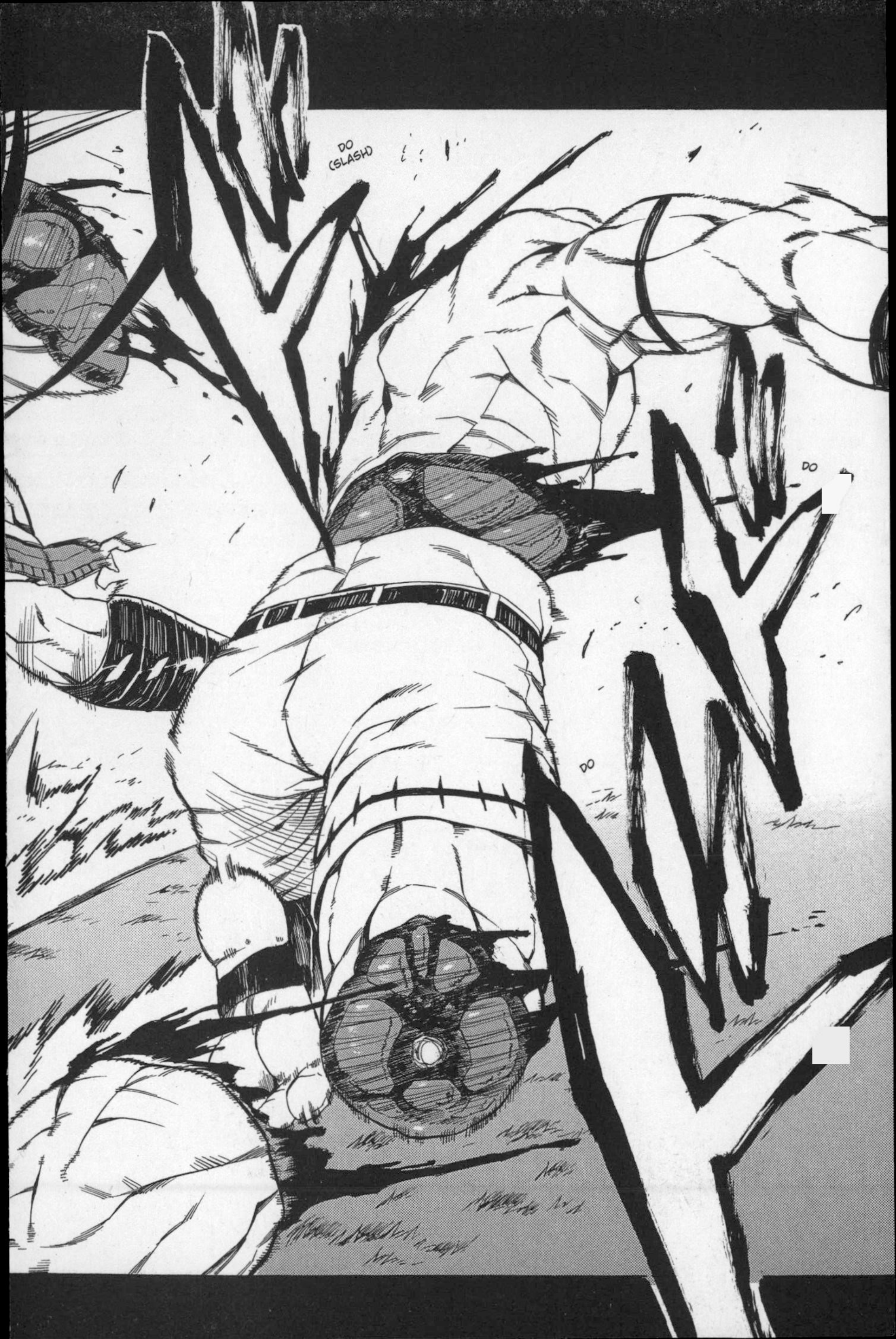
DO
(SLASH)
DO
DO

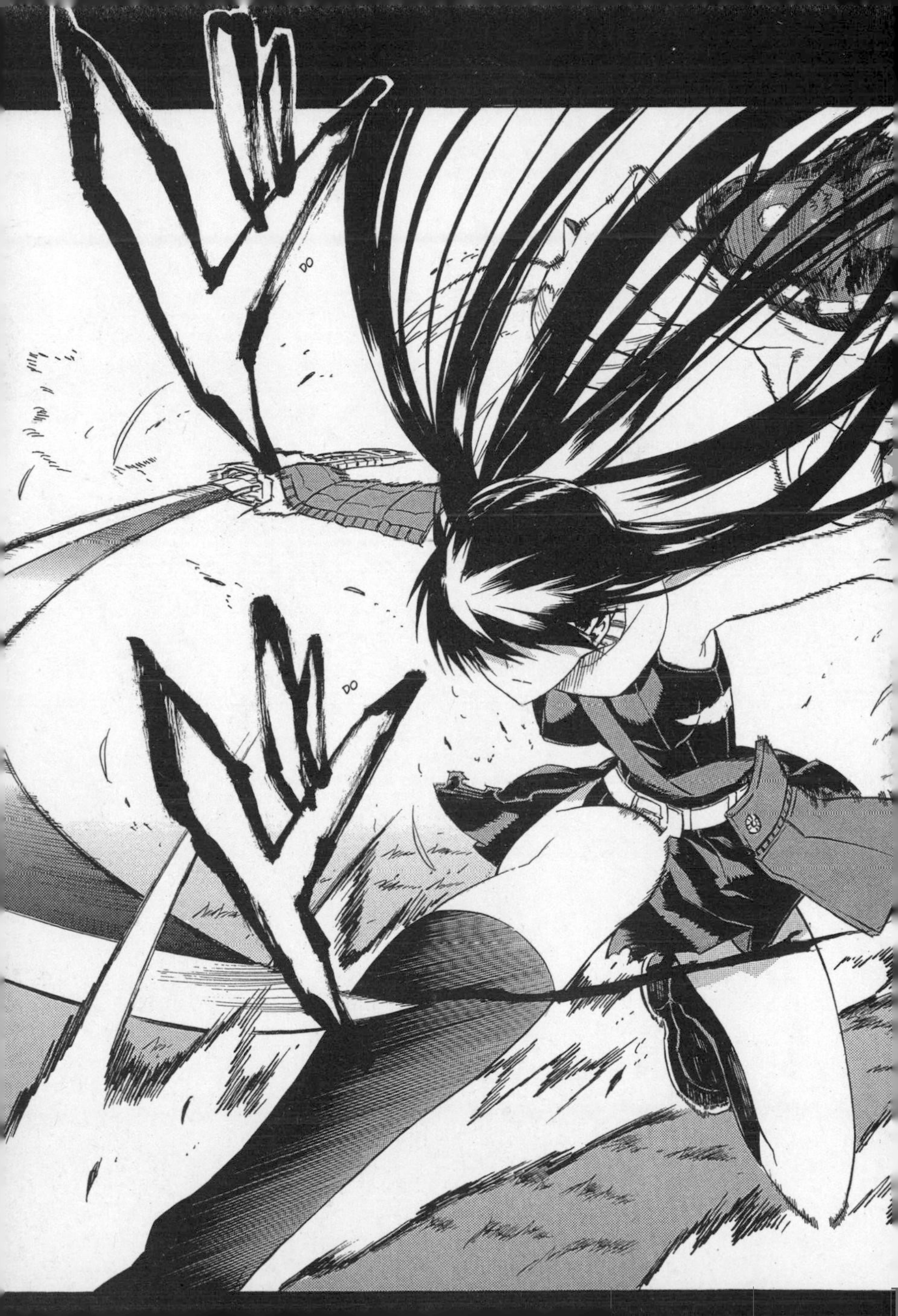
DO
DO

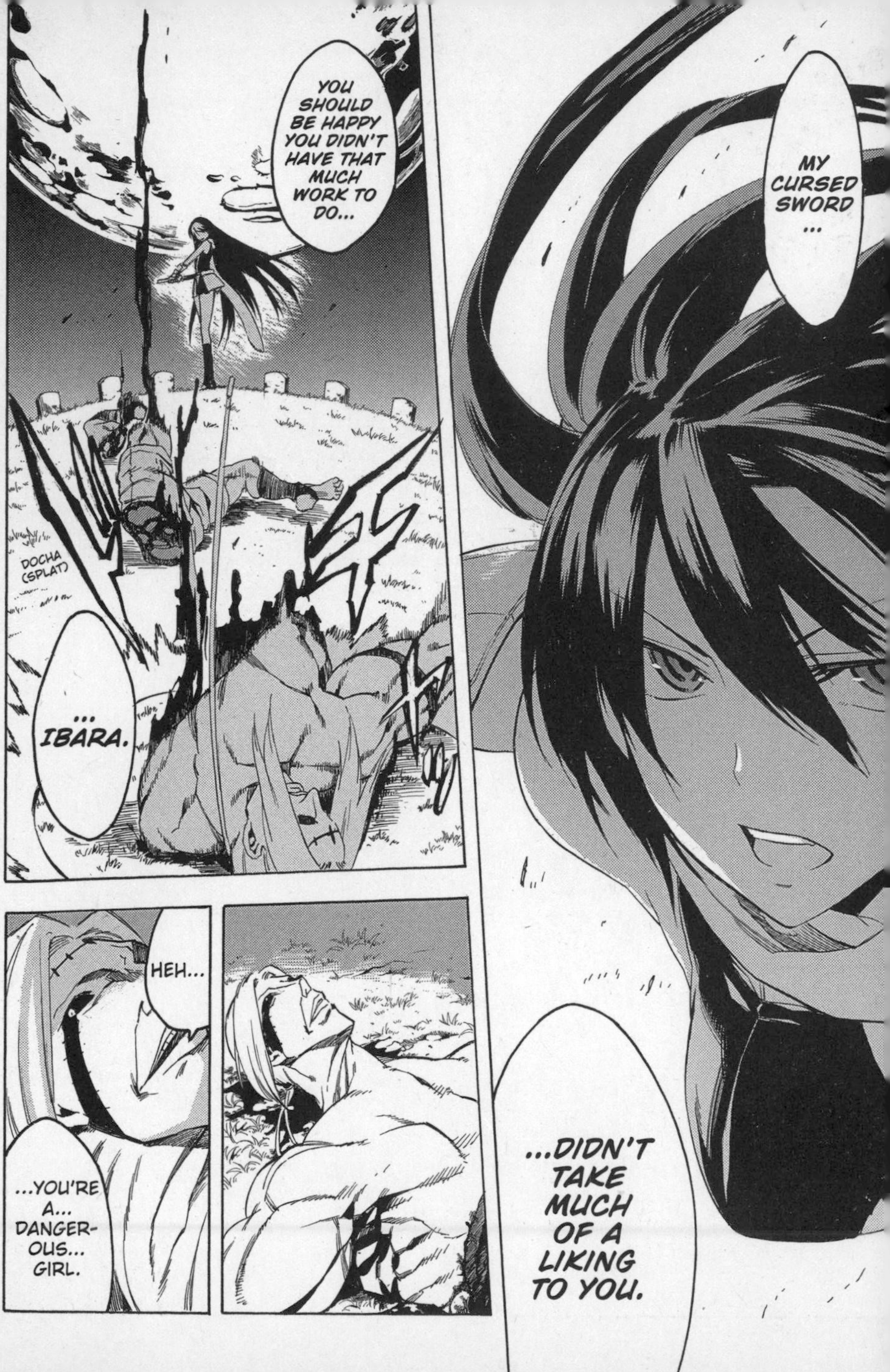
MY CURSED SWORD ...
...DIDN'T TAKE MUCH OF A LIKING TO YOU.
YOU SHOULD BE HAPPY YOU DIDN'T HAVE THAT MUCH WORK TO DO...
DOCHA (SPLAT)
... IBARA.
HEH...
...YOU'RE A... DANGER-OUS... GIRL.

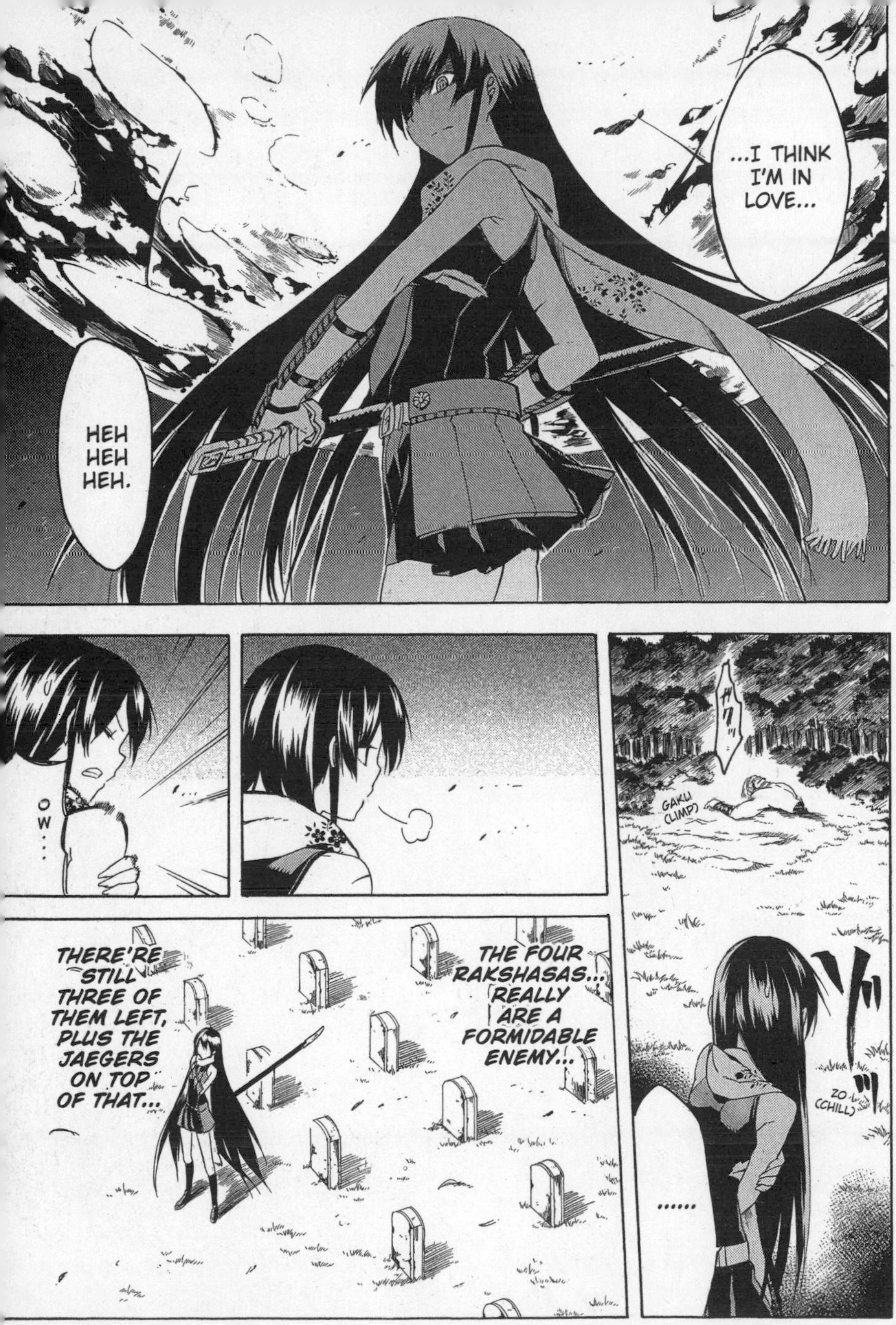
...I THINK I'M IN LOVE...
HEH HEH HEH.
GAKU (LIMP)
OW...
THE FOUR RAKSHASAS... REALLY ARE A FORMIDABLE ENEMY...
THERE'RE STILL THREE OF THEM LEFT, PLUS THE JAEGERS ON TOP OF THAT...
ZO (CHILL)
......

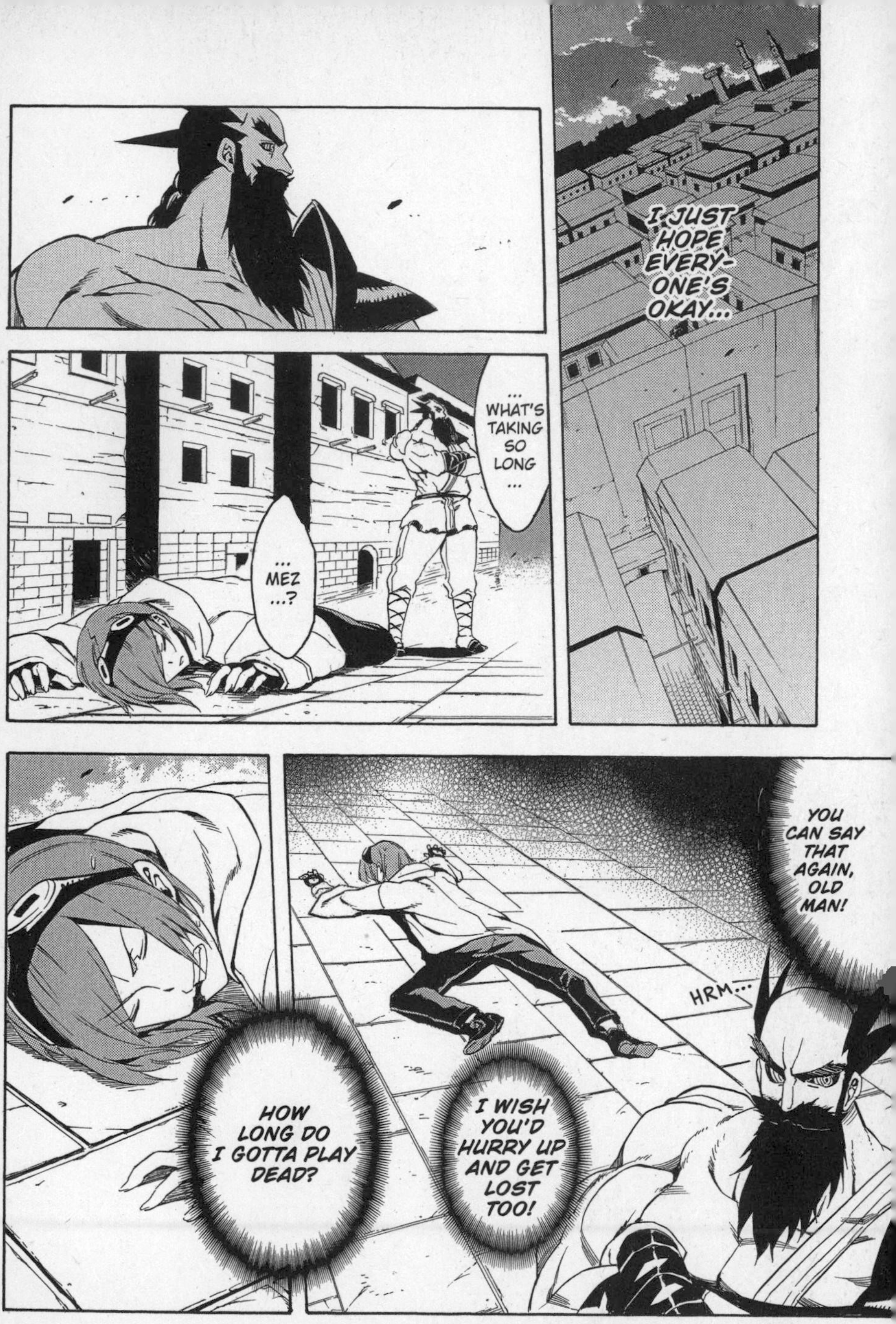
I JUST HOPE EVERY-ONE'S OKAY...
... WHAT'S TAKING SO LONG ...
... MEZ ...?
YOU CAN SAY THAT AGAIN, OLD MAN!
HRM...
I WISH YOU'D HURRY UP AND GET LOST TOO!
HOW LONG DO I GOTTA PLAY DEAD?

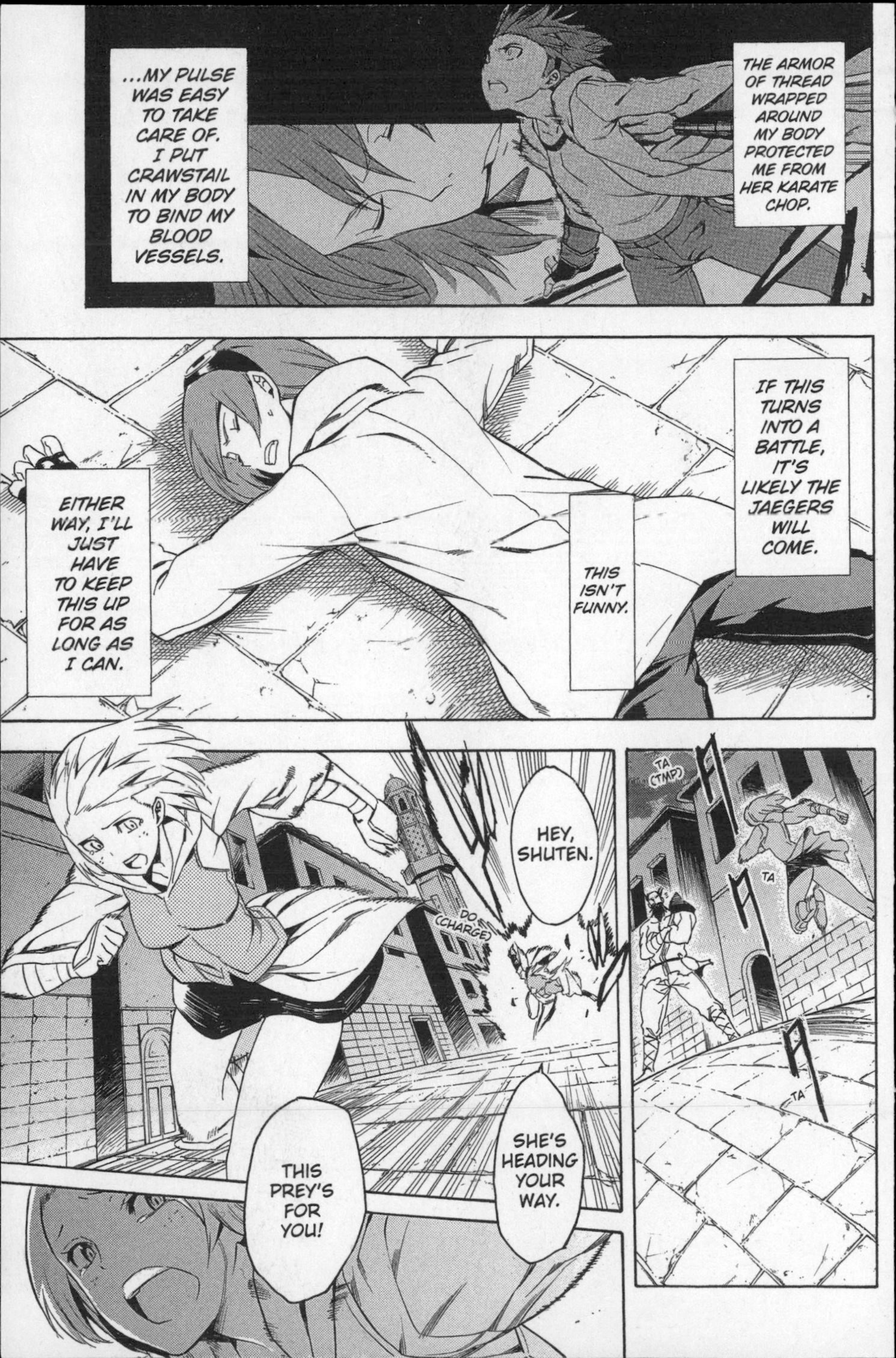
THE ARMOR OF THREAD WRAPPED AROUND MY BODY PROTECTED ME FROM HER KARATE CHOP.
...MY PULSE WAS EASY TO TAKE CARE OF. I PUT CRAWSTAIL IN MY BODY TO BIND MY BLOOD VESSELS.
IF THIS TURNS INTO A BATTLE, IT'S LIKELY THE JAEGERS WILL COME.
THIS ISN'T FUNNY.
EITHER WAY, I'LL JUST HAVE TO KEEP THIS UP FOR AS LONG AS I CAN.
TA (TMP)
TA
TA
HEY, SHUTEN.
DO (CHARGE)
SHE'S HEADING YOUR WAY.
THIS PREY'S FOR YOU!

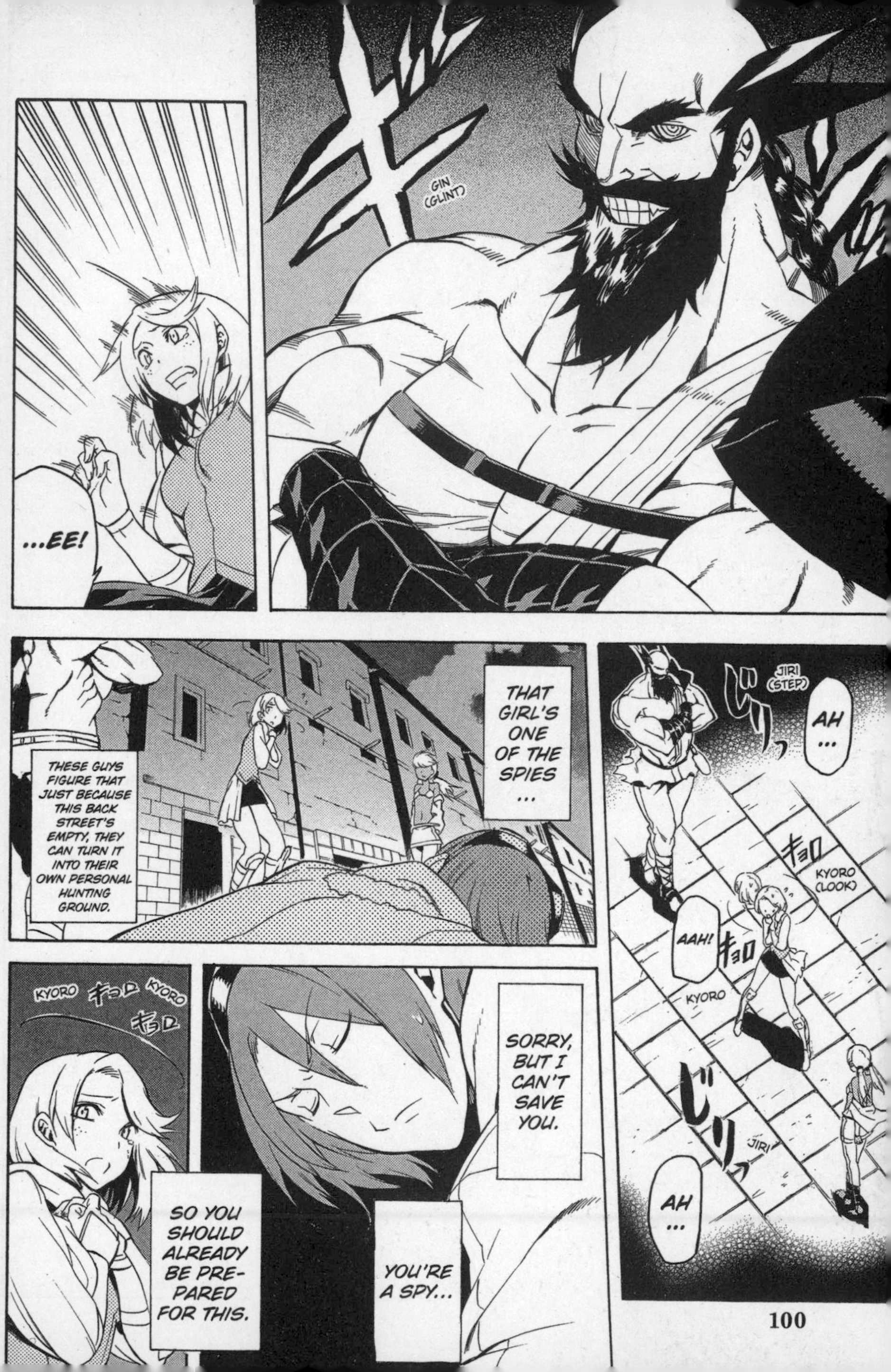

GIN (GLINT)
...EE!
JIRI (STEP)
じりっ
AH ...
キョロ
KYORO (LOOK)
AAH!
キョロ
KYORO
じりっ
JIRI
AH ...
THAT GIRL'S ONE OF THE SPIES ...
THESE GUYS FIGURE THAT JUST BECAUSE THIS BACK STREET'S EMPTY, THEY CAN TURN IT INTO THEIR OWN PERSONAL HUNTING GROUND.
SORRY, BUT I CAN'T SAVE YOU.
YOU'RE A SPY...
KYORO キョロ KYORO キョロ
SO YOU SHOULD ALREADY BE PREPARED FOR THIS.

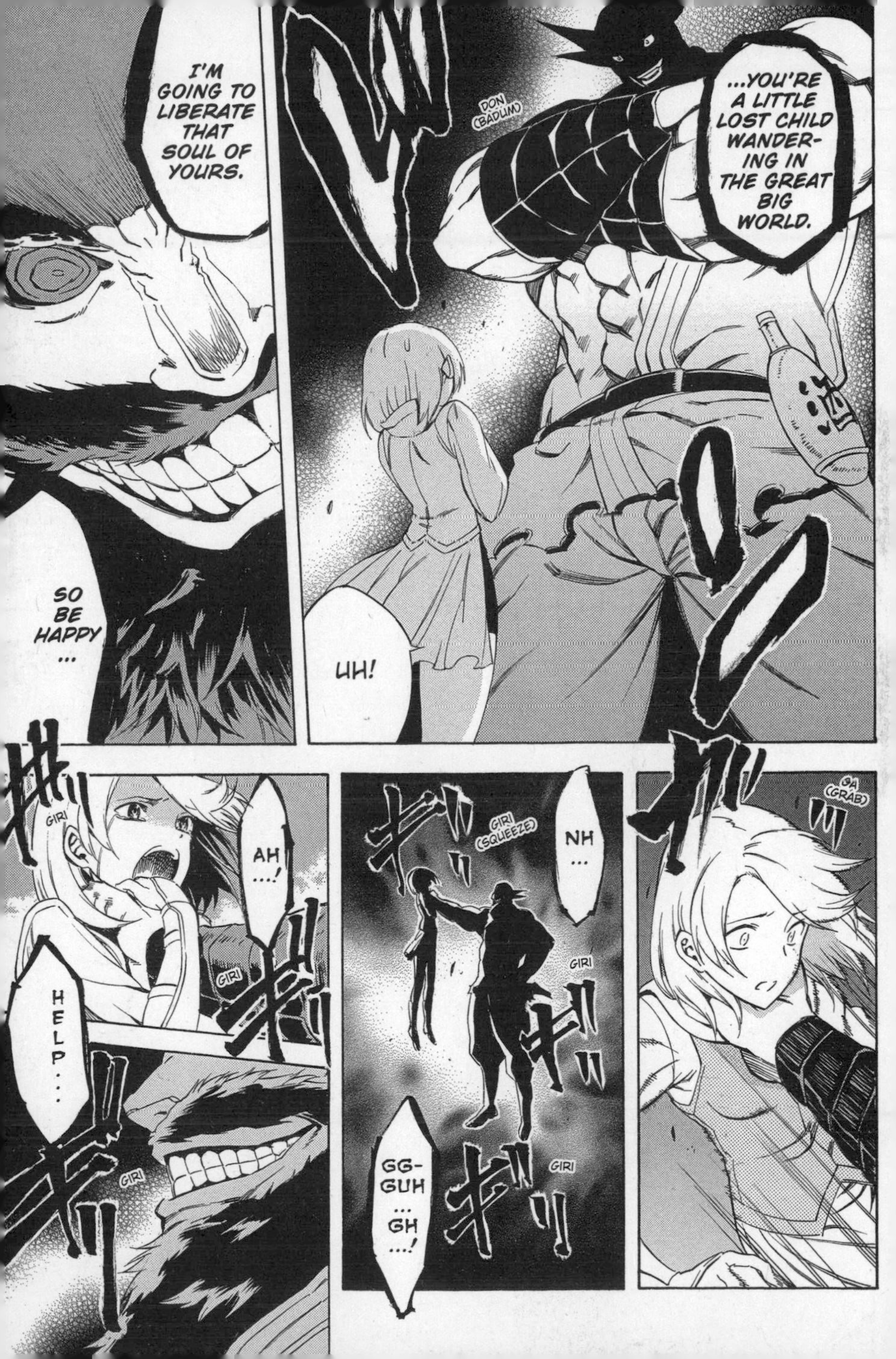
...YOU'RE A LITTLE LOST CHILD WANDERING IN THE GREAT BIG WORLD.
DON (BADUM)
UH!
I'M GOING TO LIBERATE THAT SOUL OF YOURS.
SO BE HAPPY ...
GA (GRAB)
NH ...
GIRI (SQUEEZE)
GIRI
GIRI
GG-GUH ... GH ...!
GIRI
AH ...!
GIRI
HELP...
GIRI

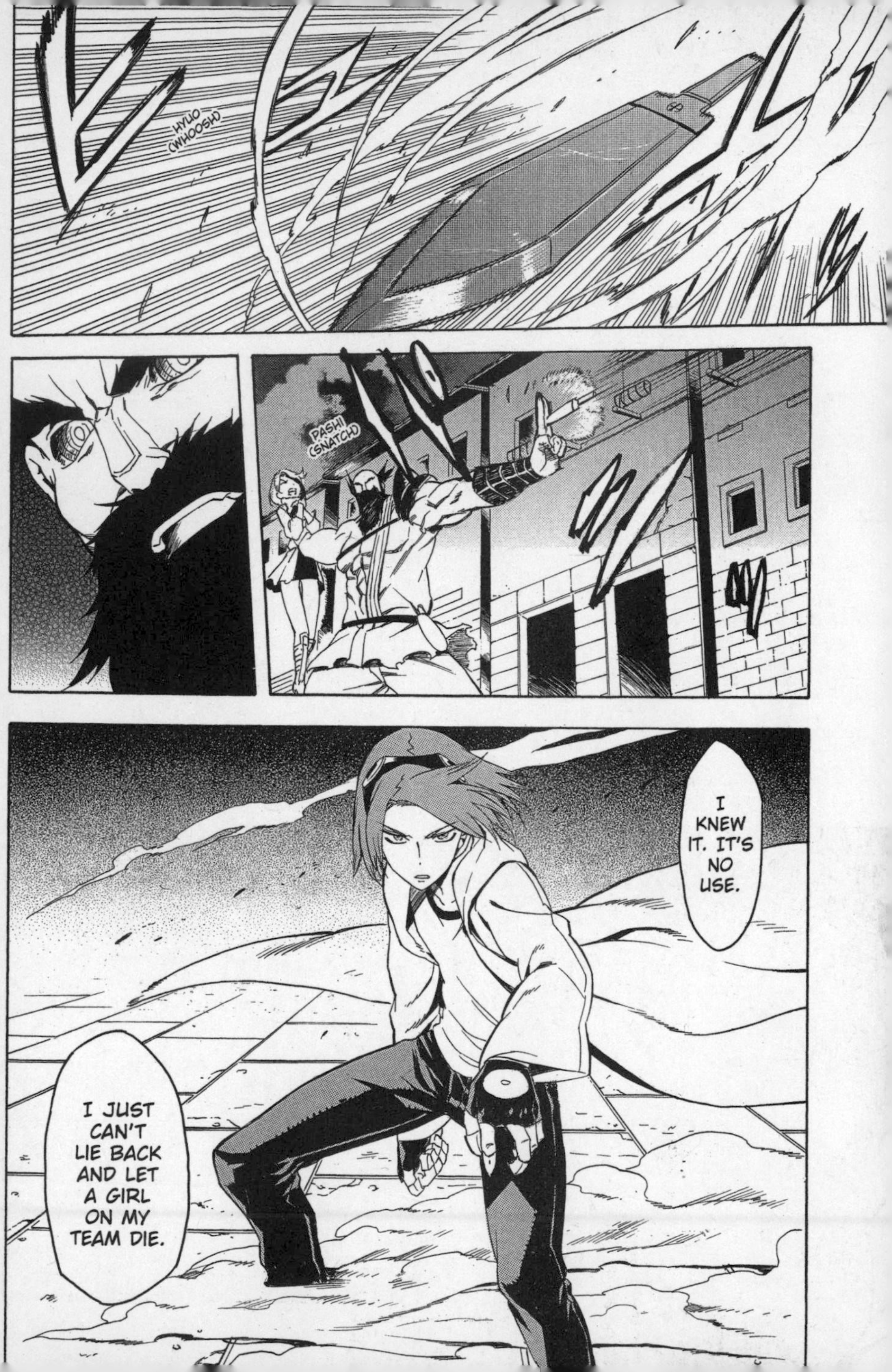
HYUO (WHOOSH)
PASHI (SNATCH)
I KNEW IT. IT'S NO USE.
I JUST CAN'T LIE BACK AND LET A GIRL ON MY TEAM DIE.

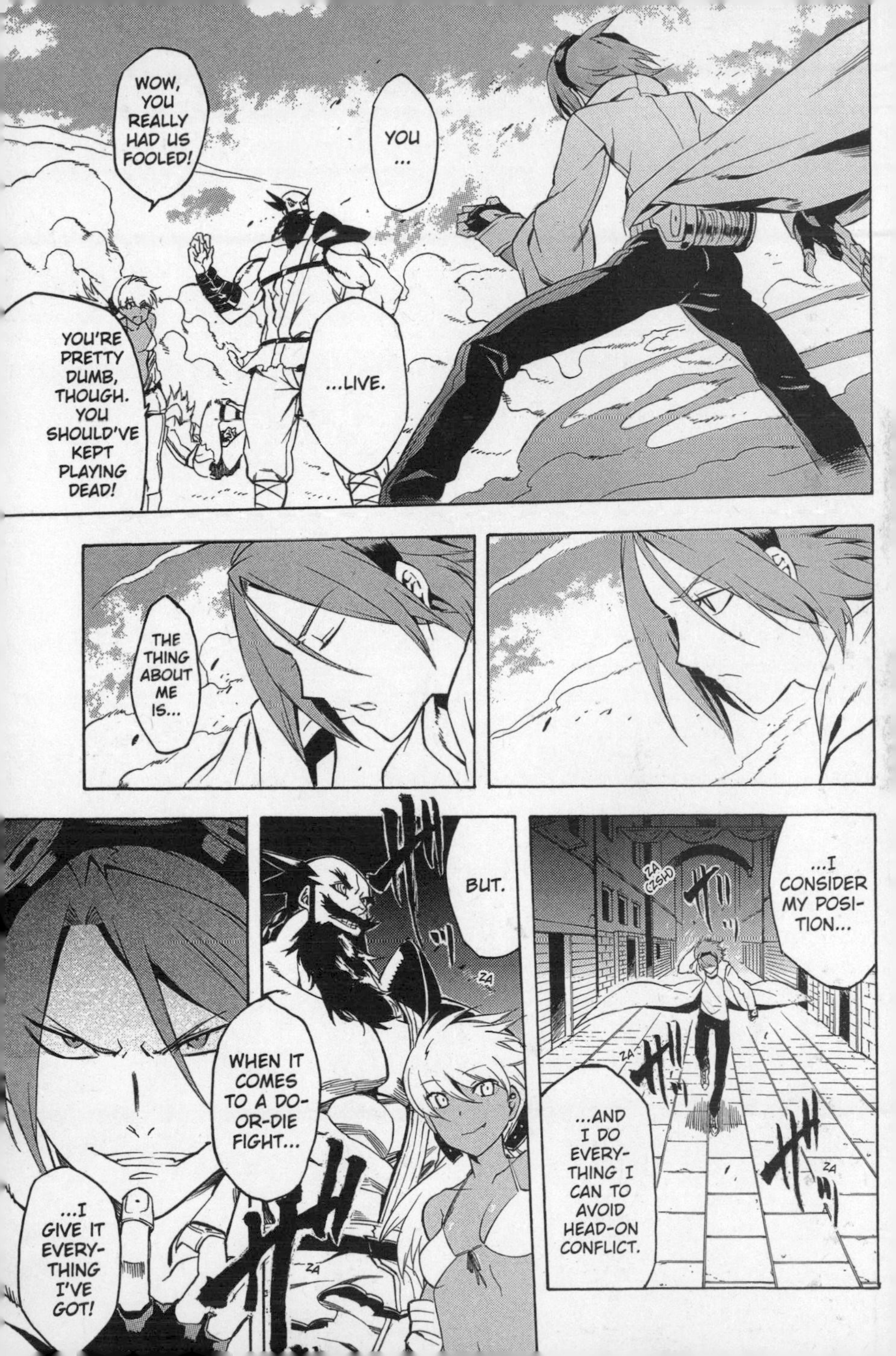
YOU ...
WOW, YOU REALLY HAD US FOOLED!
...LIVE.
YOU'RE PRETTY DUMB, THOUGH. YOU SHOULD'VE KEPT PLAYING DEAD!
THE THING ABOUT ME IS...
...I CONSIDER MY POSITION...
ZA (ZSH)
...AND I DO EVERYTHING I CAN TO AVOID HEAD-ON CONFLICT.
ZA
ZA
BUT.
ZA
WHEN IT COMES TO A DO-OR-DIE FIGHT...
ZA
...I GIVE IT EVERYTHING I'VE GOT!

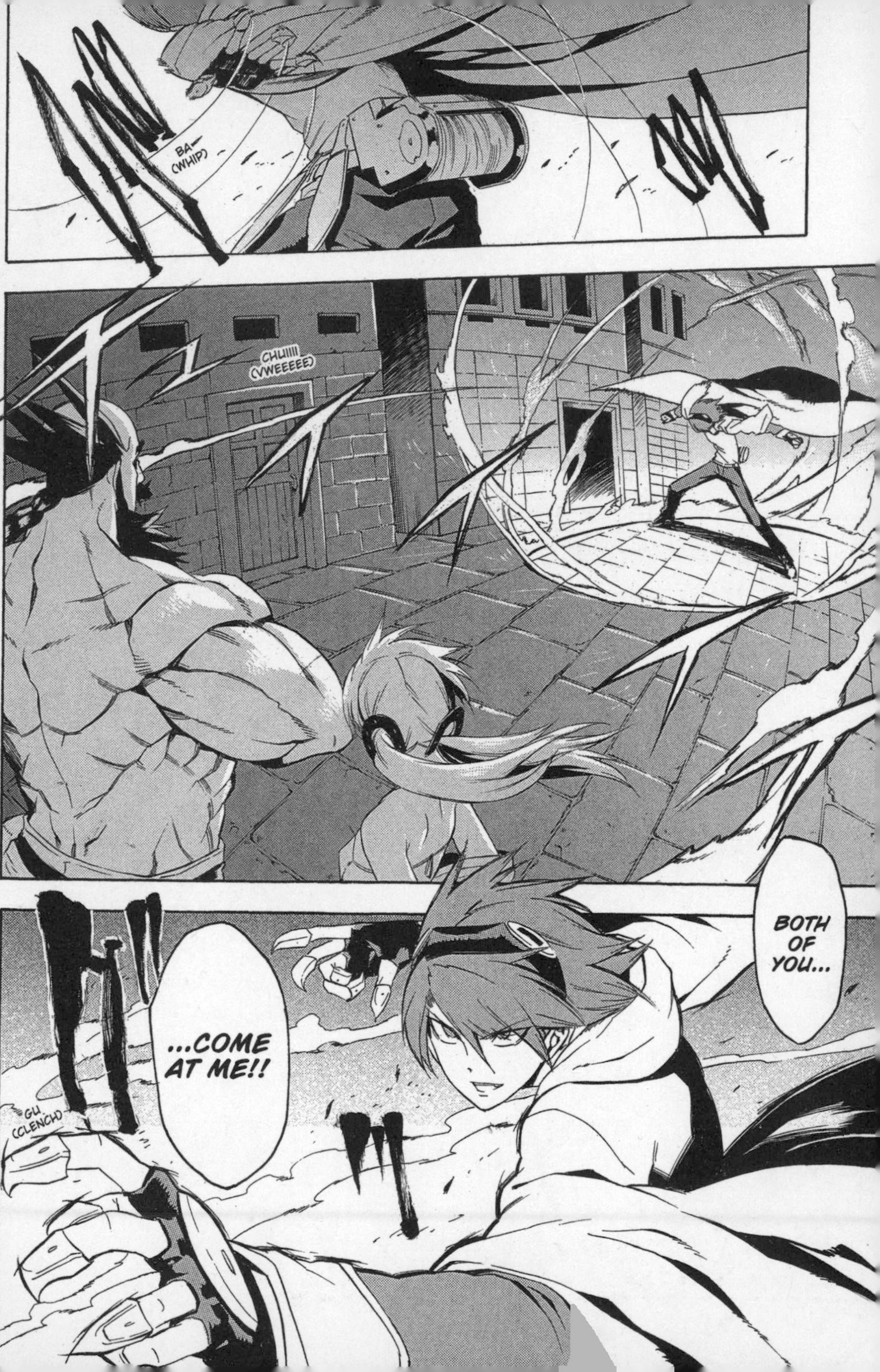
BA— (WHIP)
CHUIIII (VWEEEEE)
BOTH OF YOU...
...COME AT ME!!
GU (CLENCH)

Akame ga KILL!

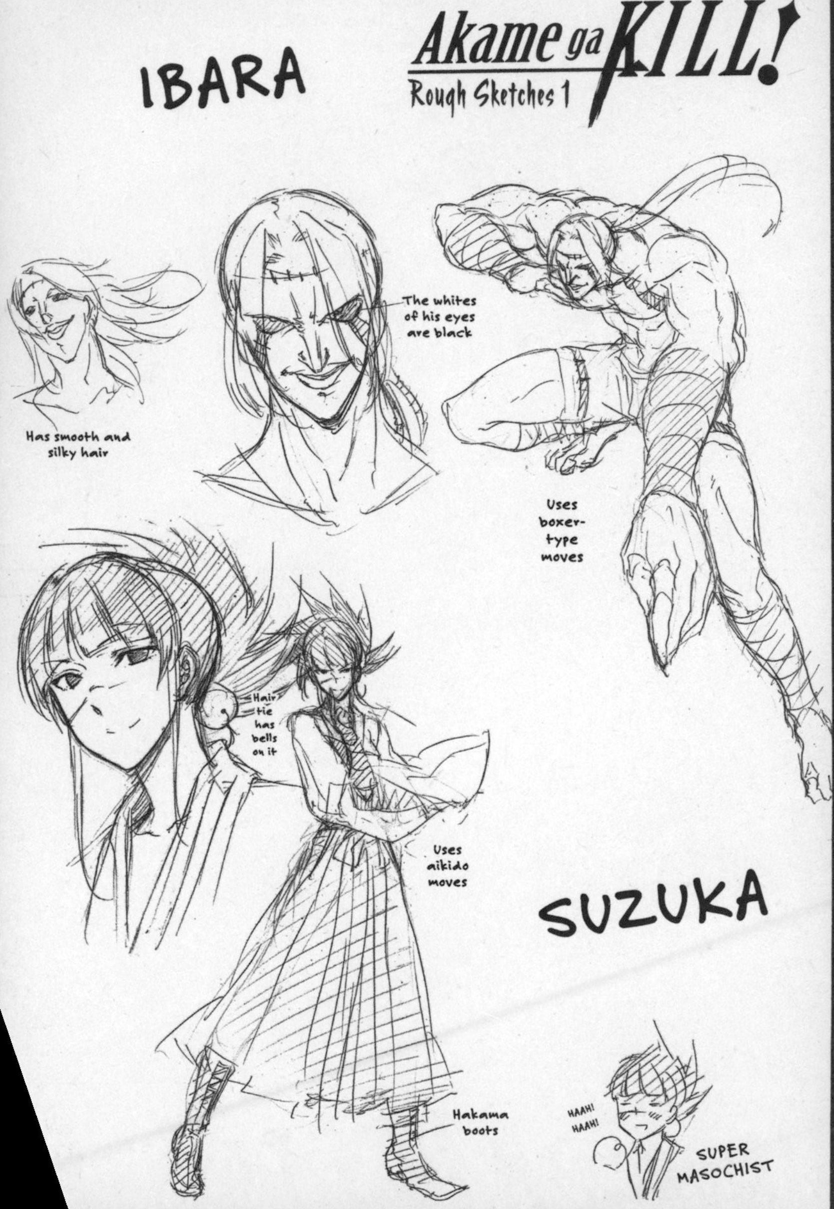
Akame ga KILL!
Rough Sketches 1
IBARA
Has smooth and silky hair
The whites of his eyes are black
Uses boxer-type moves
Hair tie has bells on it
Uses aikido moves
SUZUKA
Hakama boots
HAAH! HAAH!
SUPER MASOCHIST

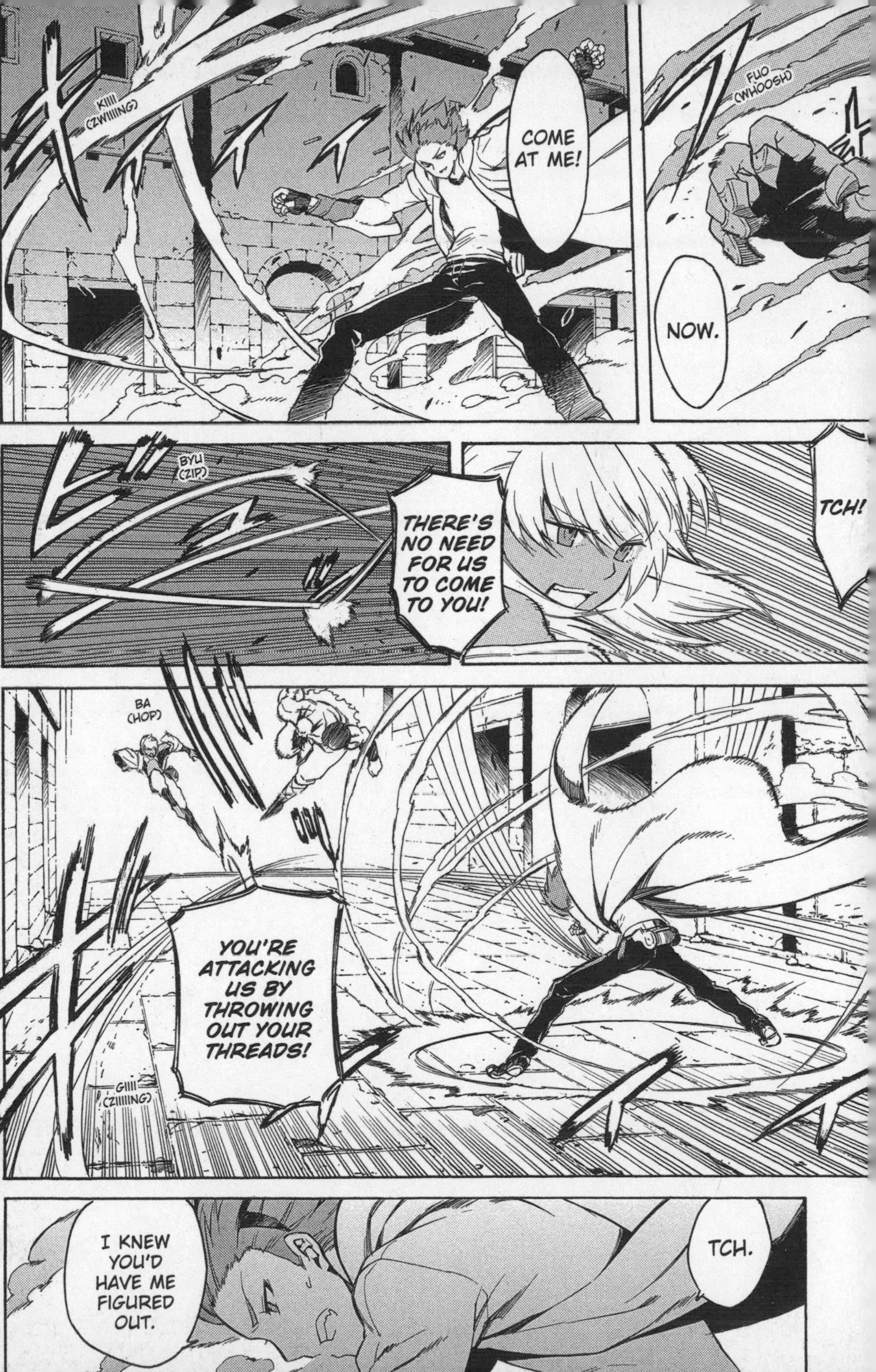
FUO (WHOOSH)
NOW.
COME AT ME!
KIIII (ZWIIIIING)
TCH!
THERE'S NO NEED FOR US TO COME TO YOU!
BYU (ZIP)
BA (HOP)
YOU'RE ATTACKING US BY THROWING OUT YOUR THREADS!
GIIII (ZIIIIING)
TCH.
I KNEW YOU'D HAVE ME FIGURED OUT.

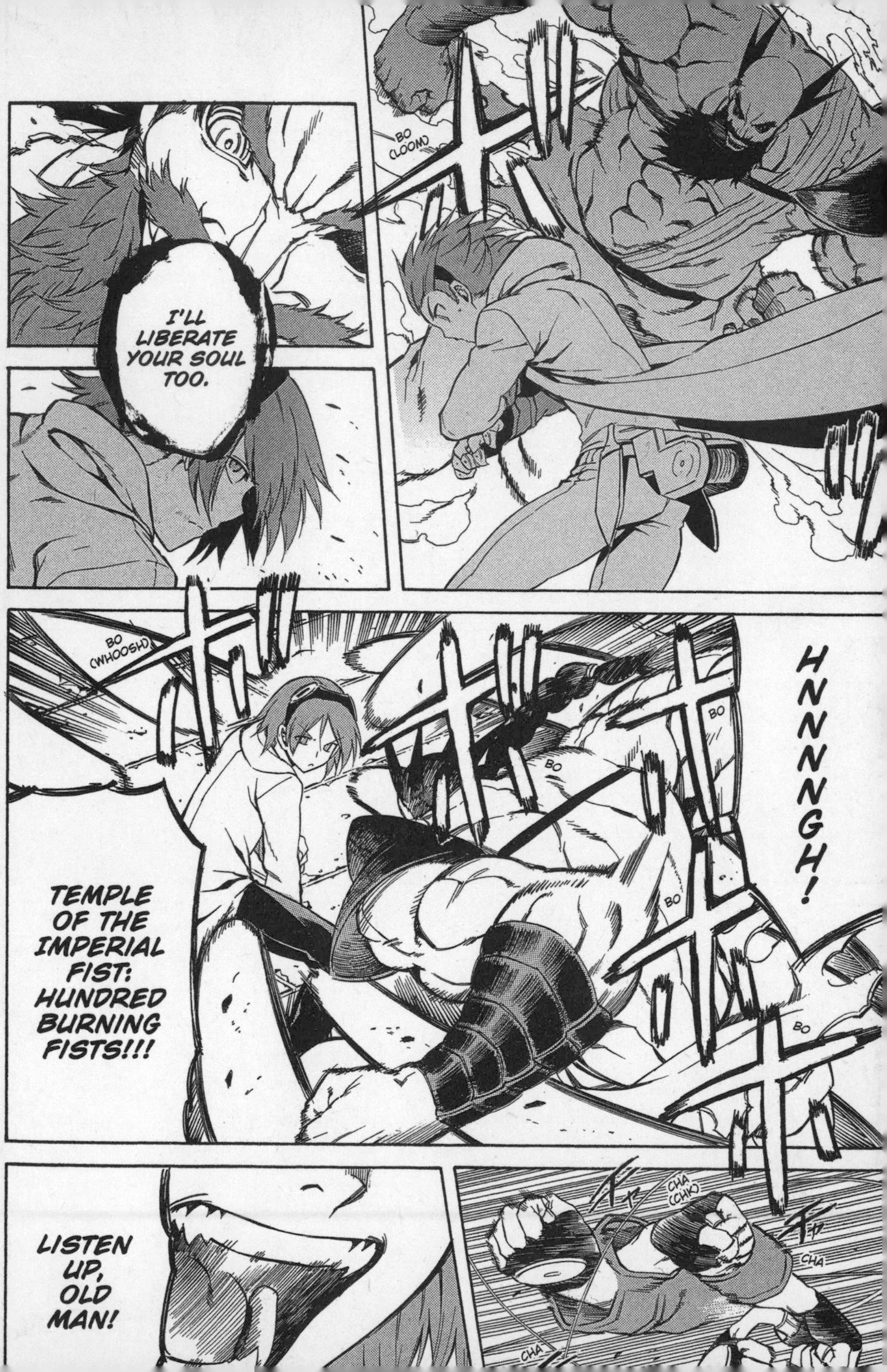
BO (LOOM)
I'LL LIBERATE YOUR SOUL TOO.
BO (WHOOSH)
HNNNNGH!
BO
BO
BO
BO
TEMPLE OF THE IMPERIAL FIST: HUNDRED BURNING FISTS!!!
CHA (CHK)
CHA
CHA
LISTEN UP, OLD MAN!

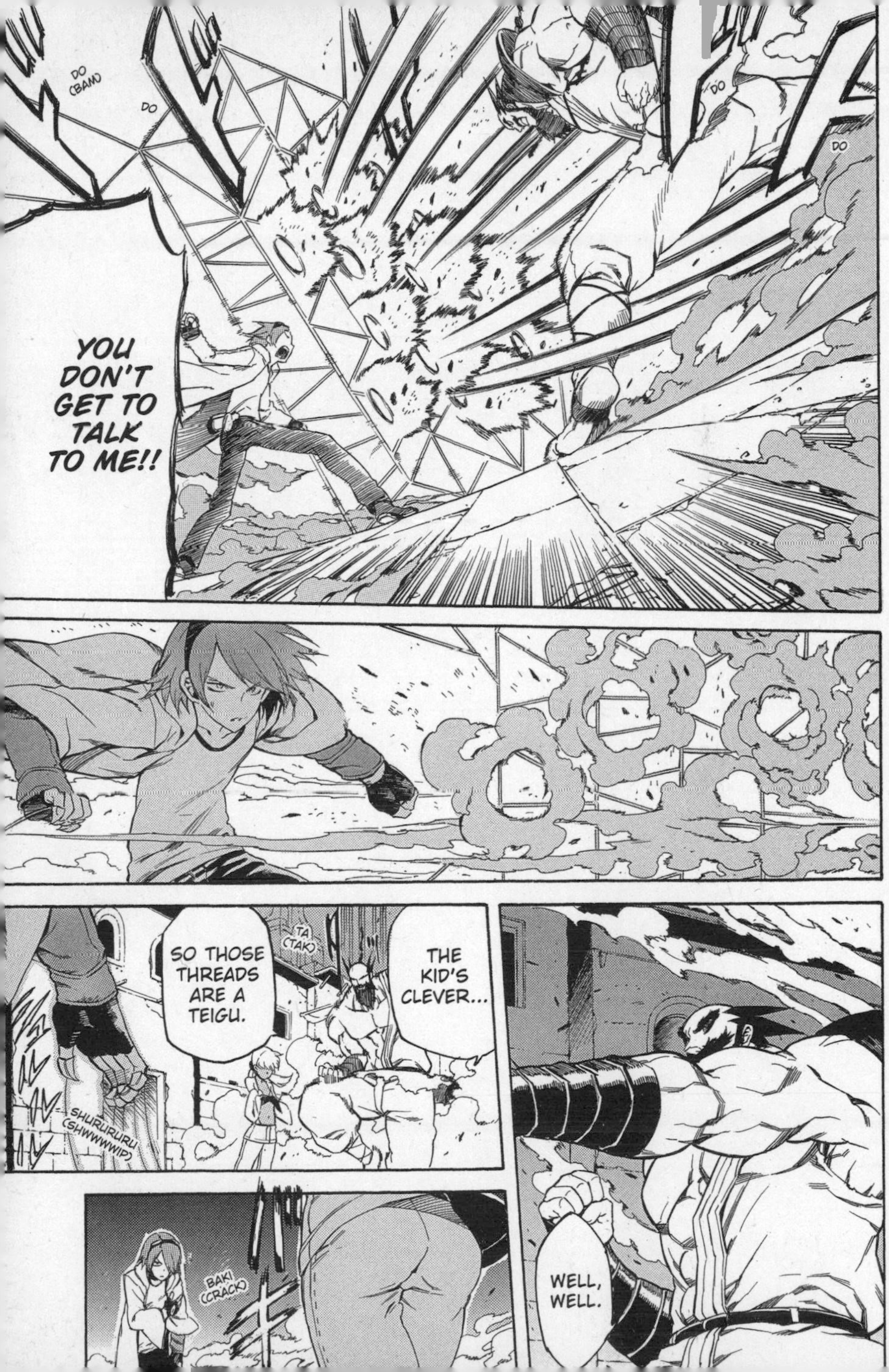
DO
DO
DO (BAM)
DO
YOU DON'T GET TO TALK TO ME!!
THE KID'S CLEVER...
TA (TAK)
SO THOSE THREADS ARE A TEIGU.
SHURURURU (SHWWWWIP)
WELL, WELL.
BAKI (CRACK)

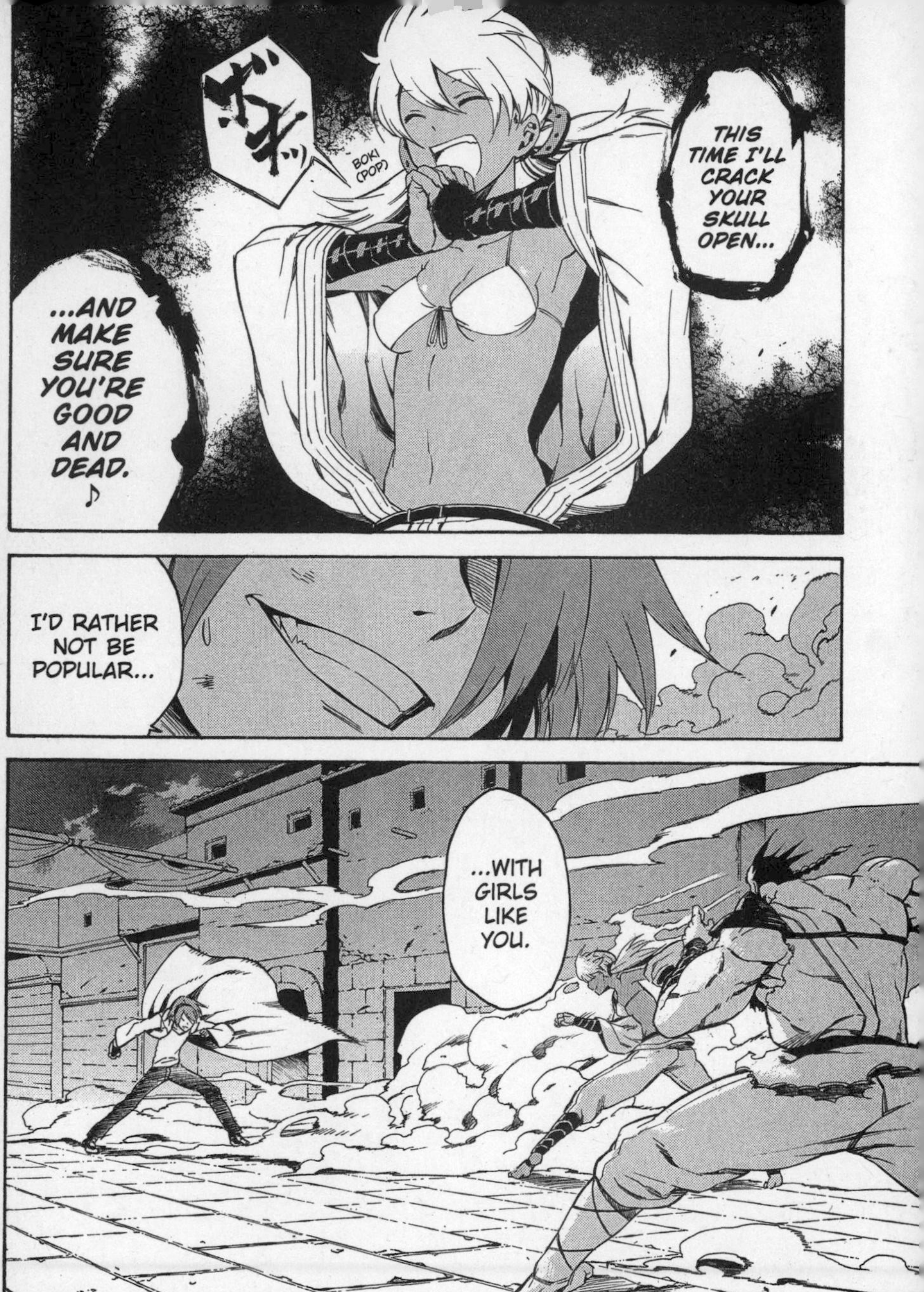
THIS TIME I'LL CRACK YOUR SKULL OPEN...
BOKI (POP)
...AND MAKE SURE YOU'RE GOOD AND DEAD. ♪
I'D RATHER NOT BE POPULAR...
...WITH GIRLS LIKE YOU.

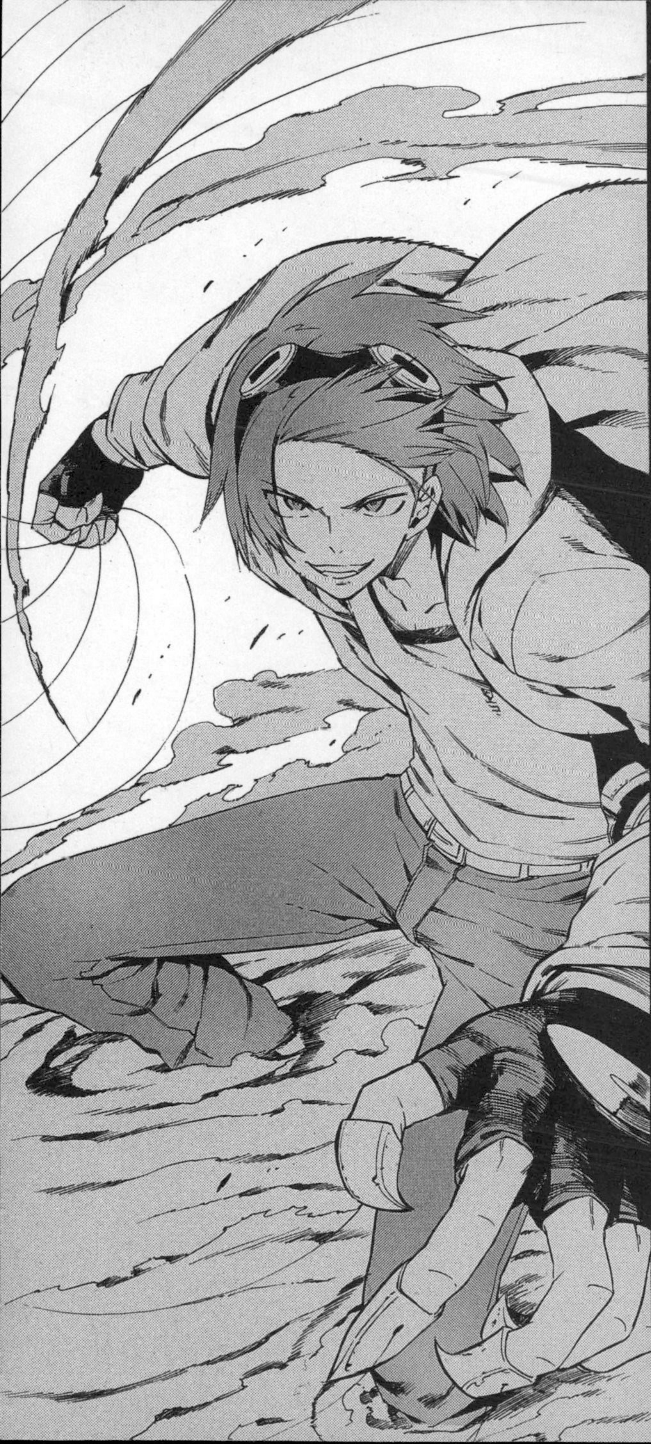

# CHAPTER 36 - KILL THE FATE (PART 1)

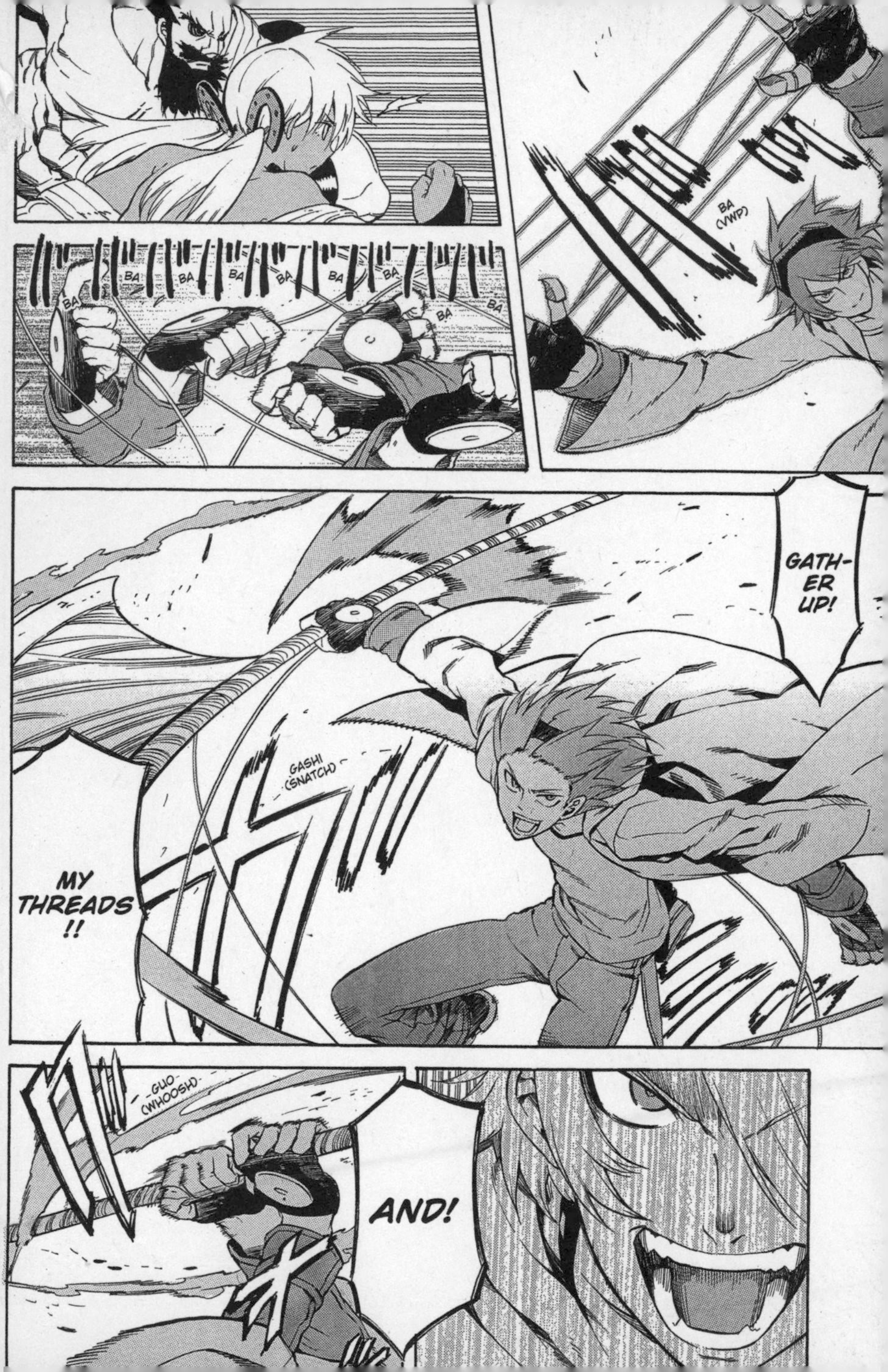
BA (VWP)
BA
BA
BA
BA
BA
BA
BA
BA
GATH-ER UP!
GASHI (SNATCH)
MY THREADS !!
GUO (WHOOSH)
AND!

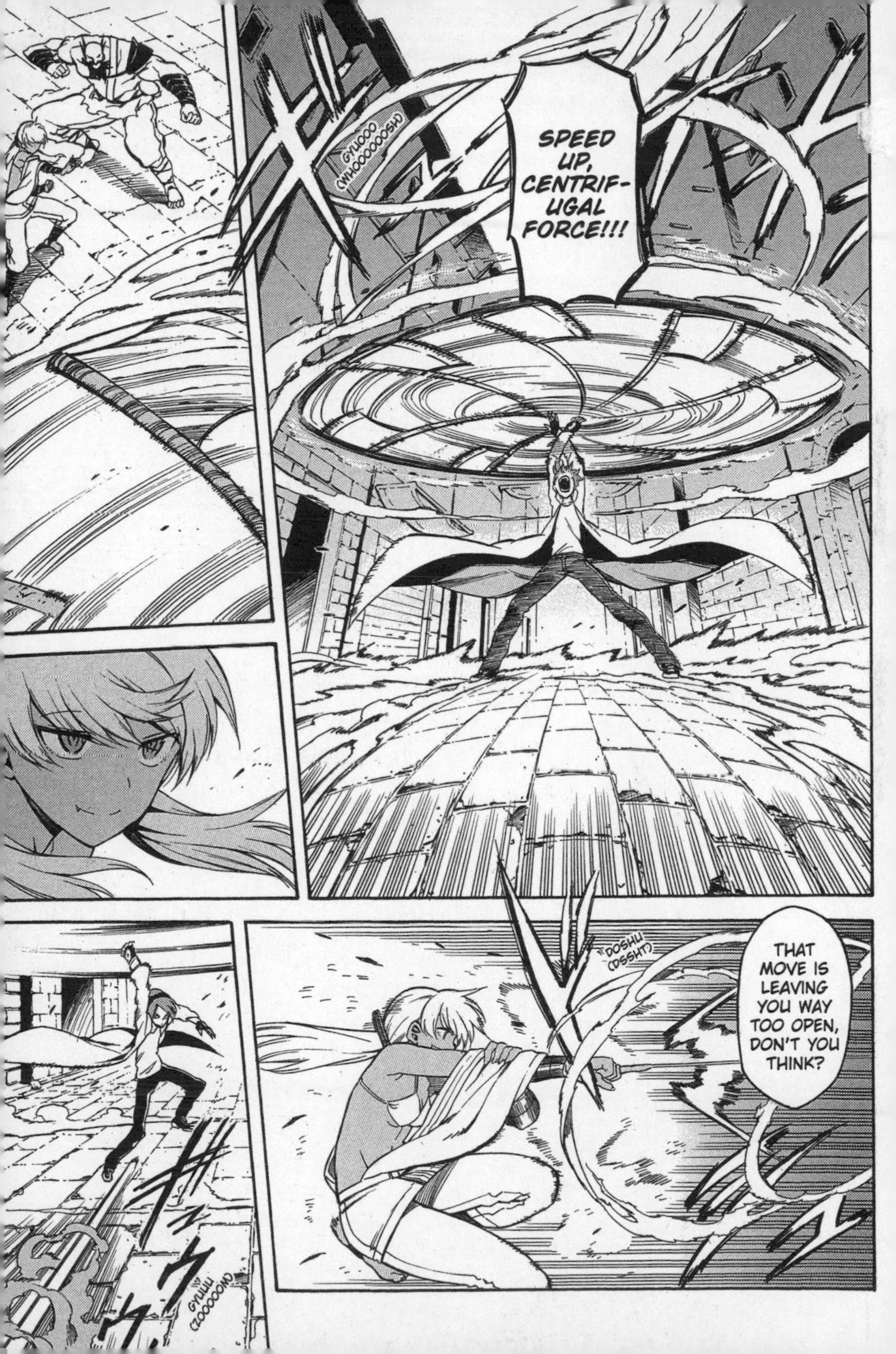

SPEED UP, CENTRIFUGAL FORCE!!!
GYUOOO (WHOOOOOOSH)
DOSHU (DSSHT)
THAT MOVE IS LEAVING YOU WAY TOO OPEN, DON'T YOU THINK?
GYULULI (ZOOOOOM)

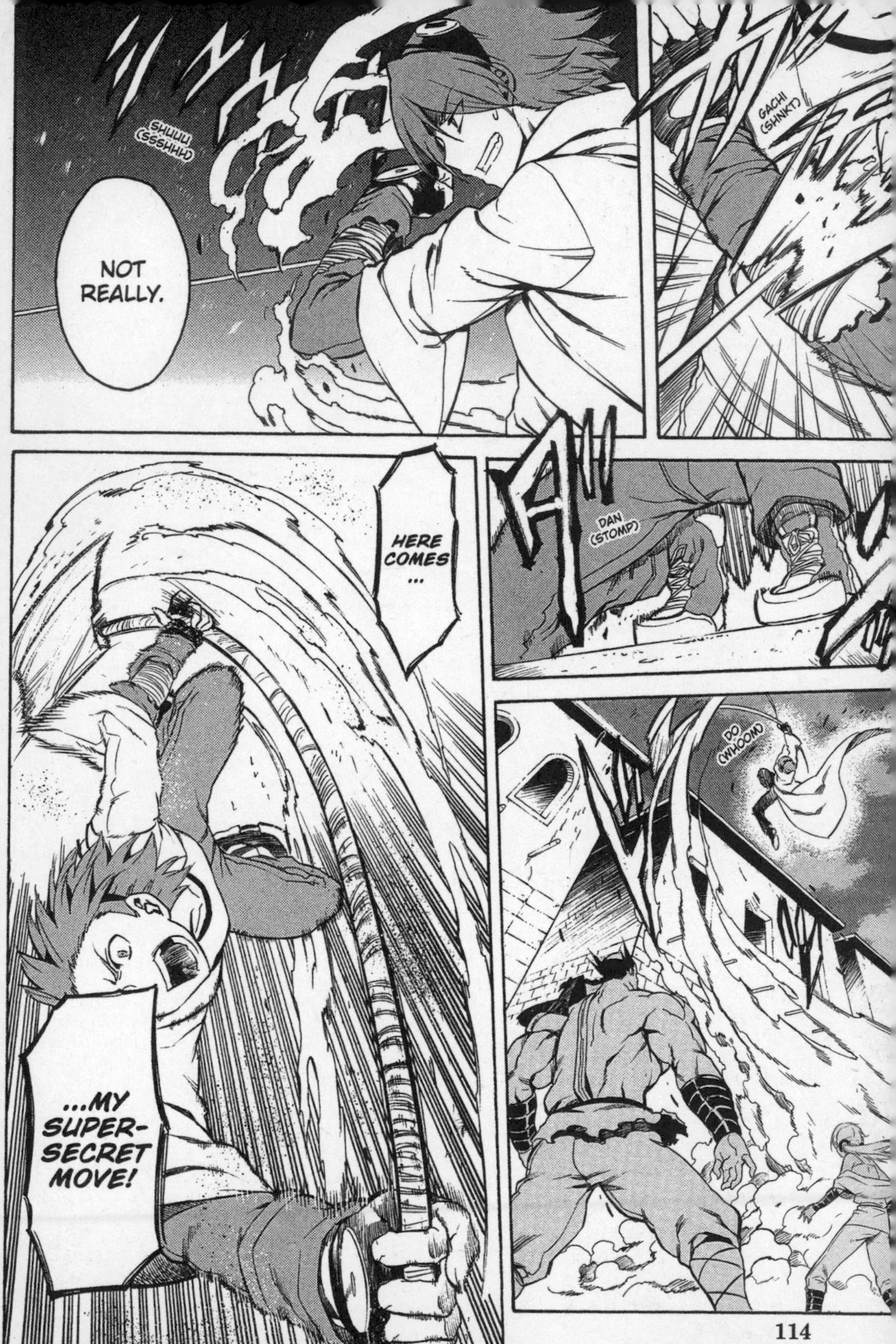
GACHI (SHNKT)
SHUUU (SSSHHH)
NOT REALLY.
DAN (STOMP)
DO (WHOOM)
HERE COMES ...
...MY SUPER-SECRET MOVE!

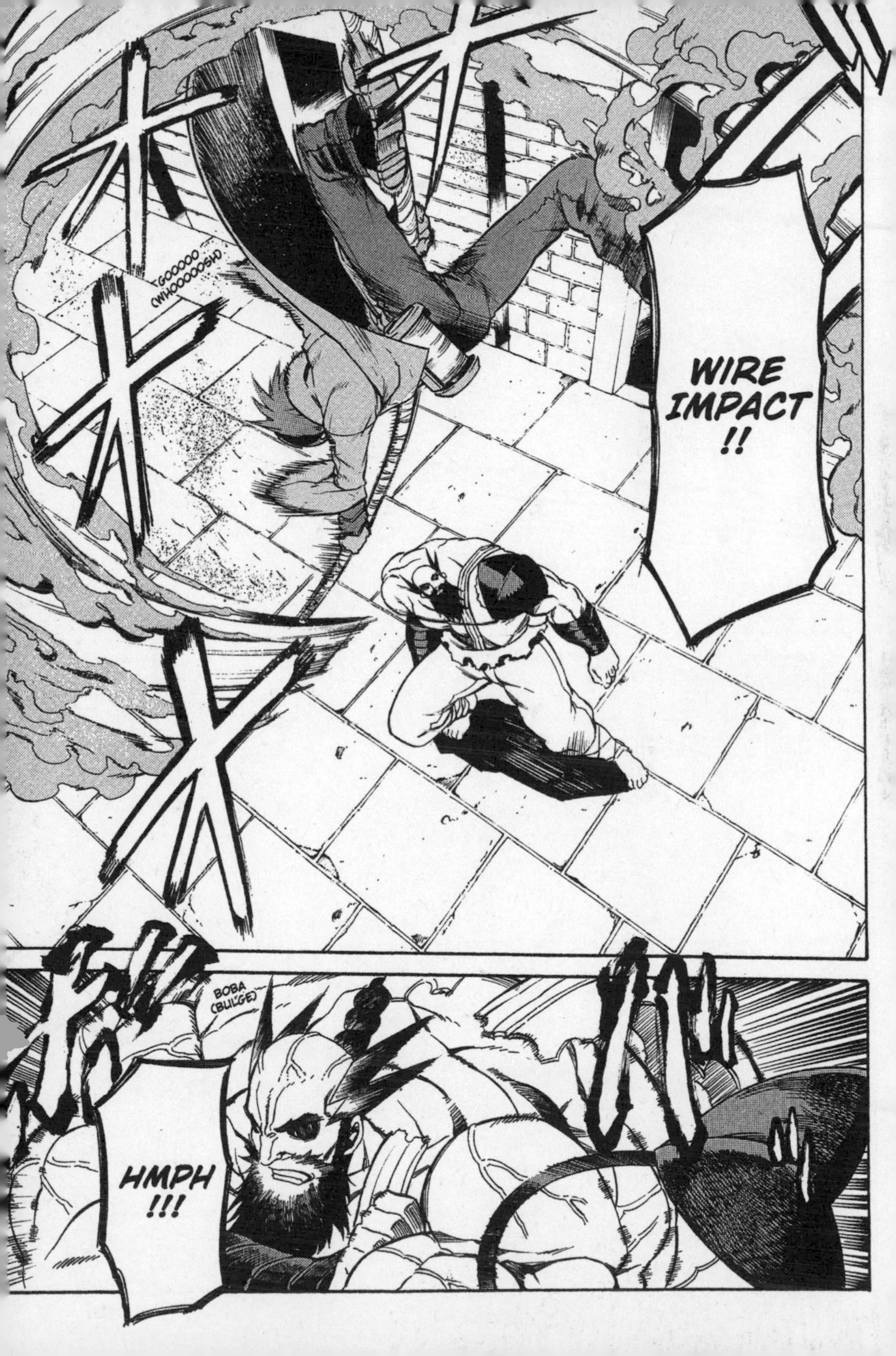
WIRE IMPACT !!
GOOOOO (WHOOOOOOSH)
BOBA (BULGE)
HMPH !!!

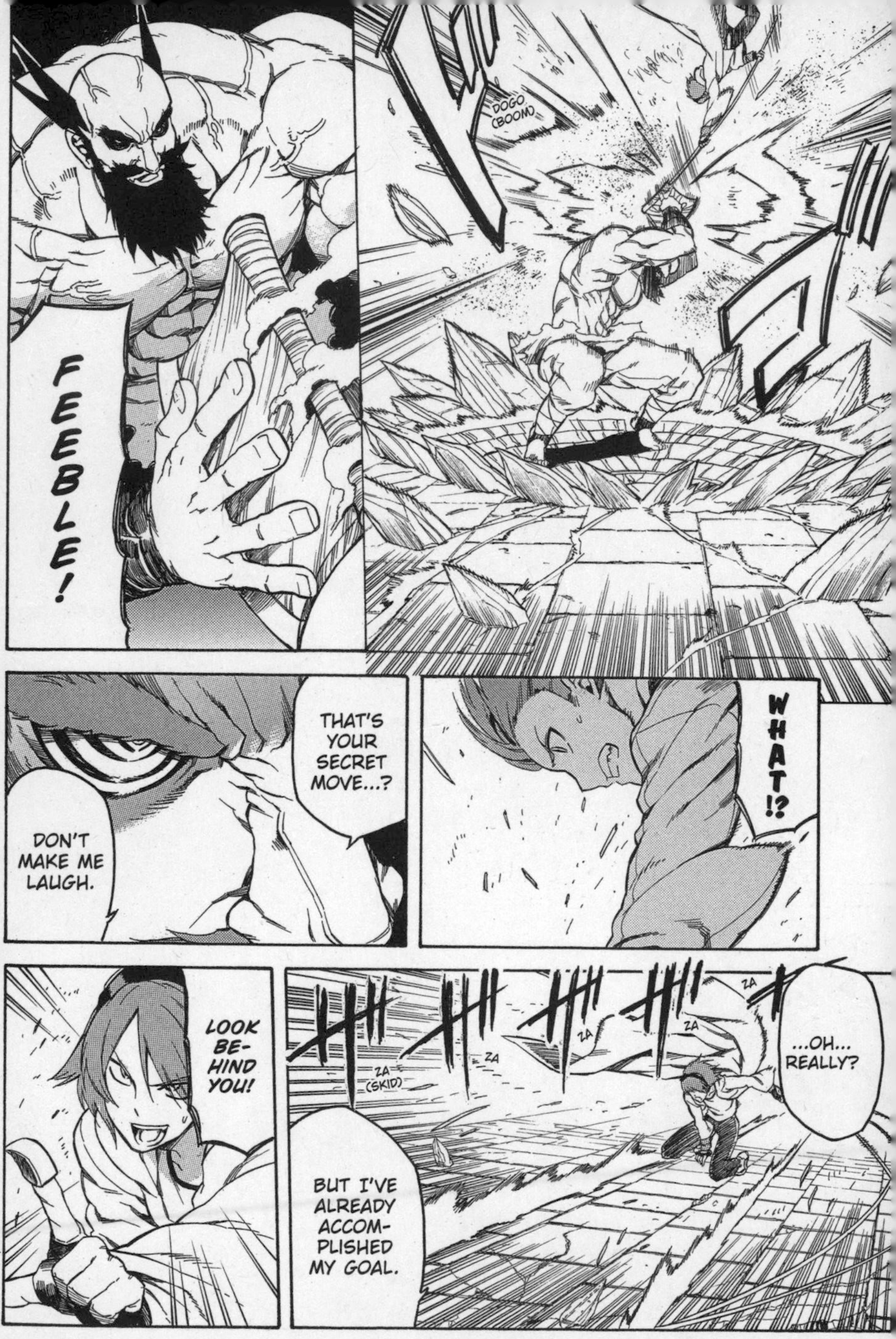
DOGO (BOOM)
FEEBLE!
THAT'S YOUR SECRET MOVE...?
DON'T MAKE ME LAUGH.
WHAT!?
...OH... REALLY?
ZA
ZA
ZA
ZA
ZA (SKID)
LOOK BE-HIND YOU!
BUT I'VE ALREADY ACCOM-PLISHED MY GOAL.

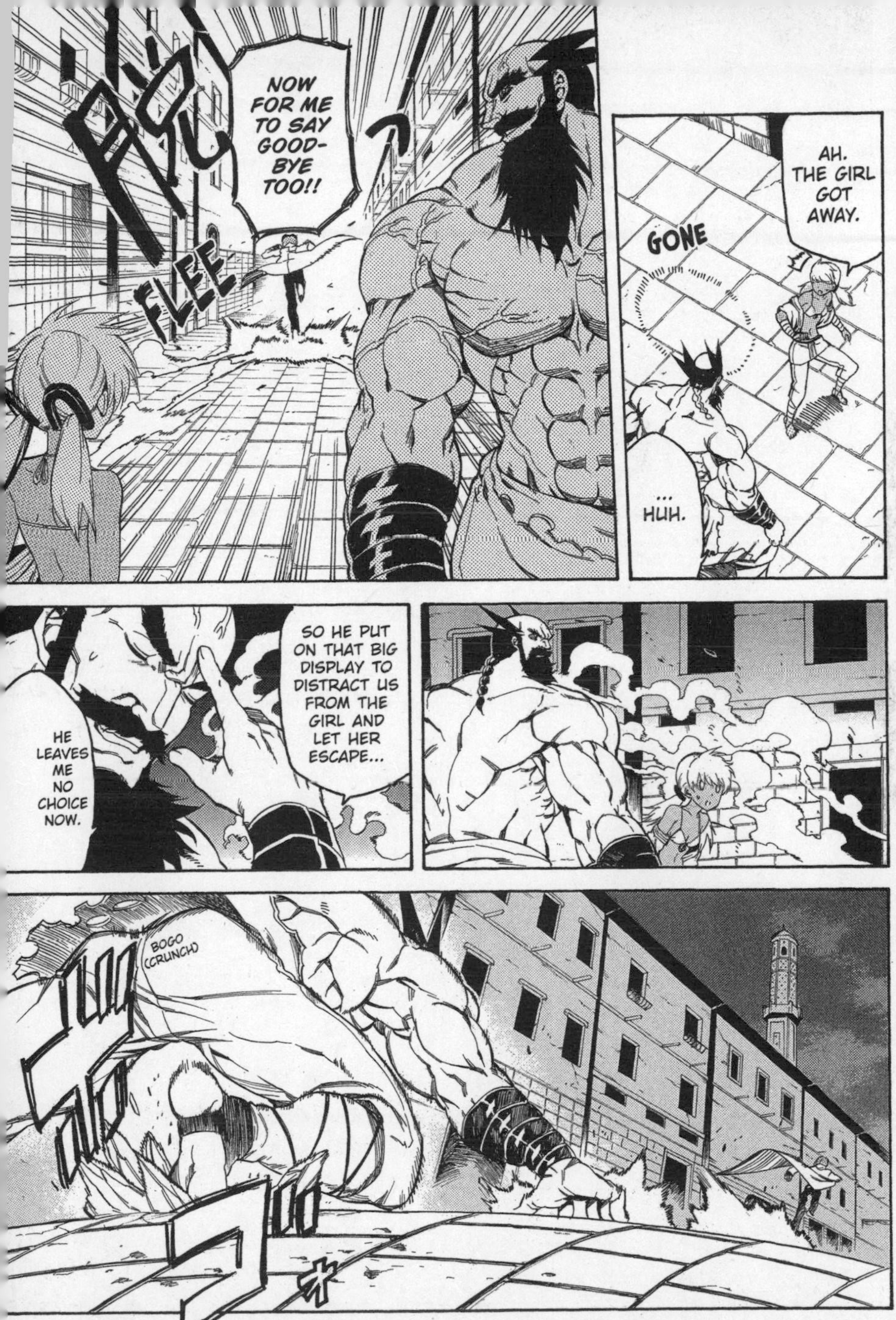

NOW FOR ME TO SAY GOOD-BYE TOO!!
FLEE
AH. THE GIRL GOT AWAY.
GONE
... HUH.
SO HE PUT ON THAT BIG DISPLAY TO DISTRACT US FROM THE GIRL AND LET HER ESCAPE...
HE LEAVES ME NO CHOICE NOW.
BOGO (CRUNCH)

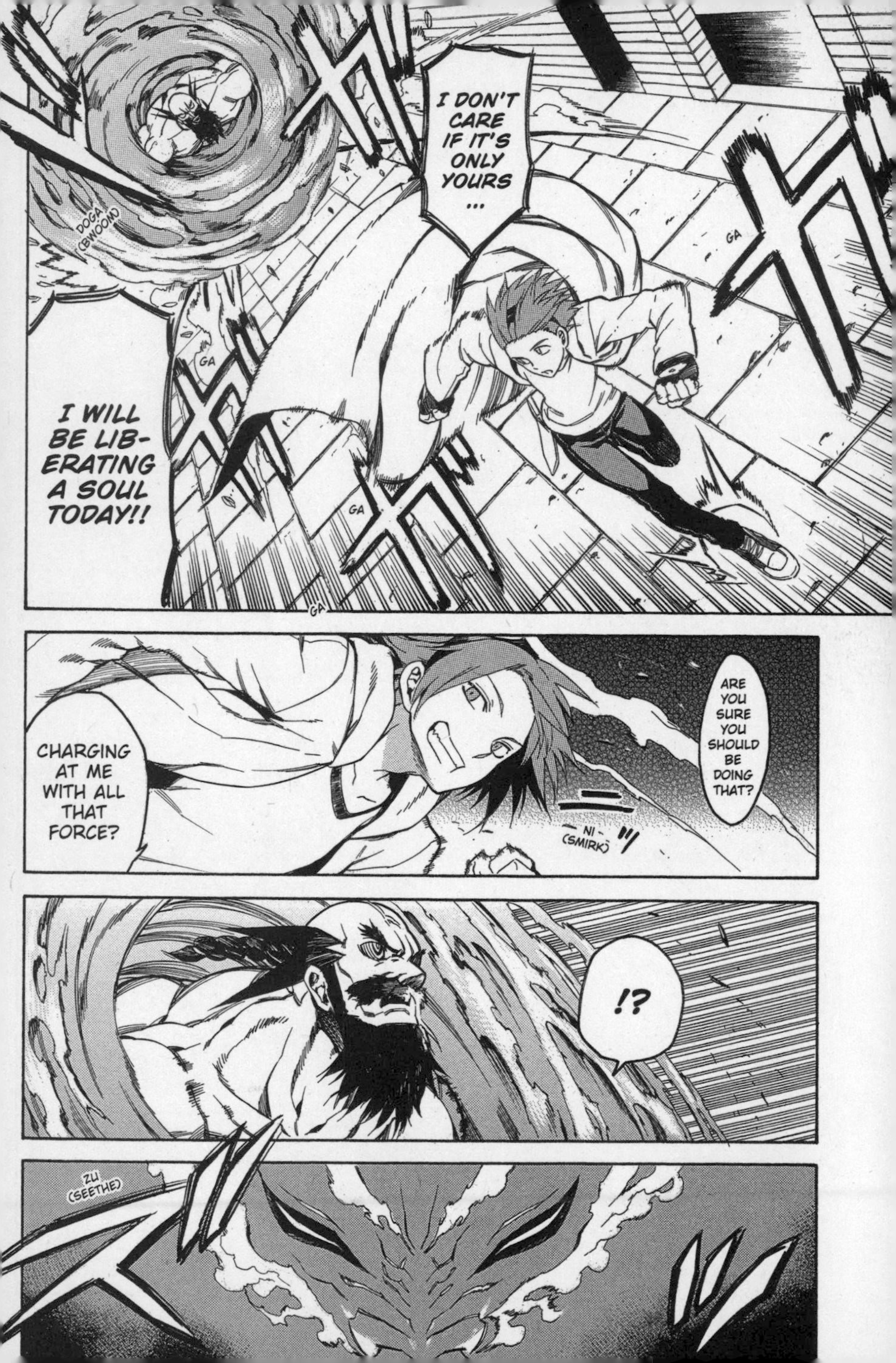
I DON'T CARE IF IT'S ONLY YOURS ...
GA
DOGA (BWOOM)
GA
I WILL BE LIBERATING A SOUL TODAY!!
GA
GA
ARE YOU SURE YOU SHOULD BE DOING THAT?
NI (SMIRK)
CHARGING AT ME WITH ALL THAT FORCE?
!?
ZU (SEETHE)

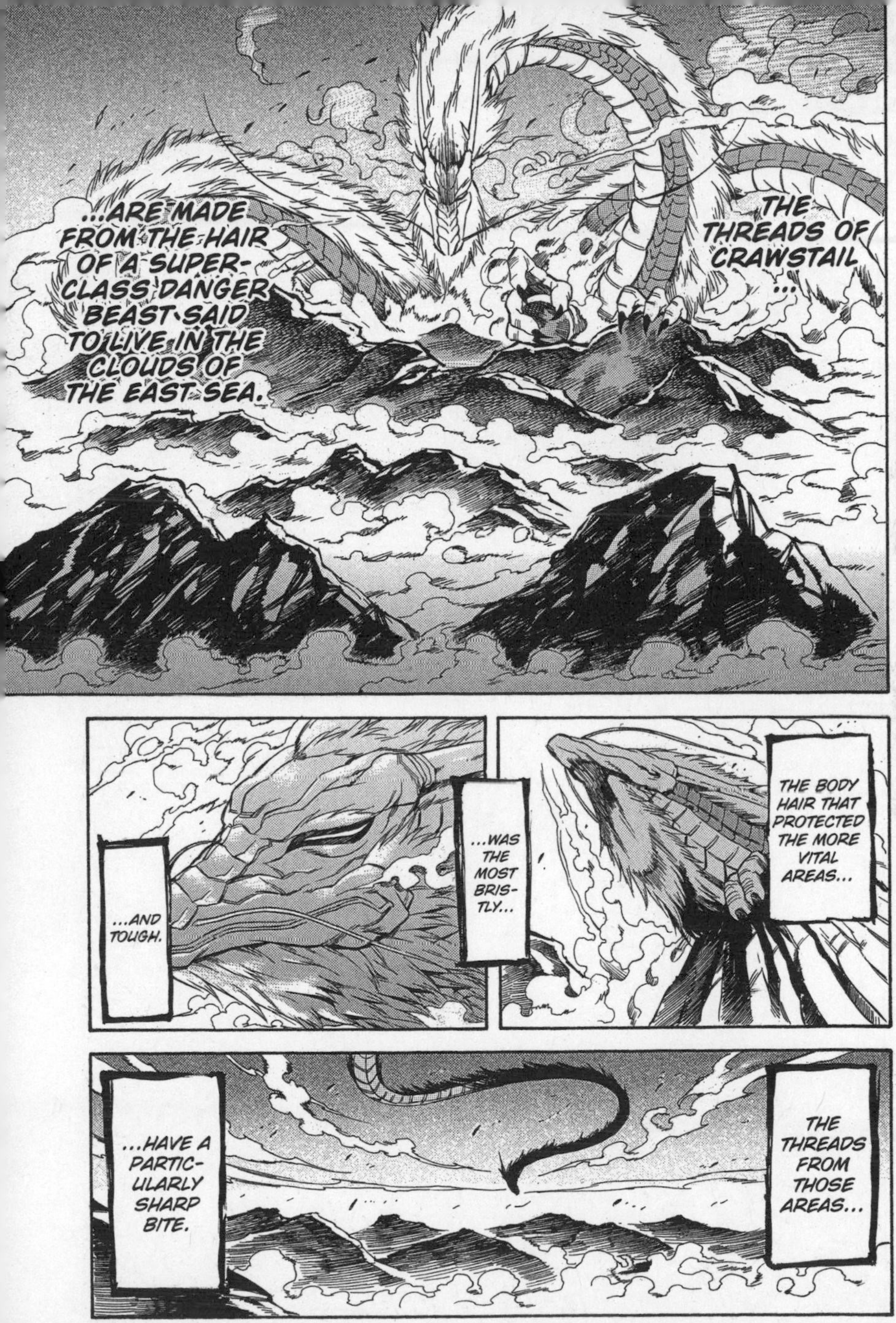
THE THREADS OF CRAWSTAIL ...
...ARE MADE FROM THE HAIR OF A SUPER-CLASS DANGER BEAST SAID TO LIVE IN THE CLOUDS OF THE EAST SEA.
THE BODY HAIR THAT PROTECTED THE MORE VITAL AREAS...
...WAS THE MOST BRIS-TLY...
...AND TOUGH.
THE THREADS FROM THOSE AREAS...
...HAVE A PARTIC-ULARLY SHARP BITE.

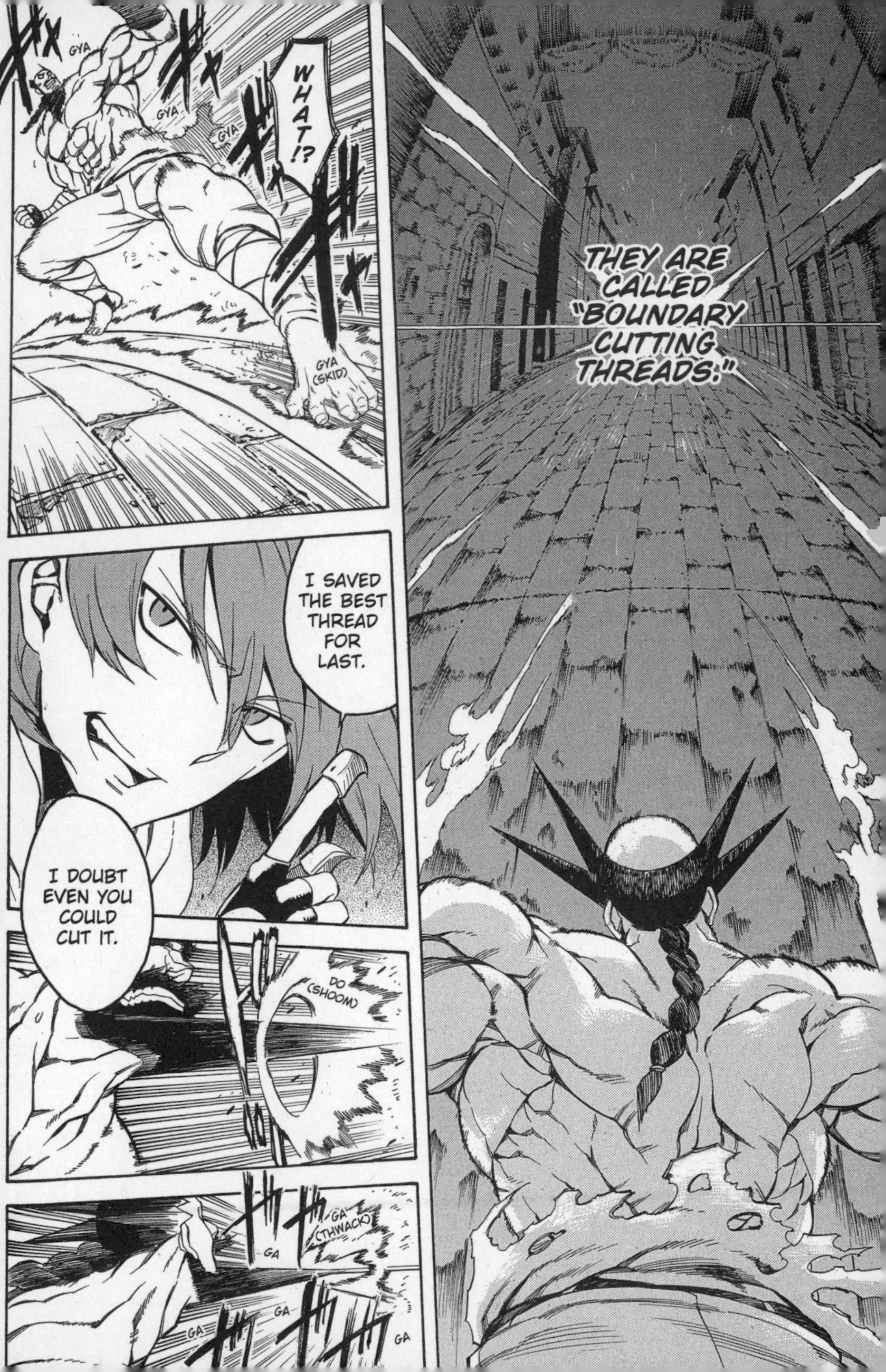
THEY ARE CALLED "BOUNDARY CUTTING THREADS."
GYA
WHAT!?
GYA
GYA
GYA (SKID)
I SAVED THE BEST THREAD FOR LAST.
I DOUBT EVEN YOU COULD CUT IT.
DO (SHOOM)
GA (THWACK)
GA
GA
GA
GA

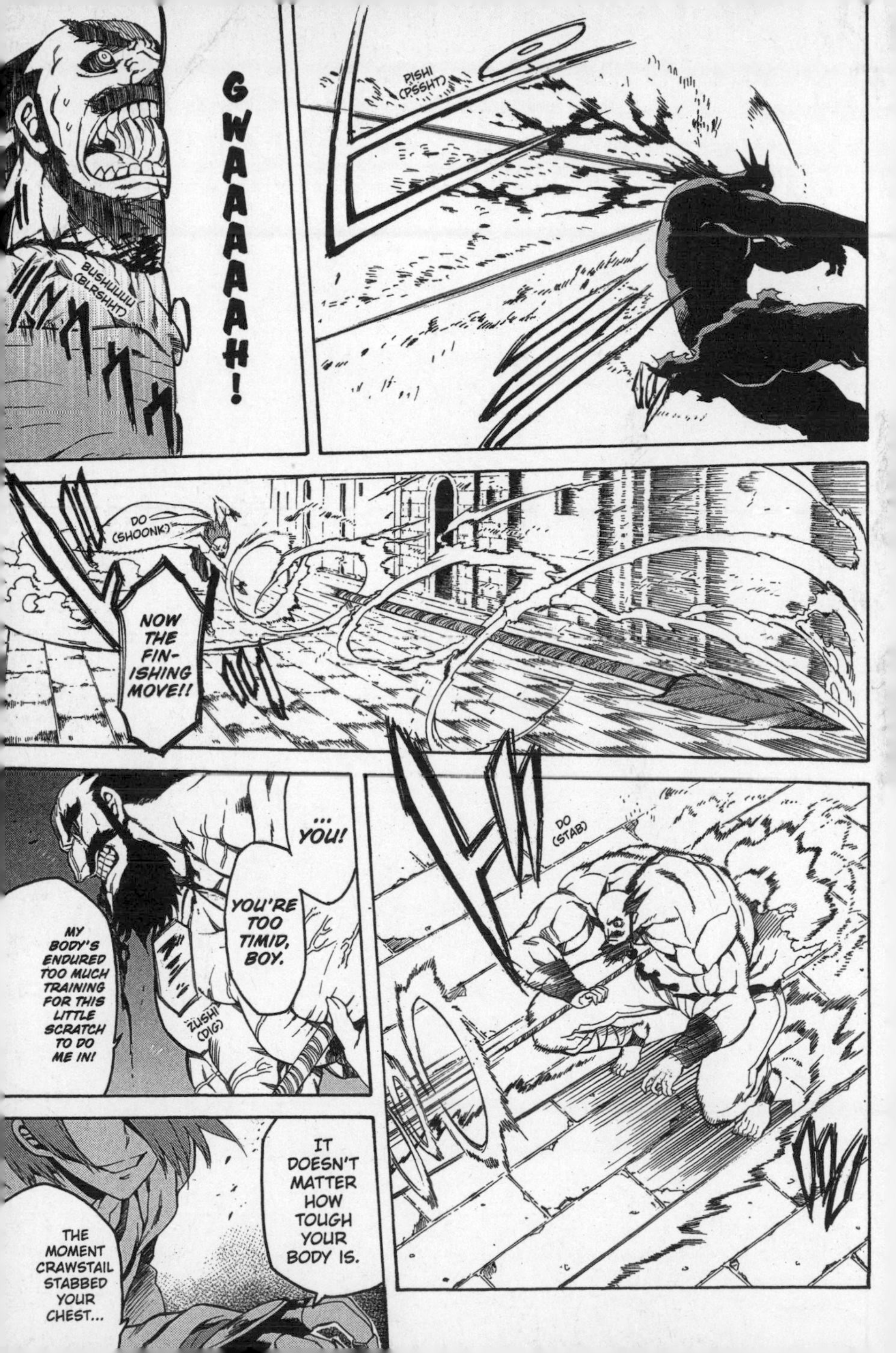
PISHI (PSSHT)
GWAAAAAAH!
BUSHUUUU (BLRSHHT)
DO (SHOONK)
NOW THE FIN-ISHING MOVE!!
DO (STAB)
...YOU!
YOU'RE TOO TIMID, BOY.
MY BODY'S ENDURED TOO MUCH TRAINING FOR THIS LITTLE SCRATCH TO DO ME IN!
ZUSHI (DIG)
IT DOESN'T MATTER HOW TOUGH YOUR BODY IS.
THE MOMENT CRAWSTAIL STABBED YOUR CHEST...

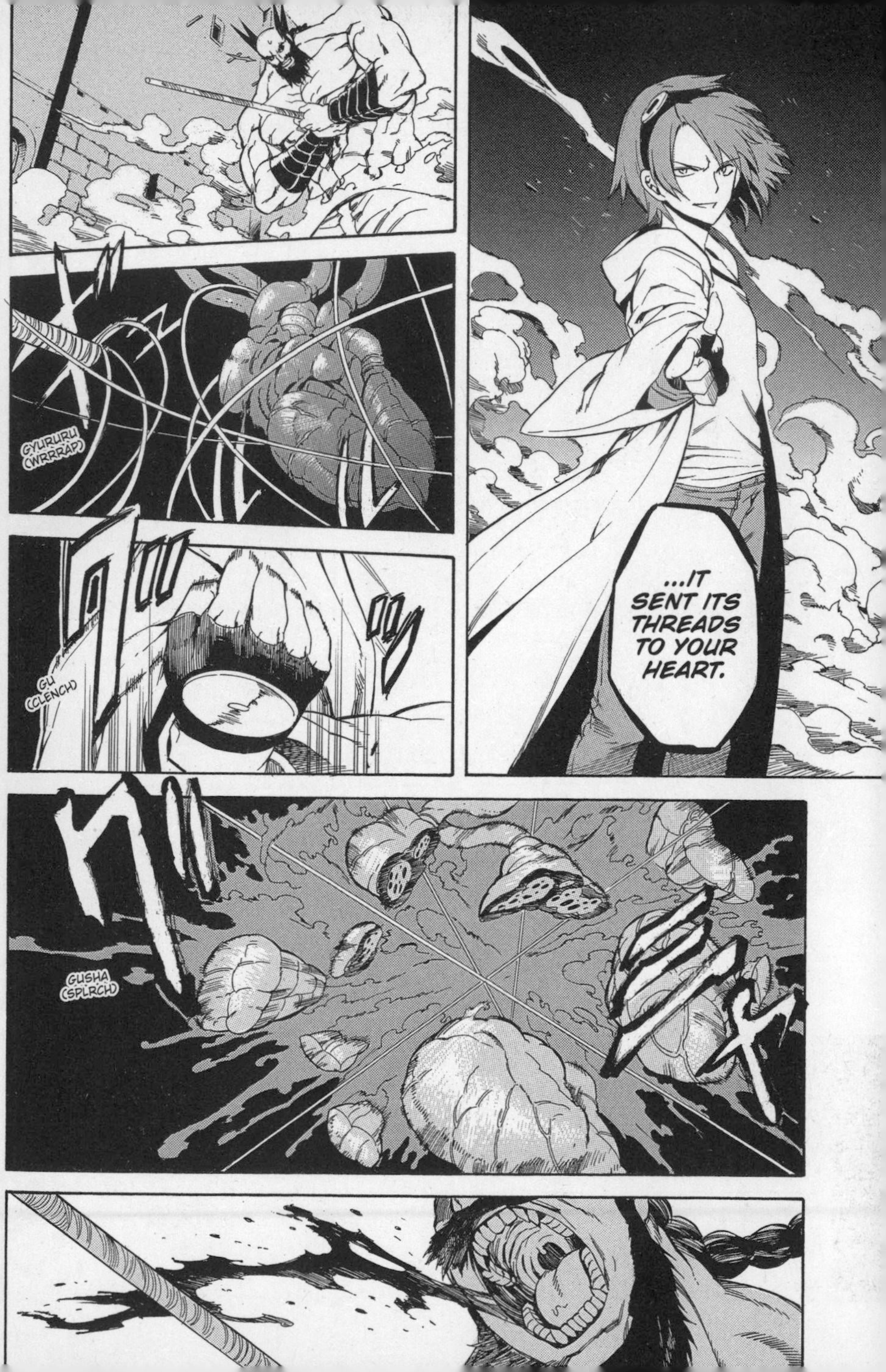
...IT SENT ITS THREADS TO YOUR HEART.
GYURURU (WRRRAP)
GU (CLENCH)
GUSHA (SPLRCH)

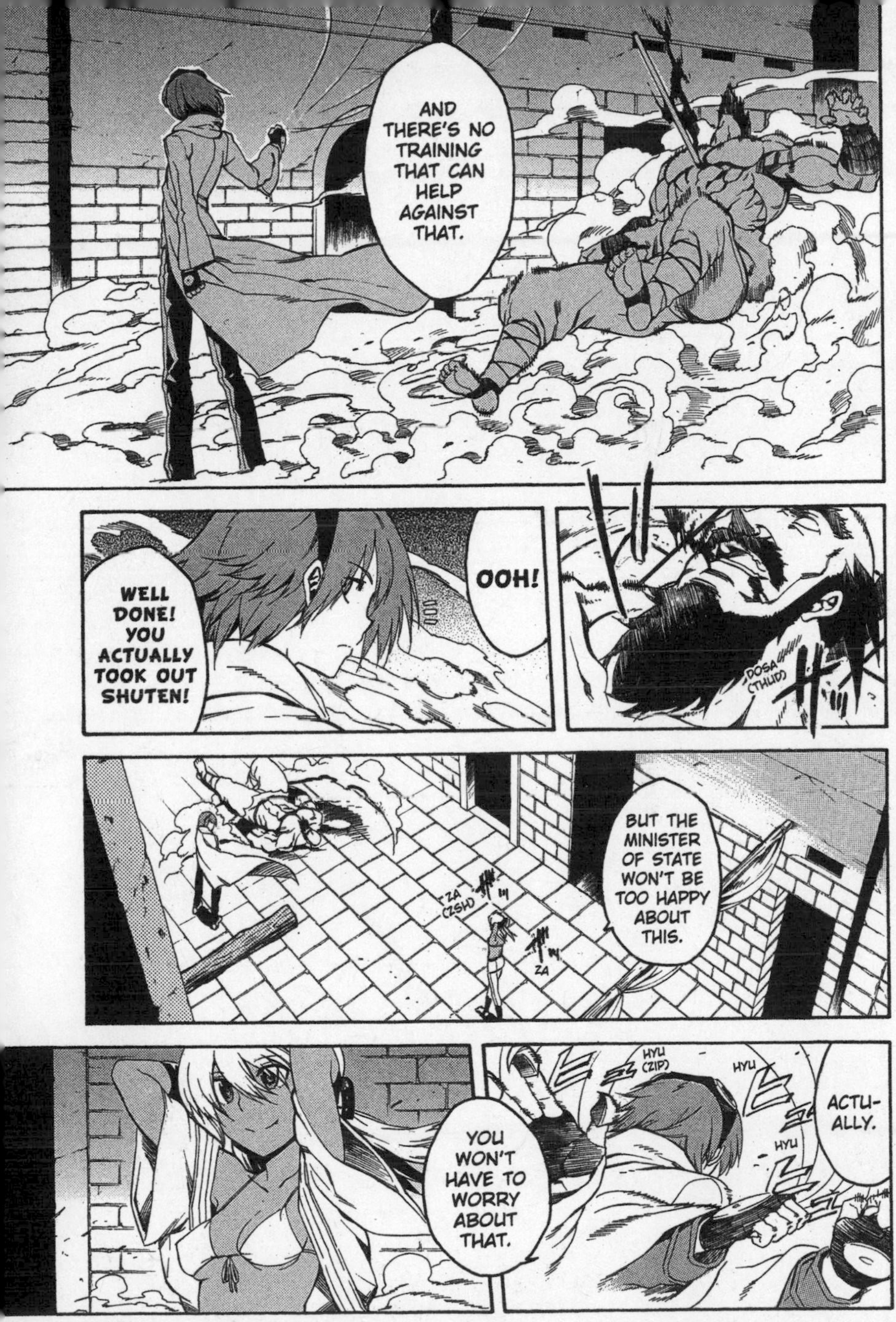

AND THERE'S NO TRAINING THAT CAN HELP AGAINST THAT.
DOSA (THUD)
OOH!
WELL DONE! YOU ACTUALLY TOOK OUT SHUTEN!
BUT THE MINISTER OF STATE WON'T BE TOO HAPPY ABOUT THIS.
ZA (ZSH)
ZA
HYU (ZIP)
HYU
HYU
ACTU-ALLY.
YOU WON'T HAVE TO WORRY ABOUT THAT.

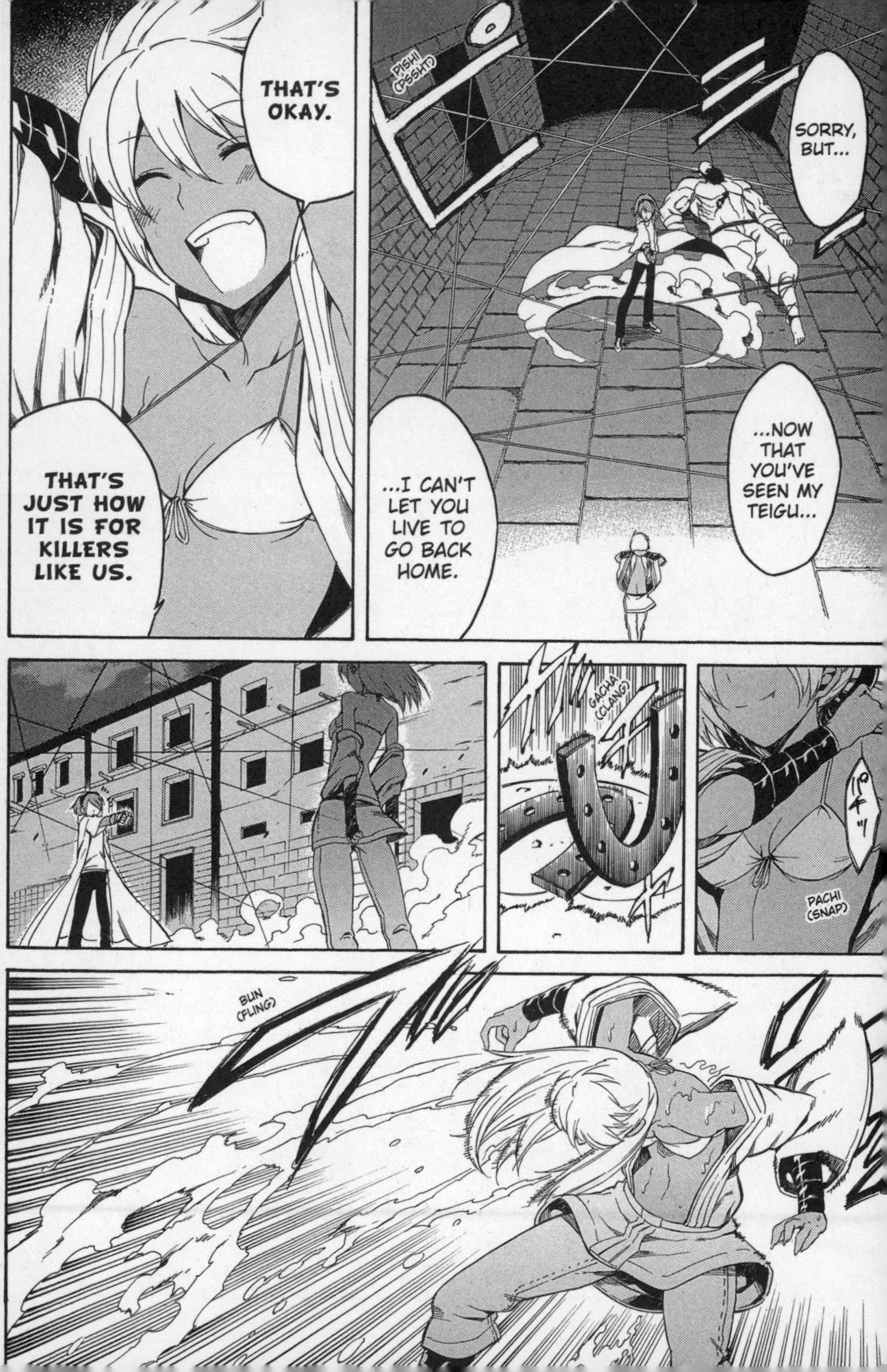
PISHI (PSSHT)
SORRY, BUT...
...NOW THAT YOU'VE SEEN MY TEIGU...
...I CAN'T LET YOU LIVE TO GO BACK HOME.
THAT'S OKAY.
THAT'S JUST HOW IT IS FOR KILLERS LIKE US.
パチッ
PACHI (SNAP)
GACHA (CLANG)
BUN (FLING)

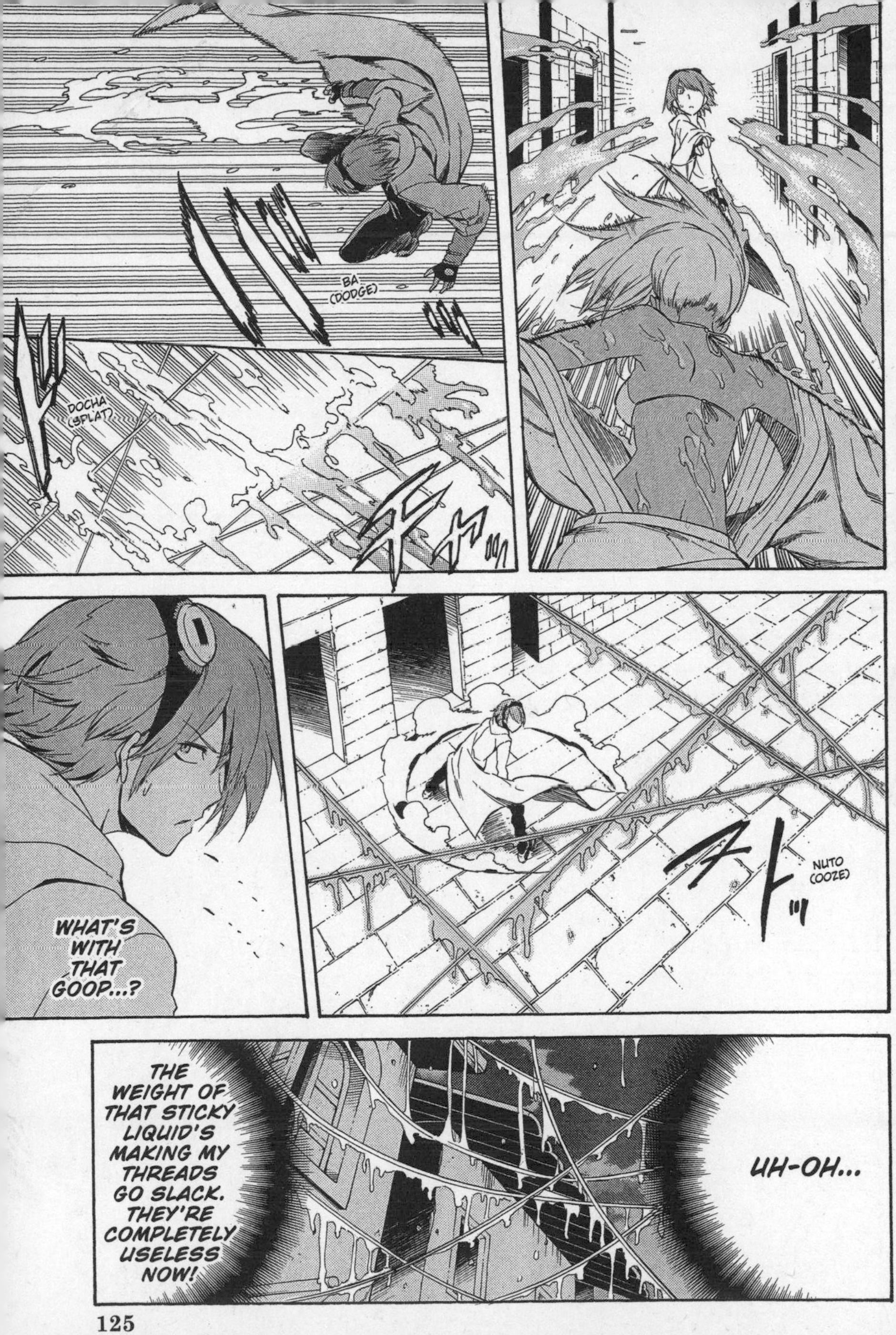
BA (DODGE)
DOCHA (SPLAT)
NUTO (OOZE)
WHAT'S WITH THAT GOOP...?
UH-OH...
THE WEIGHT OF THAT STICKY LIQUID'S MAKING MY THREADS GO SLACK. THEY'RE COMPLETELY USELESS NOW!

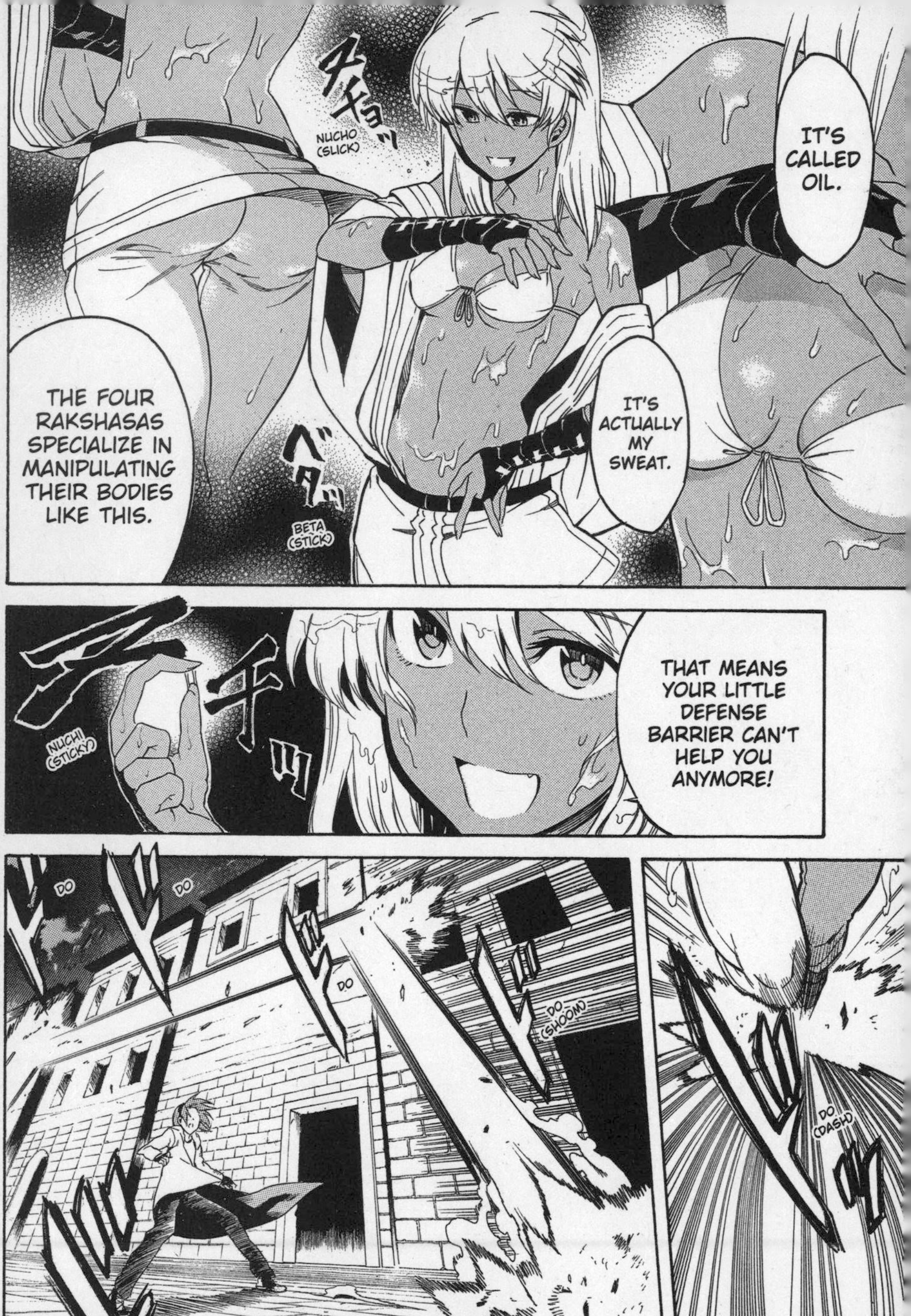
IT'S CALLED OIL.
NUCHO (SLICK)
IT'S ACTUALLY MY SWEAT.
THE FOUR RAKSHASAS SPECIALIZE IN MANIPULATING THEIR BODIES LIKE THIS.
BETA (STICK)
THAT MEANS YOUR LITTLE DEFENSE BARRIER CAN'T HELP YOU ANYMORE!
NUCHI (STICKY)
DO (DASH)
DO
DO
DO
DO (SHOOM)
DO

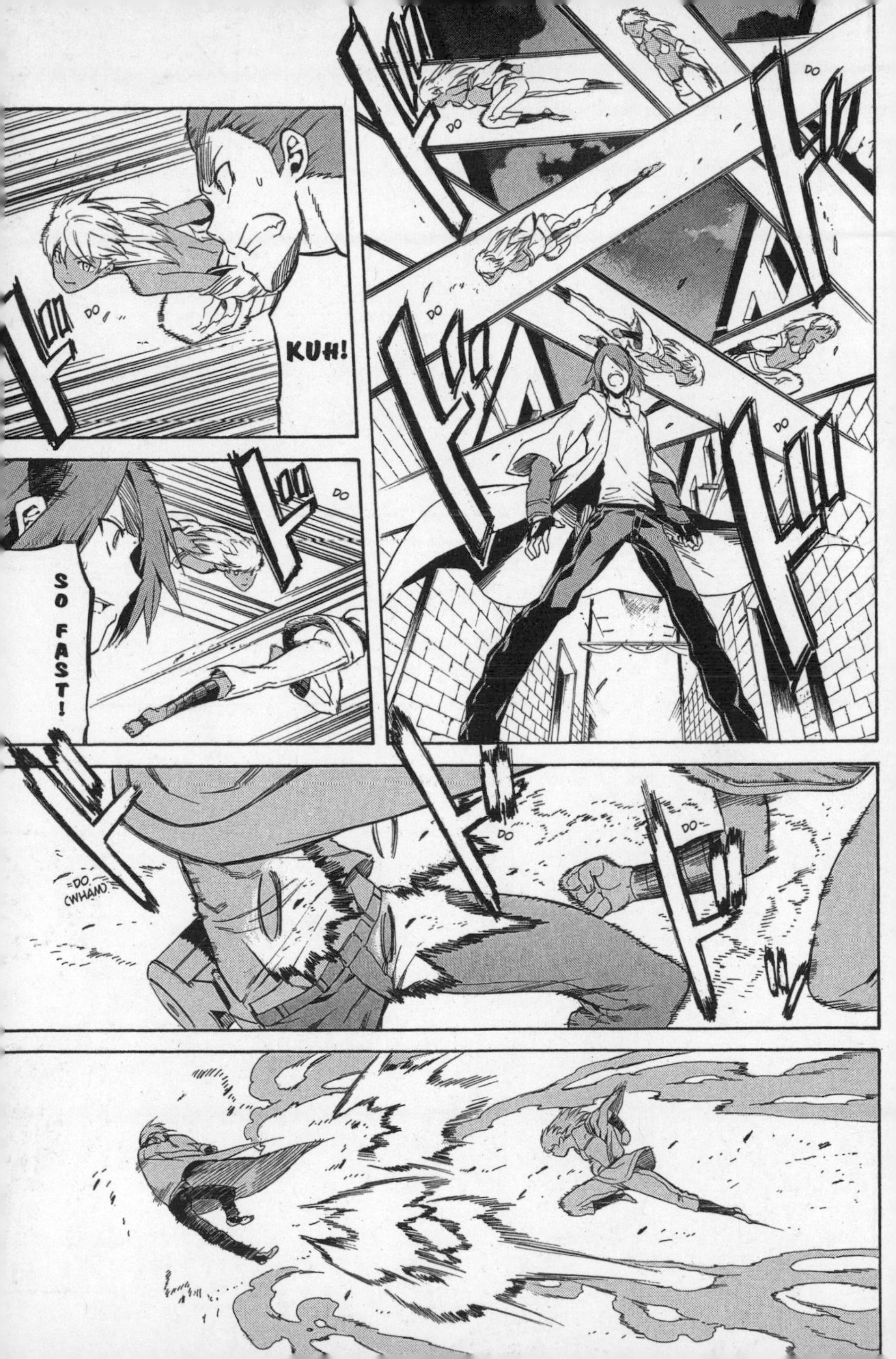 DO
DO
DO
DO
DO
KUH!
DO
DO
SO FAST!
DO
DO-
=DO
(WHAM)

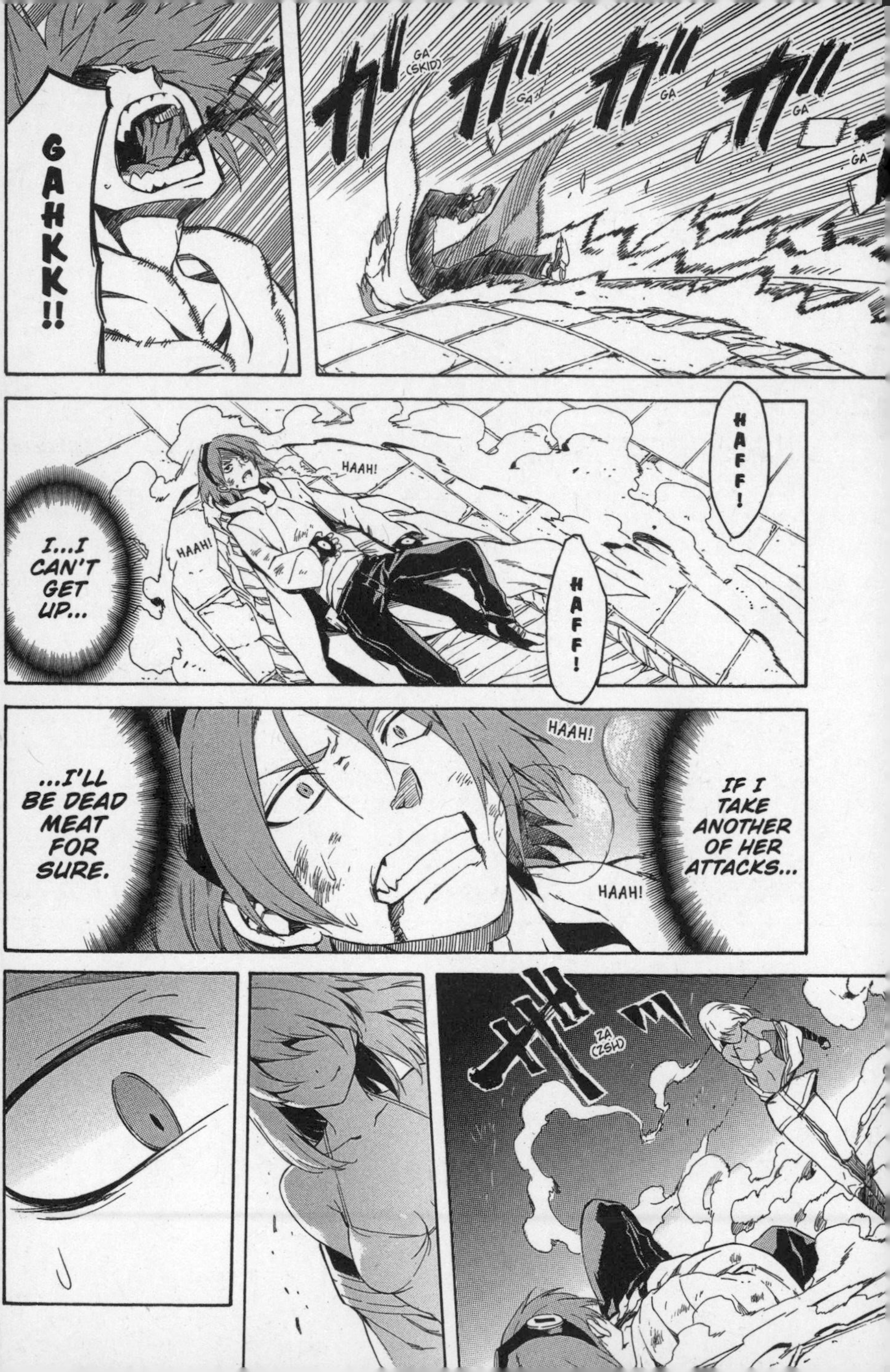

GA (SKID)
GA
GA
GA
GA
GAHKK!!
HAFF!
HAFF!
HAAH!
HAAH!
I...I CAN'T GET UP...
IF I TAKE ANOTHER OF HER ATTACKS...
HAAH!
HAAH!
...I'LL BE DEAD MEAT FOR SURE.
ZA (ZSH)

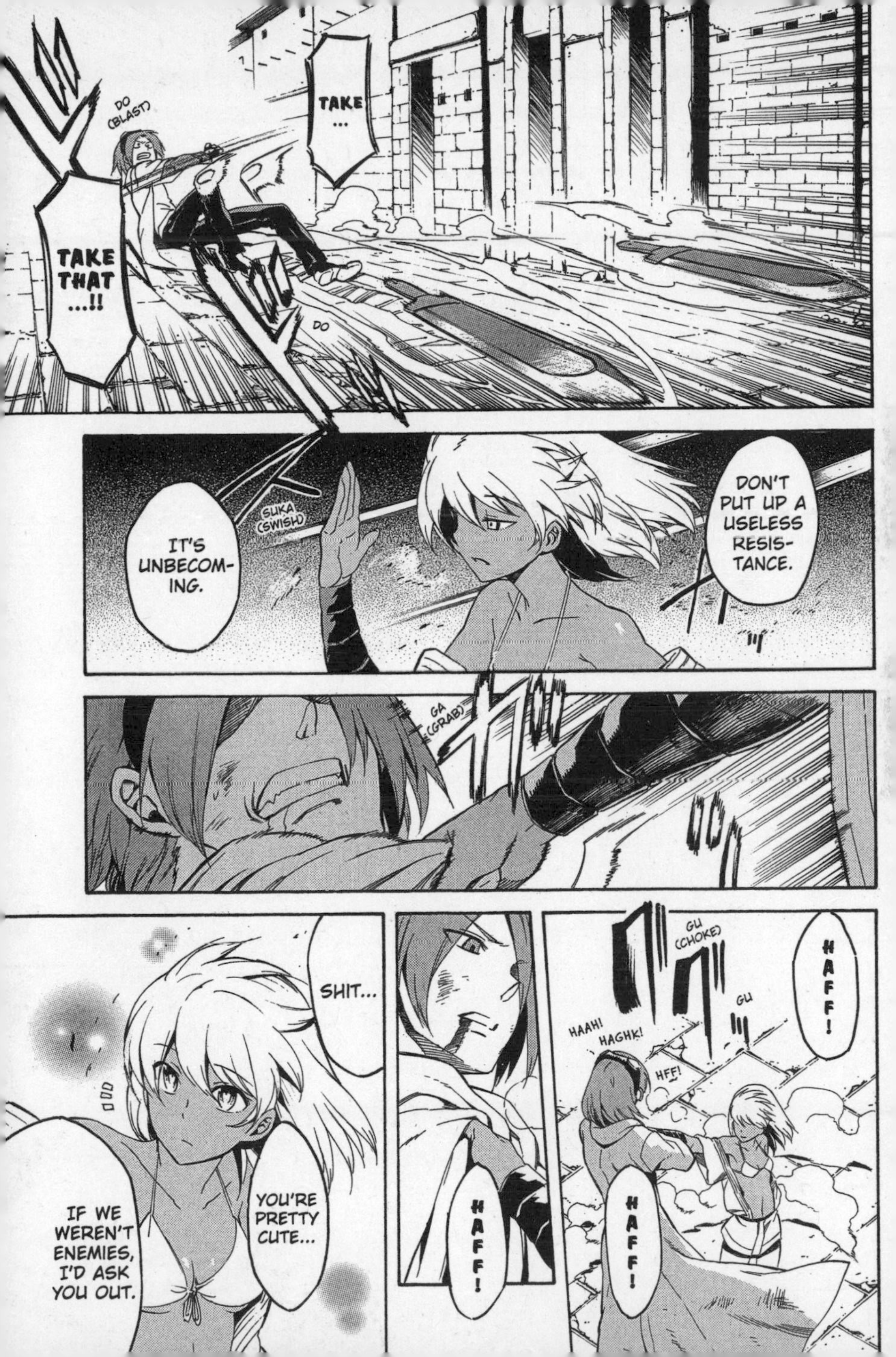
TAKE ...
DO (BLAST)
TAKE THAT ...!!
DO
DON'T PUT UP A USELESS RESIS-TANCE.
SUKA (SWISH)
IT'S UNBECOM-ING.
GA (GRAB)
HAFF!
GU (CHOKE)
GU
HAAH! HAGHK!
HFF!
HAFF!
SHIT...
HAFF!
YOU'RE PRETTY CUTE...
IF WE WEREN'T ENEMIES, I'D ASK YOU OUT.

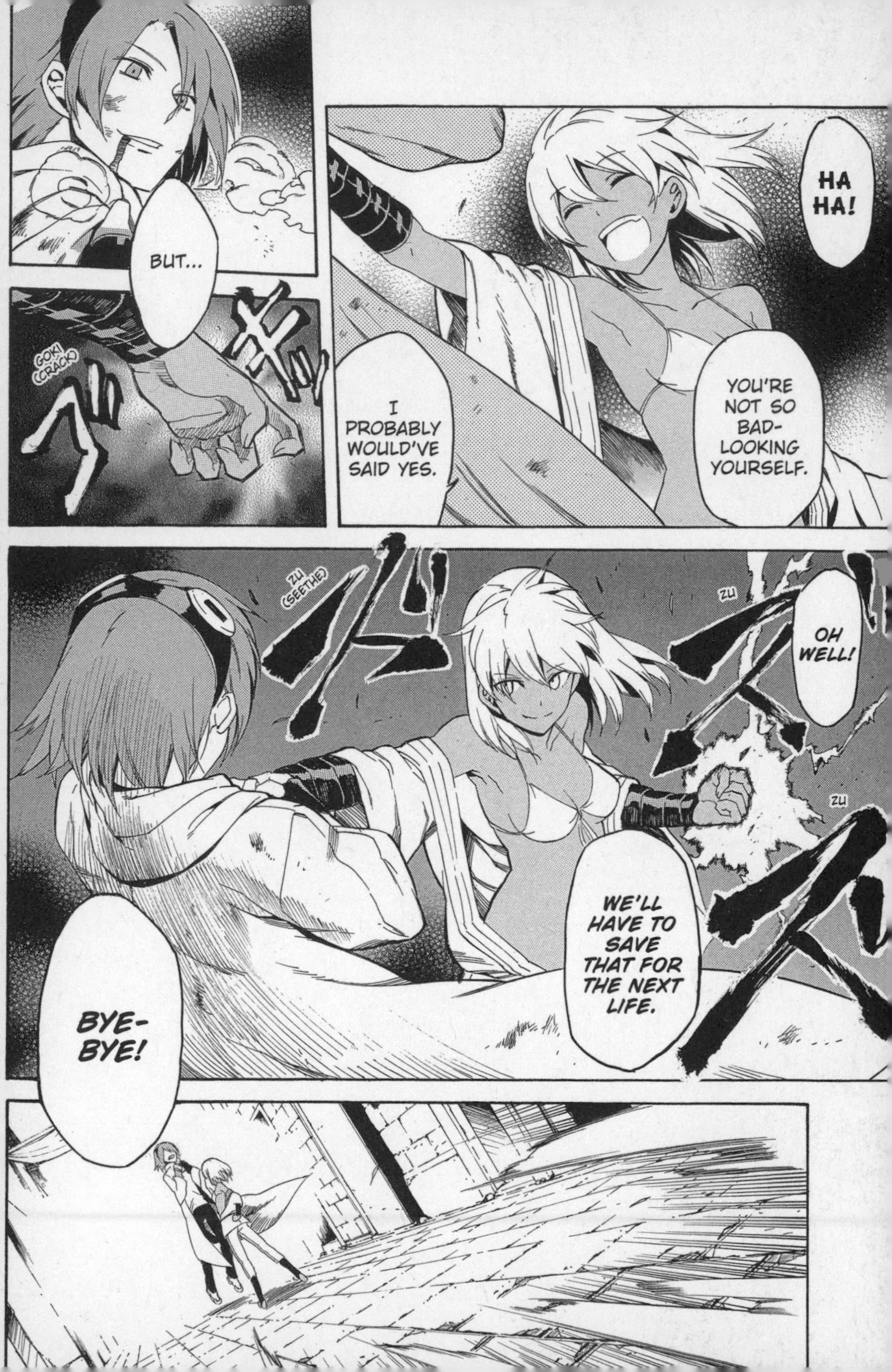
HA HA!
YOU'RE NOT SO BAD-LOOKING YOURSELF.
I PROBABLY WOULD'VE SAID YES.
BUT...
GOKI (CRACK)
OH WELL!
ZU
ZU
ZU (SEETHE)
WE'LL HAVE TO SAVE THAT FOR THE NEXT LIFE.
BYE-BYE!

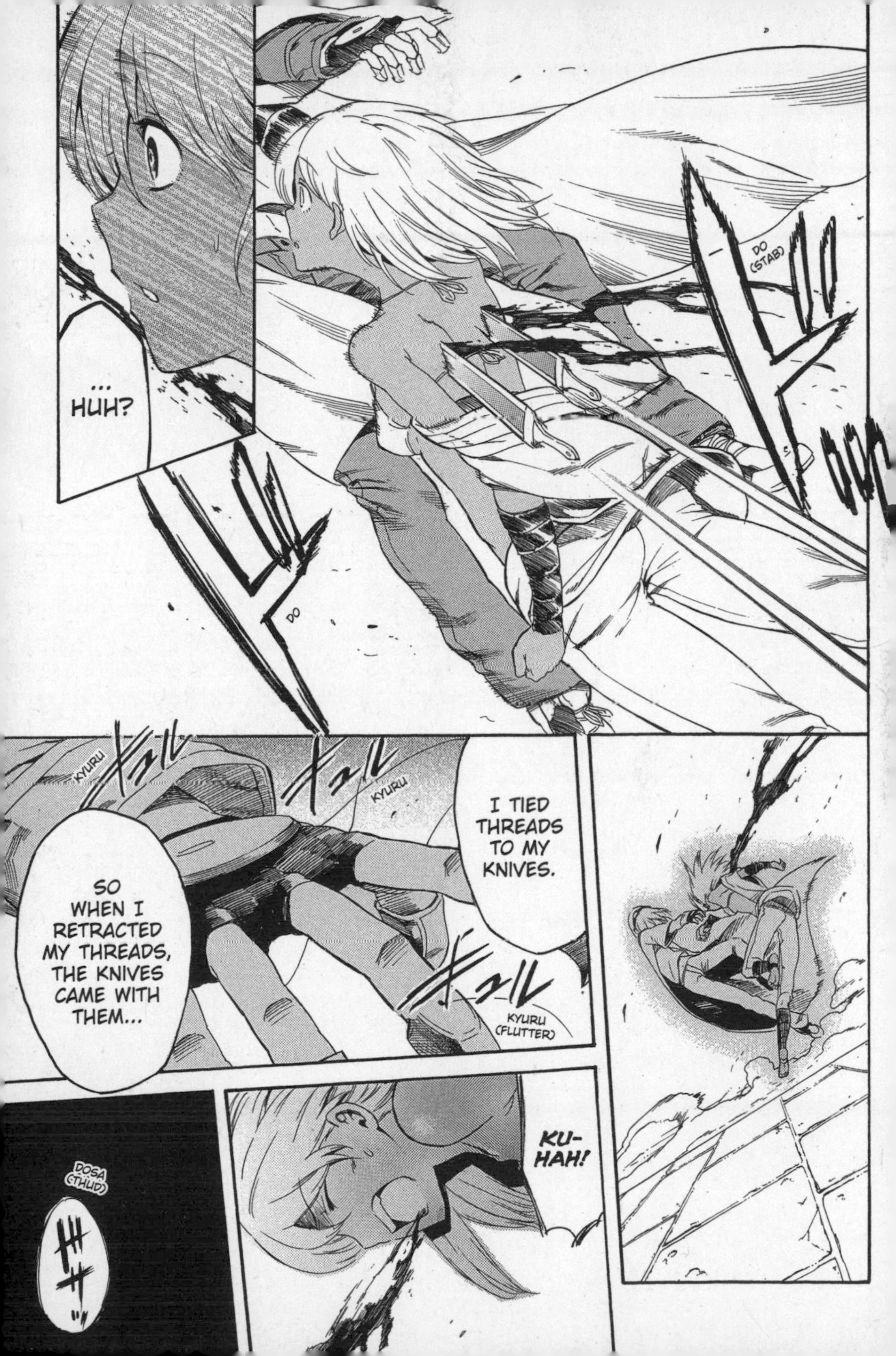

DO (STAB)
DO
... HUH?
KYURU
KYURU
I TIED THREADS TO MY KNIVES.
KYURU (FLUTTER)
SO WHEN I RETRACTED MY THREADS, THE KNIVES CAME WITH THEM...
KU-HAH!
DOSA (THUD)

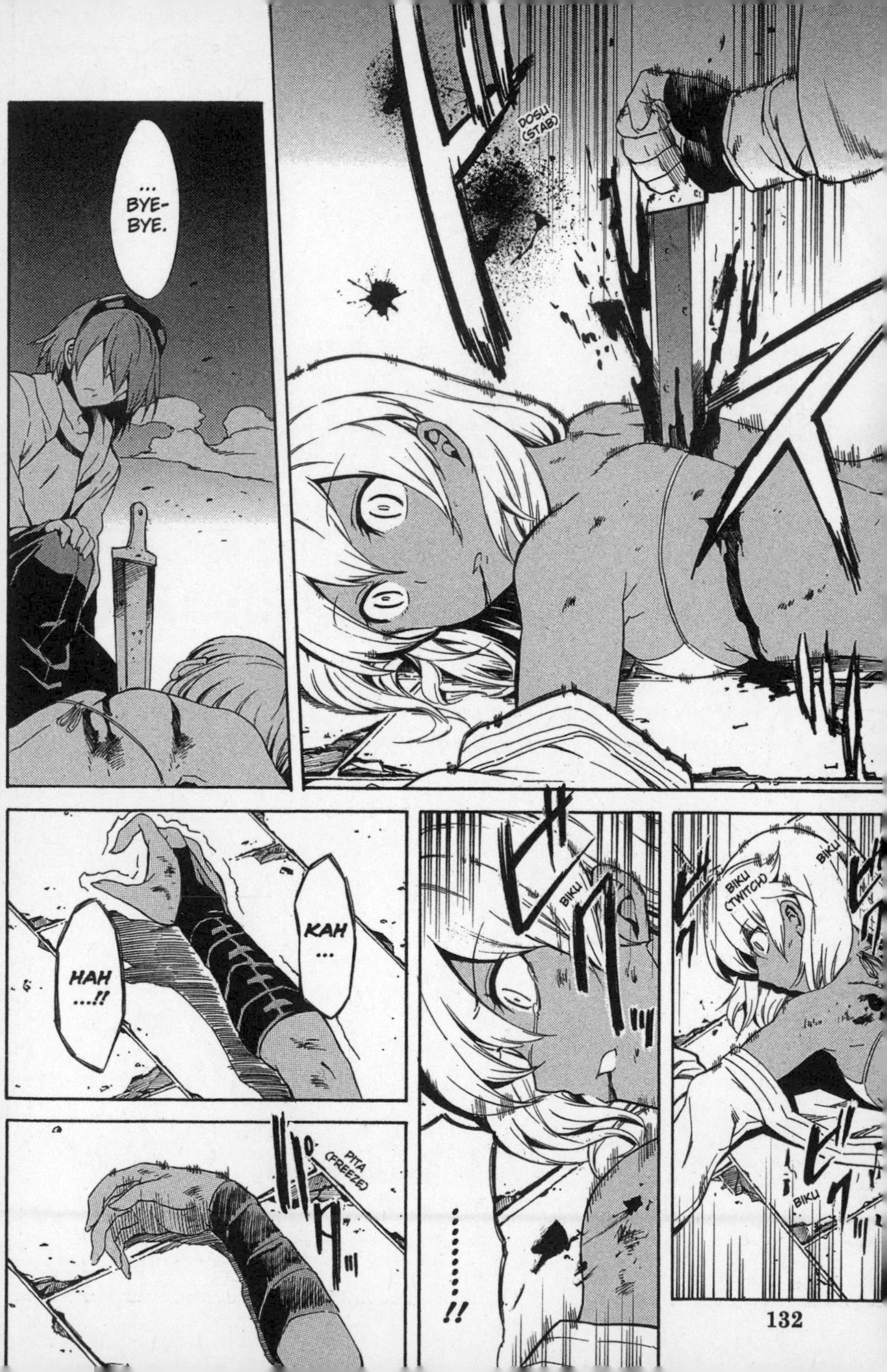
DOSU (STAB)
... BYE-BYE.
BIKU
BIKU (TWITCH)
BIKU
BIKU
KAH ...
HAH ...!!
PITA (FREEZE)
.........!!

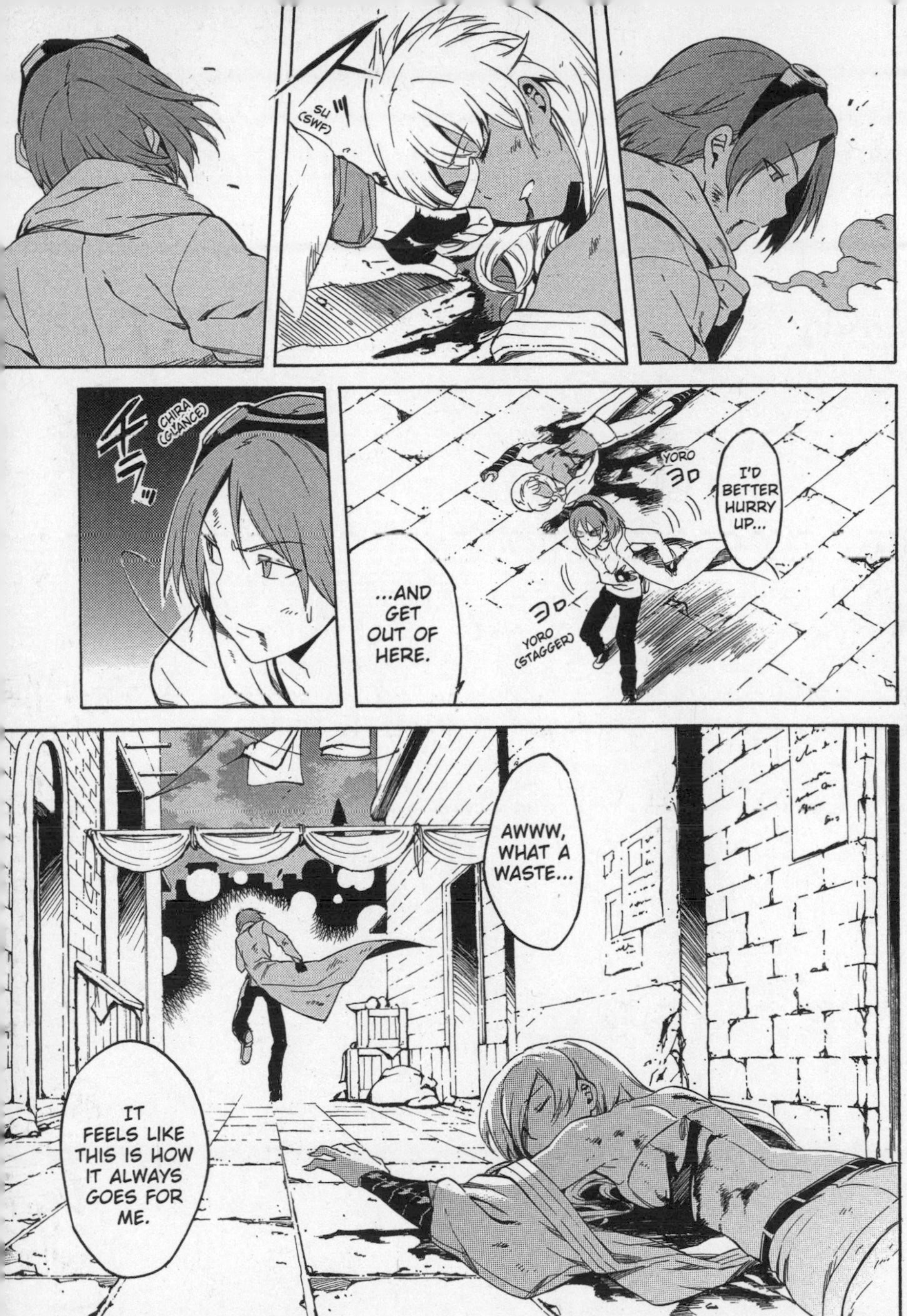
SU (SWF)
I'D BETTER HURRY UP...
YORO
...AND GET OUT OF HERE.
YORO (STAGGER)
CHIRA (GLANCE)
AWWW, WHAT A WASTE...
IT FEELS LIKE THIS IS HOW IT ALWAYS GOES FOR ME.

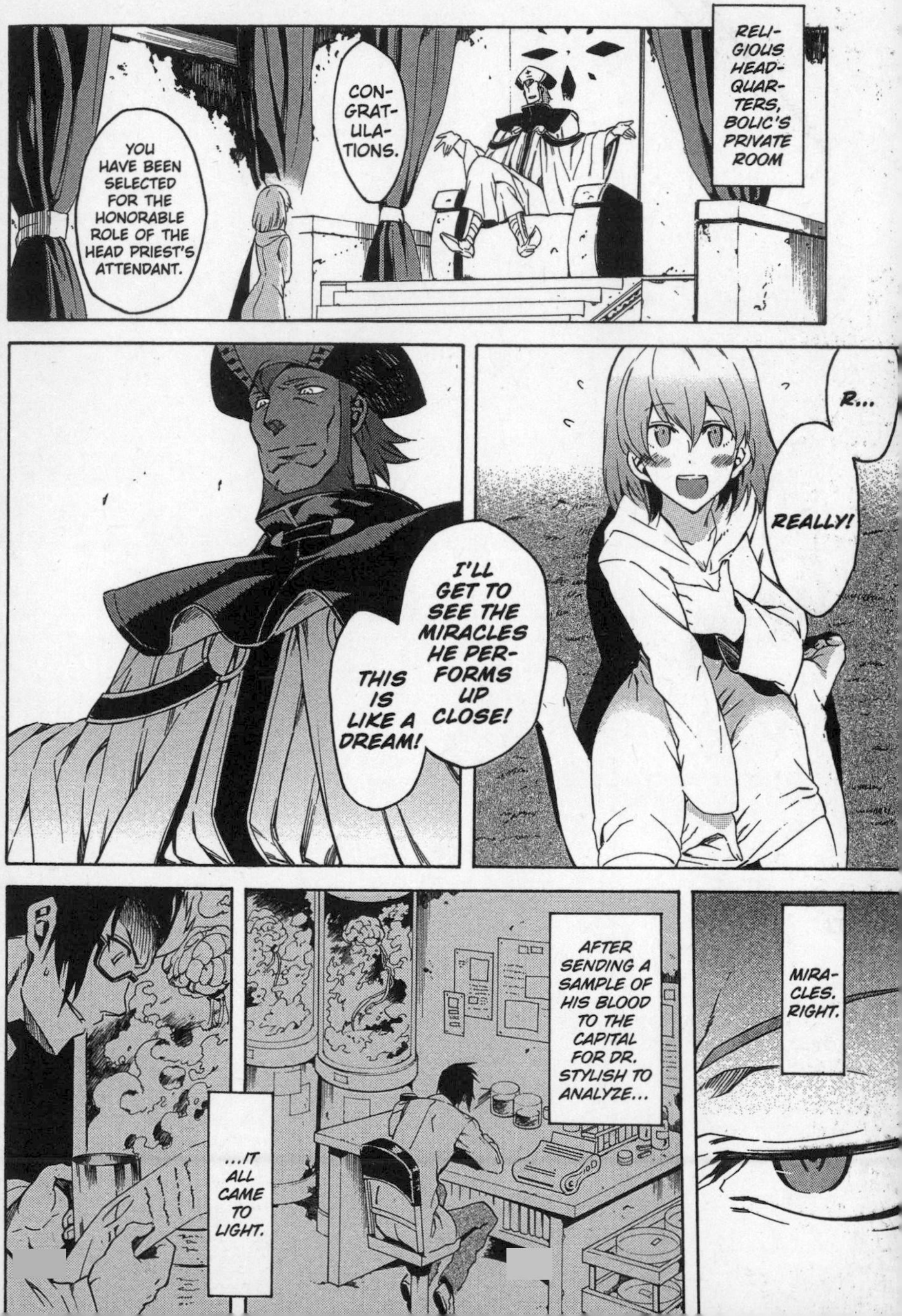
RELIGIOUS HEADQUARTERS, BOLIC'S PRIVATE ROOM
CONGRATULATIONS.
YOU HAVE BEEN SELECTED FOR THE HONORABLE ROLE OF THE HEAD PRIEST'S ATTENDANT.
R...
REALLY!
I'LL GET TO SEE THE MIRACLES HE PERFORMS UP CLOSE!
THIS IS LIKE A DREAM!
MIRACLES. RIGHT.
AFTER SENDING A SAMPLE OF HIS BLOOD TO THE CAPITAL FOR DR. STYLISH TO ANALYZE...
...IT ALL CAME TO LIGHT.

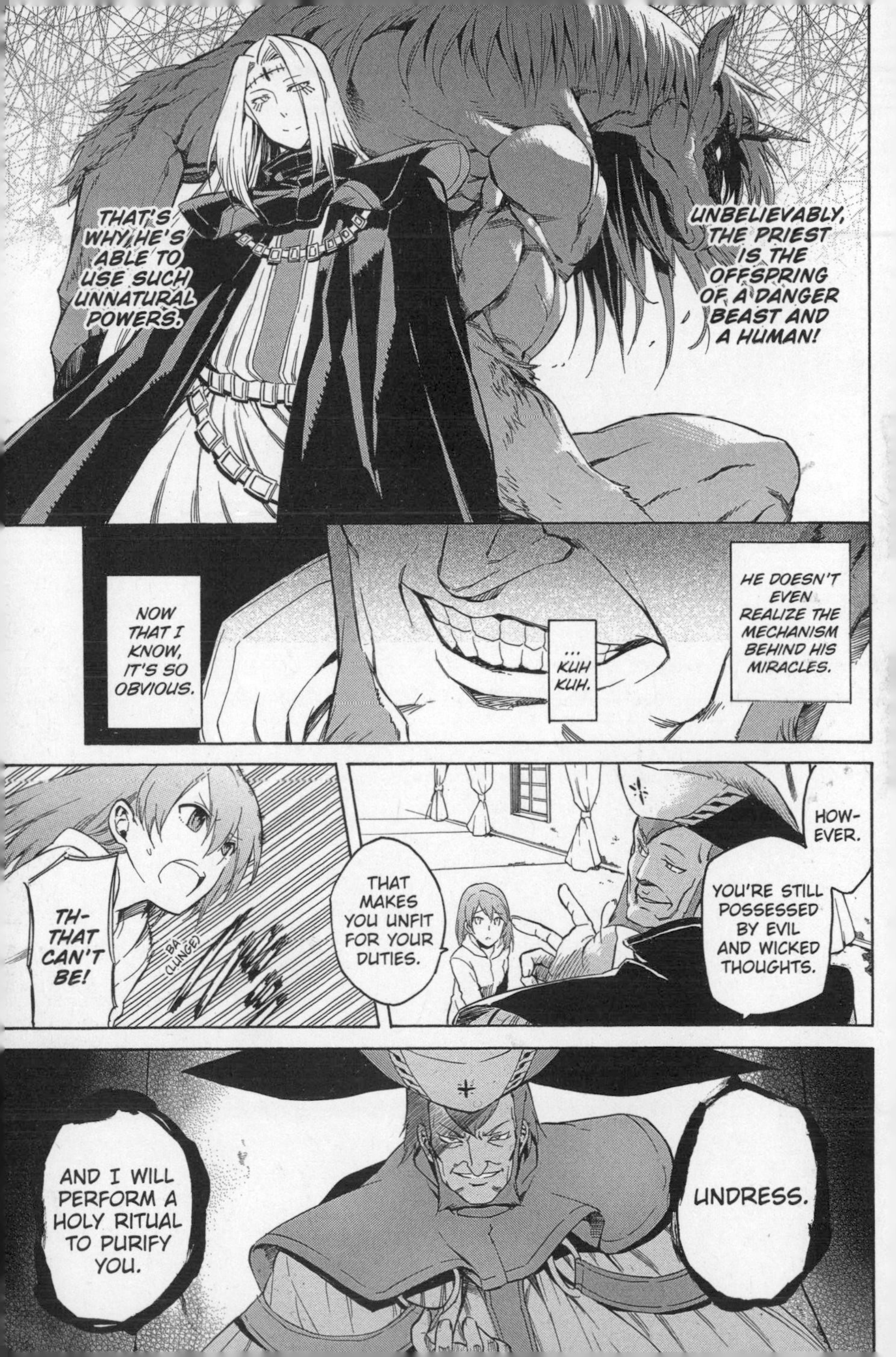
UNBELIEVABLY, THE PRIEST IS THE OFFSPRING OF A DANGER BEAST AND A HUMAN!
THAT'S WHY HE'S ABLE TO USE SUCH UNNATURAL POWERS.
HE DOESN'T EVEN REALIZE THE MECHANISM BEHIND HIS MIRACLES.
... KUH KUH.
NOW THAT I KNOW, IT'S SO OBVIOUS.
HOW-EVER.
YOU'RE STILL POSSESSED BY EVIL AND WICKED THOUGHTS.
THAT MAKES YOU UNFIT FOR YOUR DUTIES.
BA (LUNGE)
TH-THAT CAN'T BE!
UNDRESS.
AND I WILL PERFORM A HOLY RITUAL TO PURIFY YOU.

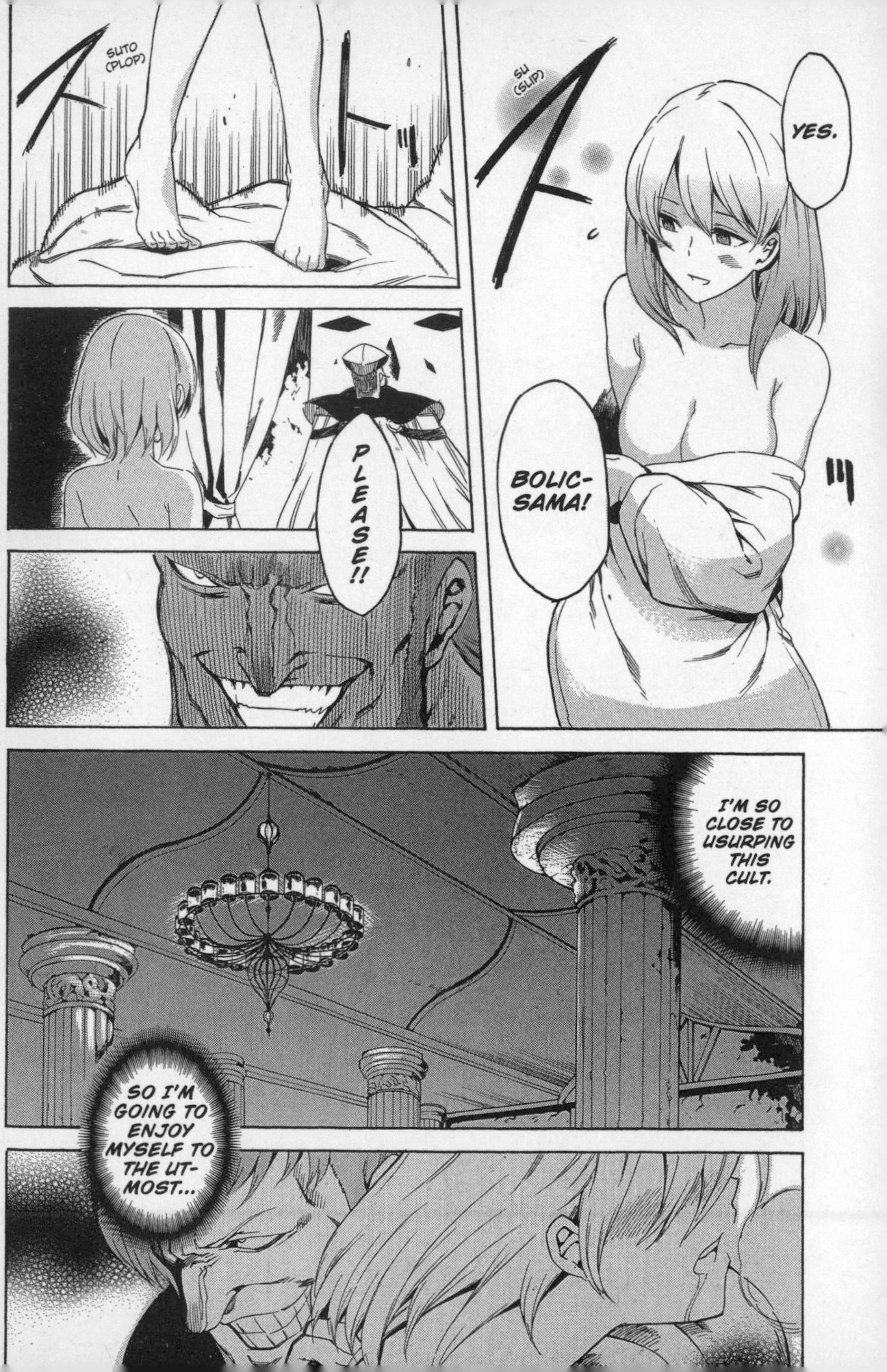
SU (SLIP)
YES.
SUTO (PLOP)
BOLIC-SAMA!
PLEASE!!
I'M SO CLOSE TO USURPING THIS CULT.
SO I'M GOING TO ENJOY MYSELF TO THE UT-MOST...

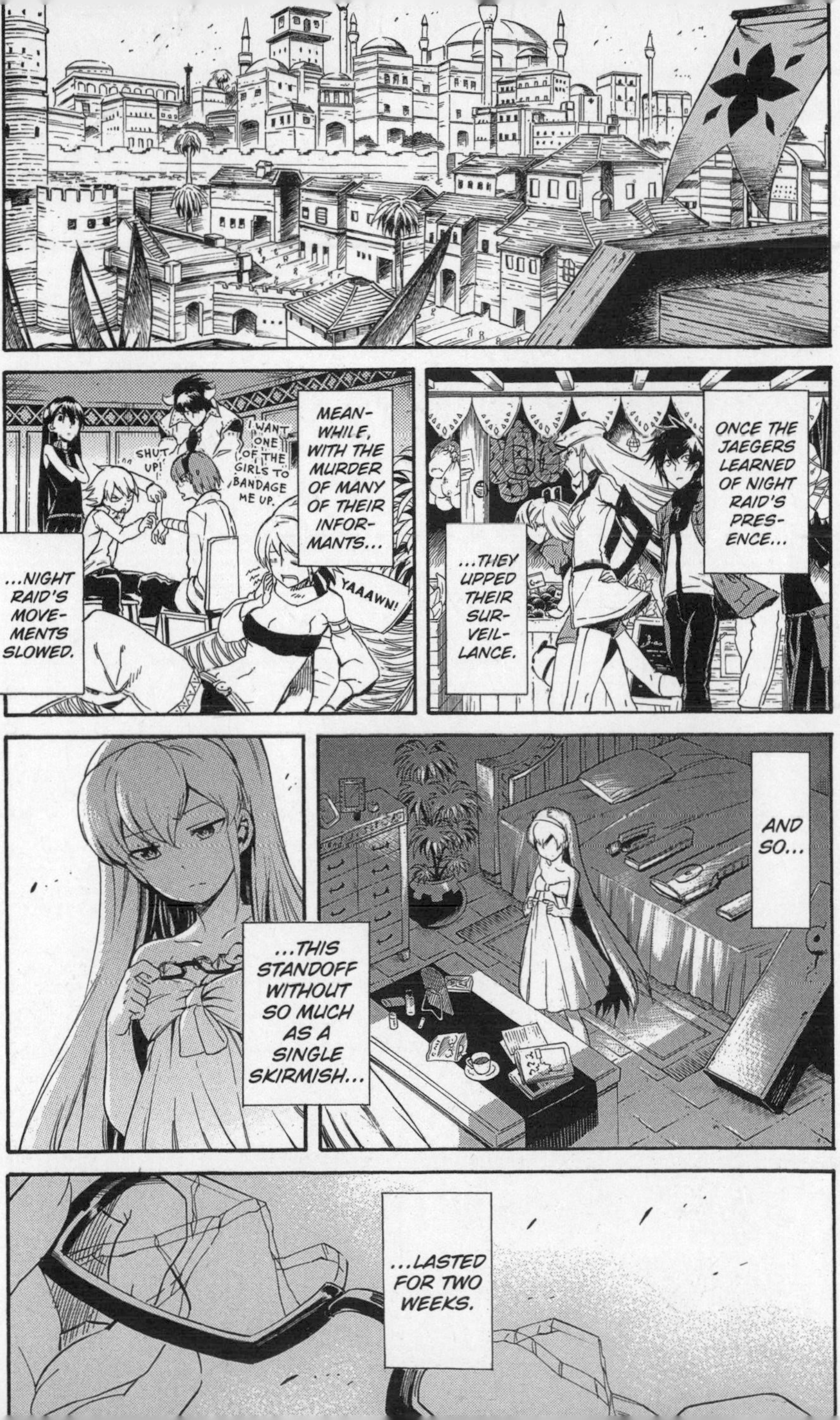
ONCE THE JAEGERS LEARNED OF NIGHT RAID'S PRESENCE...
...THEY UPPED THEIR SURVEILLANCE.
MEANWHILE, WITH THE MURDER OF MANY OF THEIR INFORMANTS...
I WANT ONE OF THE GIRLS TO BANDAGE ME UP.
SHUT UP!
YAAAAWN!
...NIGHT RAID'S MOVEMENTS SLOWED.
AND SO...
...THIS STANDOFF WITHOUT SO MUCH AS A SINGLE SKIRMISH...
...LASTED FOR TWO WEEKS.

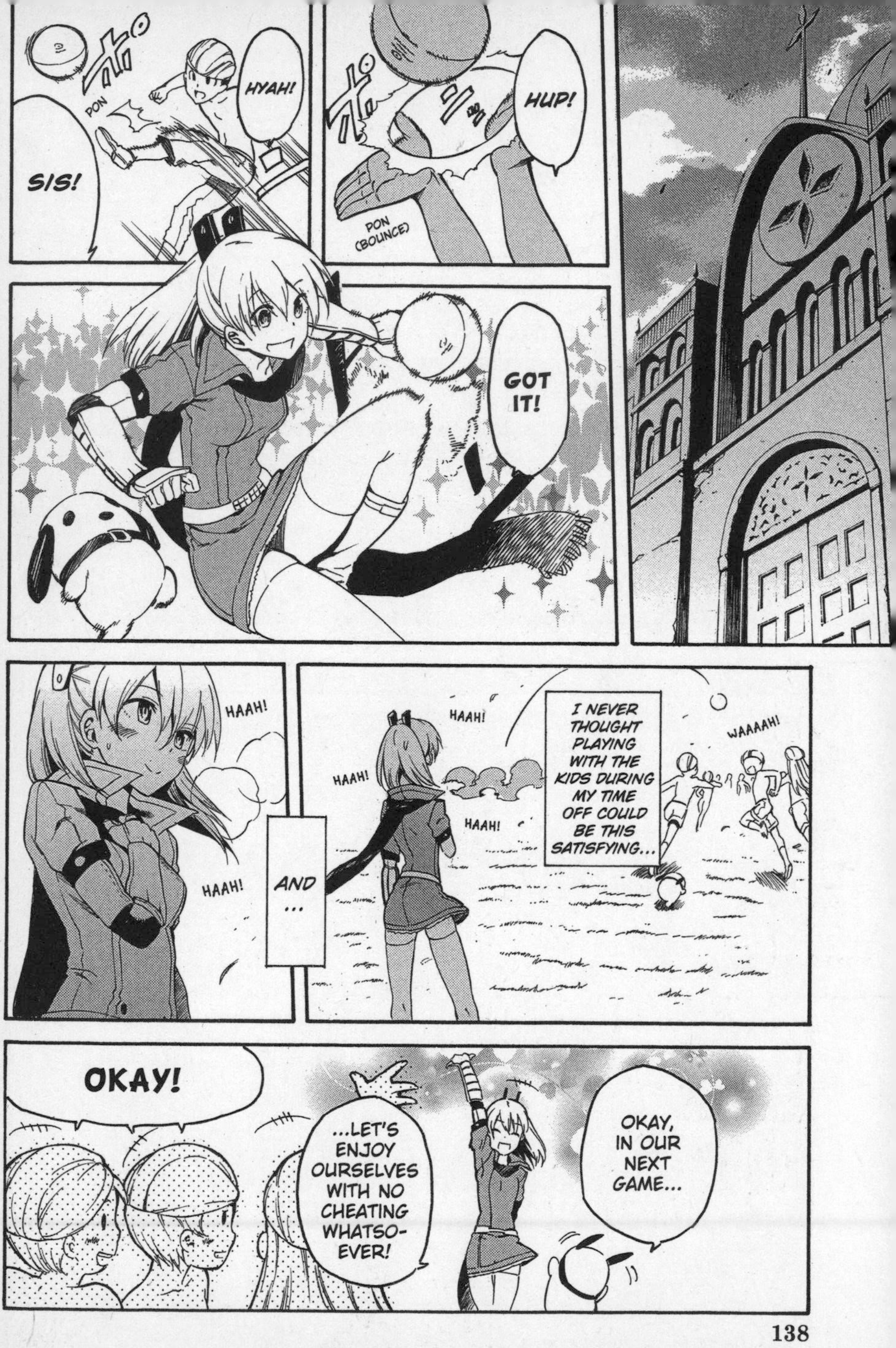
SIS!
PON
HYAH!
PON
(BOUNCE)
HUP!
GOT IT!
HAAH!
HAAH!
HAAH!
HAAH!
HAAH!
AND ...
I NEVER THOUGHT PLAYING WITH THE KIDS DURING MY TIME OFF COULD BE THIS SATISFYING...
WAAAAH!
OKAY!
...LET'S ENJOY OURSELVES WITH NO CHEATING WHATSO-EVER!
OKAY, IN OUR NEXT GAME...

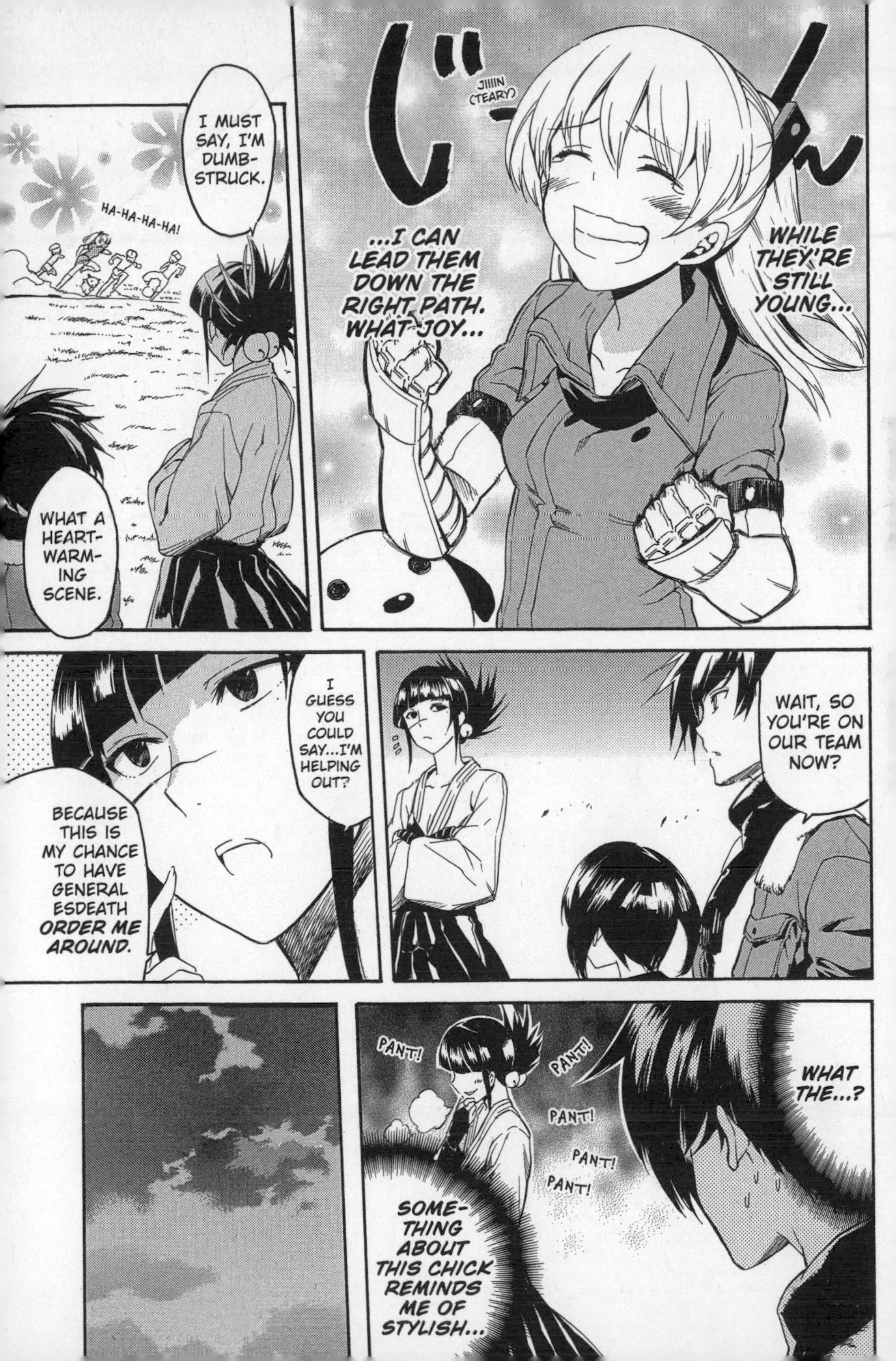
JIIIIN (TEARY)
WHILE THEY'RE STILL YOUNG...
...I CAN LEAD THEM DOWN THE RIGHT PATH. WHAT JOY...
I MUST SAY, I'M DUMBSTRUCK.
HA-HA-HA-HA!
WHAT A HEARTWARMING SCENE.
WAIT, SO YOU'RE ON OUR TEAM NOW?
I GUESS YOU COULD SAY...I'M HELPING OUT?
BECAUSE THIS IS MY CHANCE TO HAVE GENERAL ESDEATH ORDER ME AROUND.
PANT!
PANT!
PANT!
PANT!
PANT!
WHAT THE...?
SOMETHING ABOUT THIS CHICK REMINDS ME OF STYLISH...

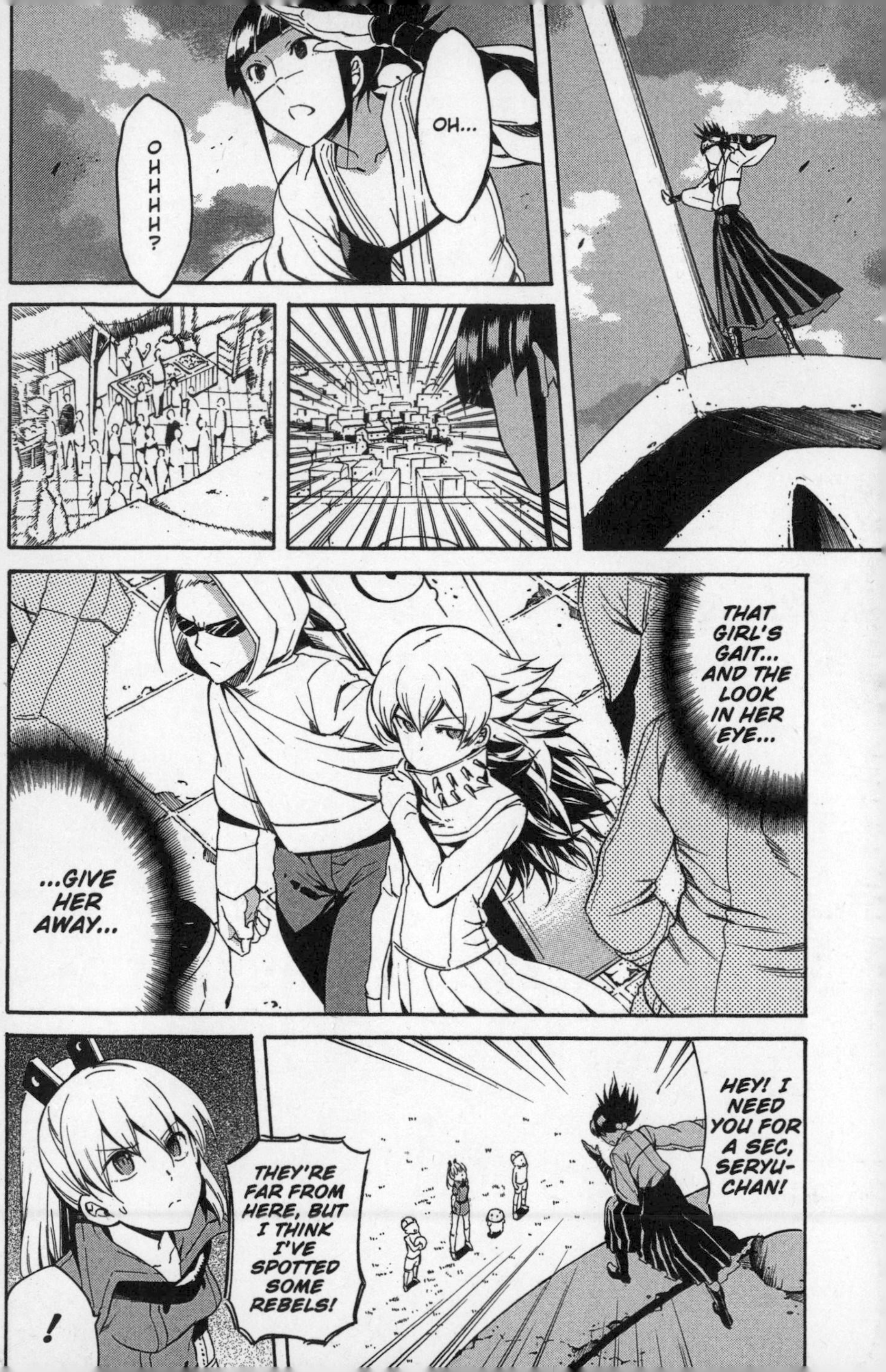
OH...
OHHHH?
THAT GIRL'S GAIT... AND THE LOOK IN HER EYE...
...GIVE HER AWAY...
HEY! I NEED YOU FOR A SEC, SERYU-CHAN!
THEY'RE FAR FROM HERE, BUT I THINK I'VE SPOTTED SOME REBELS!
!

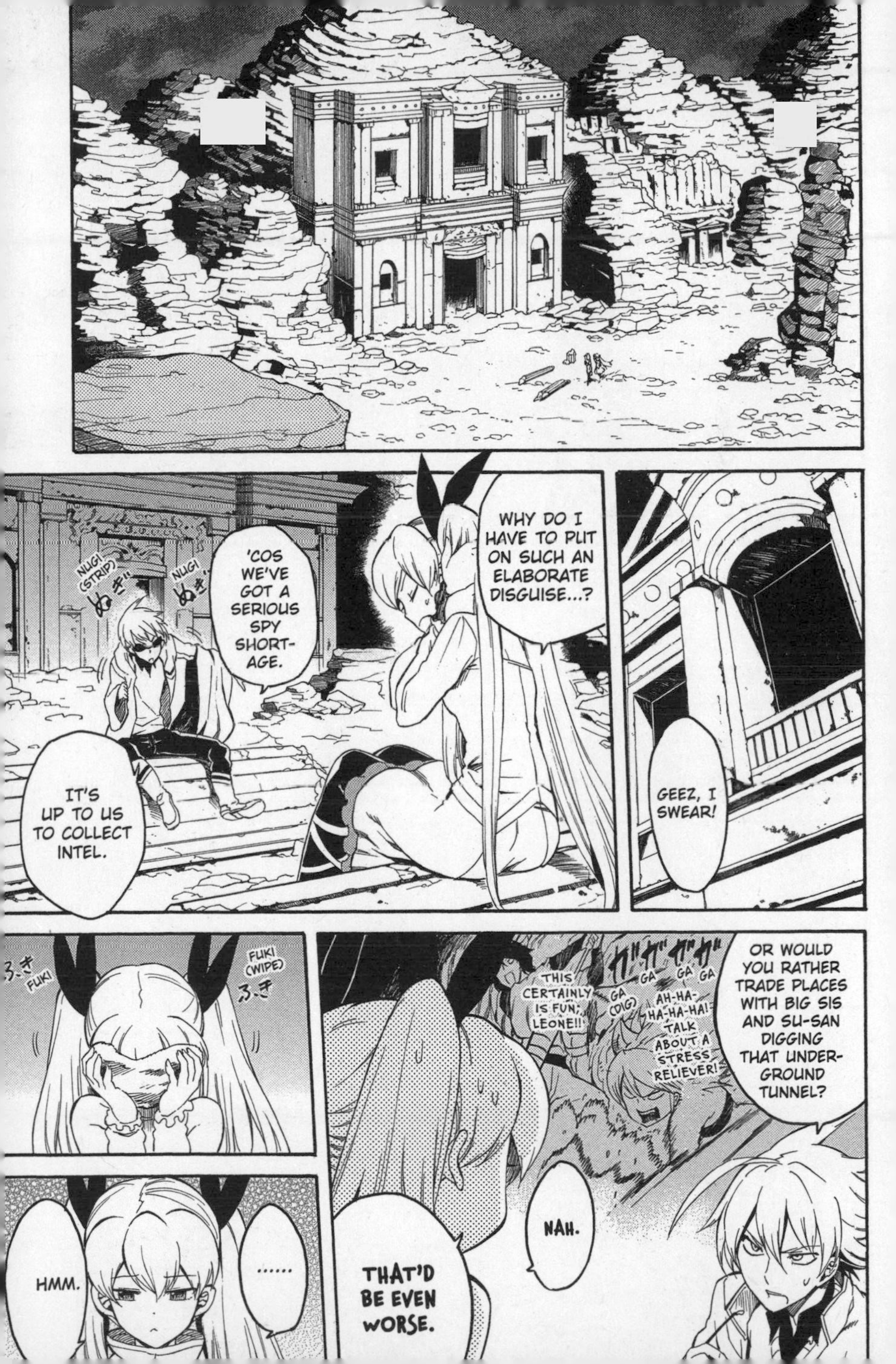
GEEZ, I SWEAR!
WHY DO I HAVE TO PUT ON SUCH AN ELABORATE DISGUISE...?
NUGI (STRIP) ぬぎ
NUGI ぬぎ
'COS WE'VE GOT A SERIOUS SPY SHORTAGE.
IT'S UP TO US TO COLLECT INTEL.
OR WOULD YOU RATHER TRADE PLACES WITH BIG SIS AND SU-SAN DIGGING THAT UNDERGROUND TUNNEL?
ガガガガ GA GA GA
AH-HA-HA-HA-HA! TALK ABOUT A STRESS RELIEVER!
GA (DIG)
THIS CERTAINLY IS FUN, LEONE!!
NAH.
THAT'D BE EVEN WORSE.
FUKI (WIPE) ふき
ふき FUKI
......
HMM.

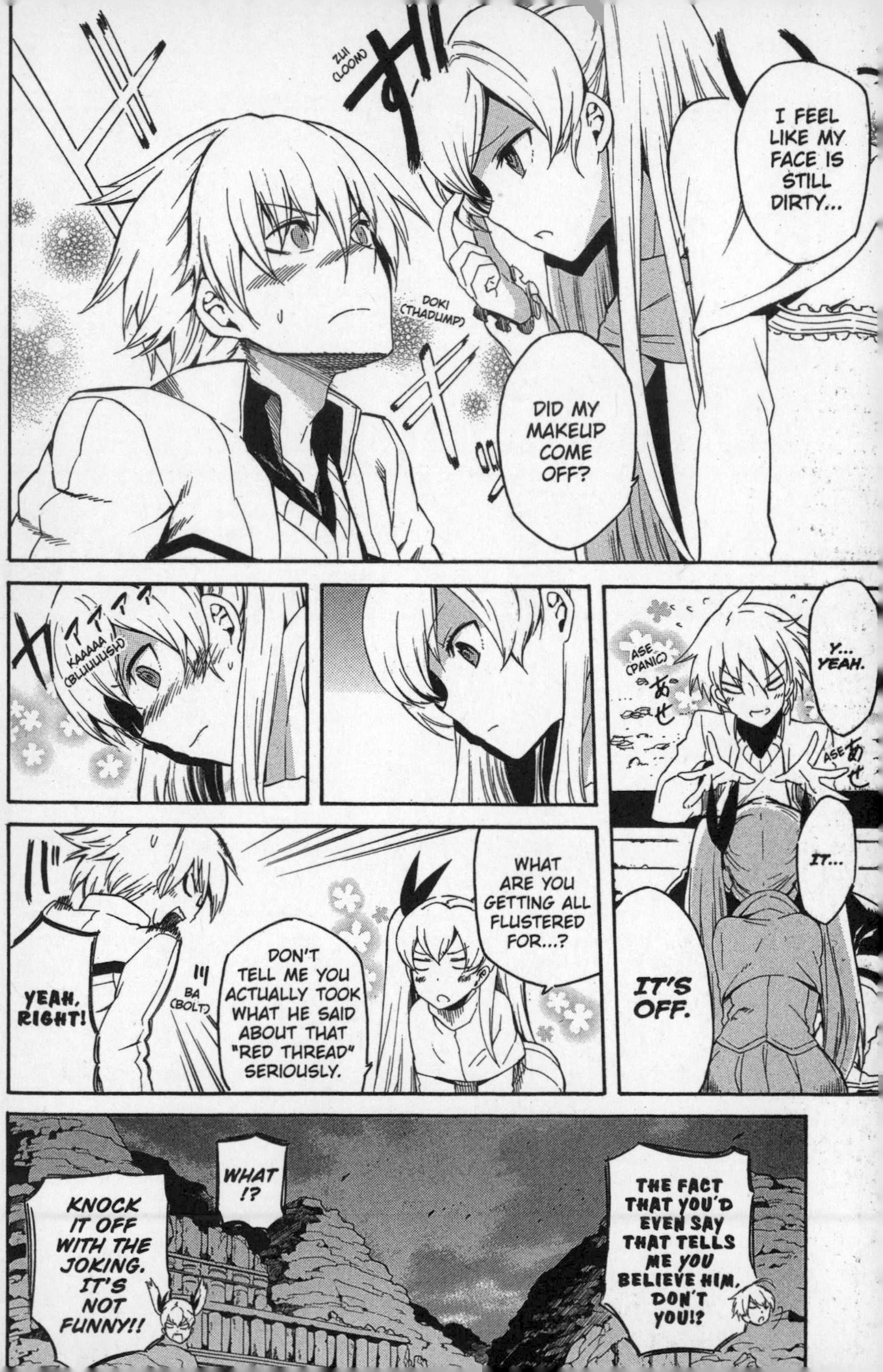
ZUI (LOOM)
I FEEL LIKE MY FACE IS STILL DIRTY...
DOKI (THADUMP)
DID MY MAKEUP COME OFF?
Y... YEAH.
ASE (PANIC)
ASE
IT...
IT'S OFF.
KAAAAA (BLUUUUSH)
WHAT ARE YOU GETTING ALL FLUSTERED FOR...?
DON'T TELL ME YOU ACTUALLY TOOK WHAT HE SAID ABOUT THAT "RED THREAD" SERIOUSLY.
BA (BOLT)
YEAH, RIGHT!
THE FACT THAT YOU'D EVEN SAY THAT TELLS ME YOU BELIEVE HIM, DON'T YOU!?
WHAT!?
KNOCK IT OFF WITH THE JOKING. IT'S NOT FUNNY!!

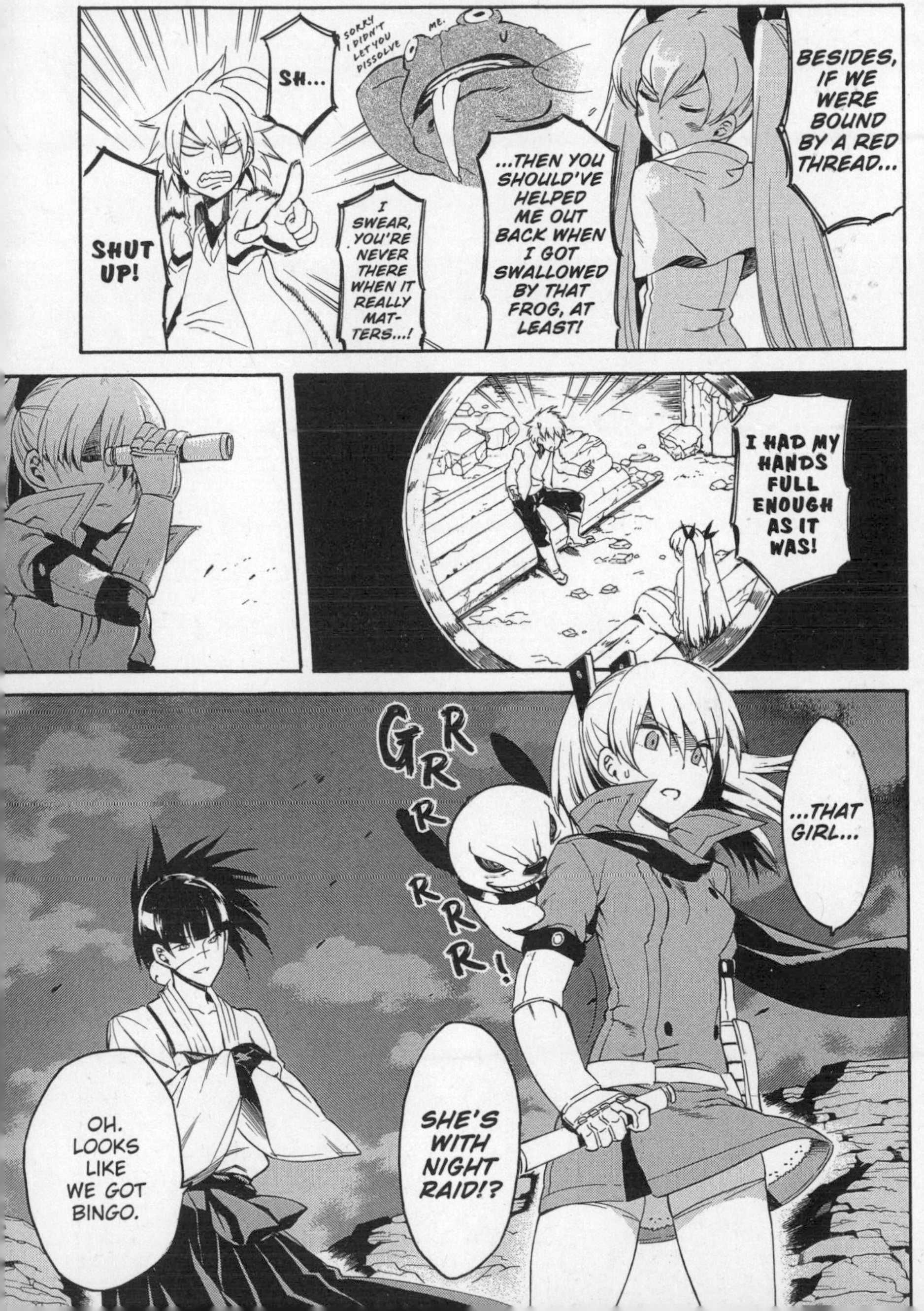
BESIDES, IF WE WERE BOUND BY A RED THREAD...
...THEN YOU SHOULD'VE HELPED ME OUT BACK WHEN I GOT SWALLOWED BY THAT FROG, AT LEAST!
I SWEAR, YOU'RE NEVER THERE WHEN IT REALLY MAT-TERS...!
SORRY I DIDN'T LET YOU DISSOLVE ME.
SH...
SHUT UP!
I HAD MY HANDS FULL ENOUGH AS IT WAS!
...THAT GIRL...
GRRRRRRR!
SHE'S WITH NIGHT RAID!?
OH. LOOKS LIKE WE GOT BINGO.

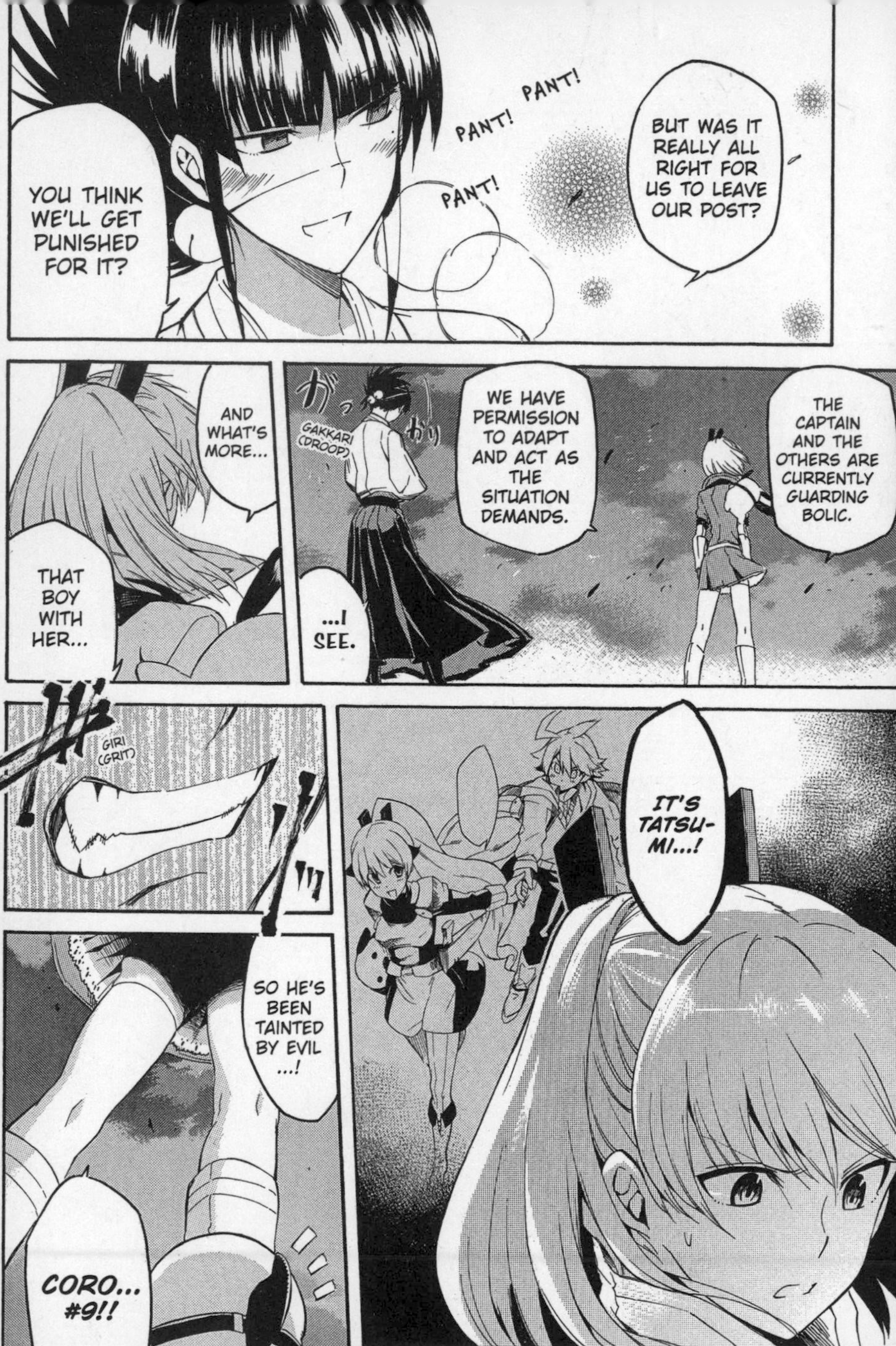
BUT WAS IT REALLY ALL RIGHT FOR US TO LEAVE OUR POST?
PANT! PANT!
PANT!
YOU THINK WE'LL GET PUNISHED FOR IT?
THE CAPTAIN AND THE OTHERS ARE CURRENTLY GUARDING BOLIC.
WE HAVE PERMISSION TO ADAPT AND ACT AS THE SITUATION DEMANDS.
GAKKARI (DROOP)
...I SEE.
AND WHAT'S MORE...
THAT BOY WITH HER...
IT'S TATSUMI...!
GIRI (GRIT)
SO HE'S BEEN TAINTED BY EVIL ...!
CORO... #9!!

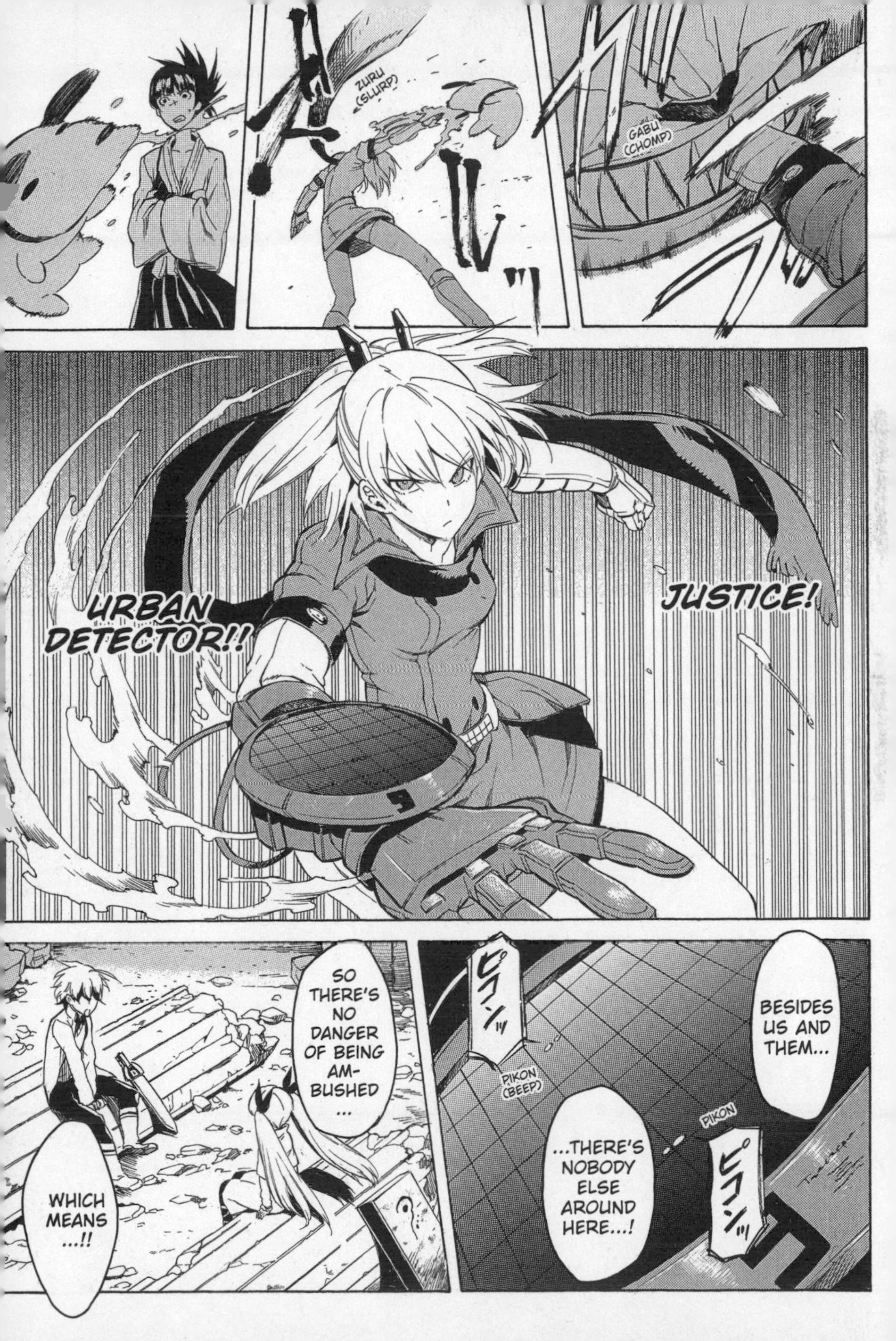
GABU (CHOMP)
ZURU (SLURP)
JUSTICE!
URBAN DETECTOR!!
BESIDES US AND THEM...
PIKON (BEEP)
PIKON
...THERE'S NOBODY ELSE AROUND HERE...!
SO THERE'S NO DANGER OF BEING AM-BUSHED...
WHICH MEANS ...!!

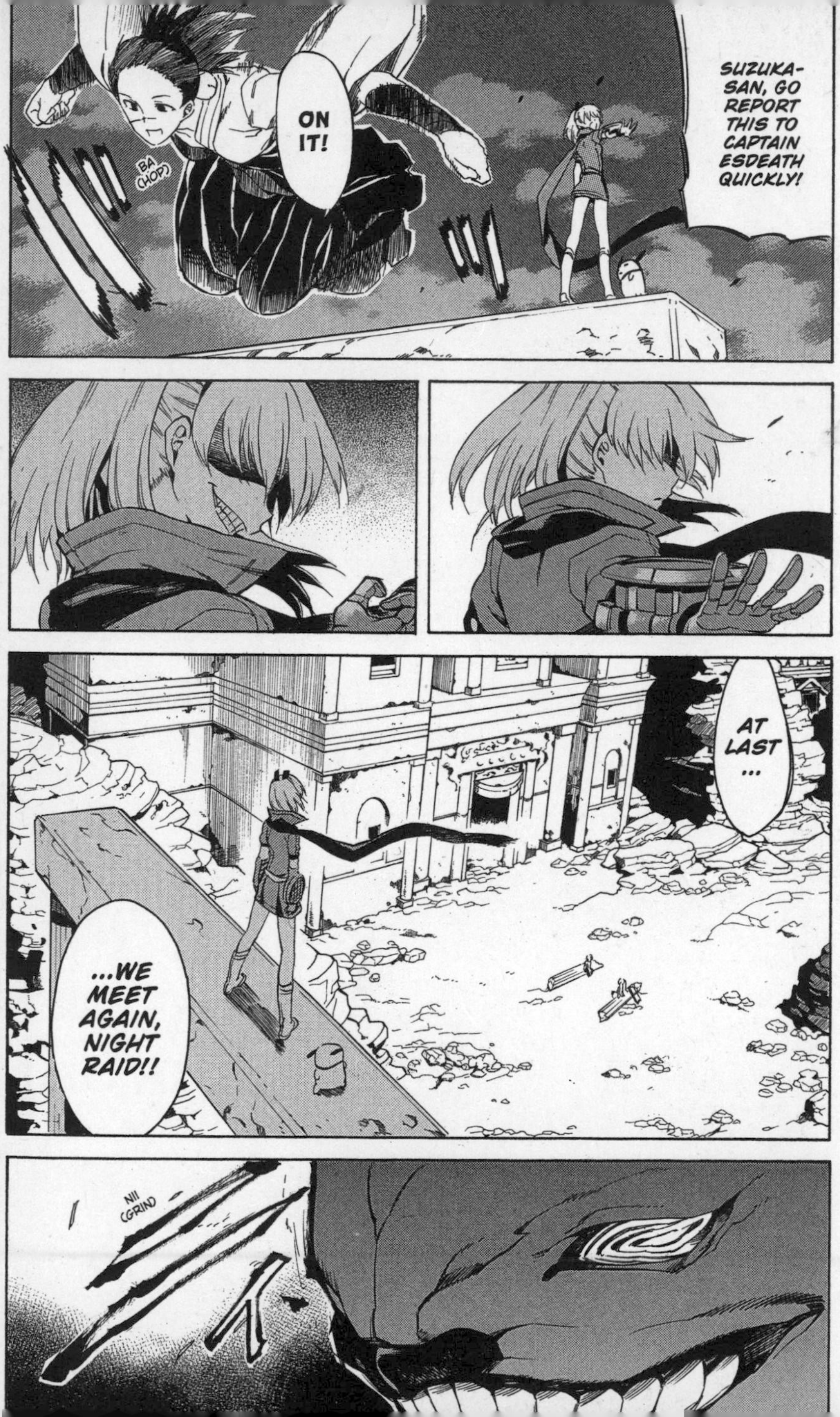
SUZUKA-SAN, GO REPORT THIS TO CAPTAIN ESDEATH QUICKLY!
ON IT!
BA (HOP)
AT LAST...
...WE MEET AGAIN, NIGHT RAID!!
NII (GRIND)

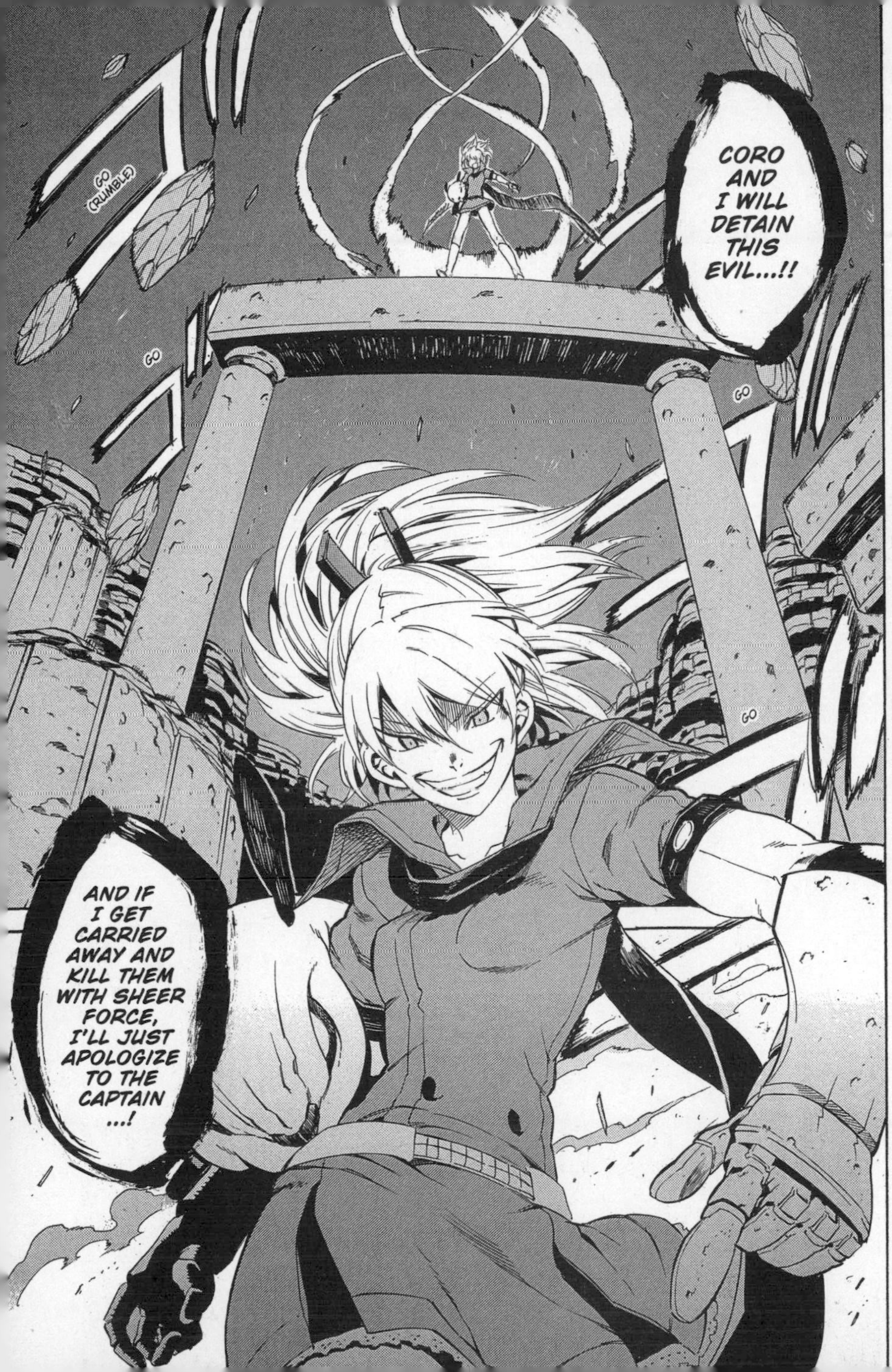
GO (RUMBLE)
CORO AND I WILL DETAIN THIS EVIL...!!
GO
GO
GO
AND IF I GET CARRIED AWAY AND KILL THEM WITH SHEER FORCE, I'LL JUST APOLOGIZE TO THE CAPTAIN ...!

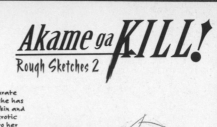

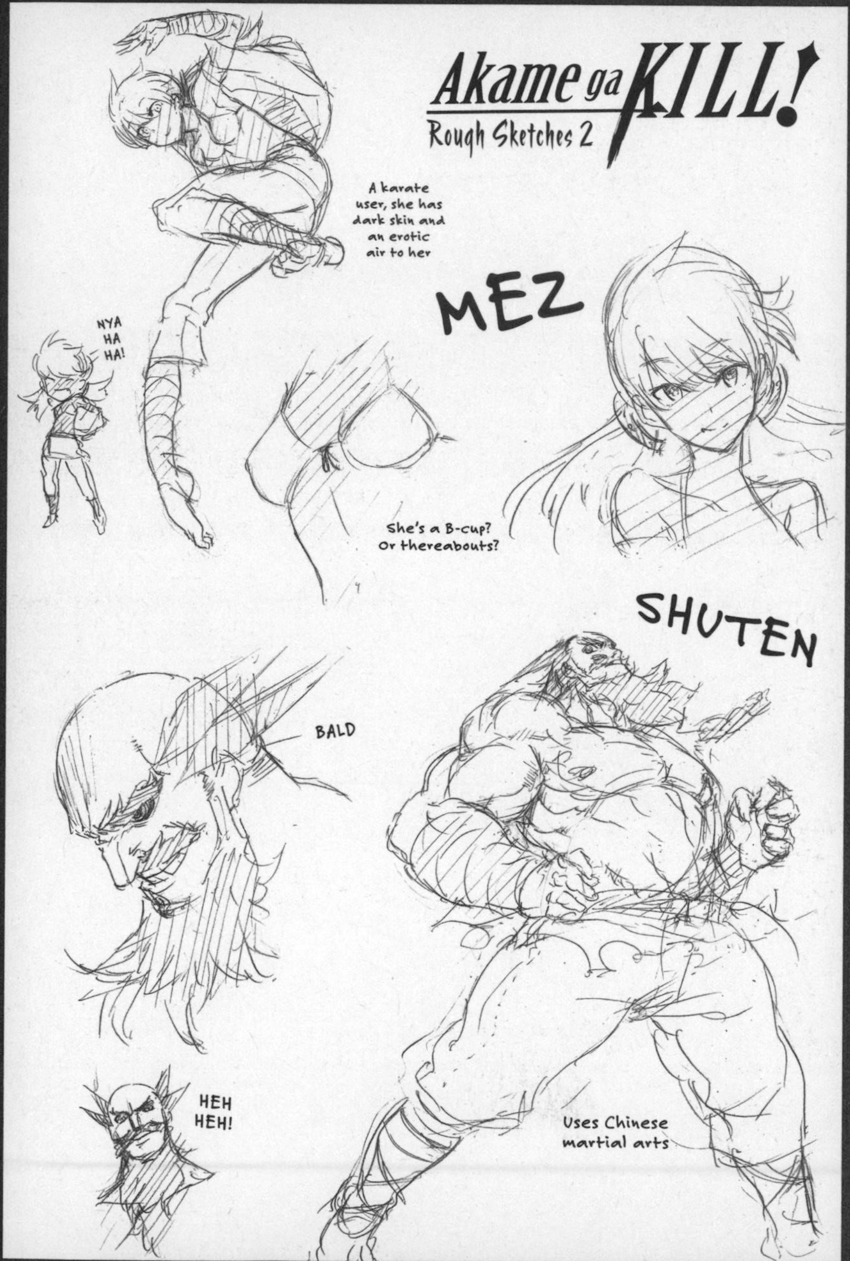

# Akame ga KILL!
## Rough Sketches 2

A karate user, she has dark skin and an erotic air to her

**MEZ**

NYA HA HA!

She's a B-cup? Or thereabouts?

**SHUTEN**

BALD

HEH HEH!

Uses Chinese martial arts

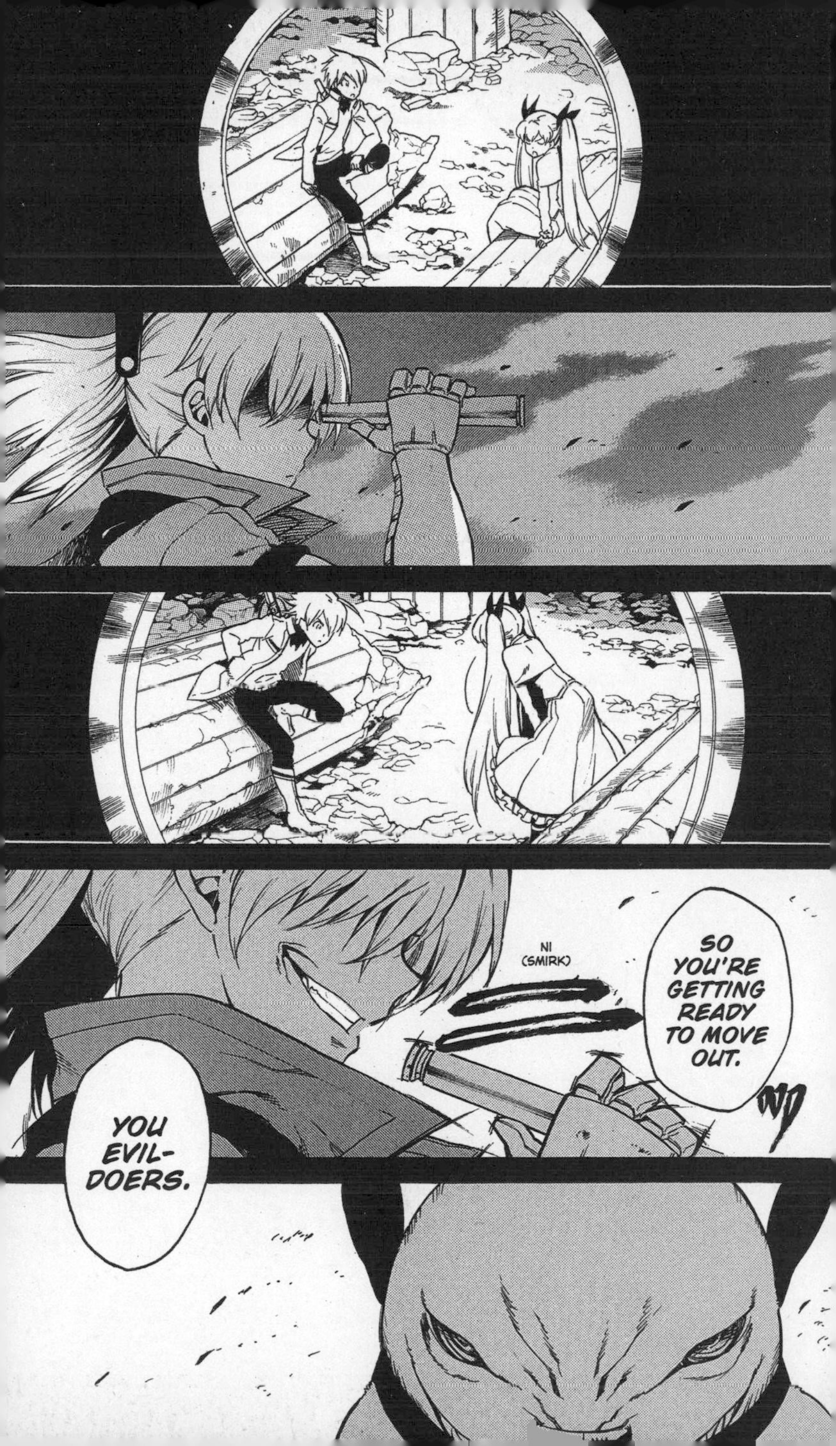
SO YOU'RE GETTING READY TO MOVE OUT.
NI (SMIRK)
YOU EVIL-DOERS.

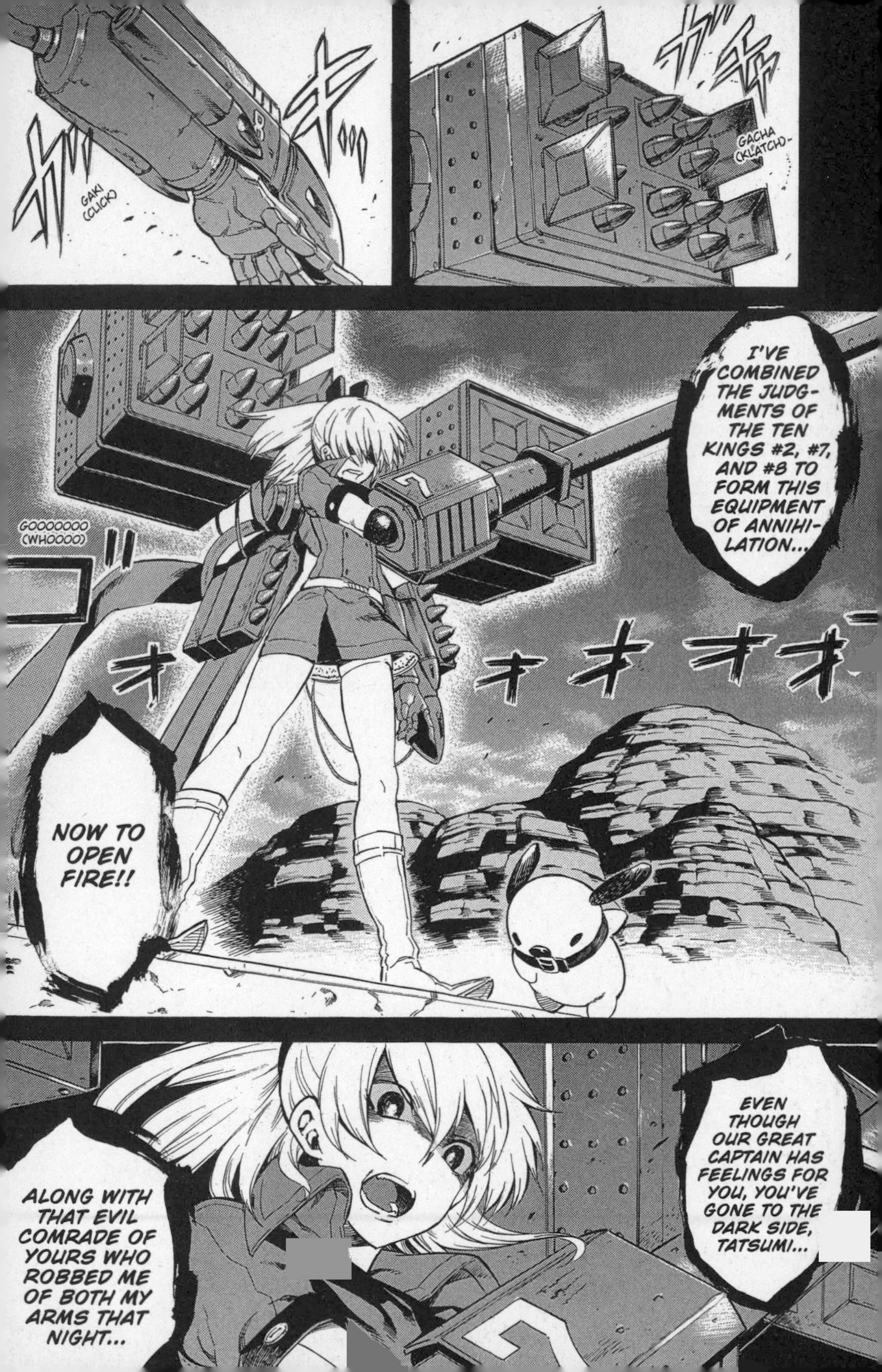
GACHA (KLATCH)
GAKI (CLICK)
I'VE COMBINED THE JUDGMENTS OF THE TEN KINGS #2, #7, AND #8 TO FORM THIS EQUIPMENT OF ANNIHILATION...
GOOOOOOO (WHOOOO)
NOW TO OPEN FIRE!!
EVEN THOUGH OUR GREAT CAPTAIN HAS FEELINGS FOR YOU, YOU'VE GONE TO THE DARK SIDE, TATSUMI...
ALONG WITH THAT EVIL COMRADE OF YOURS WHO ROBBED ME OF BOTH MY ARMS THAT NIGHT...

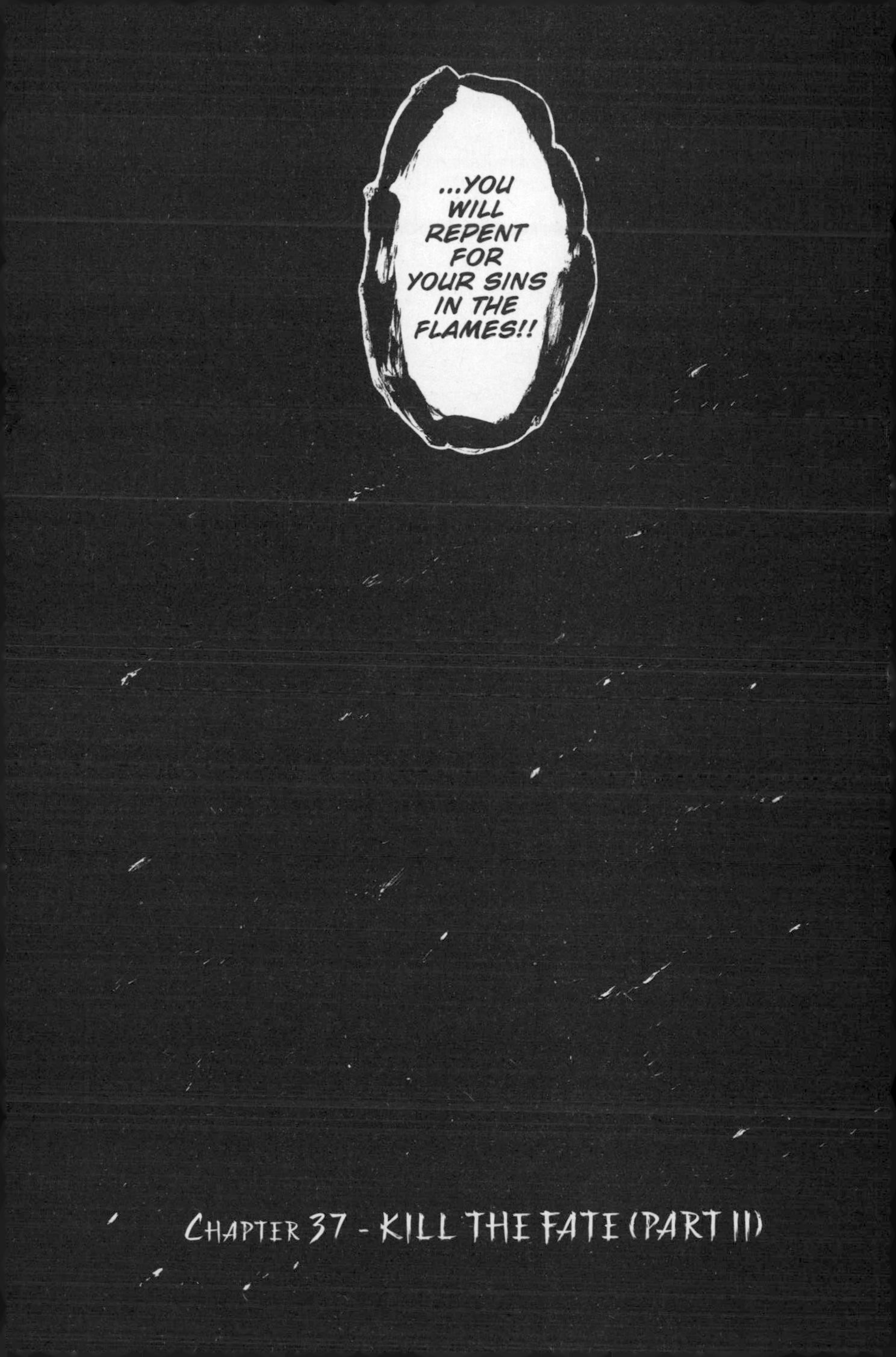
...YOU WILL REPENT FOR YOUR SINS IN THE FLAMES!!

## CHAPTER 37 - KILL THE FATE (PART II)

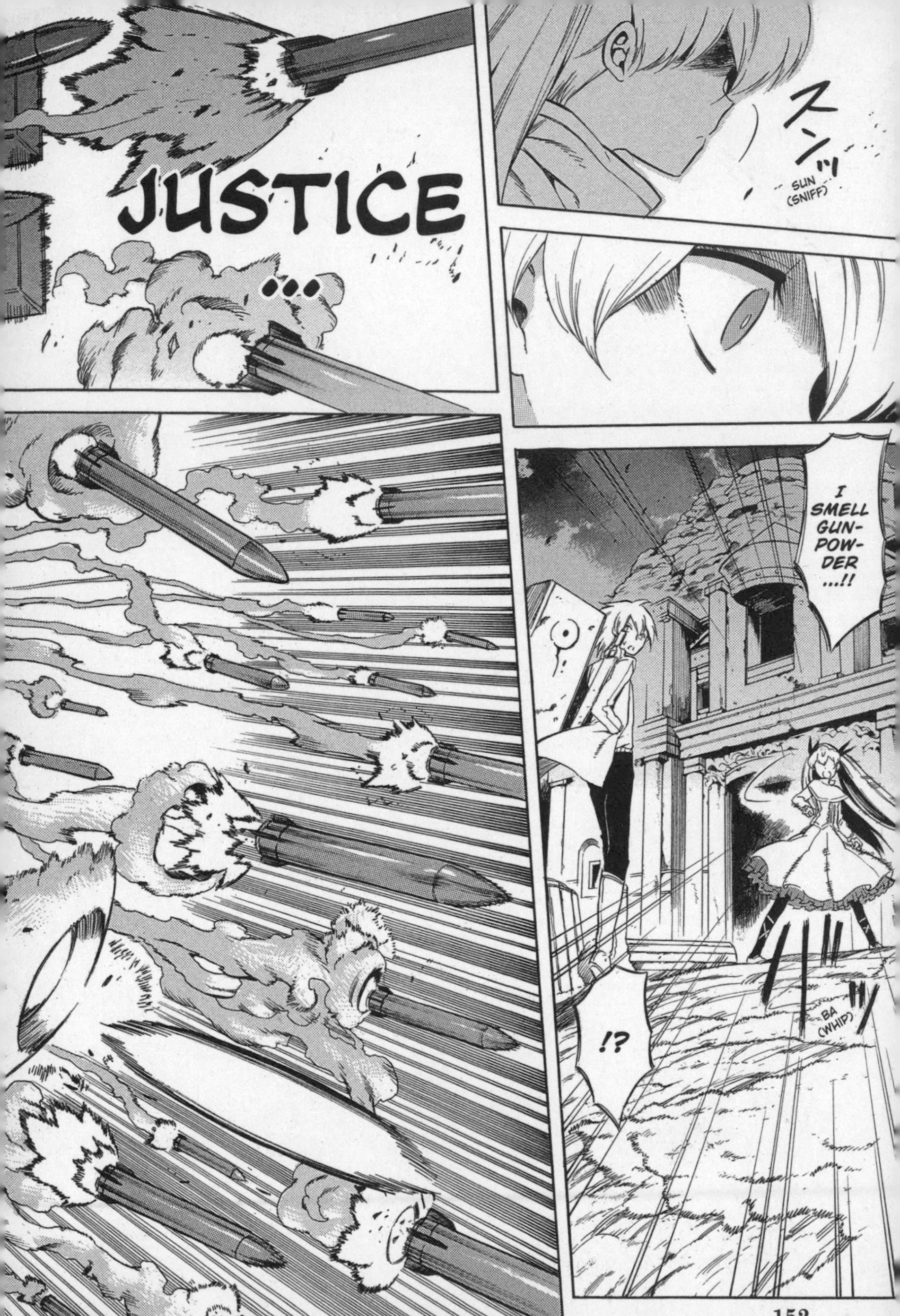

SUN (SNIFF)
I SMELL GUN-POW-DER ...!!
BA (WHIP)
!?
JUSTICE
...

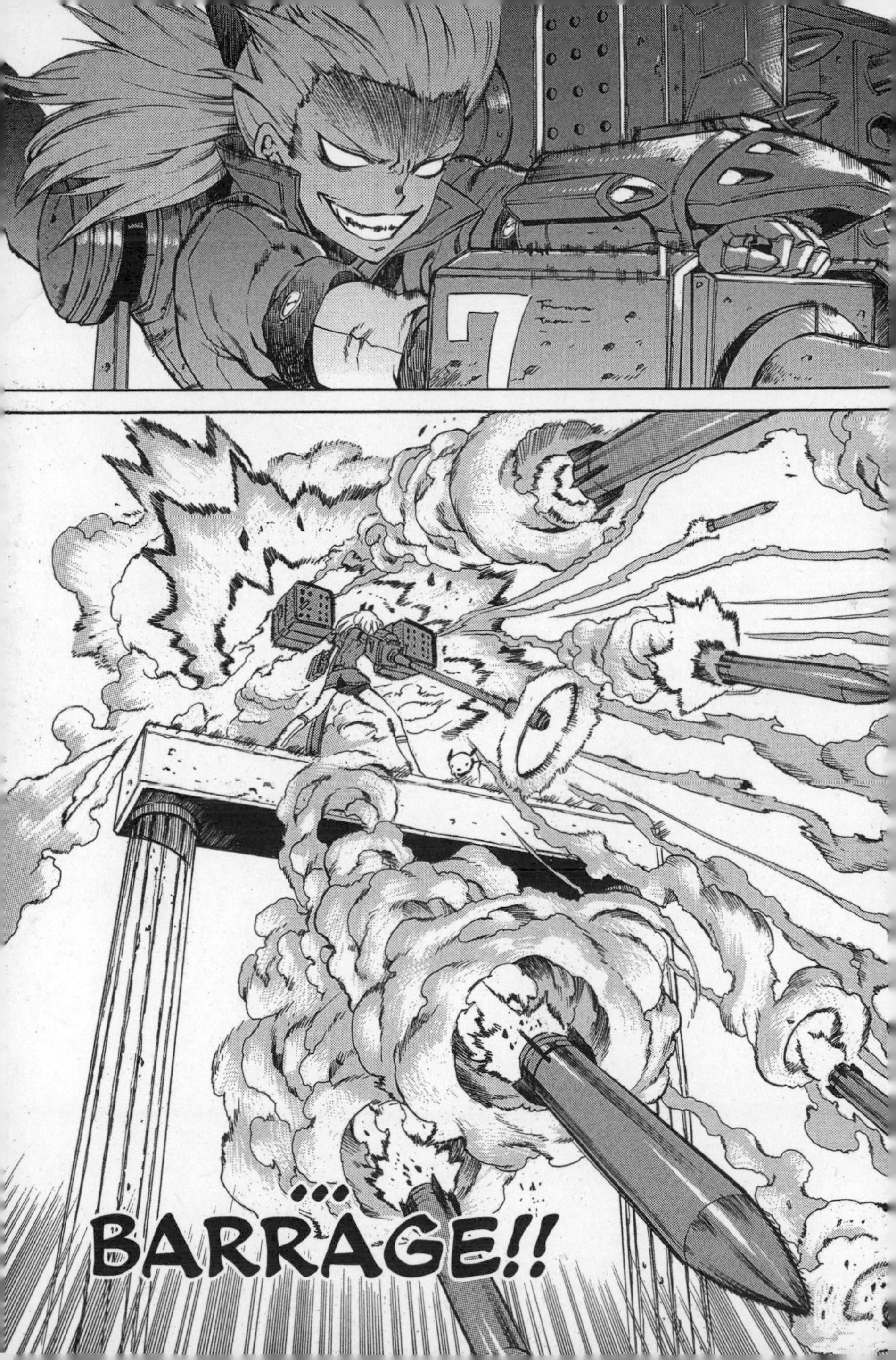
...BARRAGE!!

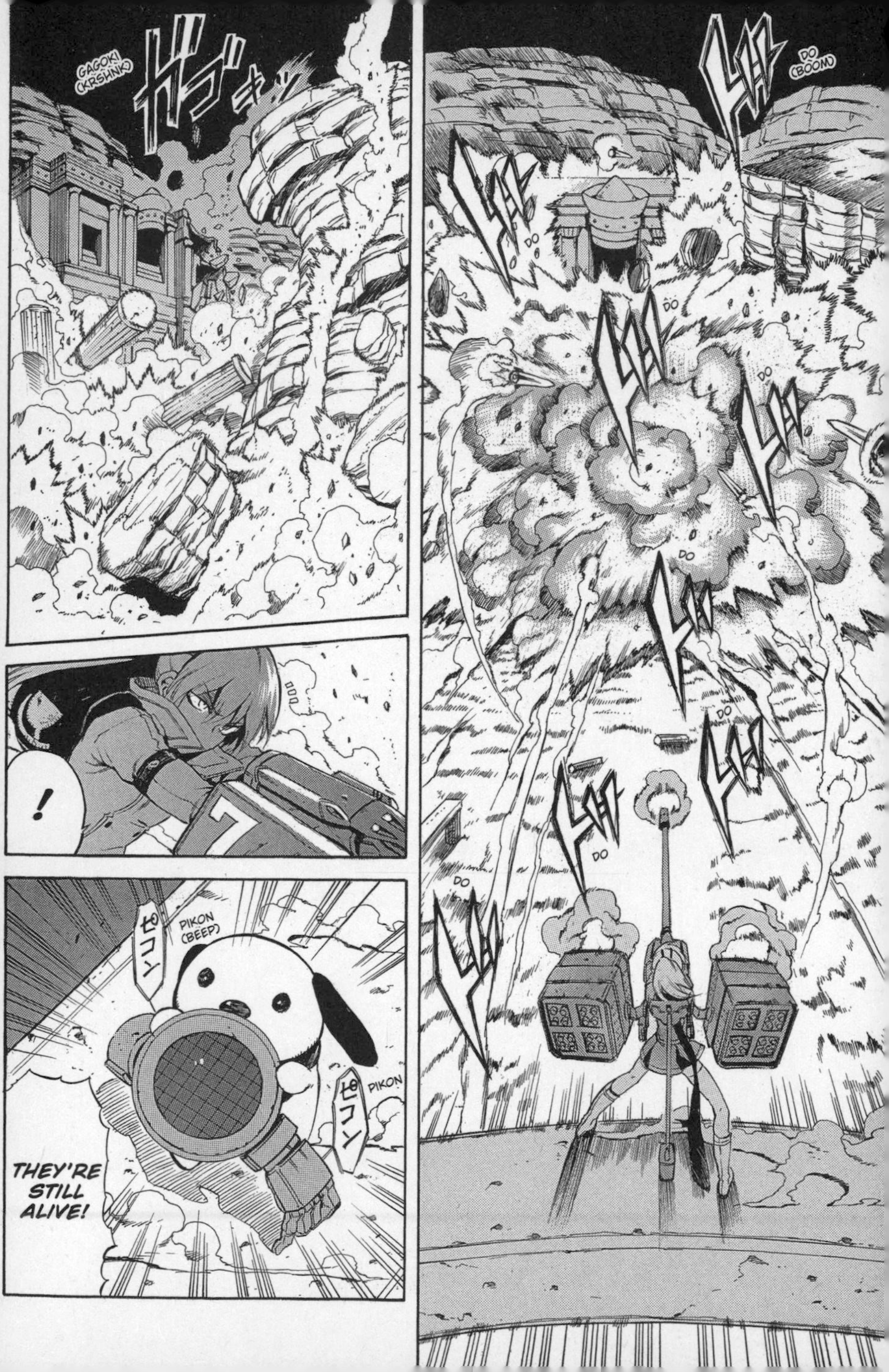
DO (BOOM)
DO
DO
DO
DO
DO
DO
DO
GAGOKI (KRSHNK)
ガゴキッ
!
ピコン
PIKON (BEEP)
ピコン
PIKON
THEY'RE STILL ALIVE!

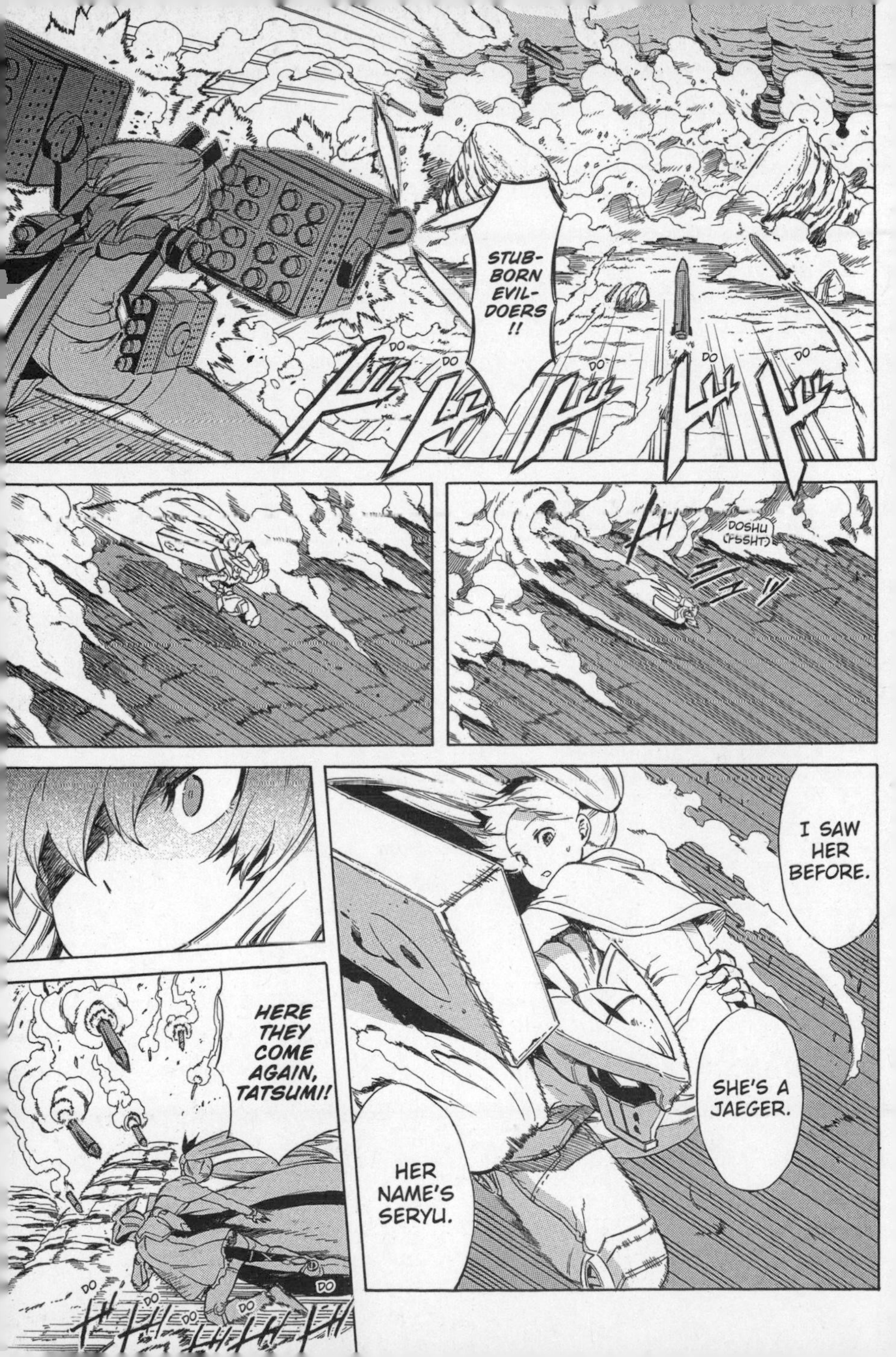
STUB-BORN EVIL-DOERS!!
DO DO DO DO DO
DOSHU (FSSHT)
I SAW HER BEFORE.
SHE'S A JAEGER.
HER NAME'S SERYU.
HERE THEY COME AGAIN, TATSUMI!
DO DO DO DO DO

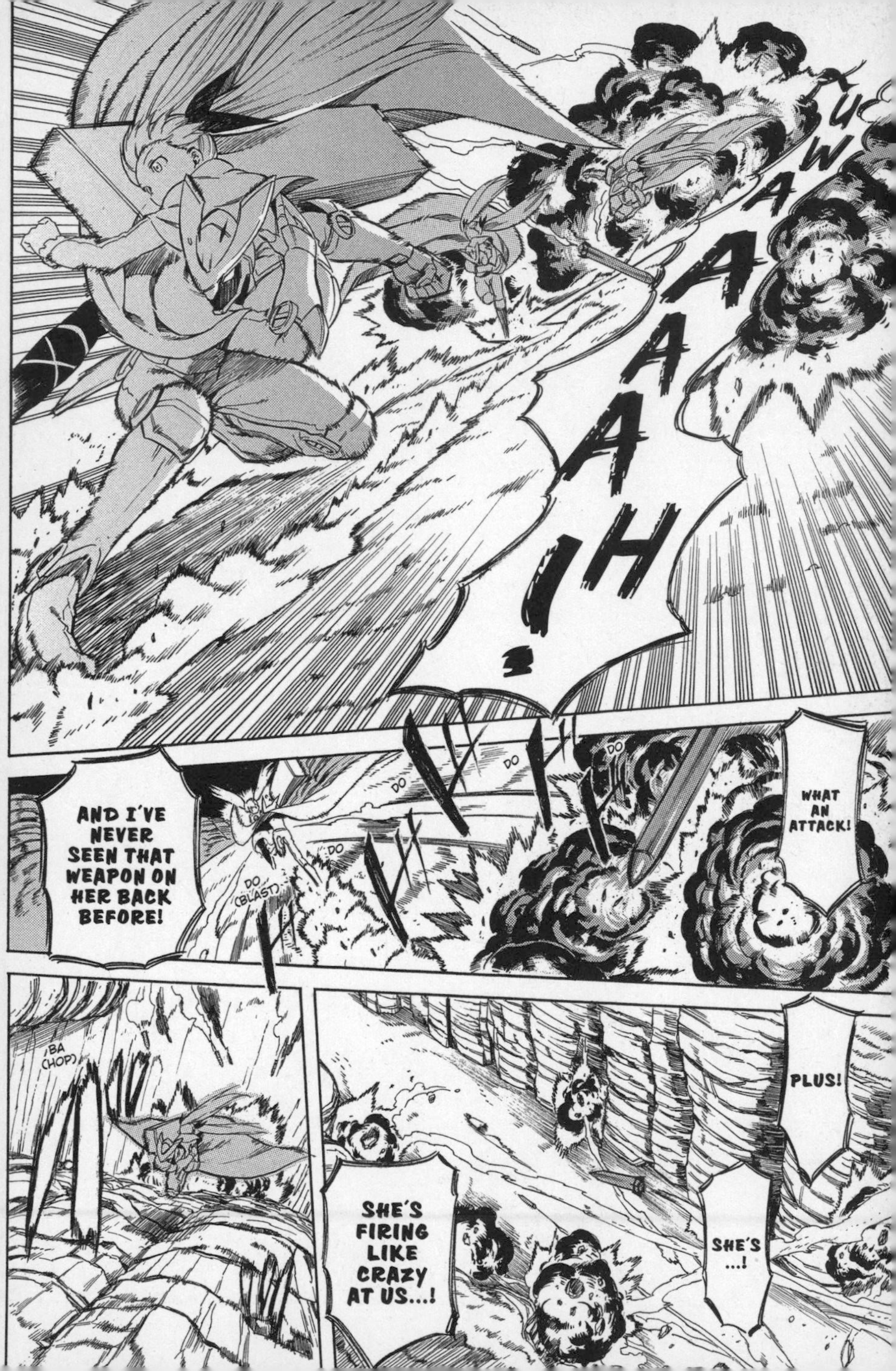

UGWAAAAH!
WHAT AN ATTACK!
DO
DO
DO
DO
DO (BLAST)
AND I'VE NEVER SEEN THAT WEAPON ON HER BACK BEFORE!
PLUS!
SHE'S ...!
SHE'S FIRING LIKE CRAZY AT US...!
BA (HOP)

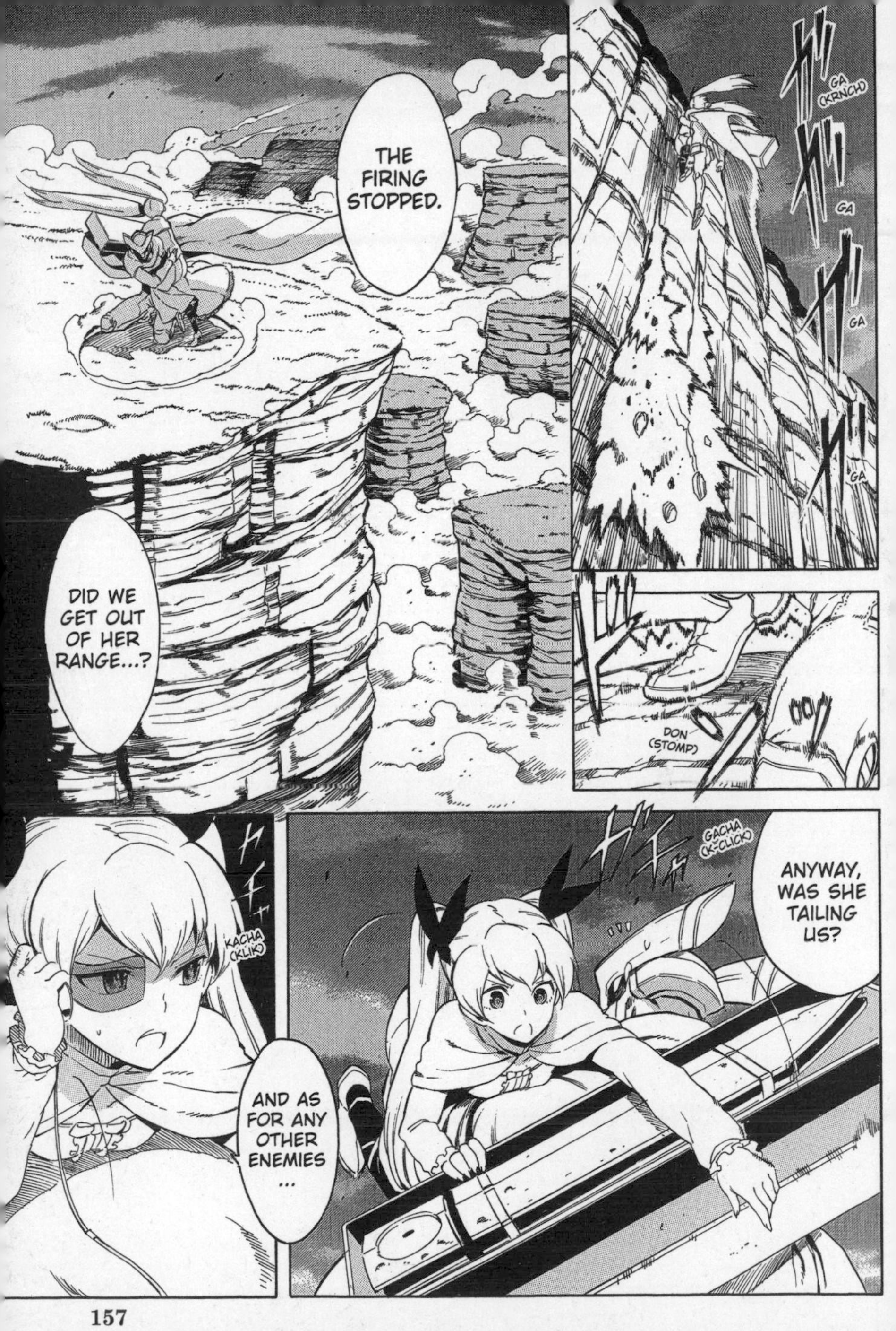
GA
(KRNCH)
GA
GA
GA
THE FIRING STOPPED.
DID WE GET OUT OF HER RANGE...?
DON
(STOMP)
GACHA
(K-CLICK)
ANYWAY, WAS SHE TAILING US?
KACHA
(KLIK)
AND AS FOR ANY OTHER ENEMIES ...

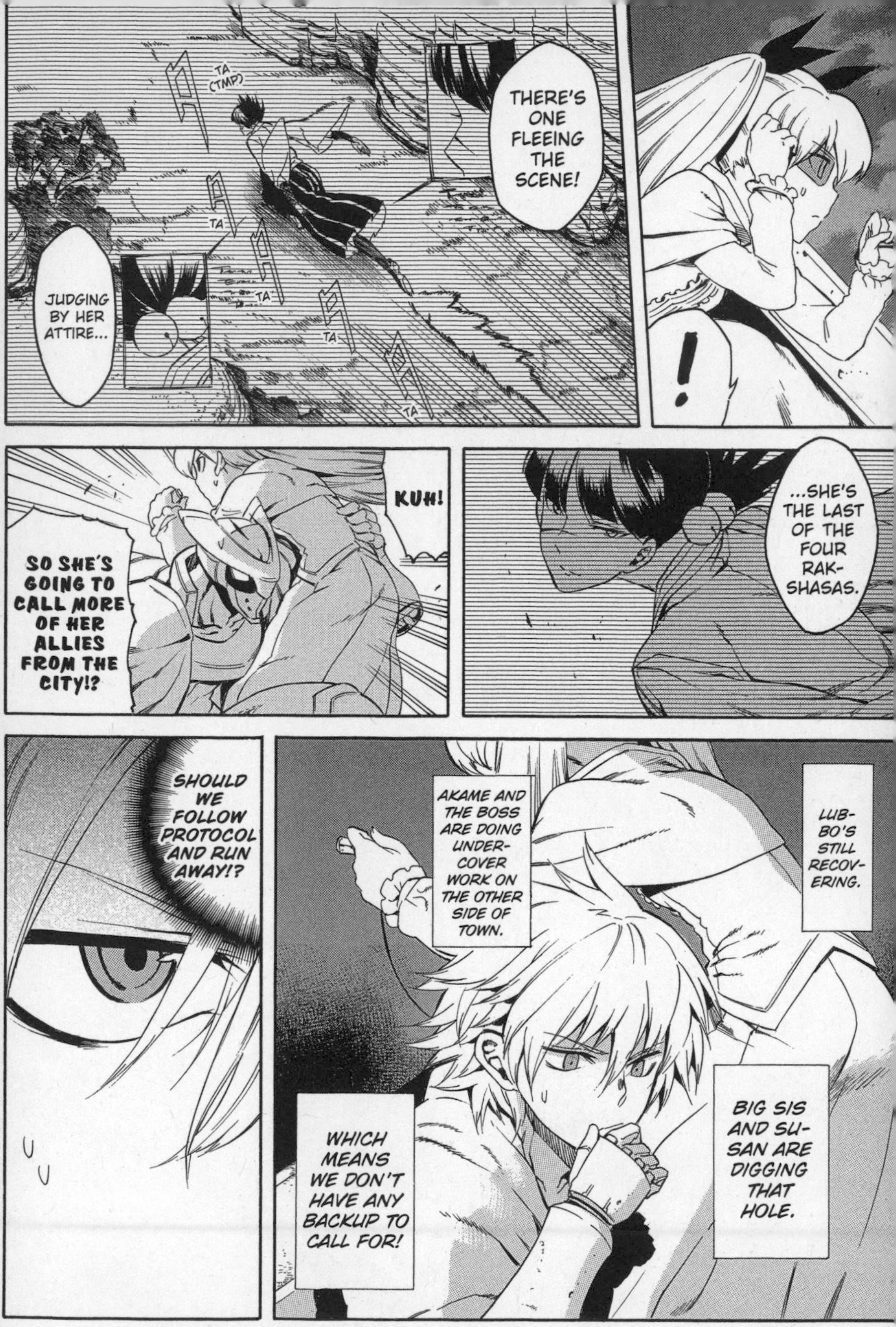
!
THERE'S ONE FLEEING THE SCENE!
TA (TMP)
TA
TA
TA
TA
JUDGING BY HER ATTIRE...
...SHE'S THE LAST OF THE FOUR RAK-SHASAS.
KUH!
SO SHE'S GOING TO CALL MORE OF HER ALLIES FROM THE CITY!?
LUB-BO'S STILL RECOV-ERING.
AKAME AND THE BOSS ARE DOING UNDER-COVER WORK ON THE OTHER SIDE OF TOWN.
BIG SIS AND SU-SAN ARE DIGGING THAT HOLE.
WHICH MEANS WE DON'T HAVE ANY BACKUP TO CALL FOR!
SHOULD WE FOLLOW PROTOCOL AND RUN AWAY!?

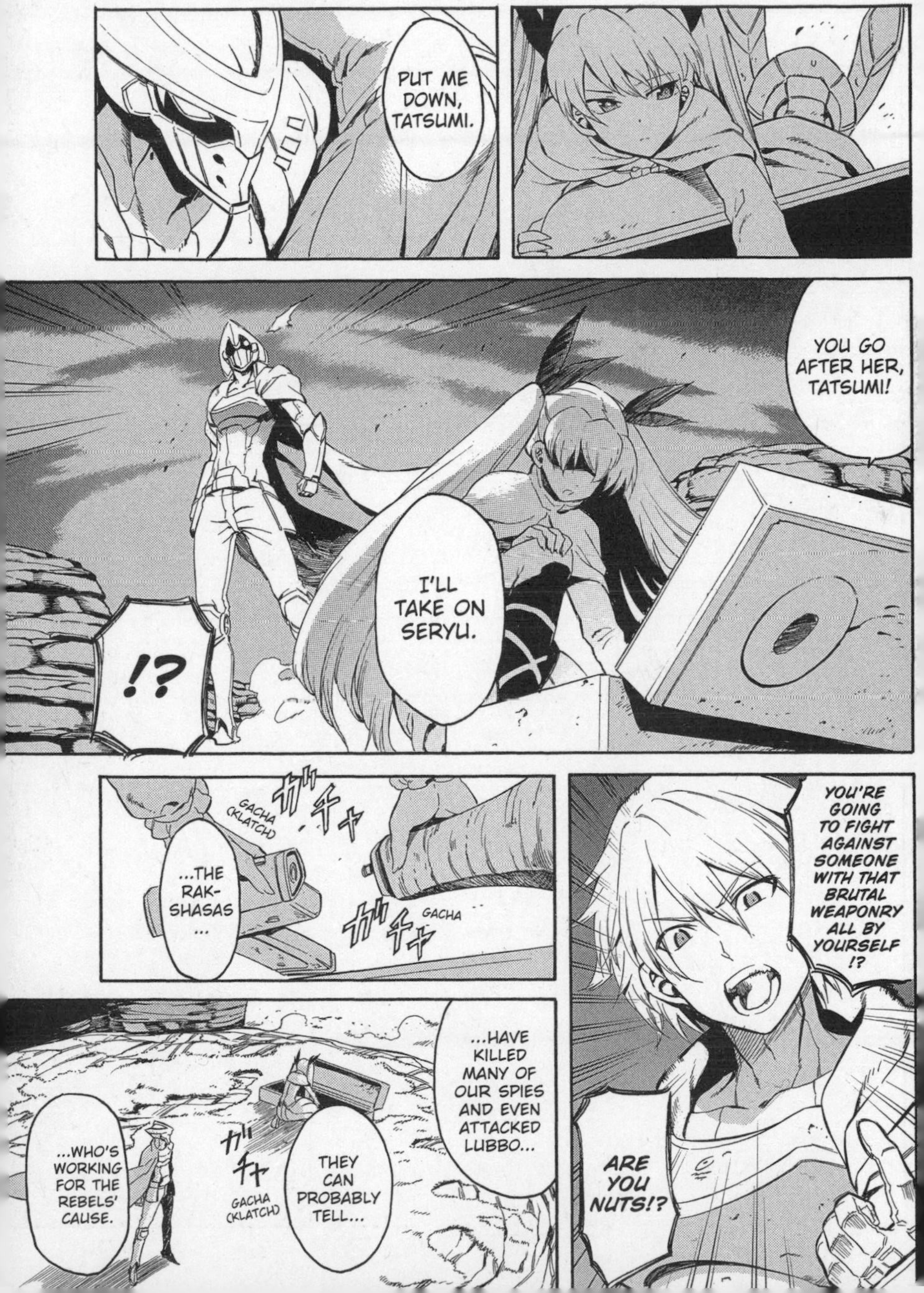
PUT ME DOWN, TATSUMI.
YOU GO AFTER HER, TATSUMI!
I'LL TAKE ON SERYU.
!?
YOU'RE GOING TO FIGHT AGAINST SOMEONE WITH THAT BRUTAL WEAPONRY ALL BY YOURSELF!?
ARE YOU NUTS!?
ガチャ
GACHA (KLATCH)
ガチャ
GACHA
...THE RAK-SHASAS...
...HAVE KILLED MANY OF OUR SPIES AND EVEN ATTACKED LUBBO...
ガチャ
GACHA (KLATCH)
THEY CAN PROBABLY TELL...
...WHO'S WORKING FOR THE REBELS' CAUSE.

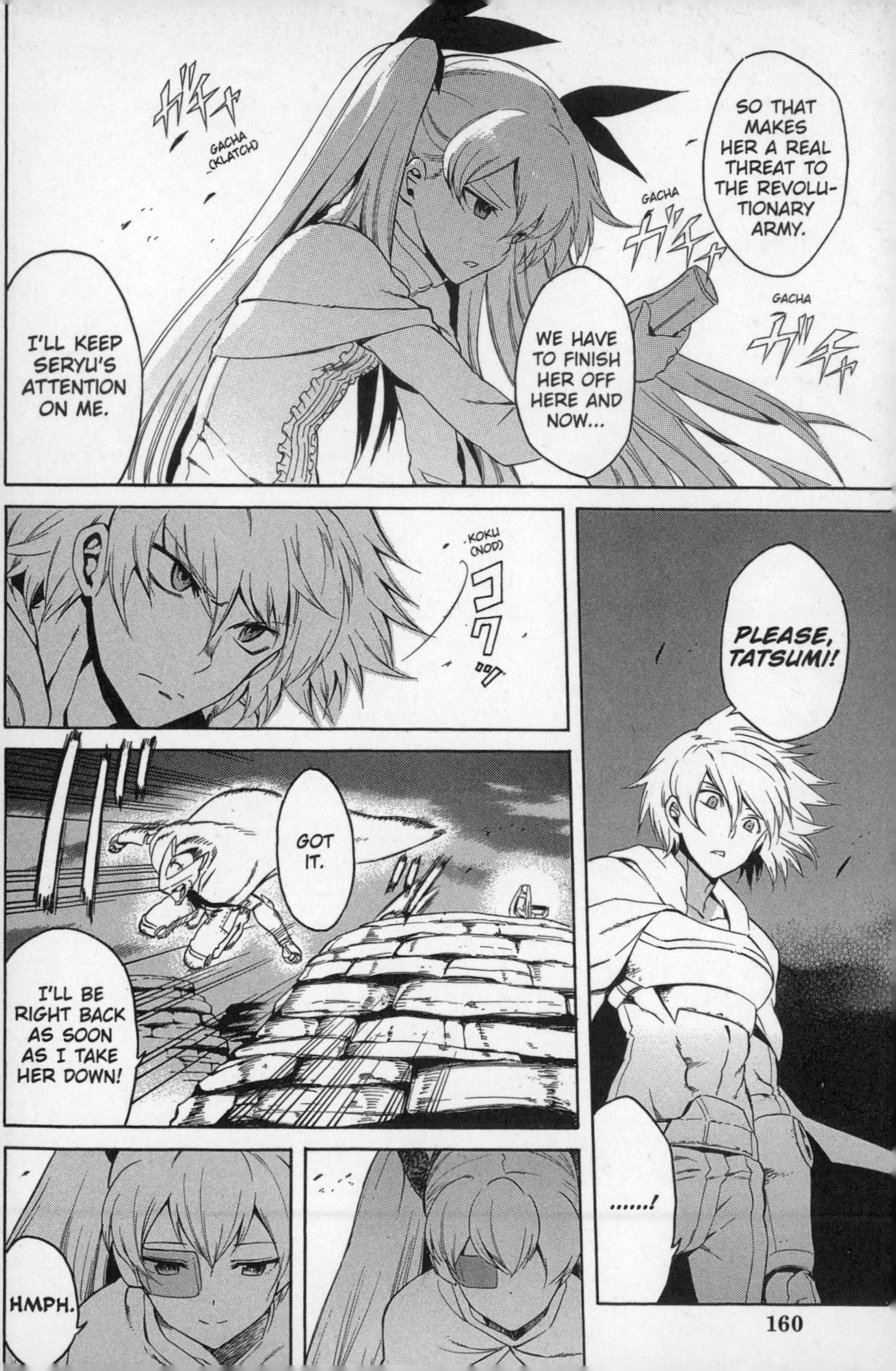
ガチャ
GACHA (KLATCH)
SO THAT MAKES HER A REAL THREAT TO THE REVOLUTIONARY ARMY.
GACHA
ガチャ
GACHA
ガチャ
WE HAVE TO FINISH HER OFF HERE AND NOW...
I'LL KEEP SERYU'S ATTENTION ON ME.
PLEASE, TATSUMI!
KOKU (NOD)
コク
GOT IT.
I'LL BE RIGHT BACK AS SOON AS I TAKE HER DOWN!
......!
HMPH.

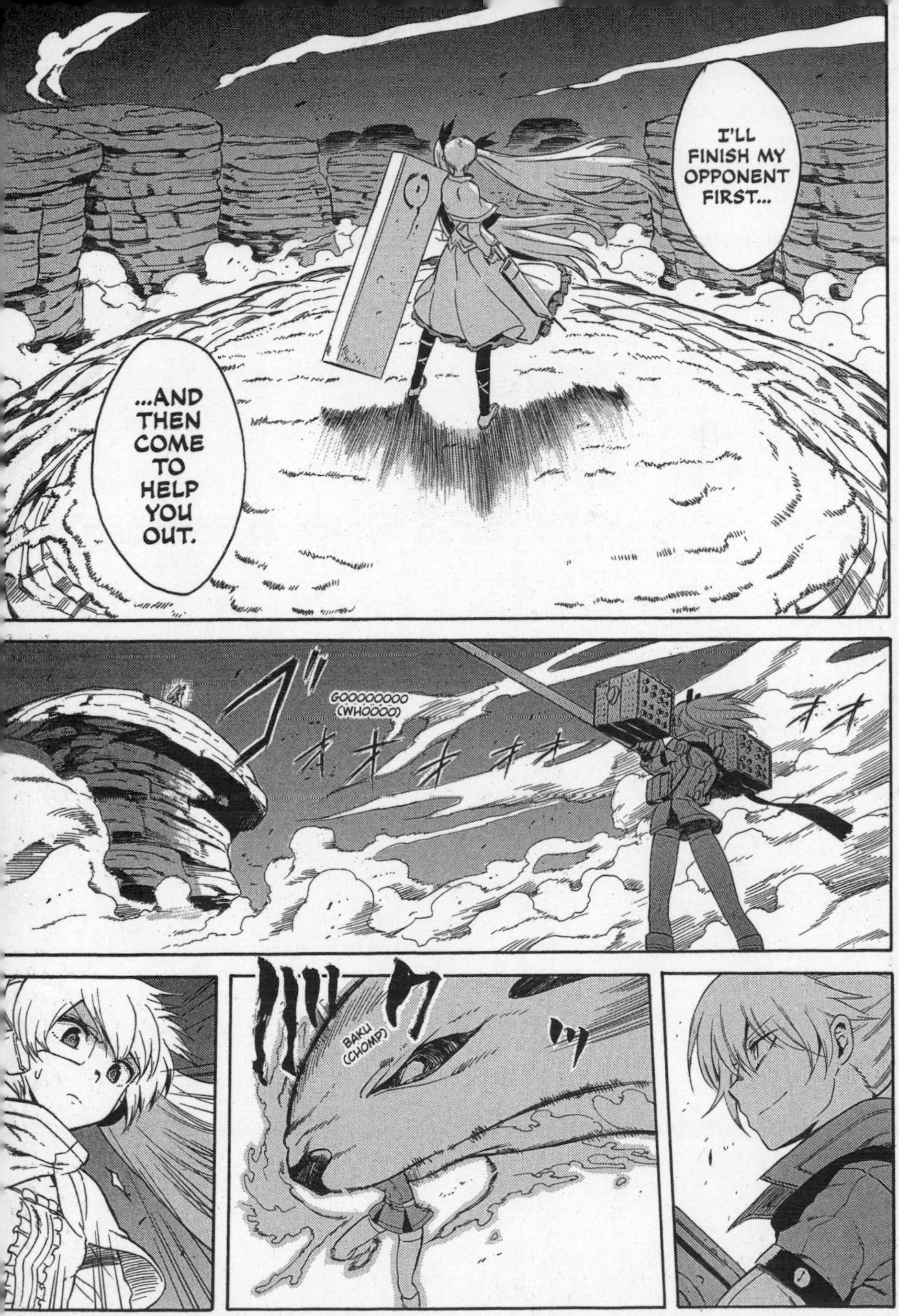
I'LL FINISH MY OPPONENT FIRST...
...AND THEN COME TO HELP YOU OUT.
GOOOOOOOO (WHOOOO)
BAKU (CHOMP)

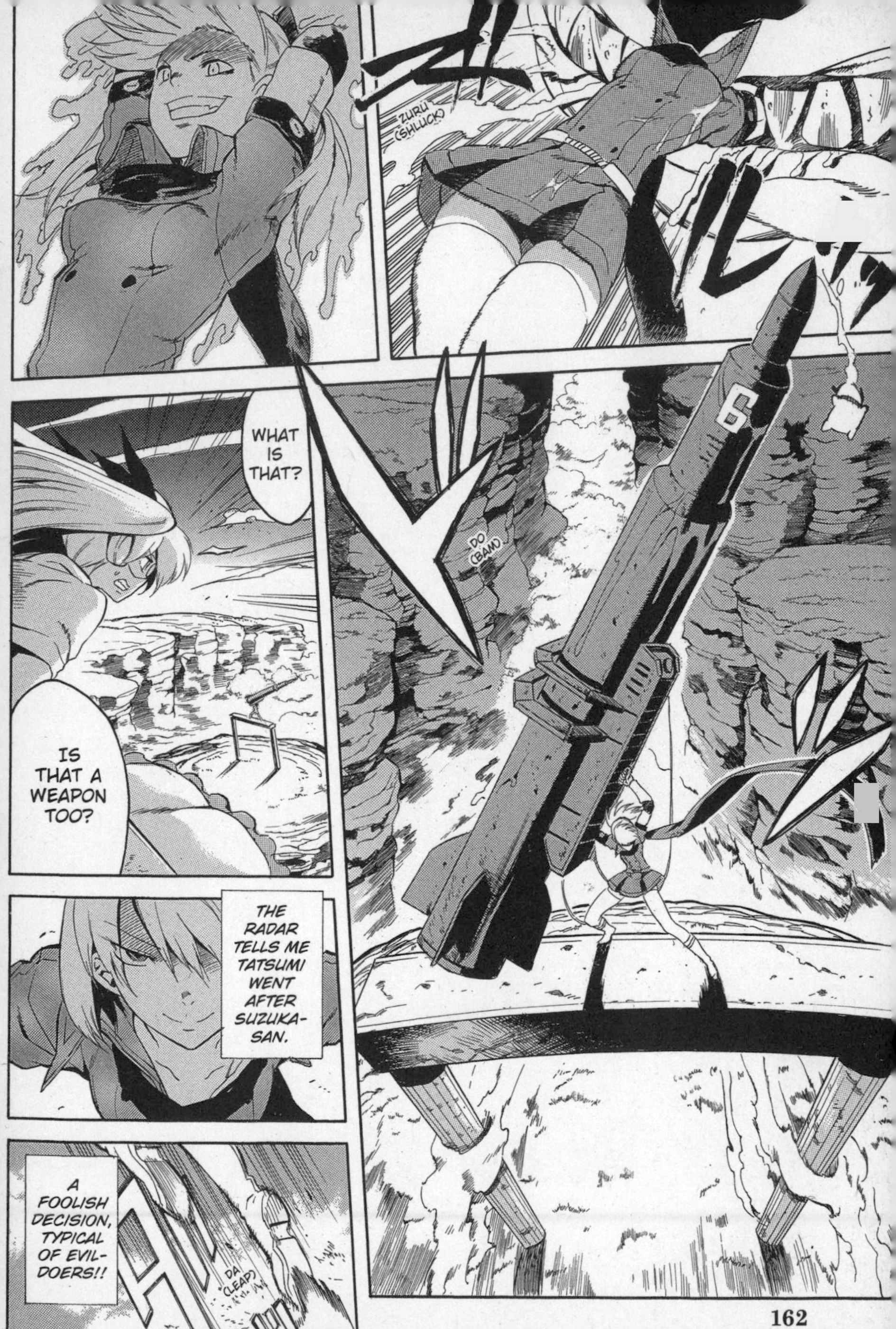

ZURU (SHLUCK)
WHAT IS THAT?
IS THAT A WEAPON TOO?
DO (BAM)
THE RADAR TELLS ME TATSUMI WENT AFTER SUZUKA-SAN.
A FOOLISH DECISION, TYPICAL OF EVIL-DOERS!!
DA (LEAP)

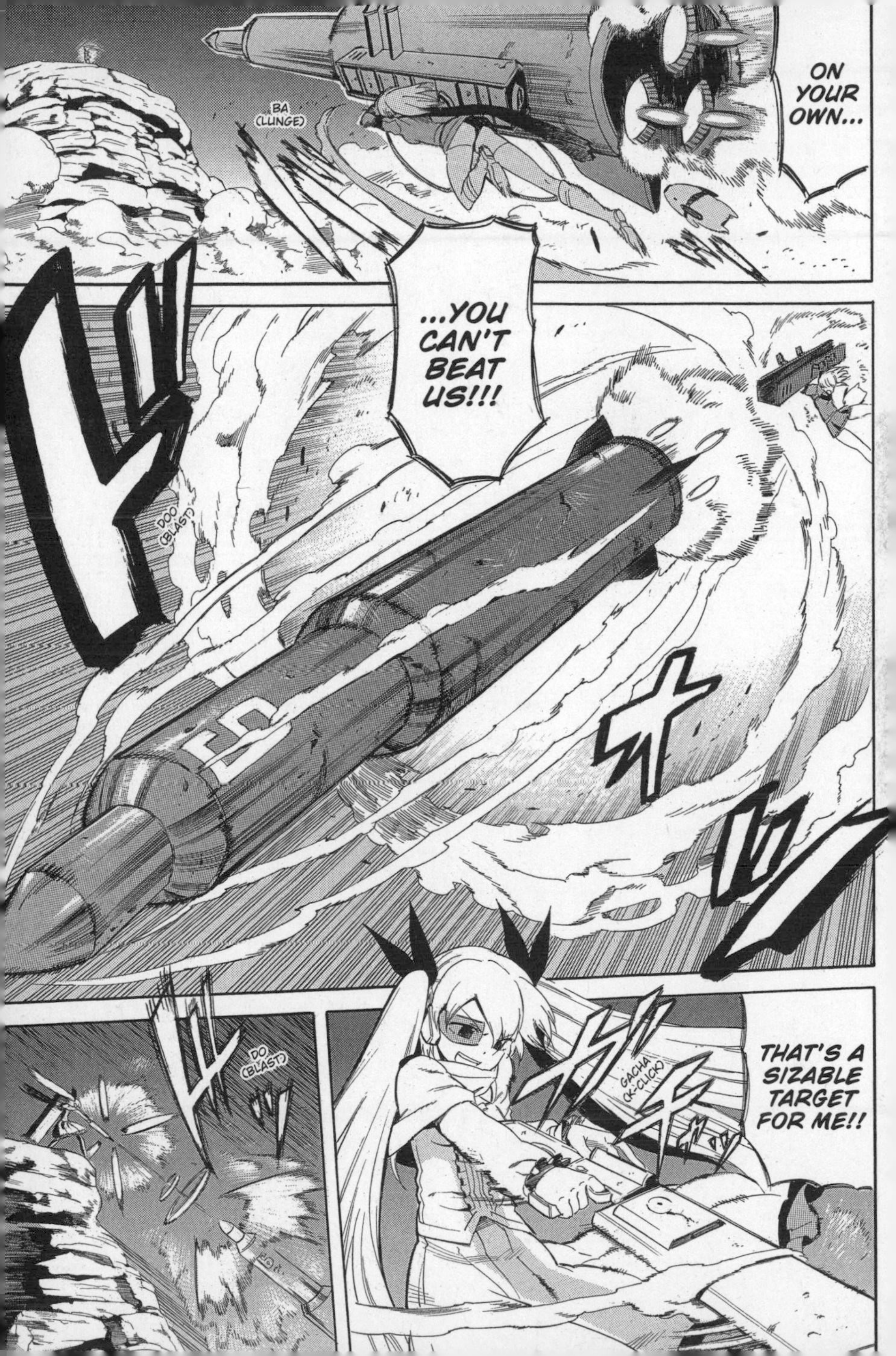
ON YOUR OWN...
BA (LUNGE)
...YOU CAN'T BEAT US!!!
DOO (BLAST)
THAT'S A SIZABLE TARGET FOR ME!!
GACHA (K-CLICK)
DO (BLAST)

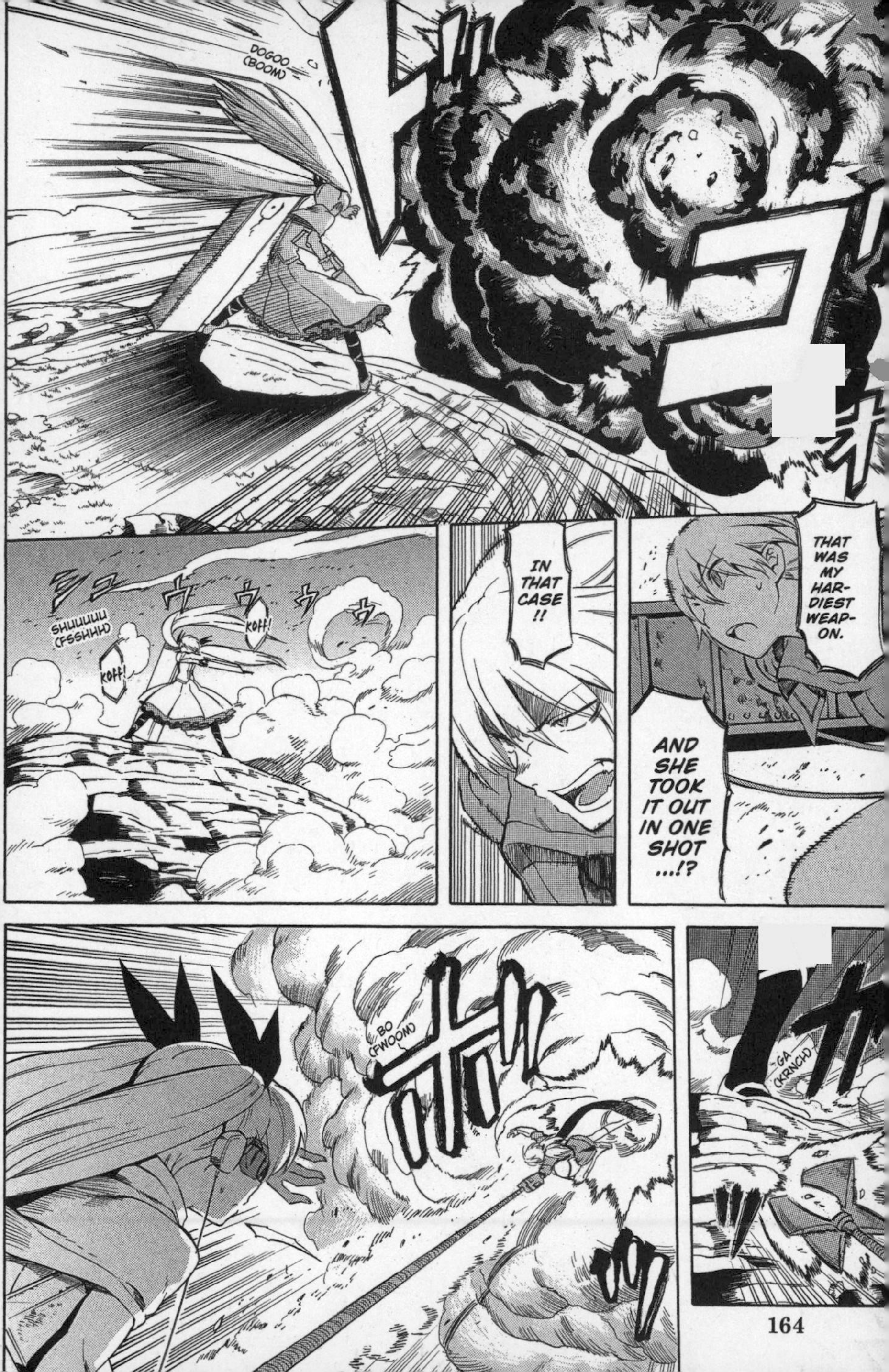
DOGOO (BOOM)
THAT WAS MY HARDIEST WEAPON.
AND SHE TOOK IT OUT IN ONE SHOT ...!?
IN THAT CASE !!
SHUUUUU (FSSHHH)
KOFF!
KOFF!
GA (KRNCH)
BO (FWOOM)

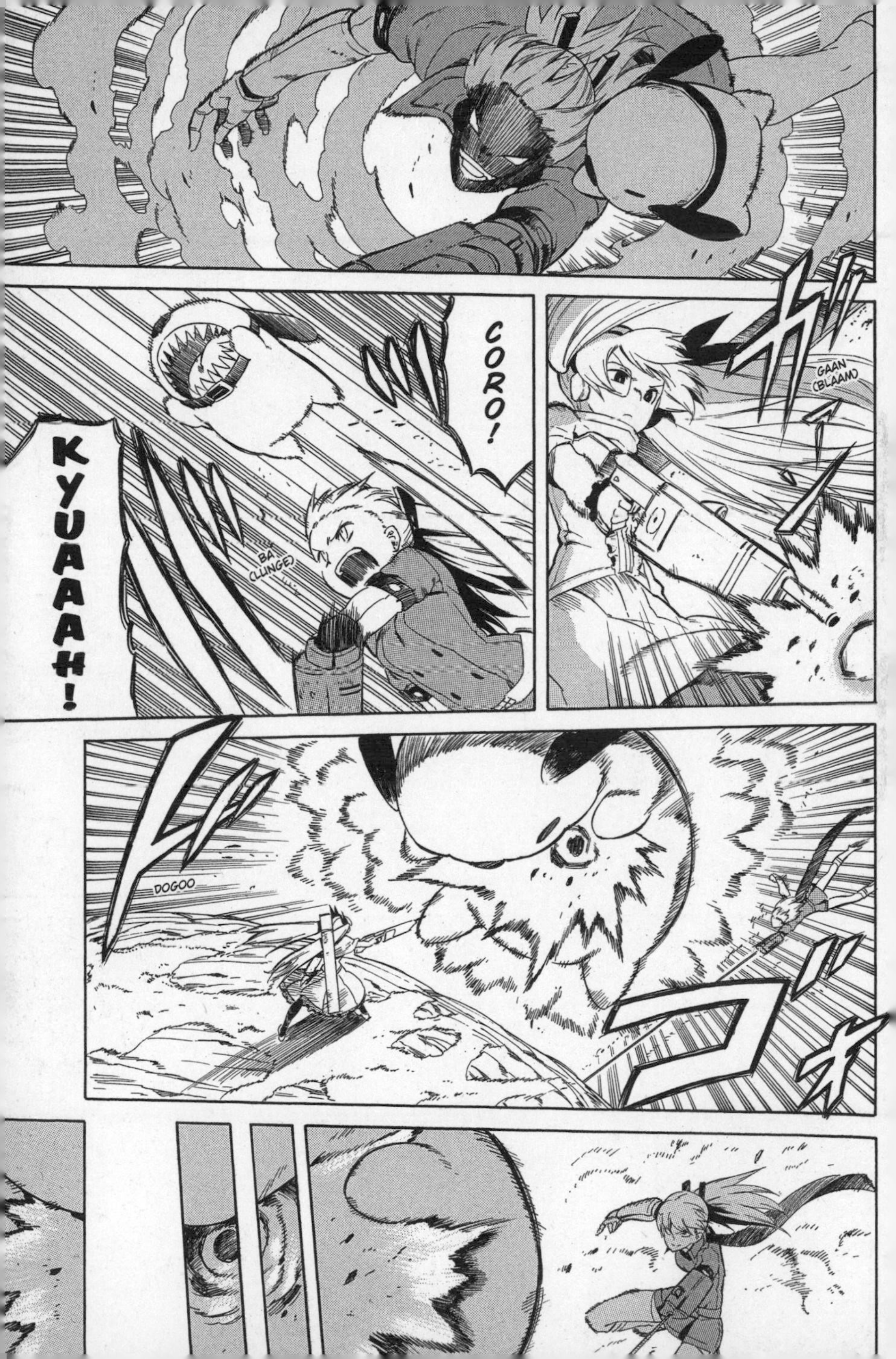
GAAN (BLAAM)
CORO!
KYUAAAAH!
BA (LUNGE)
DOGOO

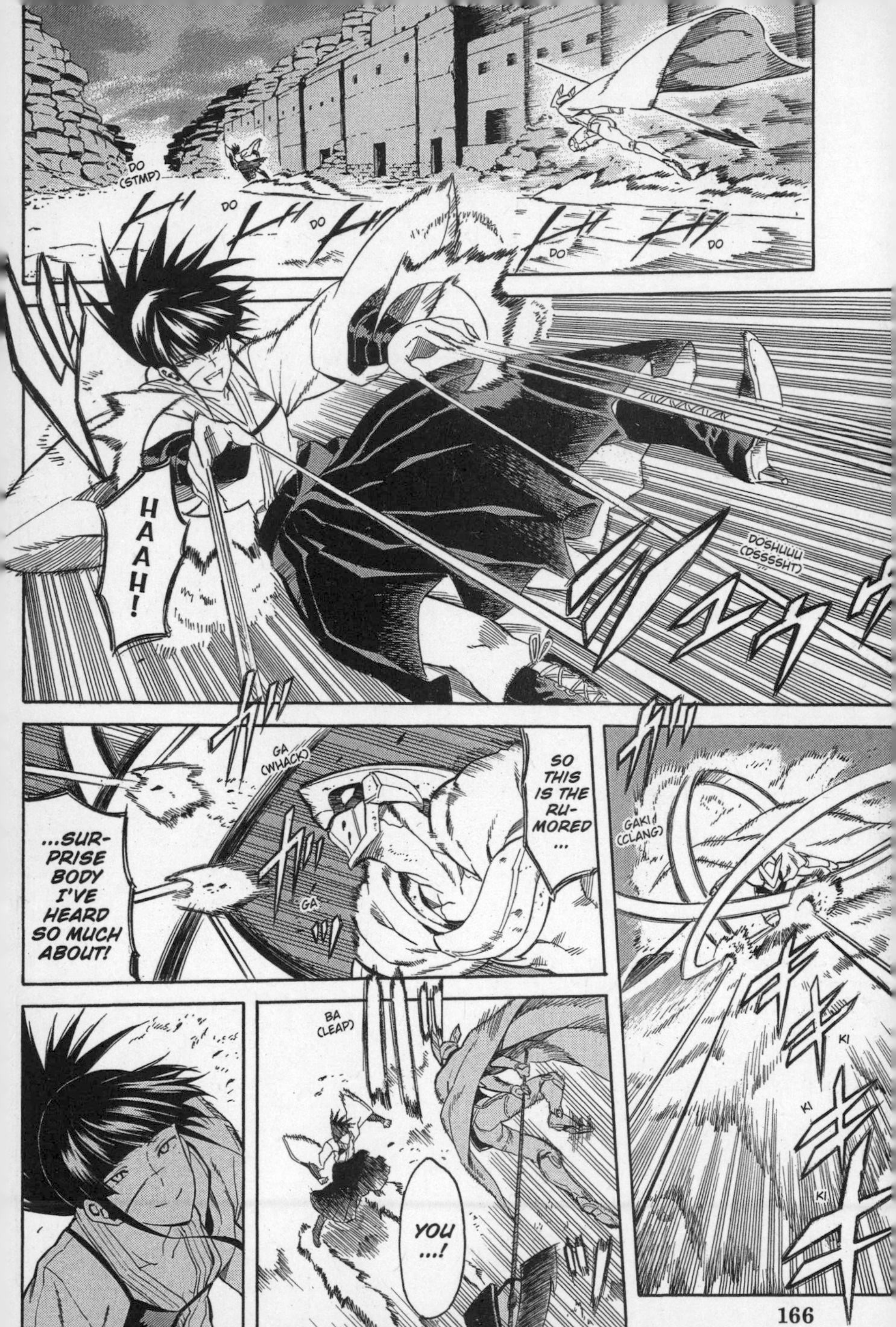
DO (STMP)
DO
DO
DO
DO
HAAAH!
DOSHUUU (DSSSSHT)
GA (WHACK)
GA
SO THIS IS THE RU-MORED ...
...SUR-PRISE BODY I'VE HEARD SO MUCH ABOUT!
GAKI (CLANG)
KI
KI
KI
BA (LEAP)
YOU ...!

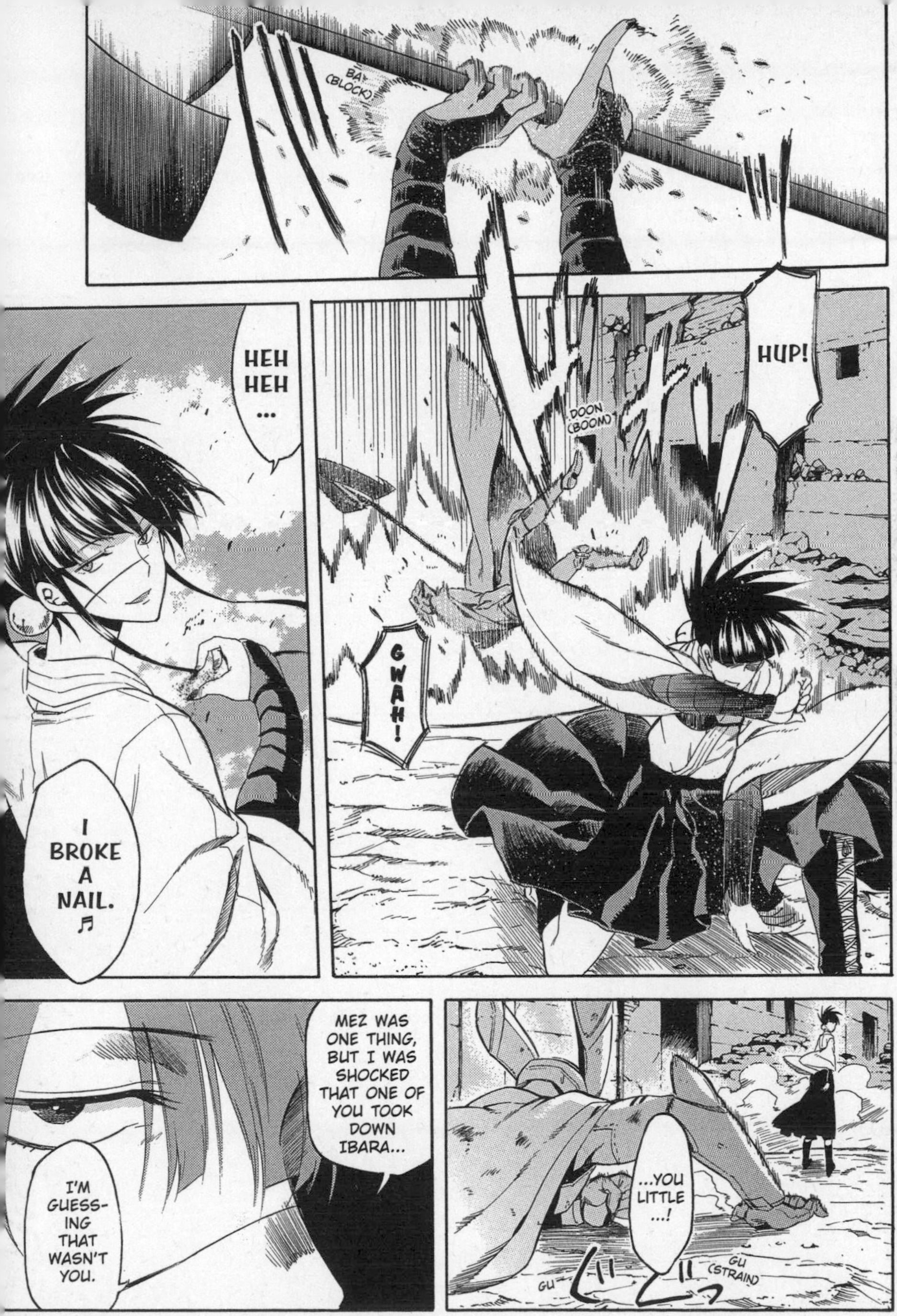
BA (BLOCK)
HUP!
DOON (BOOM)
GWAH!
HEH HEH ...
I BROKE A NAIL. ♫
...YOU LITTLE ...!
GU GU (STRAIN)
MEZ WAS ONE THING, BUT I WAS SHOCKED THAT ONE OF YOU TOOK DOWN IBARA...
I'M GUESSING THAT WASN'T YOU.

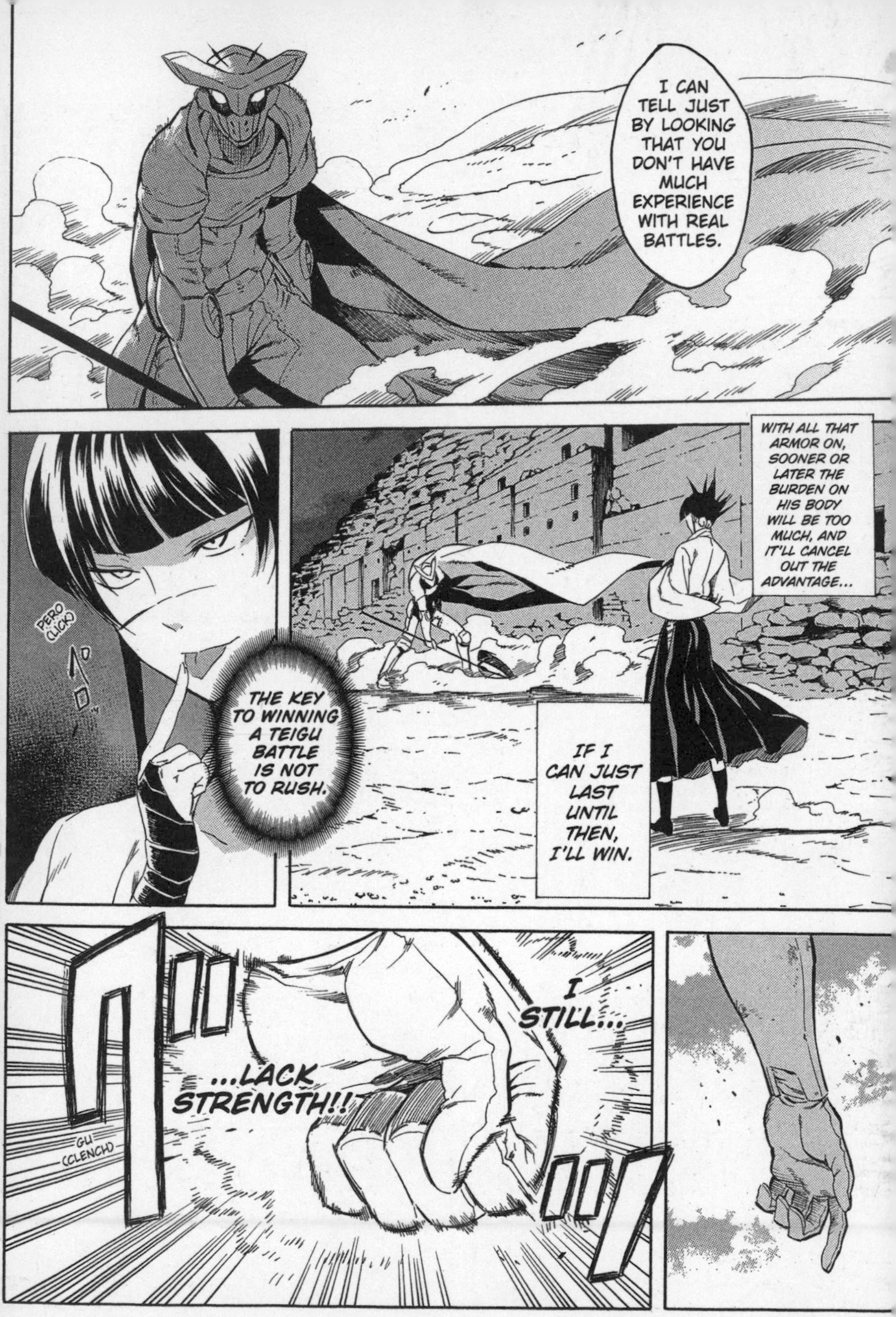
I CAN TELL JUST BY LOOKING THAT YOU DON'T HAVE MUCH EXPERIENCE WITH REAL BATTLES.
WITH ALL THAT ARMOR ON, SOONER OR LATER THE BURDEN ON HIS BODY WILL BE TOO MUCH, AND IT'LL CANCEL OUT THE ADVANTAGE...
IF I CAN JUST LAST UNTIL THEN, I'LL WIN.
THE KEY TO WINNING A TEIGU BATTLE IS NOT TO RUSH.
PERO (LICK)
I STILL...
...LACK STRENGTH!!
GU (CLENCH)

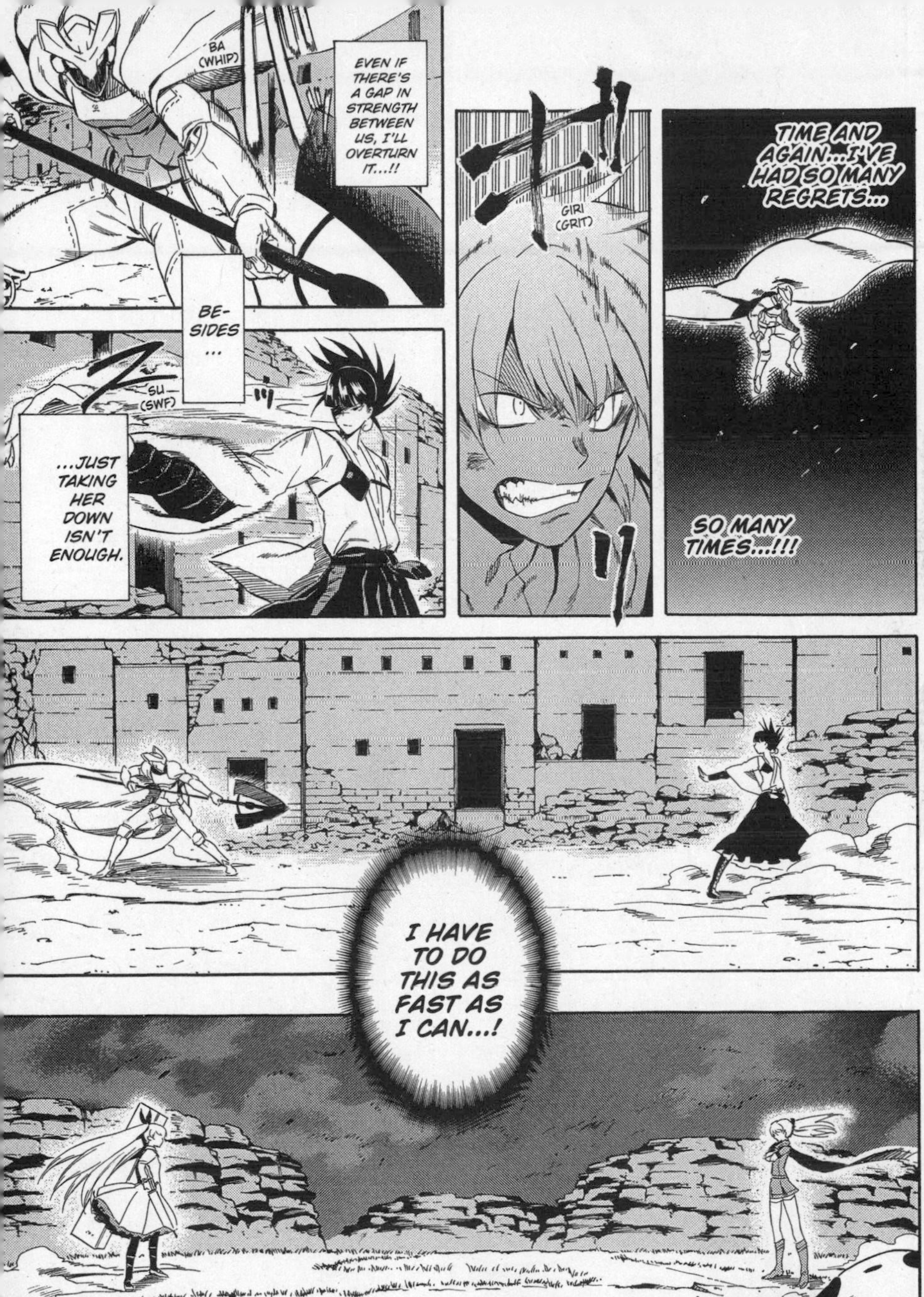
TIME AND AGAIN...I'VE HAD SO MANY REGRETS...
SO MANY TIMES...!!!
GIRI (GRIT)
EVEN IF THERE'S A GAP IN STRENGTH BETWEEN US, I'LL OVERTURN IT...!!
BA (WHIP)
BE- SIDES ...
SU (SWF)
...JUST TAKING HER DOWN ISN'T ENOUGH.
I HAVE TO DO THIS AS FAST AS I CAN...!

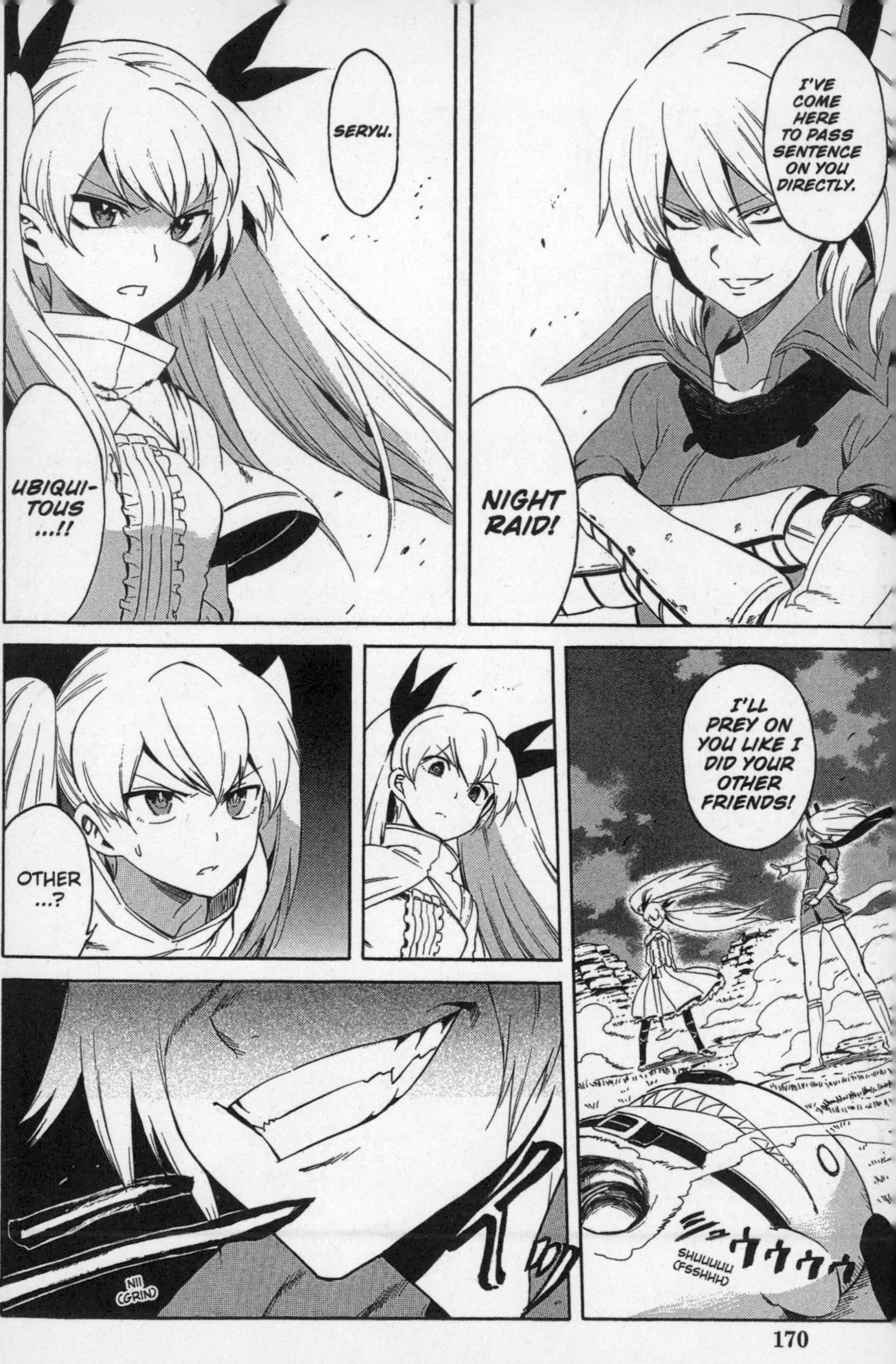
I'VE COME HERE TO PASS SENTENCE ON YOU DIRECTLY.
NIGHT RAID!
SERYU.
UBIQUITOUS ...!!
I'LL PREY ON YOU LIKE I DID YOUR OTHER FRIENDS!
OTHER ...?
SHUUUUU (FSSHHH)
NII (GRIN)

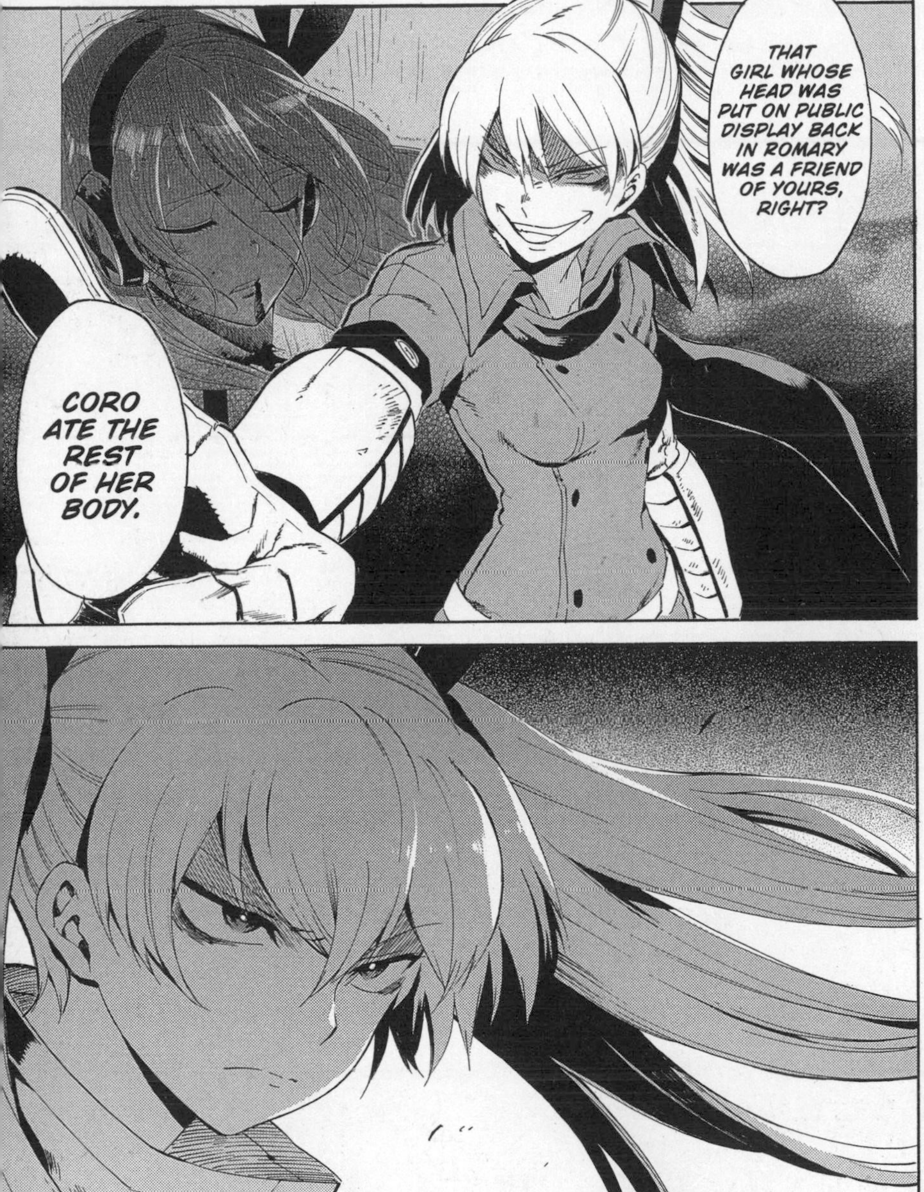
THAT GIRL WHOSE HEAD WAS PUT ON PUBLIC DISPLAY BACK IN ROMARY WAS A FRIEND OF YOURS, RIGHT?
CORO ATE THE REST OF HER BODY.

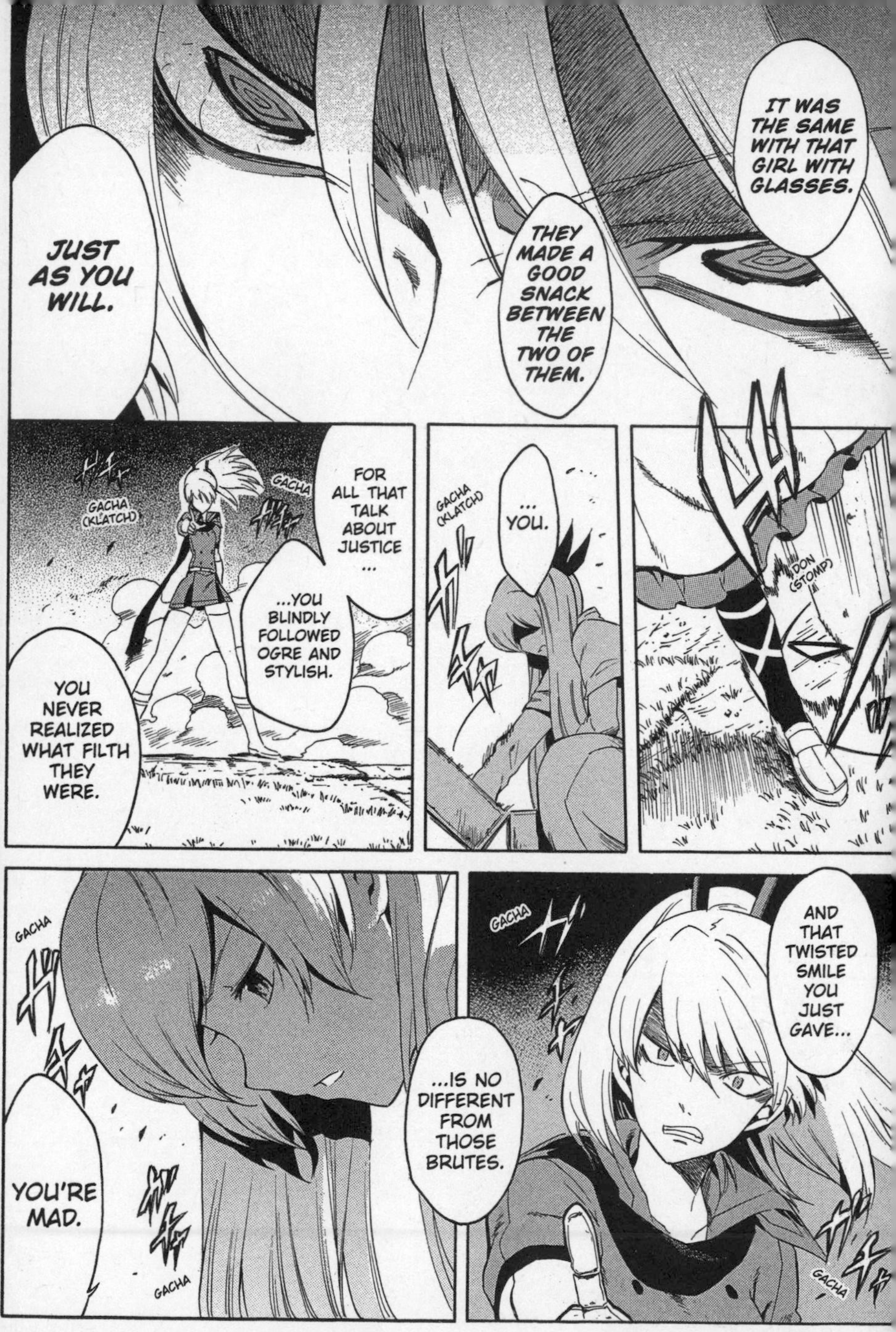
IT WAS THE SAME WITH THAT GIRL WITH GLASSES.
THEY MADE A GOOD SNACK BETWEEN THE TWO OF THEM.
JUST AS YOU WILL.
DON (STOMP)
GACHA (KLATCH)
... YOU.
FOR ALL THAT TALK ABOUT JUSTICE ...
...YOU BLINDLY FOLLOWED OGRE AND STYLISH.
GACHA
GACHA (KLATCH)
YOU NEVER REALIZED WHAT FILTH THEY WERE.
AND THAT TWISTED SMILE YOU JUST GAVE...
GACHA
...IS NO DIFFERENT FROM THOSE BRUTES.
GACHA
GACHA
YOU'RE MAD.
GACHA

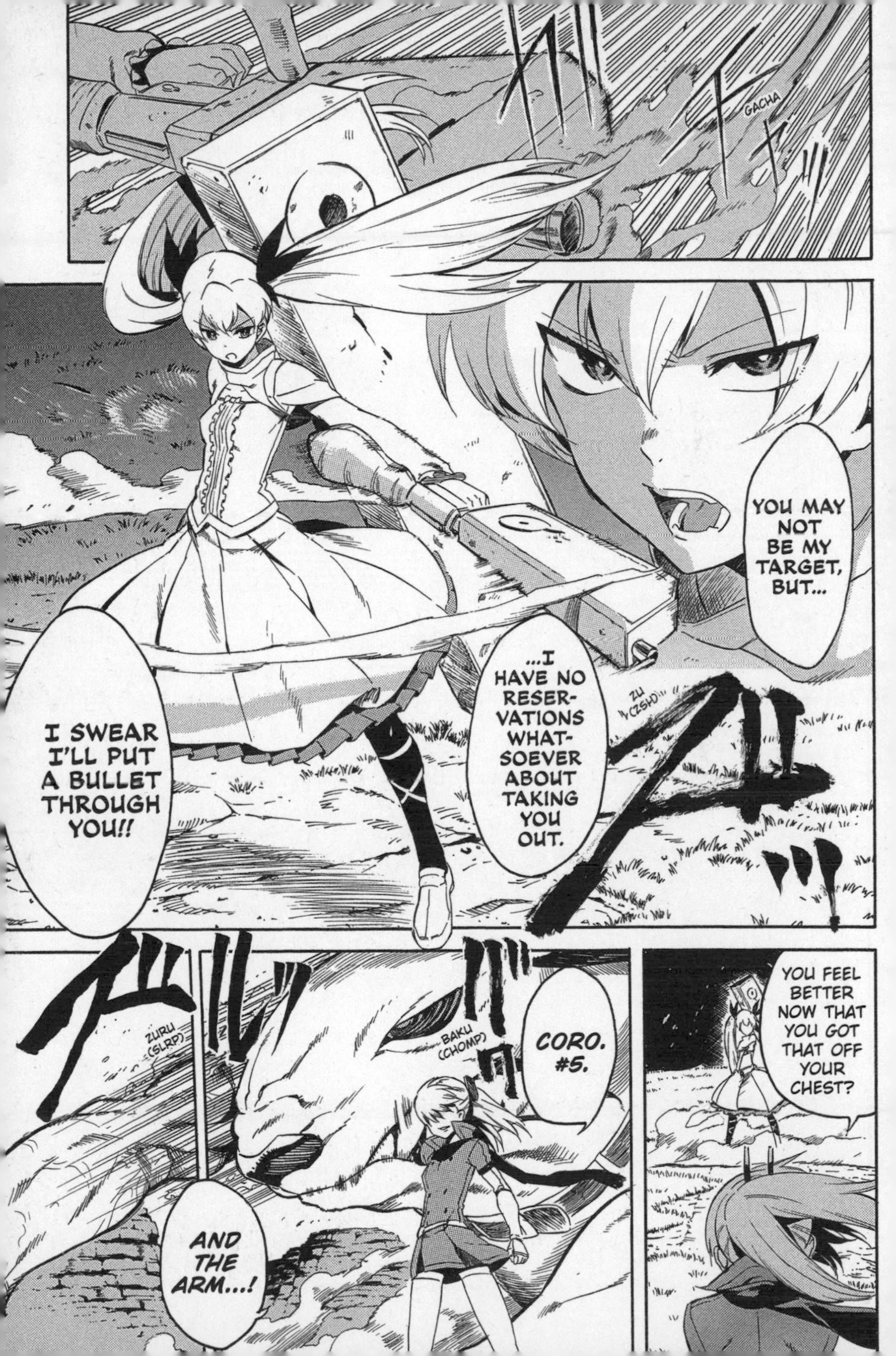
GACHA
YOU MAY NOT BE MY TARGET, BUT...
...I HAVE NO RESERVATIONS WHATSOEVER ABOUT TAKING YOU OUT.
ZU (ZSH)
I SWEAR I'LL PUT A BULLET THROUGH YOU!!
YOU FEEL BETTER NOW THAT YOU GOT THAT OFF YOUR CHEST?
CORO. #5.
BAKU (CHOMP)
ZURU (SLRP)
AND THE ARM...!

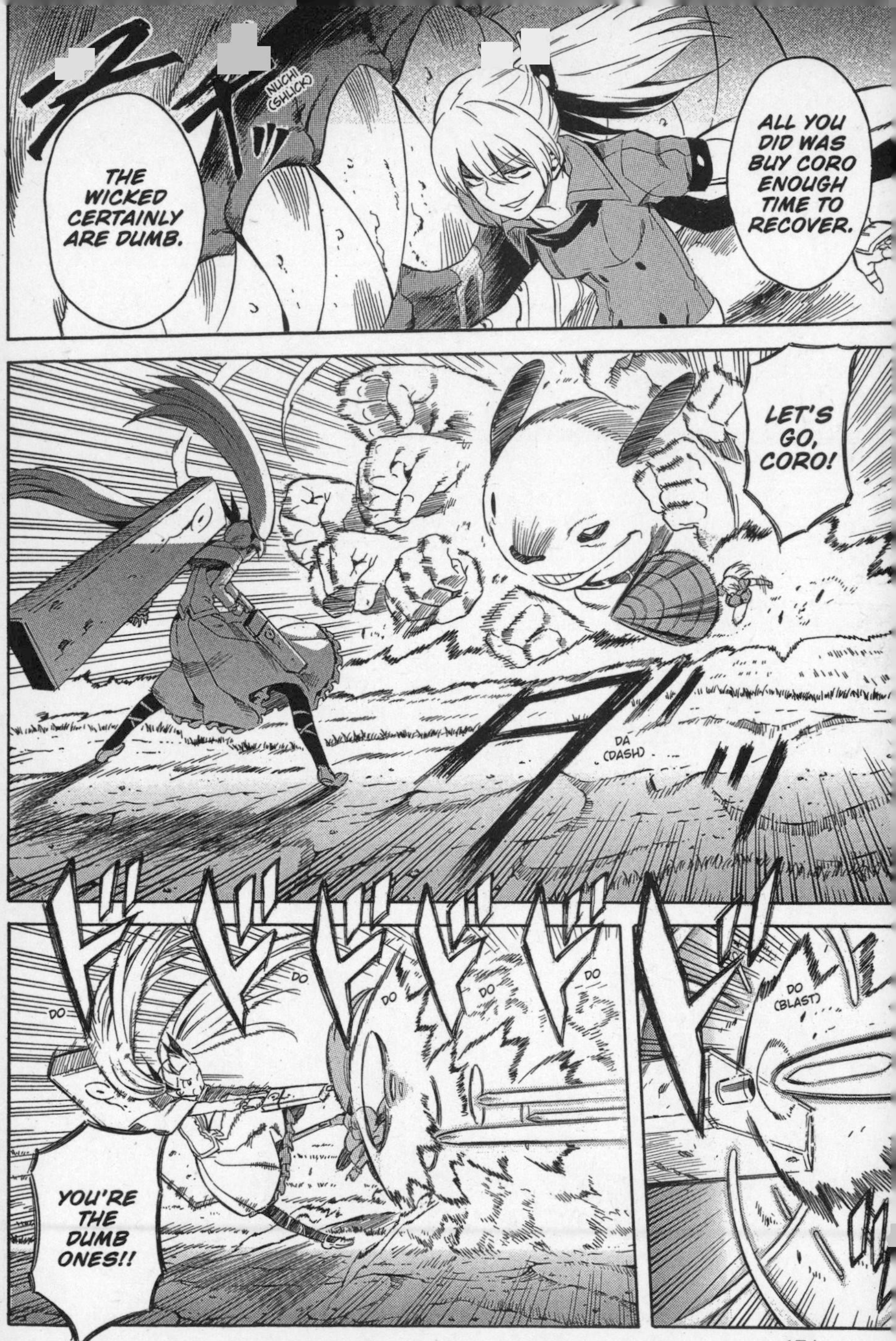

ALL YOU DID WAS BUY CORO ENOUGH TIME TO RECOVER.
NUCHI (SHLICK)
THE WICKED CERTAINLY ARE DUMB.
LET'S GO, CORO!
DA (DASH)
DO (BLAST)
DO
DO
DO
DO
DO
YOU'RE THE DUMB ONES!!

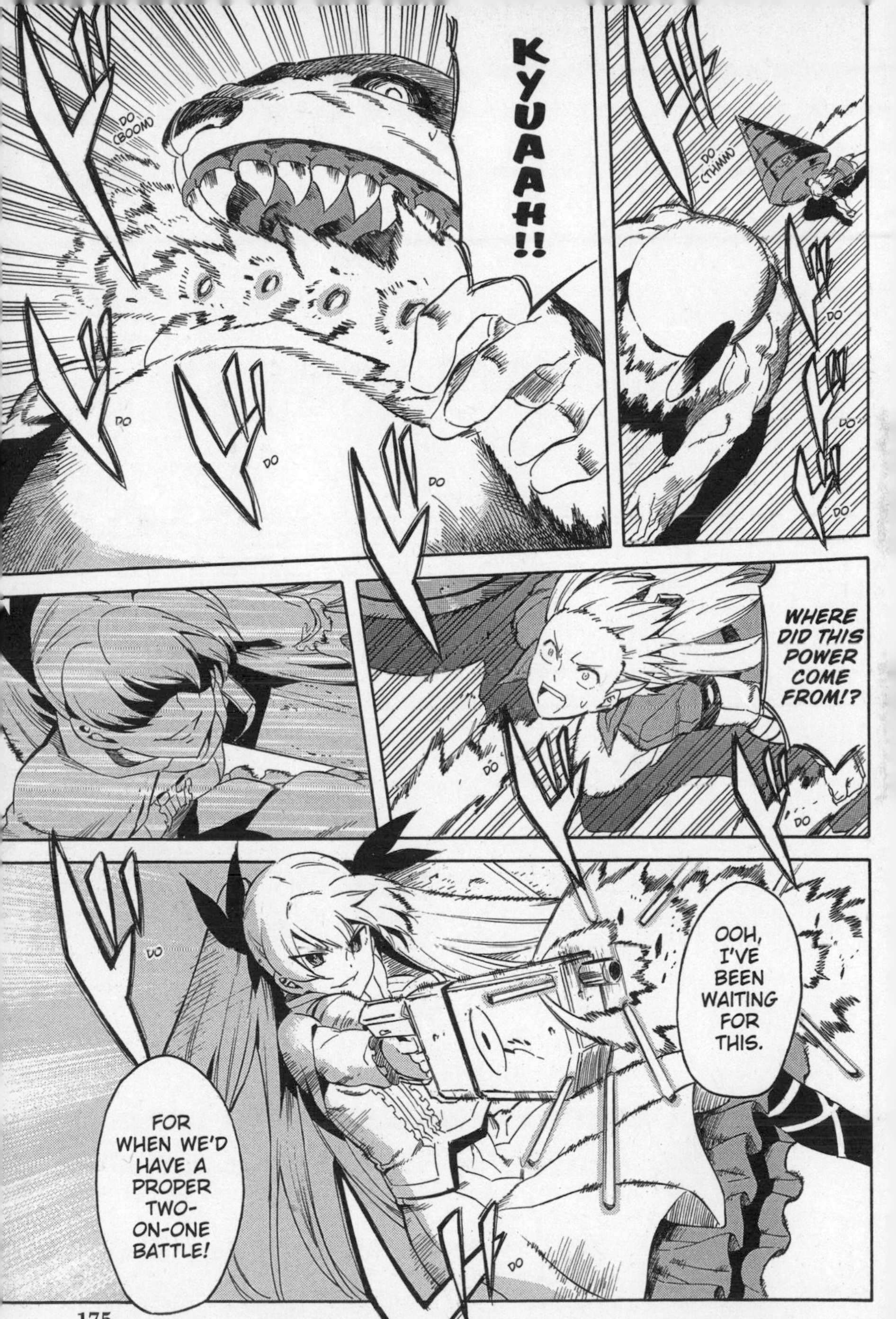
DO (THMM)
DO
DO
DO
DO (BOOM)
KYUAAH!!
DO
DO
DO
WHERE DID THIS POWER COME FROM!?
DO
DO
OOH, I'VE BEEN WAITING FOR THIS.
FOR WHEN WE'D HAVE A PROPER TWO-ON-ONE BATTLE!
DO
DO

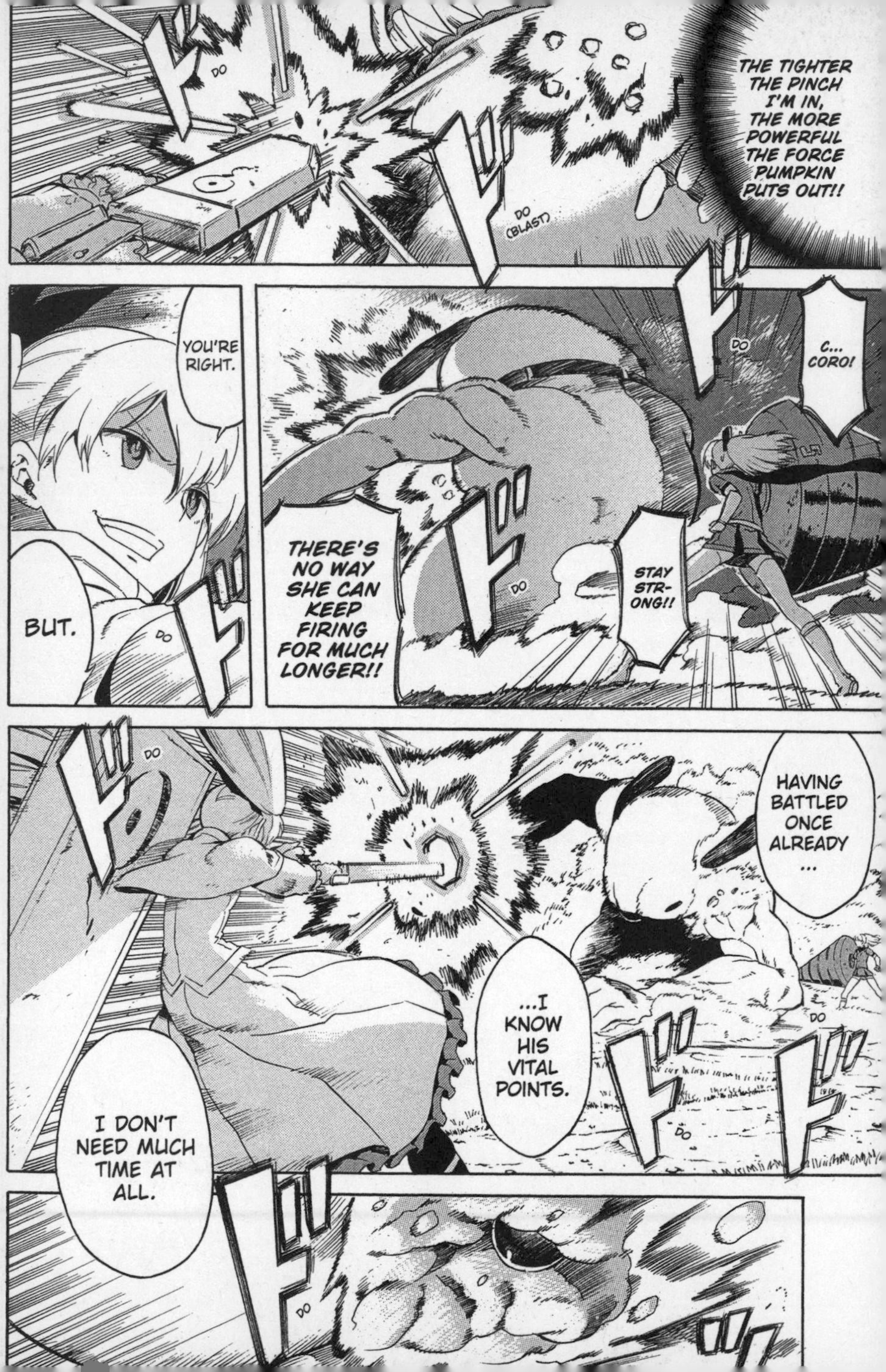
THE TIGHTER THE PINCH I'M IN, THE MORE POWERFUL THE FORCE PUMPKIN PUTS OUT!!
DO (BLAST)
DO
C... CORO!
DO
STAY STR-ONG!!
THERE'S NO WAY SHE CAN KEEP FIRING FOR MUCH LONGER!!
DO
YOU'RE RIGHT.
BUT.
DO
HAVING BATTLED ONCE ALREADY...
...I KNOW HIS VITAL POINTS.
I DON'T NEED MUCH TIME AT ALL.
DO
DO
DO
DO

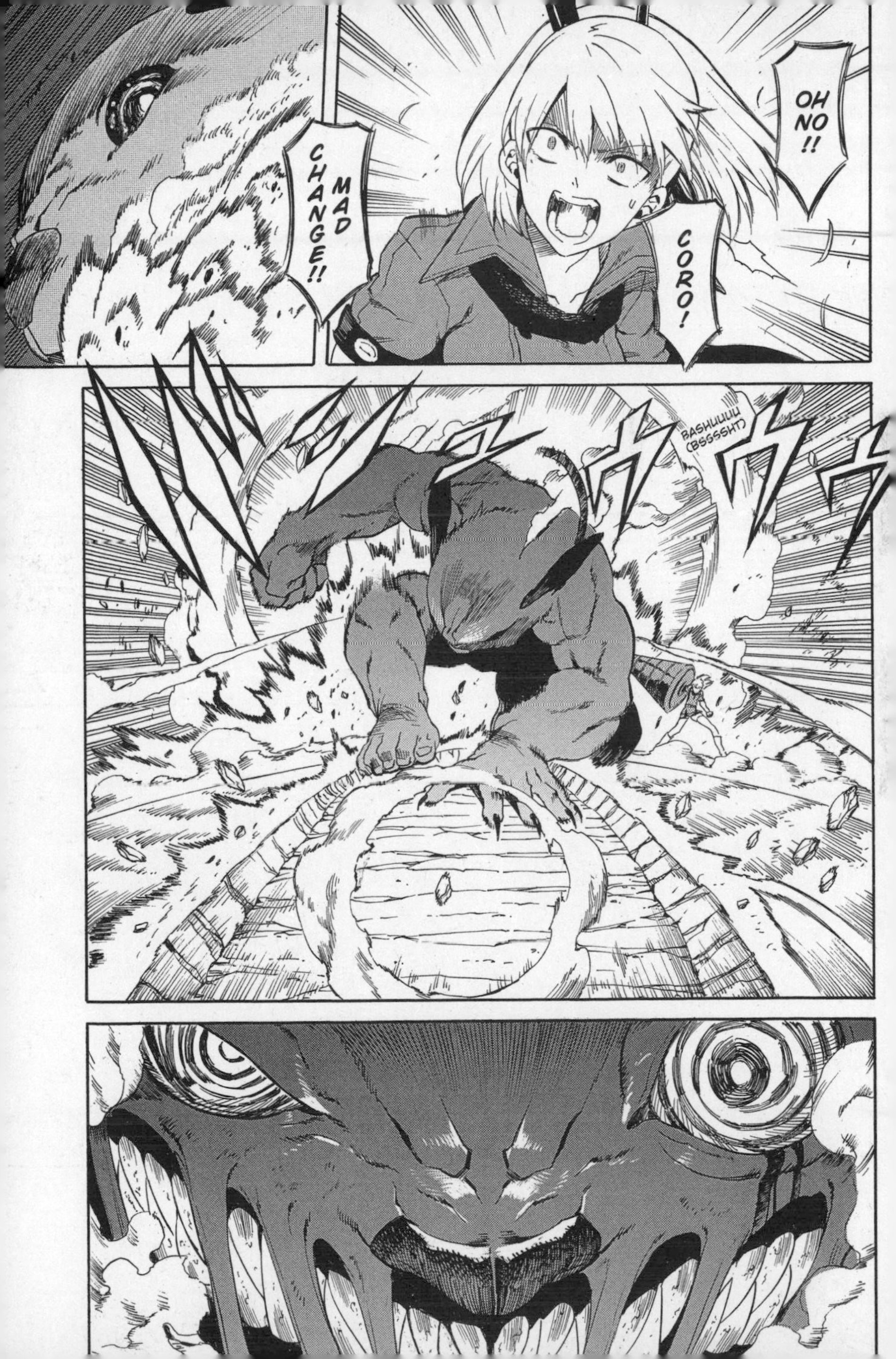
OH NO!!
CORO!
MAD CHANGE!!
BASHUUUU (BSGSSHT)

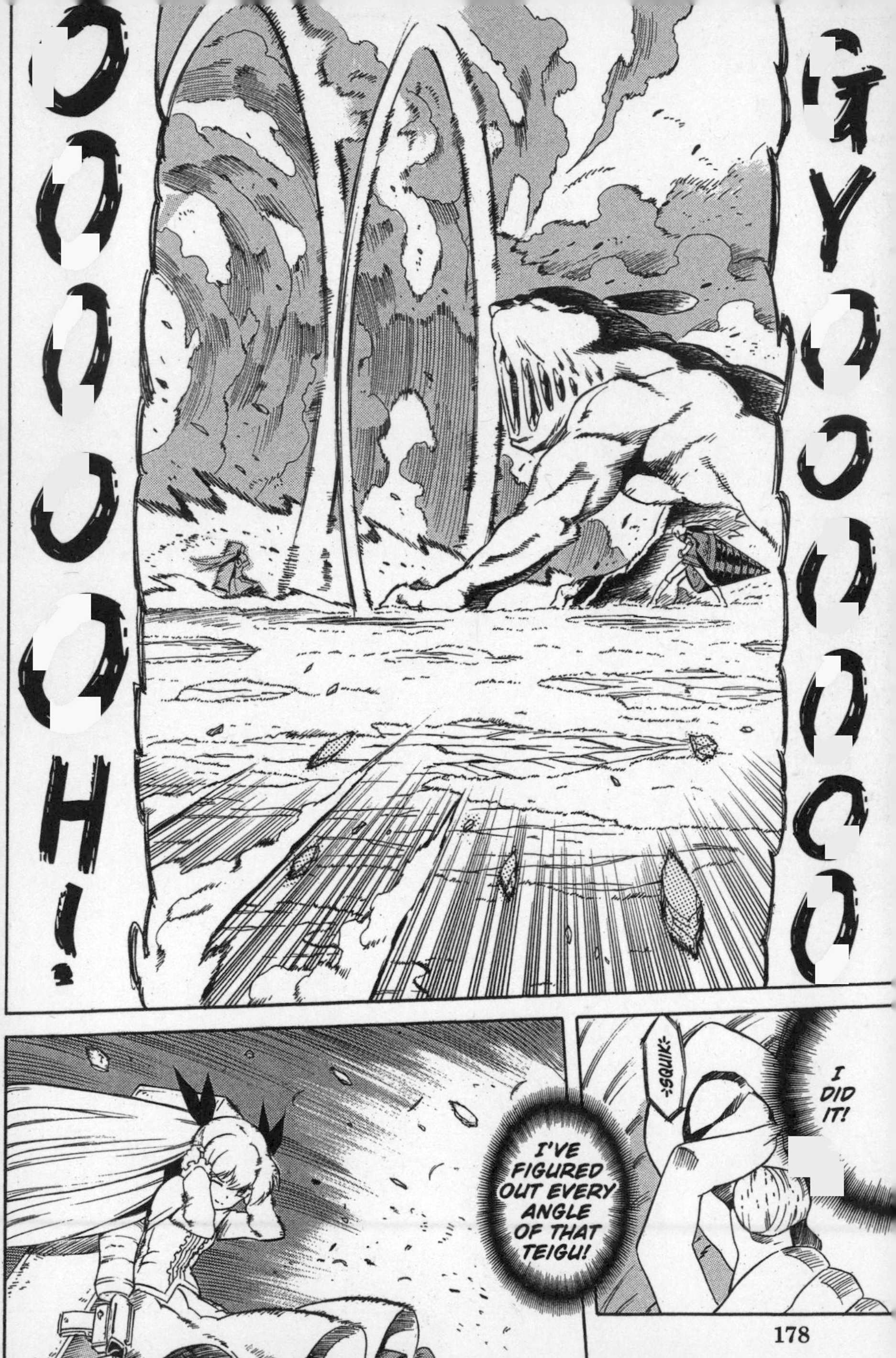
GYOOOOOO
OOOOOH!
SQUIK
I DID IT!
I'VE FIGURED OUT EVERY ANGLE OF THAT TEIGU!

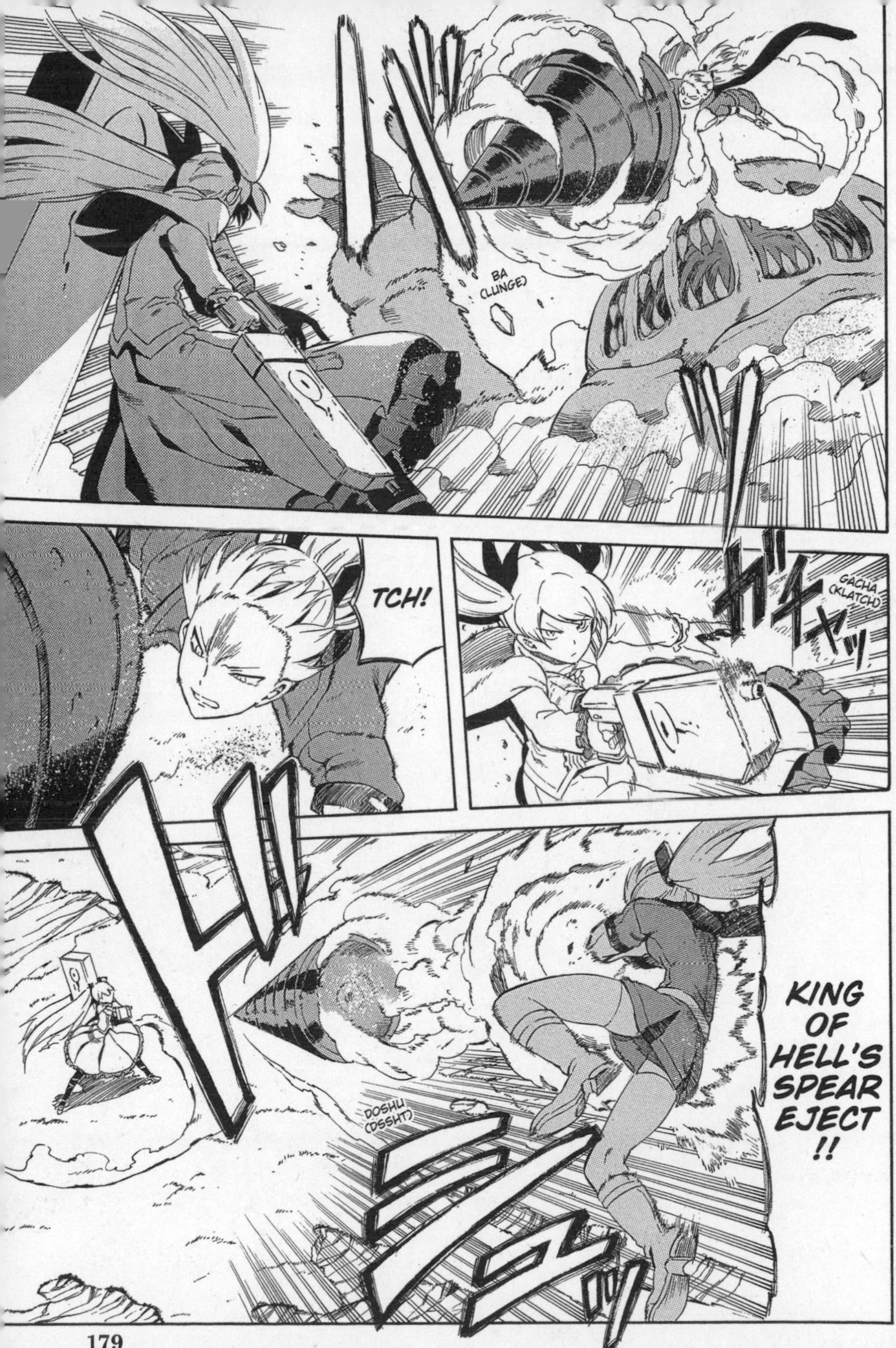
BA
(LUNGE)
GACHA
(KLATCH)
TCH!
KING OF HELL'S SPEAR EJECT!!
DOSHU
(DSSHT)

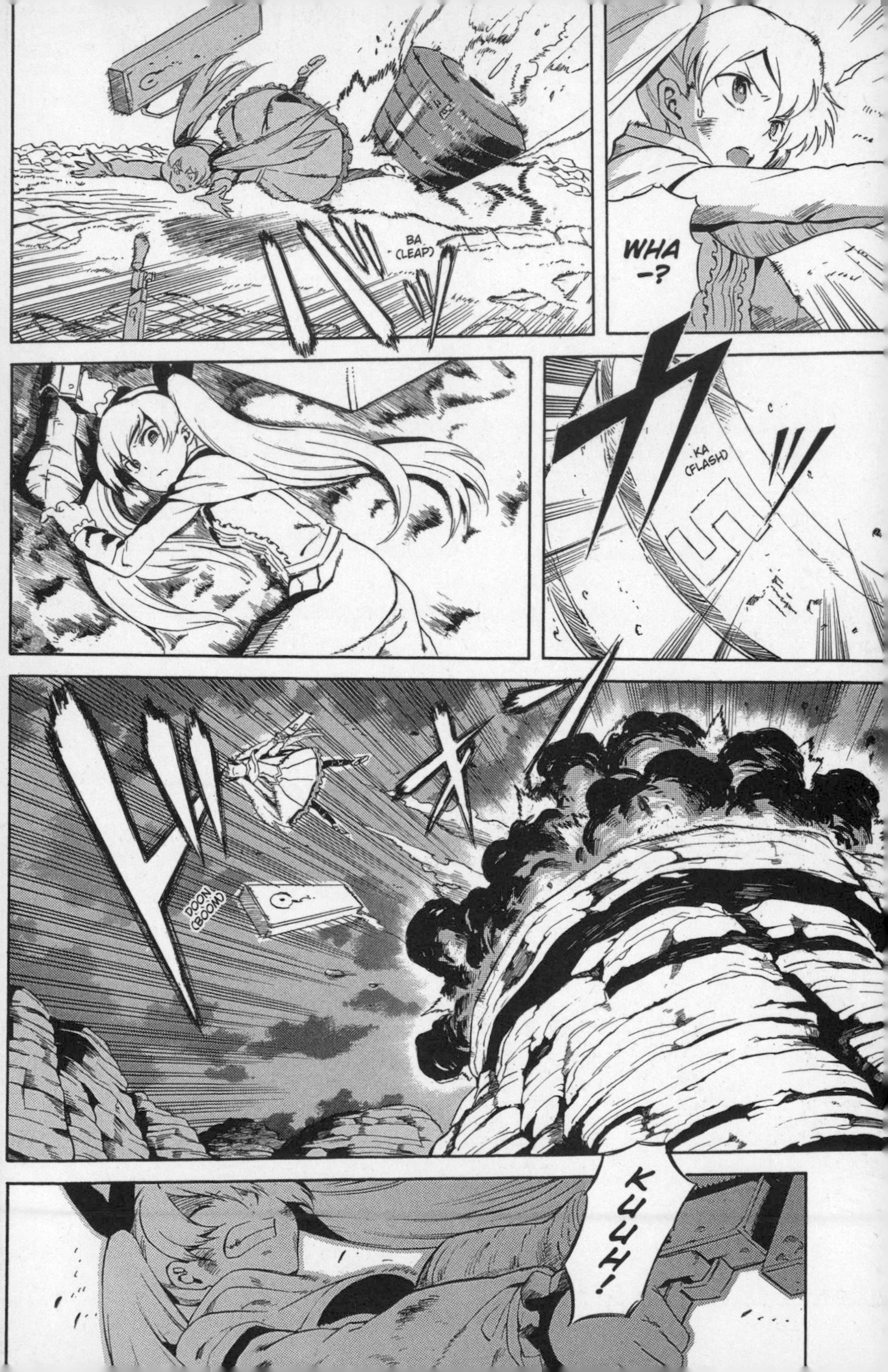
WHA
-?
BA
(LEAP)
KA
(FLASH)
DOON
(BOOM)
KUUH!

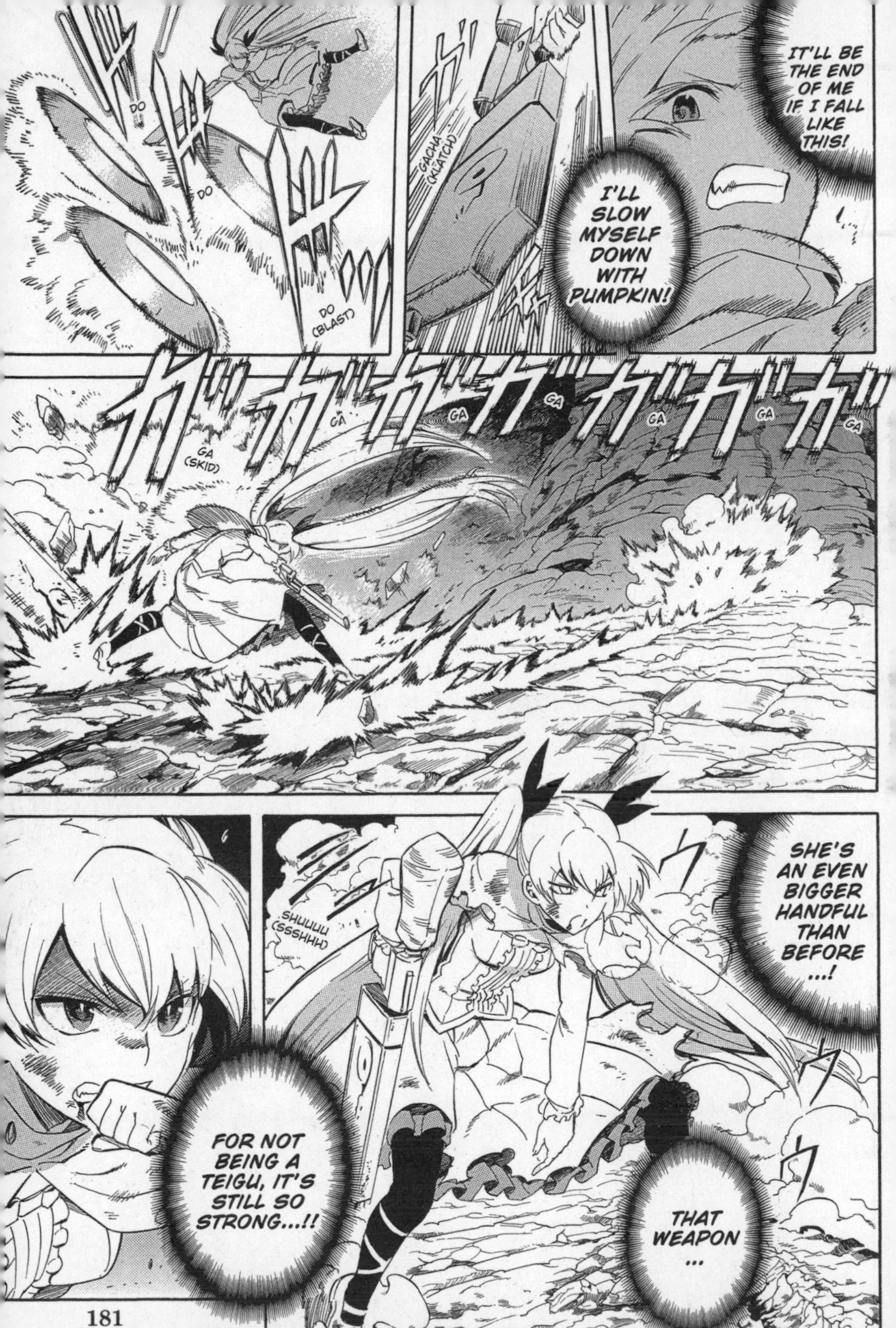
IT'LL BE THE END OF ME IF I FALL LIKE THIS!
I'LL SLOW MYSELF DOWN WITH PUMPKIN!
GACHA (KLATCH)
DO
DO
DO (BLAST)
GA (SKID)
GA
GA
GA
GA
GA
GA
SHE'S AN EVEN BIGGER HANDFUL THAN BEFORE ...!
SHUUUU (SSSHHH)
THAT WEAPON ...
FOR NOT BEING A TEIGU, IT'S STILL SO STRONG...!!

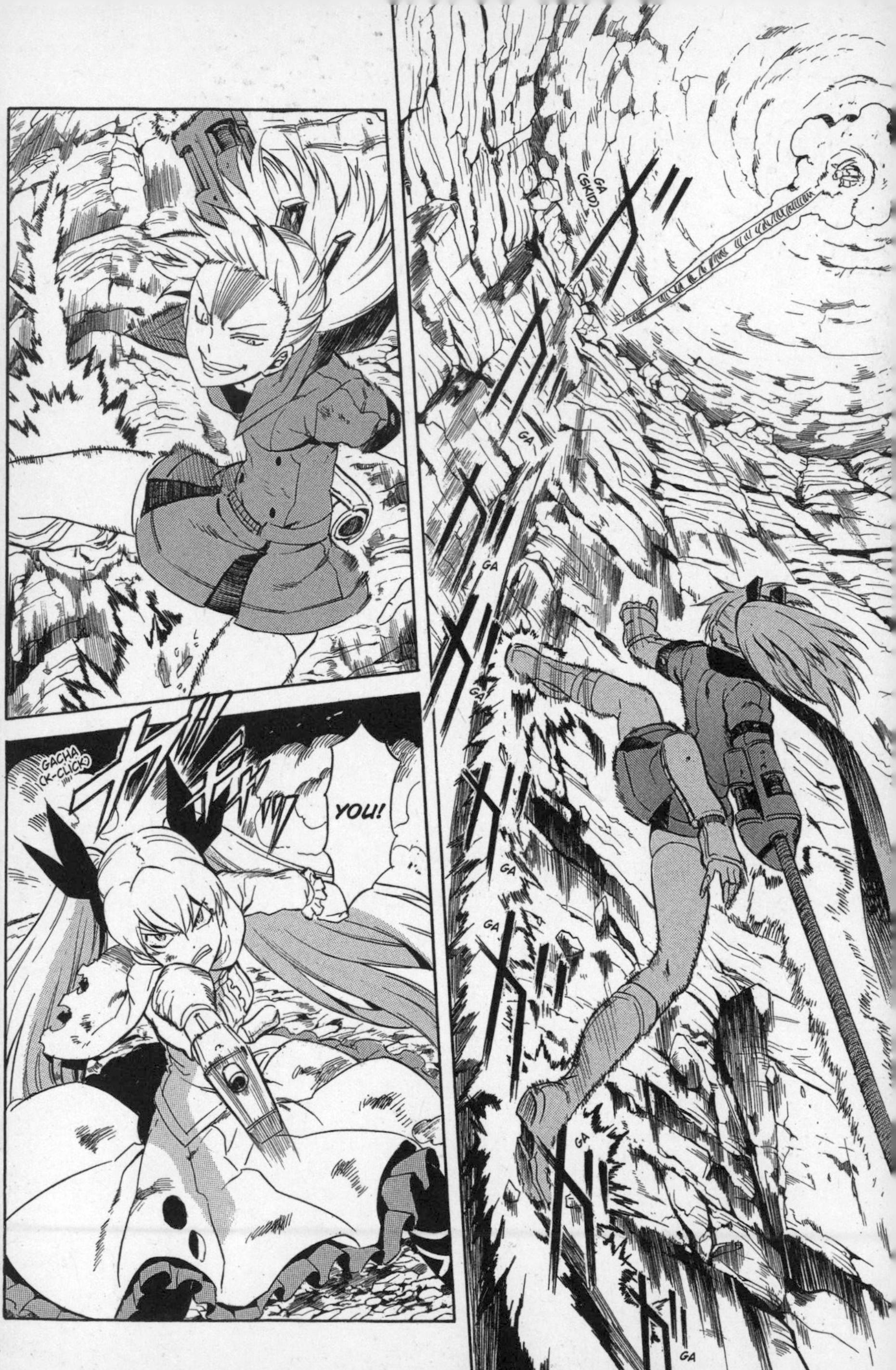
GA (SKID)
GA
GA
GA
GA
GA
GA
GA
GACHA (K-CLICK)
YOU!

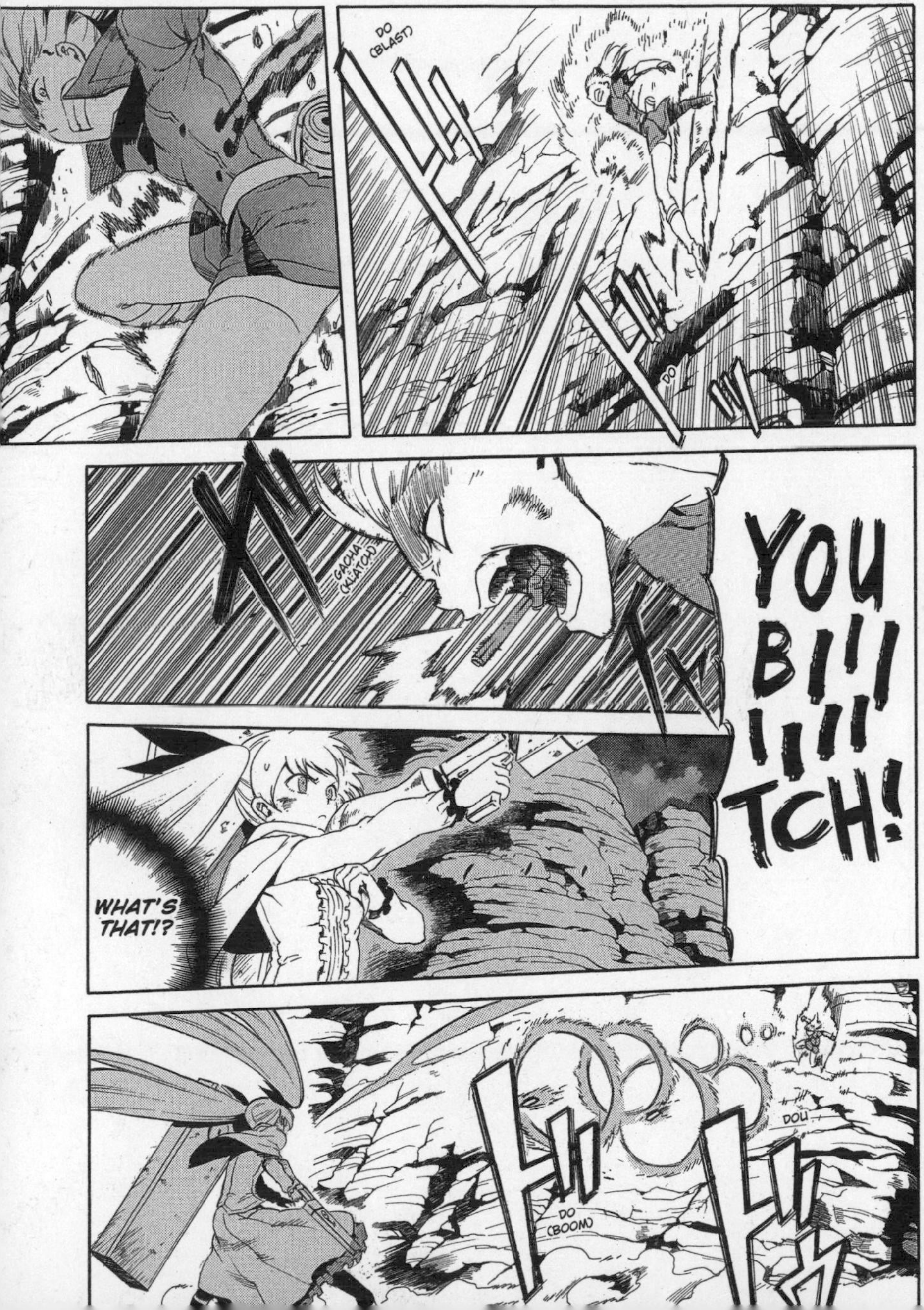
DO (BLAST)
DO
GACHA (KLATCH)
YOU BIIIIIIITCH!
WHAT'S THAT!?
DOU
DO (BOOM)

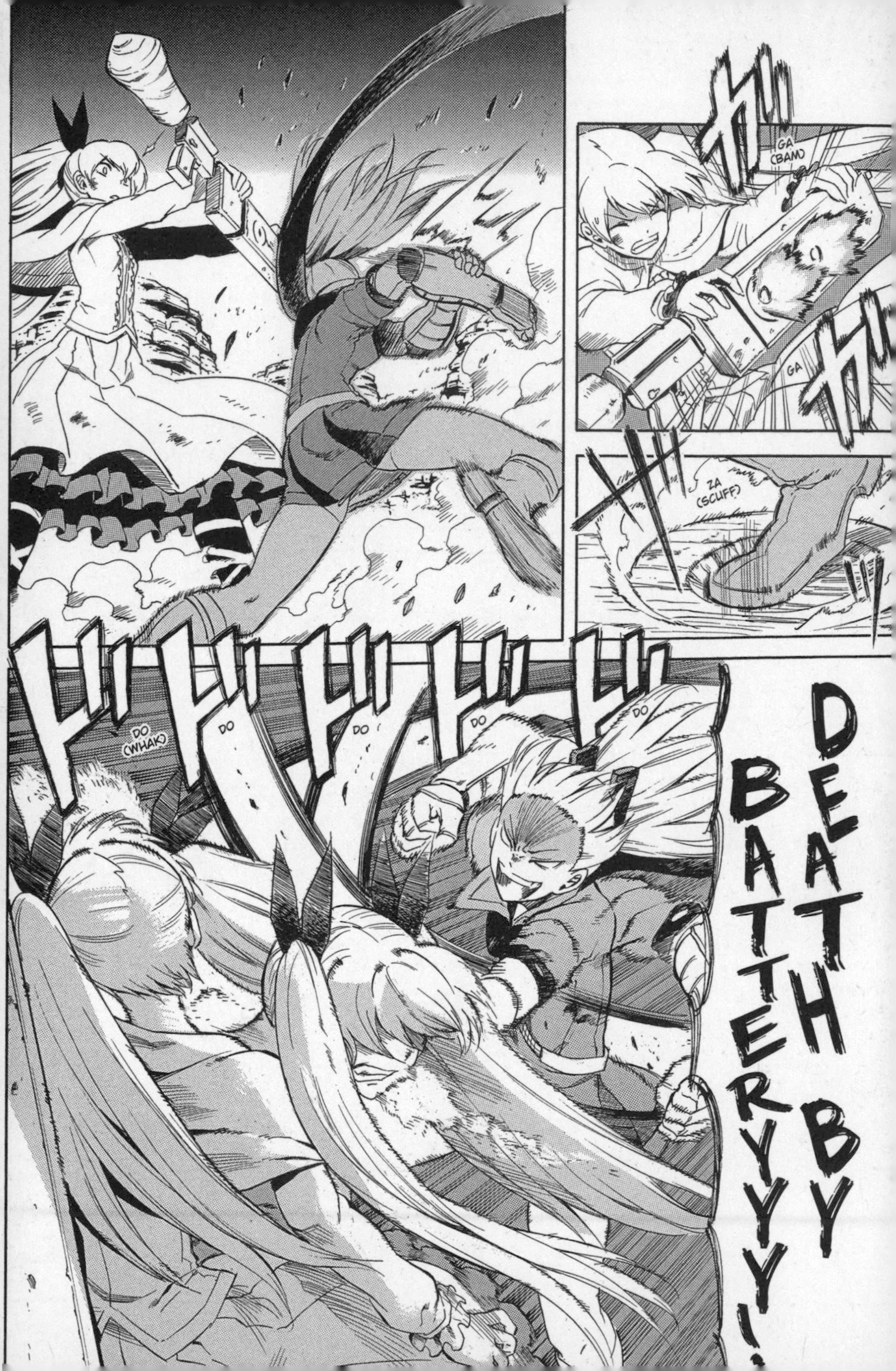
GA
(BAM)
GA
ZA
(SCUFF)
DO
(WHAK)
DO
DO
DO
DO
DEATH BY
BATTERYYY!

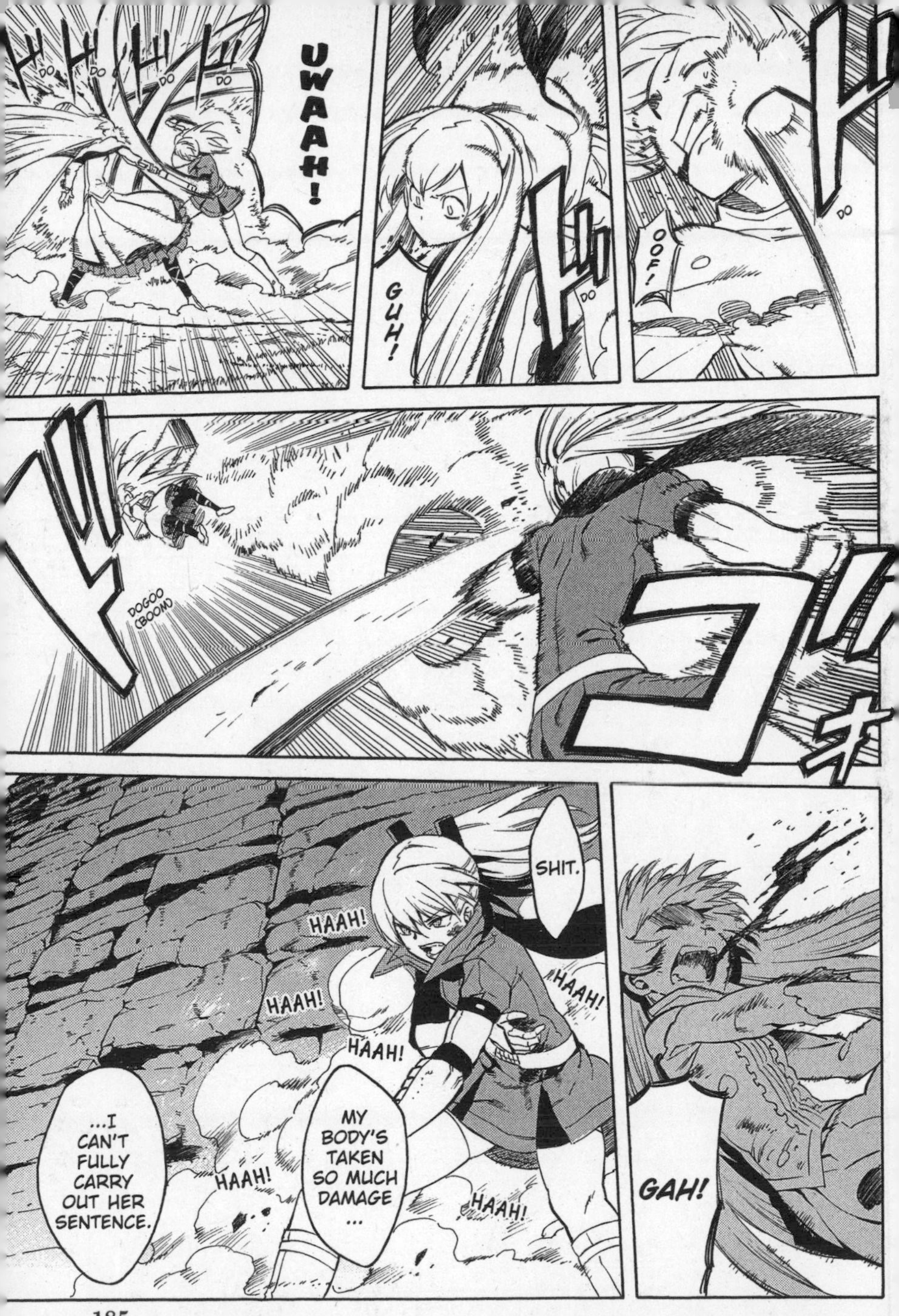
DO
OOF!
DO
GUH!
UWAAH!
DO
DO
DO
DO
DOGOO (BOOM)
GAH!
SHIT.
HAAH!
HAAH!
HAAH!
HAAH!
HAAH!
HAAH!
MY BODY'S TAKEN SO MUCH DAMAGE...
...I CAN'T FULLY CARRY OUT HER SENTENCE.

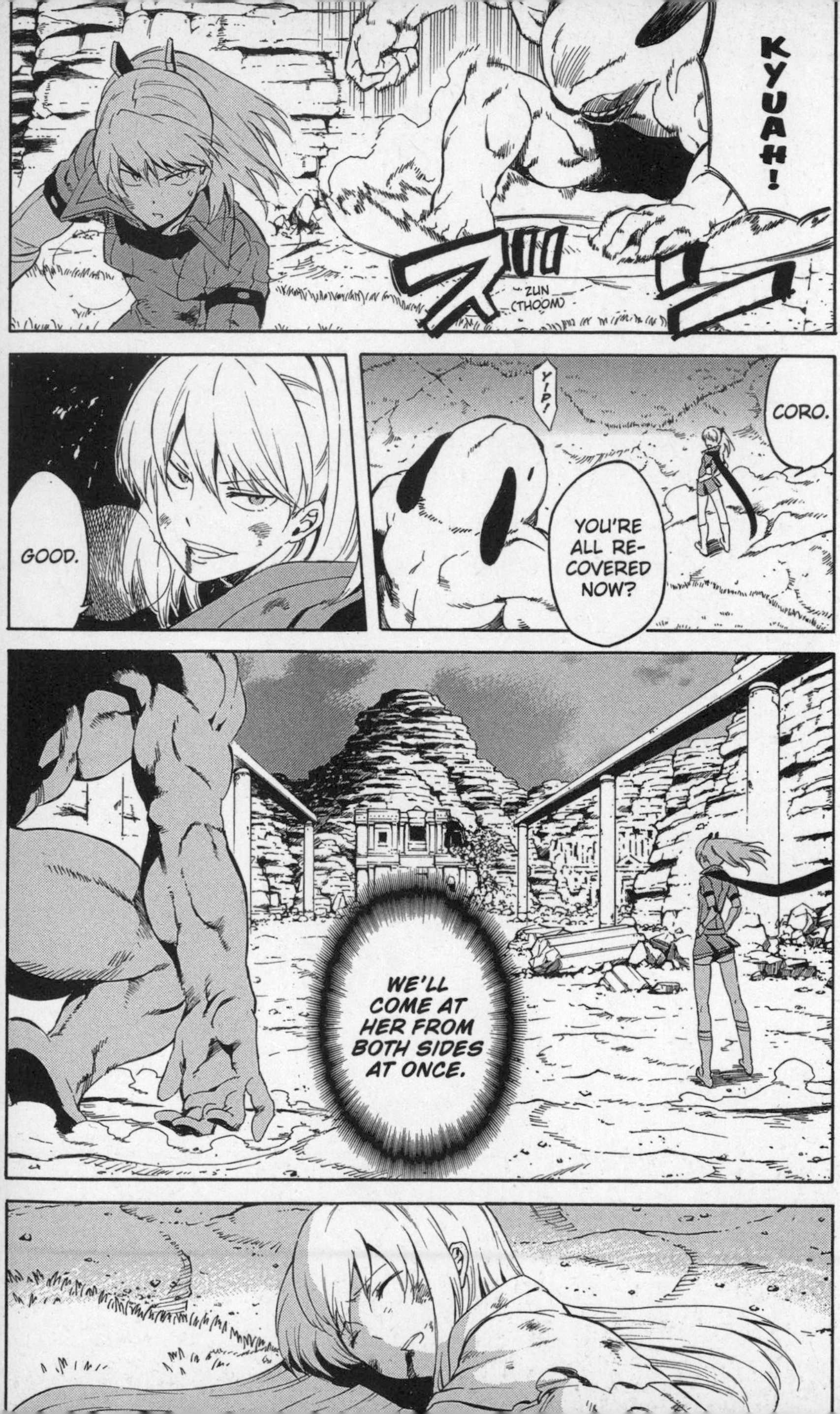
KYUAH!
ZUN (THOOM)
CORO.
YIP!
YOU'RE ALL RE-COVERED NOW?
GOOD.
WE'LL COME AT HER FROM BOTH SIDES AT ONCE.

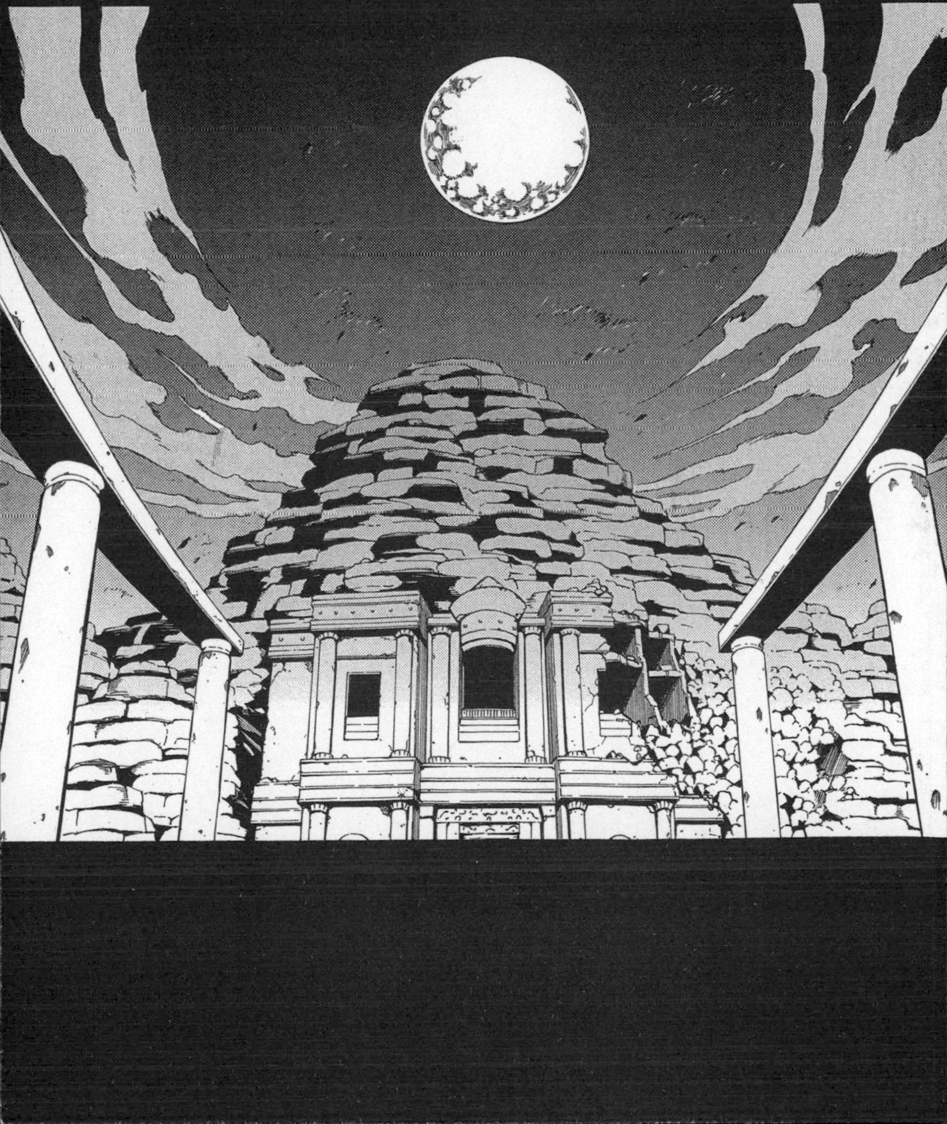

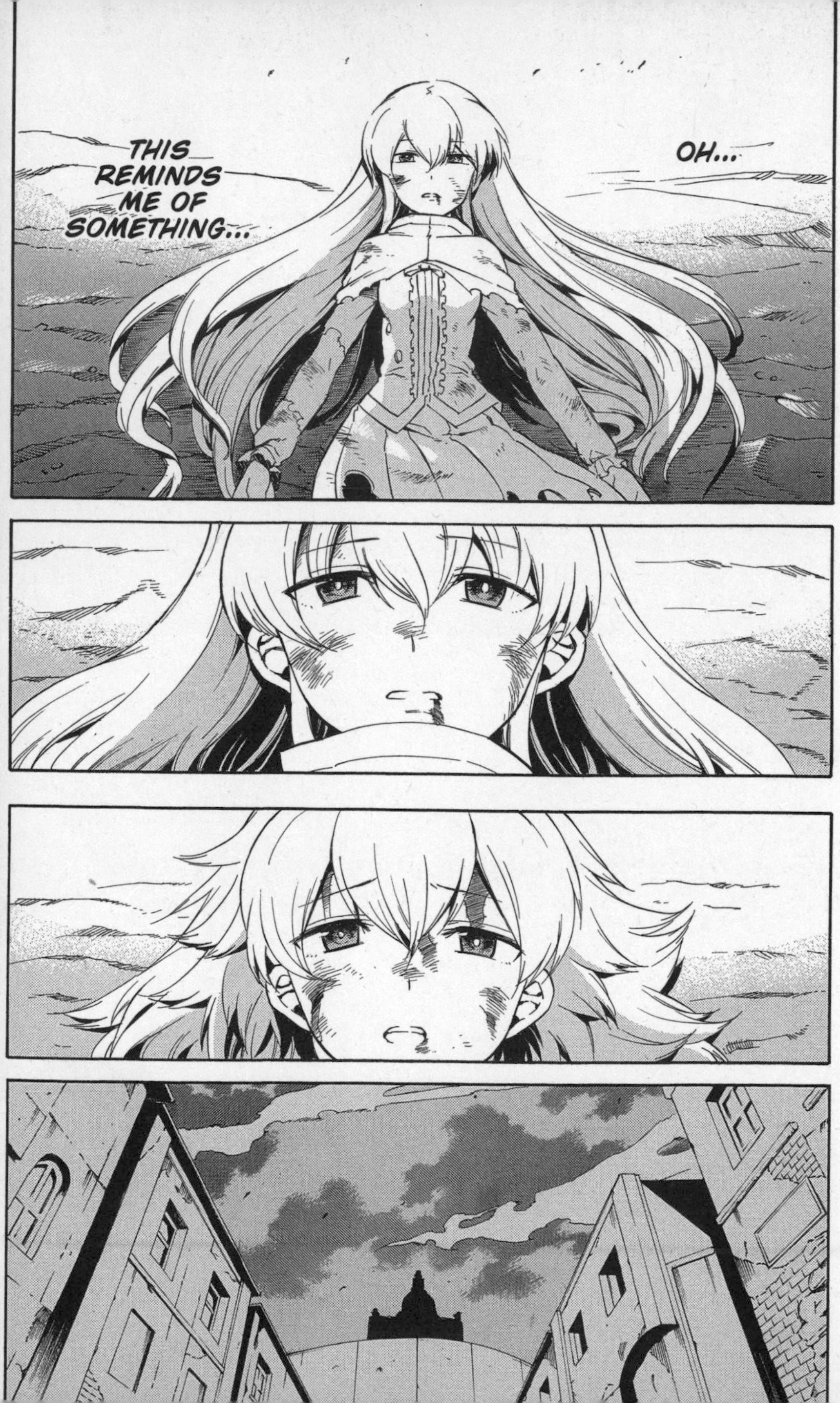
OH...
THIS REMINDS ME OF SOMETHING...

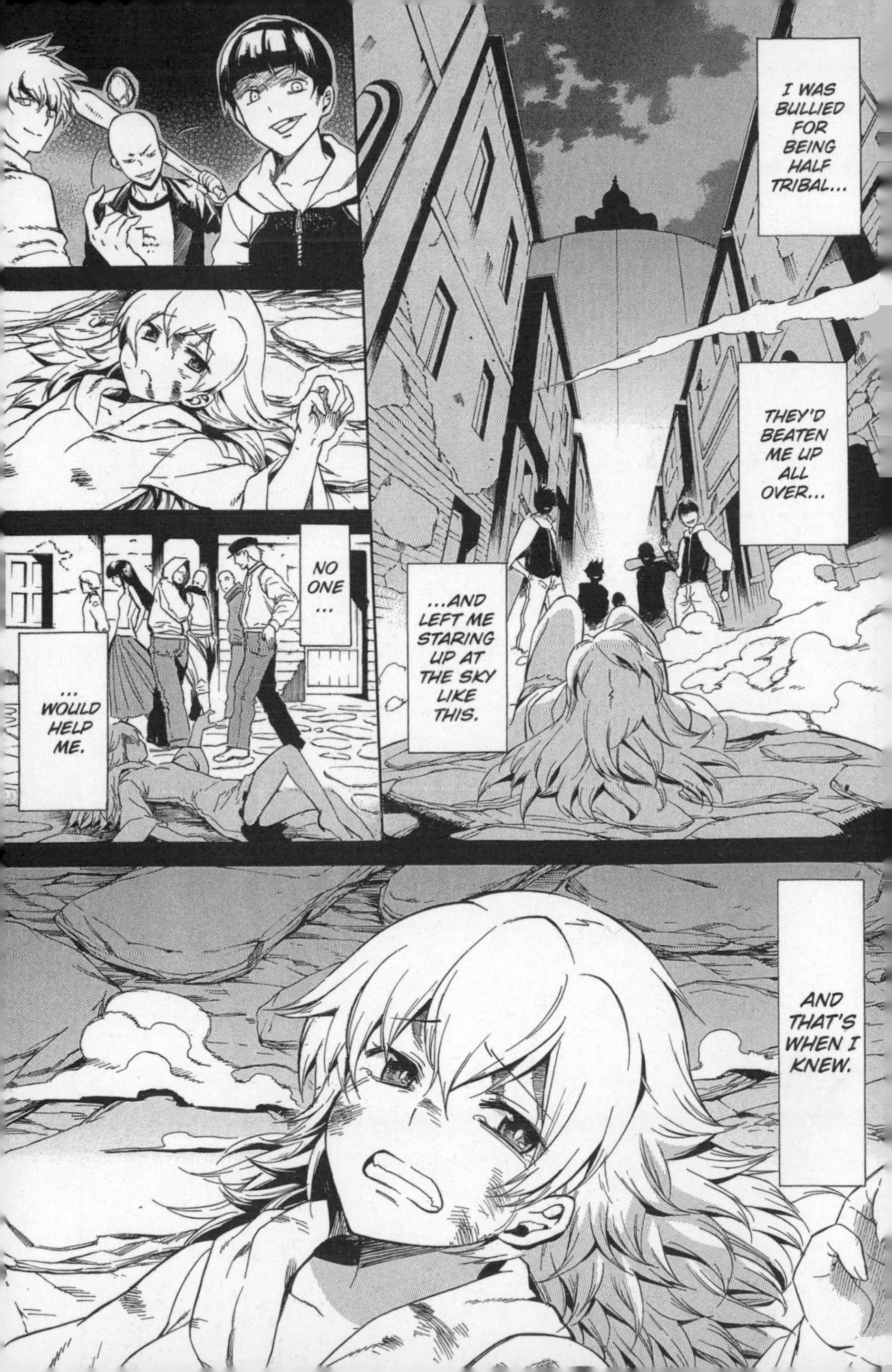
I WAS BULLIED FOR BEING HALF TRIBAL...
THEY'D BEATEN ME UP ALL OVER...
...AND LEFT ME STARING UP AT THE SKY LIKE THIS.
NO ONE...
...WOULD HELP ME.
AND THAT'S WHEN I KNEW.

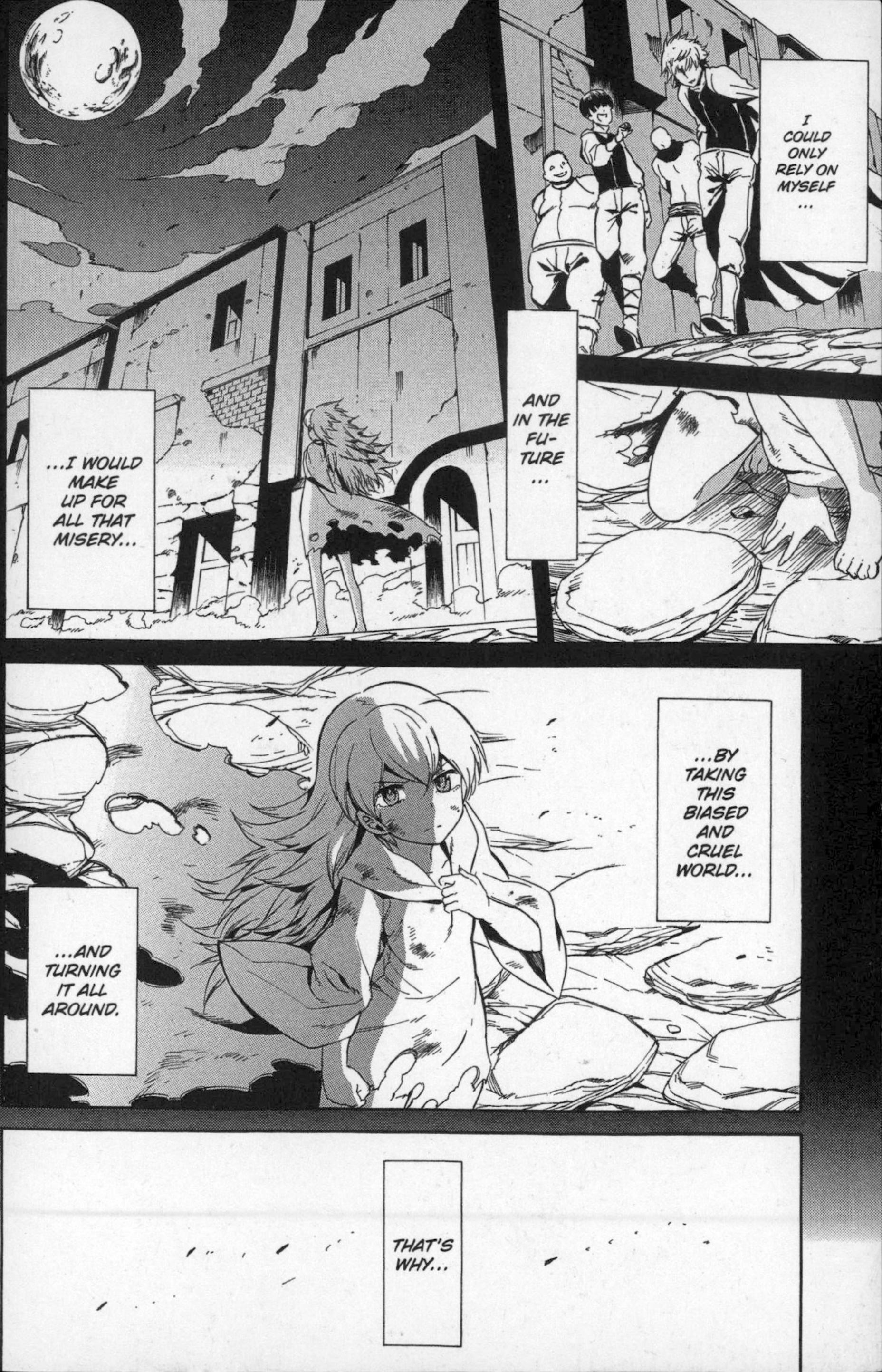
I COULD ONLY RELY ON MYSELF...
AND IN THE FU-TURE...
...I WOULD MAKE UP FOR ALL THAT MISERY...
...BY TAKING THIS BIASED AND CRUEL WORLD...
...AND TURNING IT ALL AROUND.
THAT'S WHY...

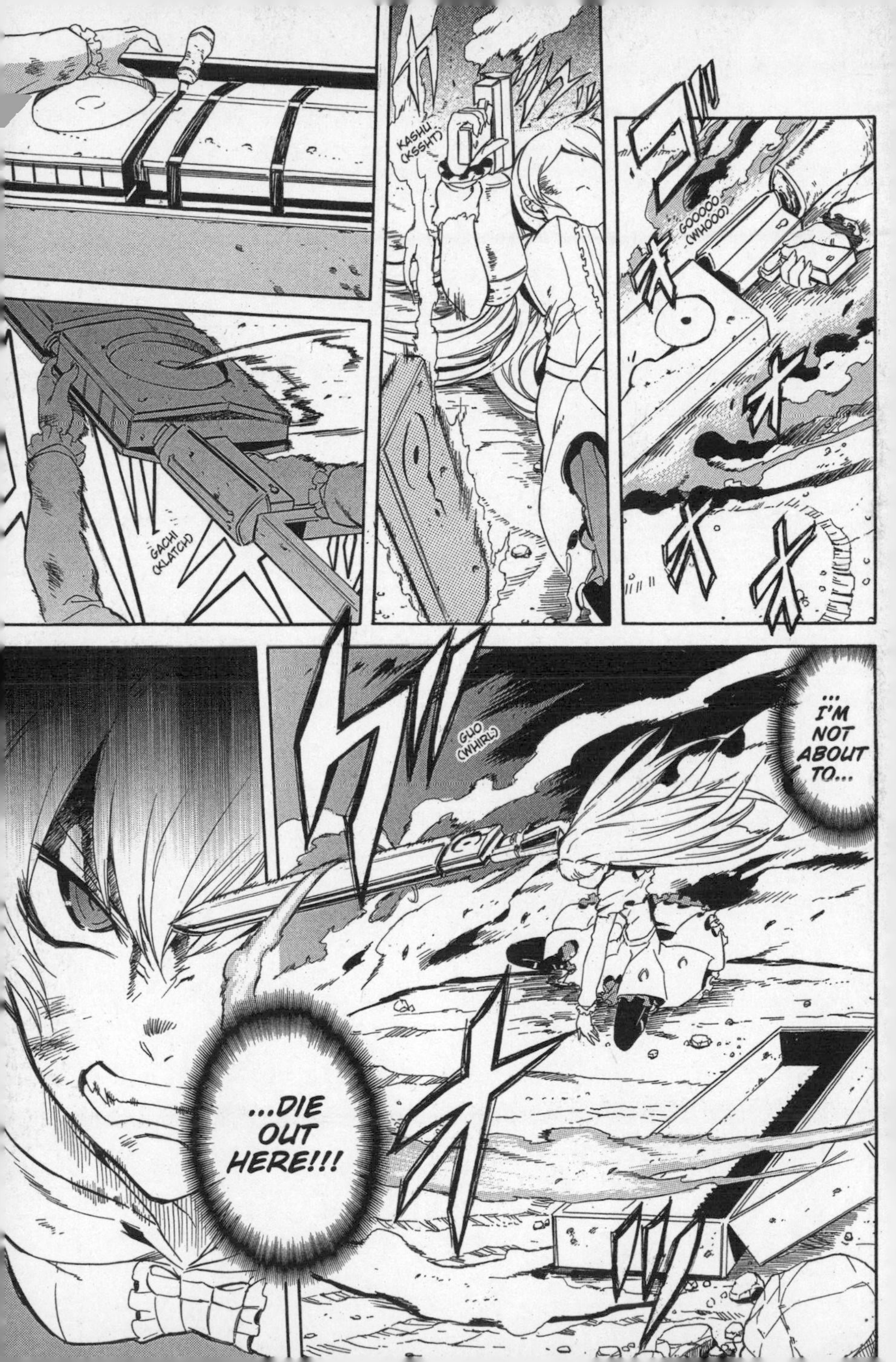

KASHU (KSSHT)
GOOOOO (WHOOO)
GACHI (KLATCH)
GUO (WHIRL)
...I'M NOT ABOUT TO...
...DIE OUT HERE!!!

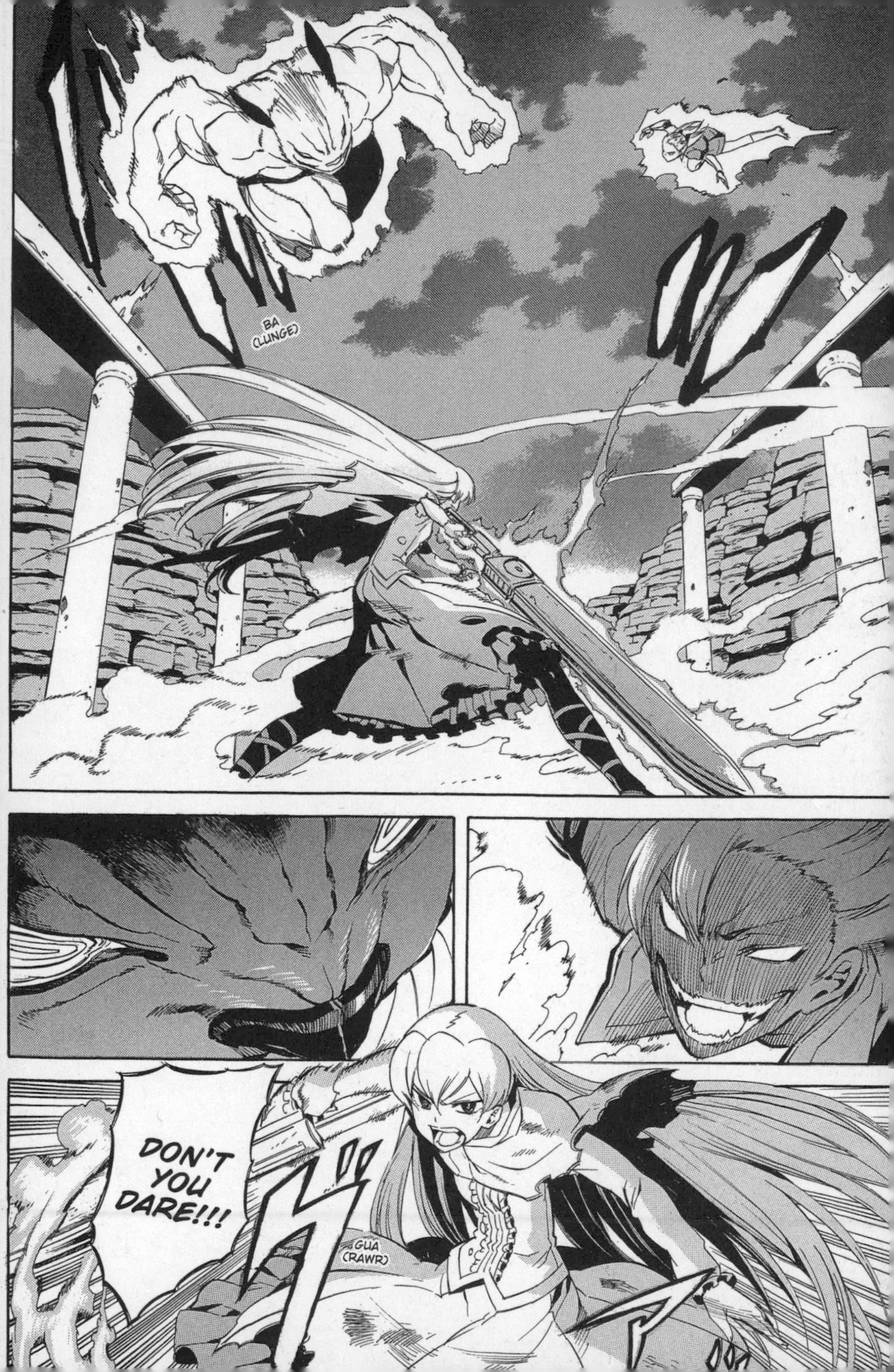
BA
(LUNGE)
DON'T YOU DARE!!!
GUA
(RAWR)

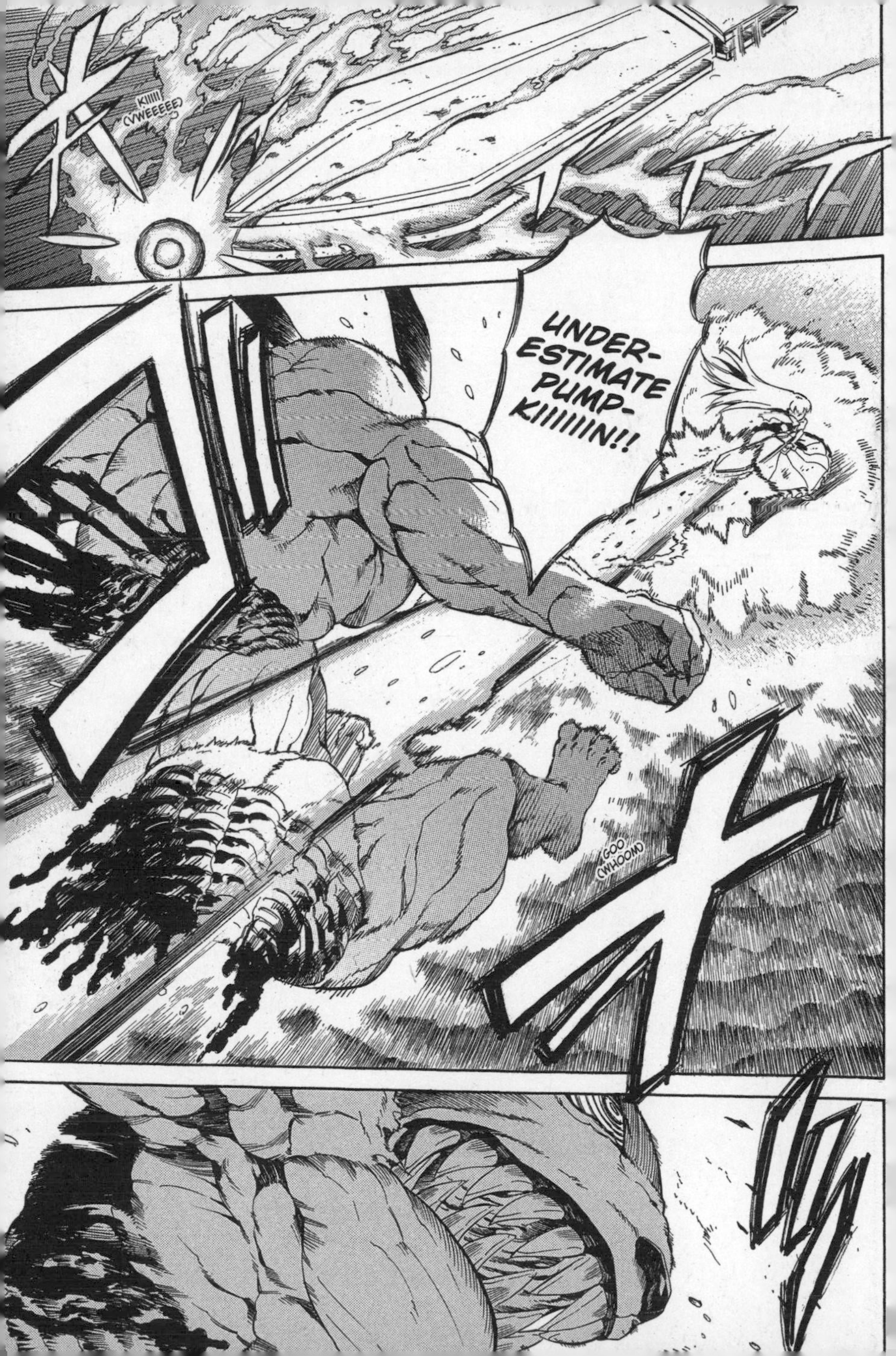
KIIIII (VWEEEEE)
UNDER-ESTIMATE PUMP-KIIIIIIN!!
GOO (WHOOM)

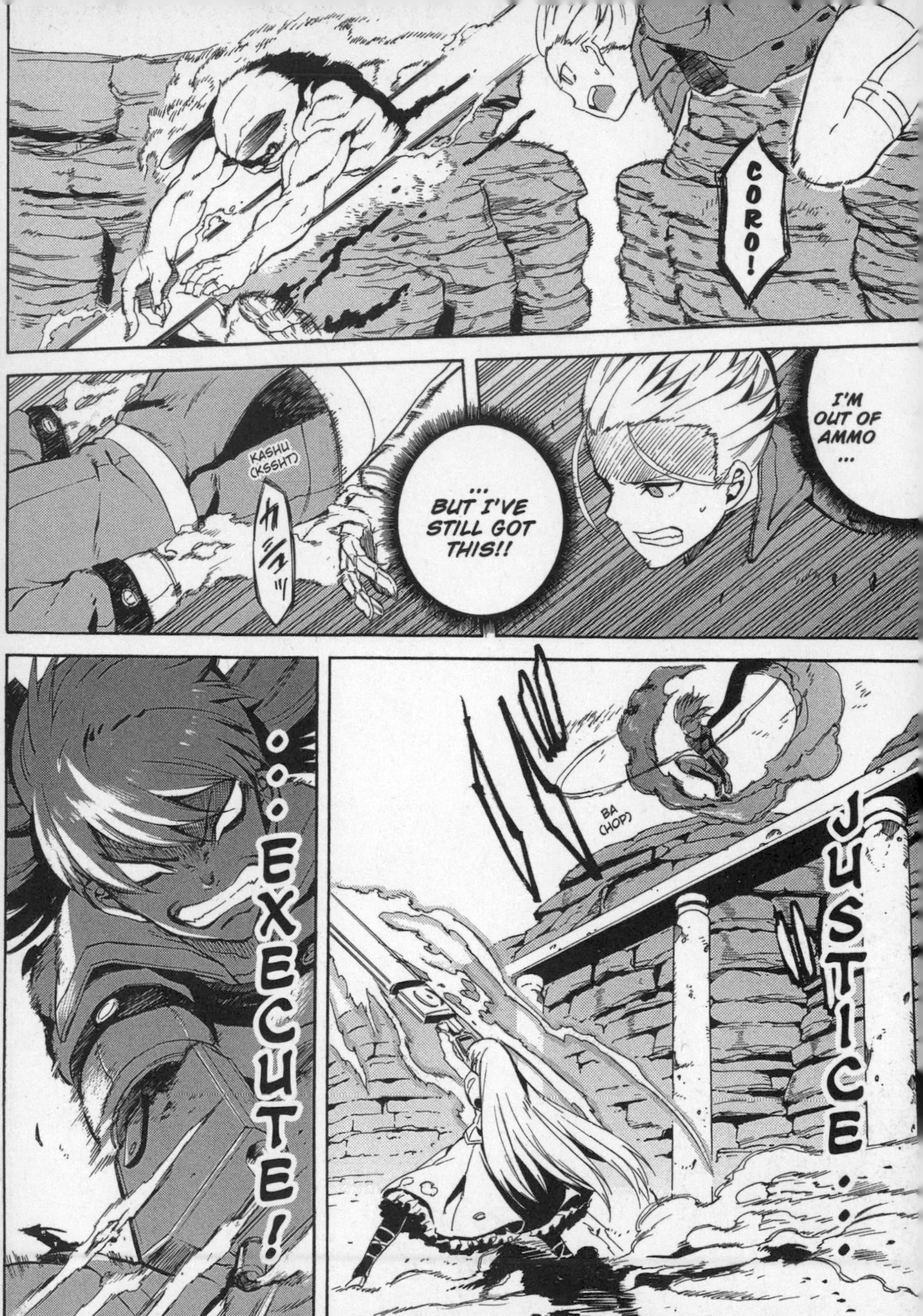

CORO!
I'M OUT OF AMMO...
... BUT I'VE STILL GOT THIS!!
KASHU (KSSHT)
カシュッ
BA (HOP)
JUSTICE...
...EXECUTE!

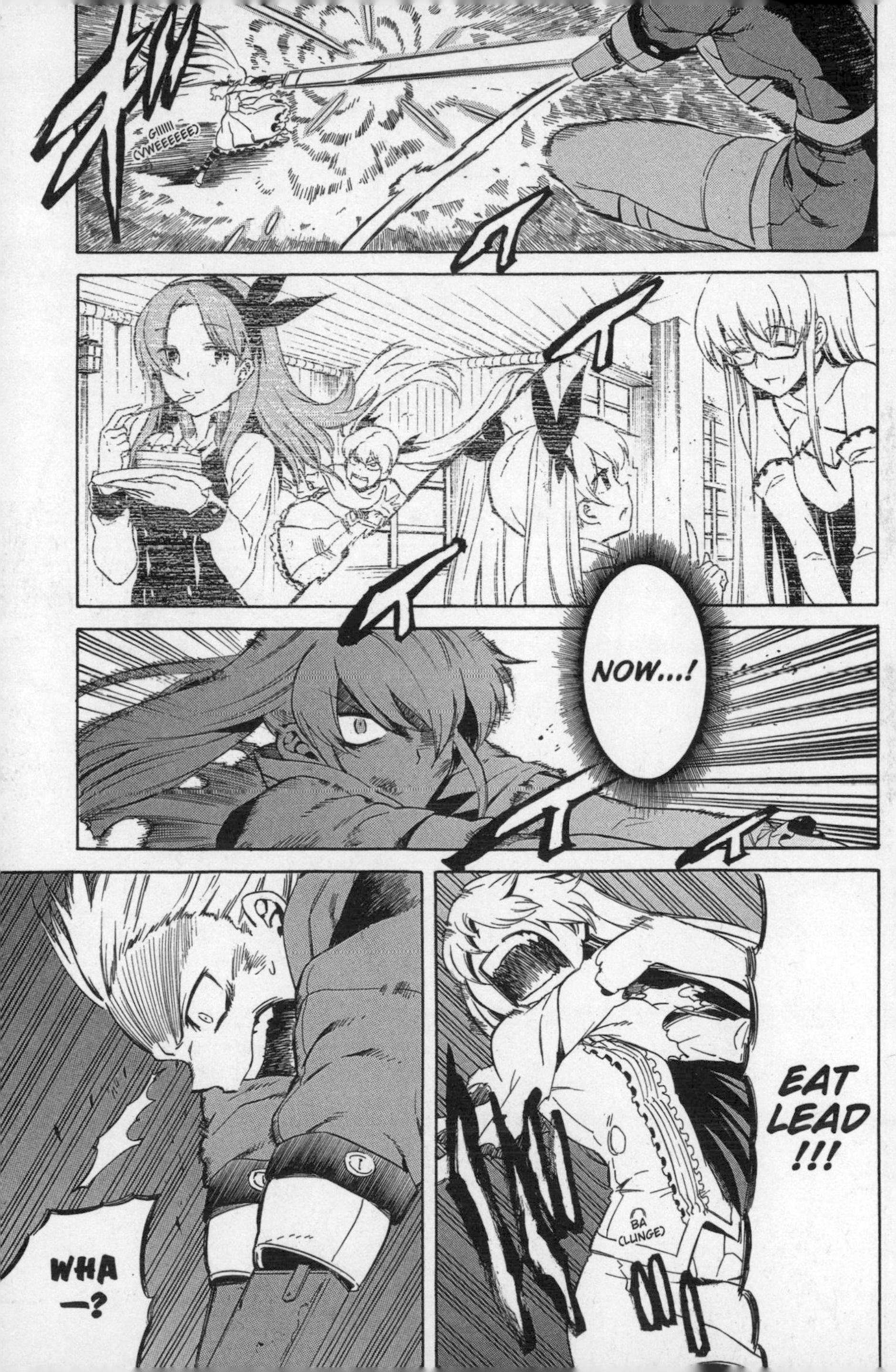
GI!!!!!
(VWEEEEEE)
NOW...!
EAT LEAD!!!
BA
(LUNGE)
WHA—?

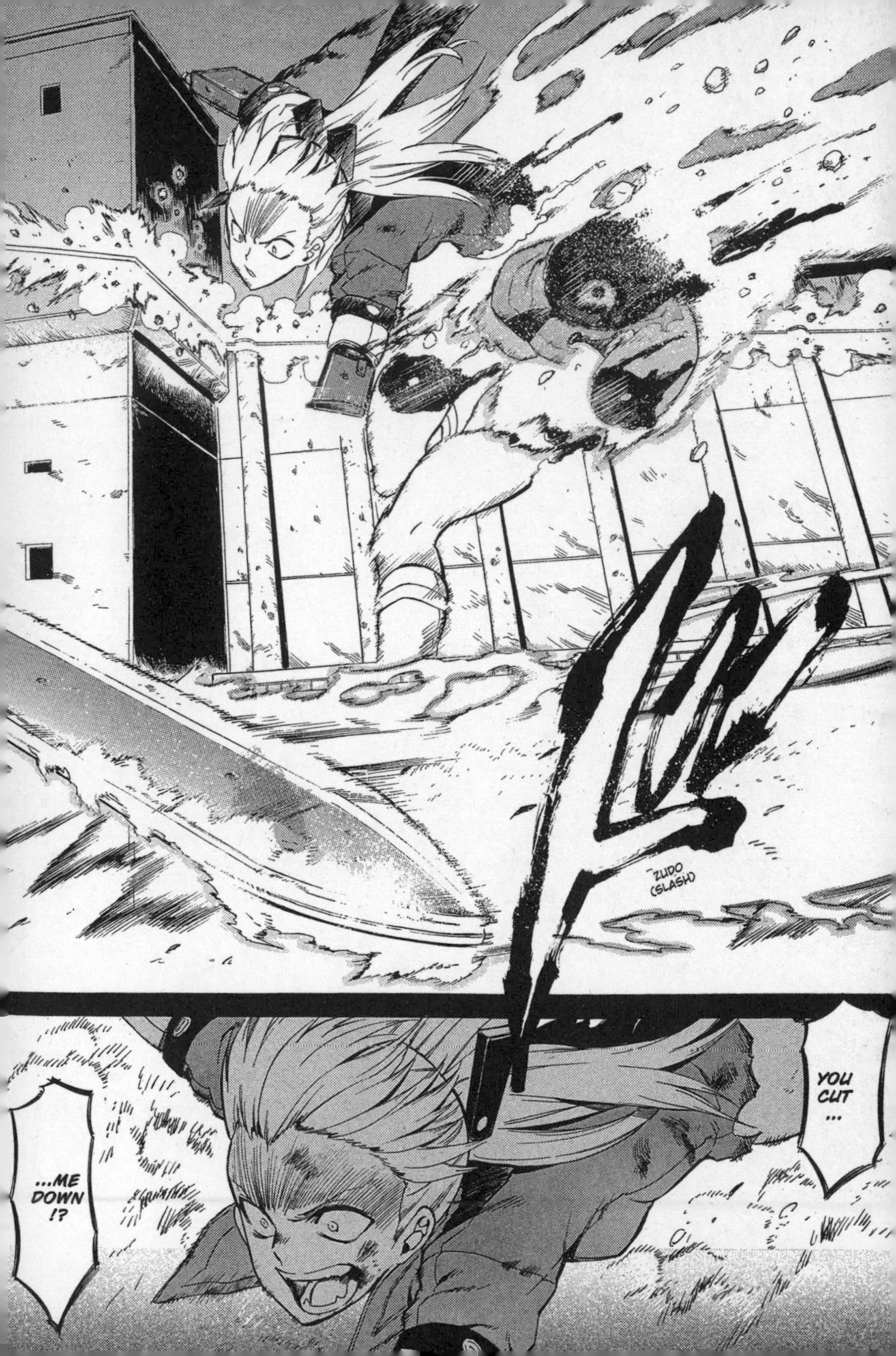
ZUDO
(SLASH)
YOU CUT...
...ME DOWN!?

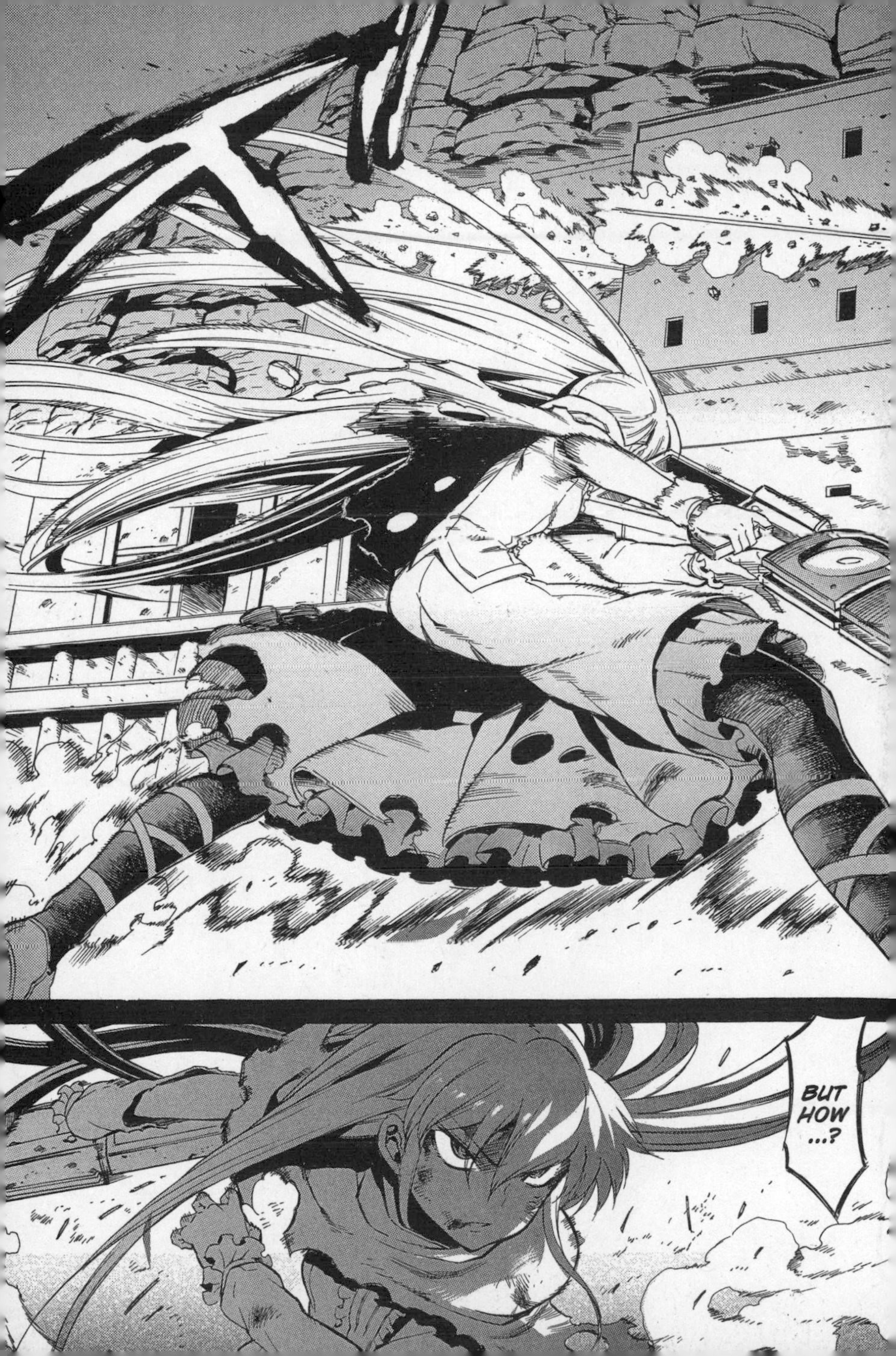
BUT HOW ...?

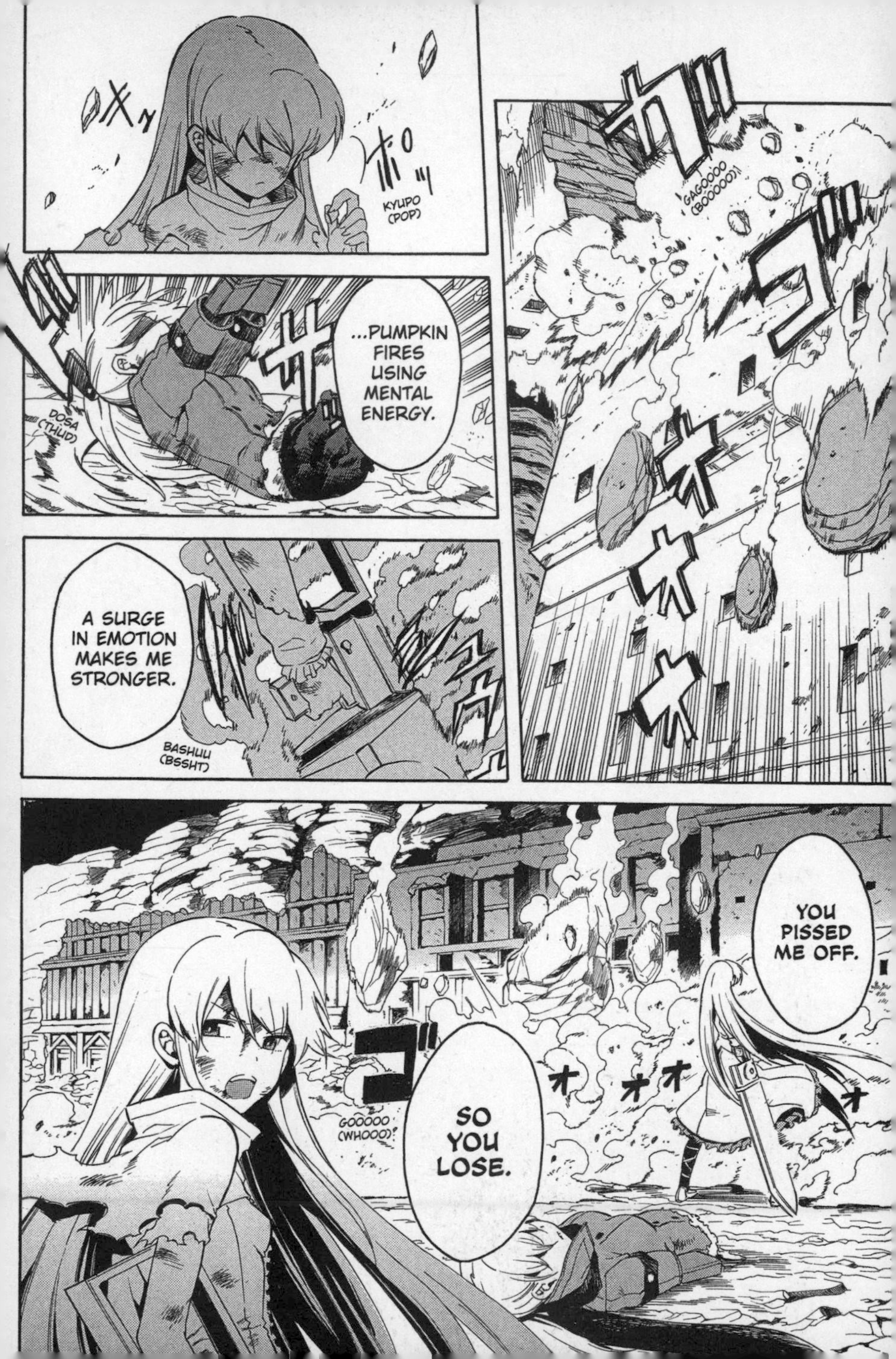
GAGOOOO (BOOOOO)
KYUPO (POP)
...PUMPKIN FIRES USING MENTAL ENERGY.
DOSA (THUD)
A SURGE IN EMOTION MAKES ME STRONGER.
BASHUU (BSSHT)
YOU PISSED ME OFF.
SO YOU LOSE.
GOOOOO (WHOOO)

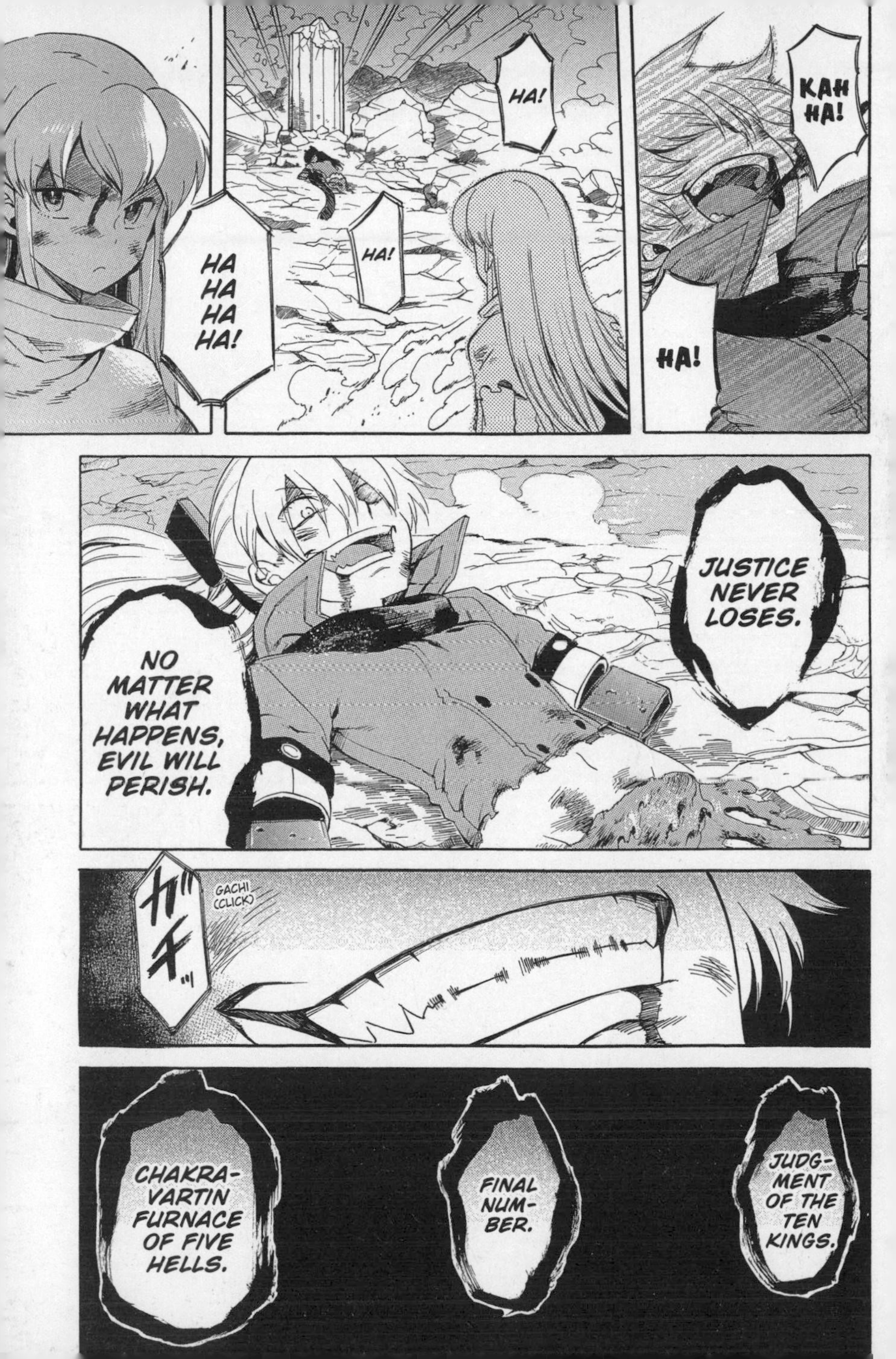
KAH HA!
HA!
HA!
HA!
HA HA HA HA!
JUSTICE NEVER LOSES.
NO MATTER WHAT HAPPENS, EVIL WILL PERISH.
ガチッ
GACHI (CLICK)
JUDGMENT OF THE TEN KINGS.
FINAL NUMBER.
CHAKRAVARTIN FURNACE OF FIVE HELLS.

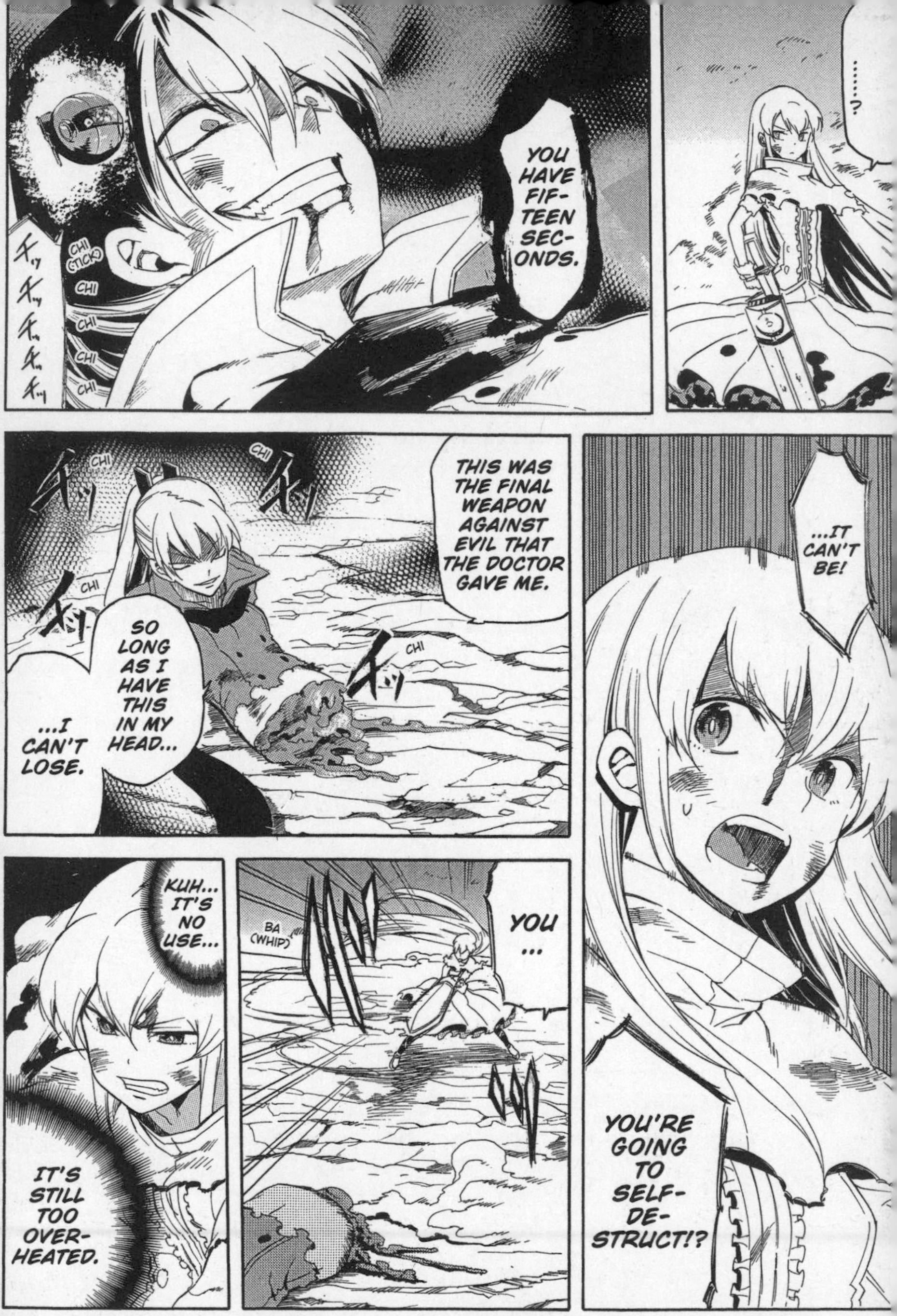
?......
YOU HAVE FIF-TEEN SEC-ONDS.
CHI (TICK)
CHI
CHI
CHI
CHI
...IT CAN'T BE!
YOU'RE GOING TO SELF-DE-STRUCT!?
CHI
CHI
CHI
CHI
THIS WAS THE FINAL WEAPON AGAINST EVIL THAT THE DOCTOR GAVE ME.
SO LONG AS I HAVE THIS IN MY HEAD...
...I CAN'T LOSE.
BA (WHIP)
YOU ...
KUH... IT'S NO USE...
IT'S STILL TOO OVER-HEATED.

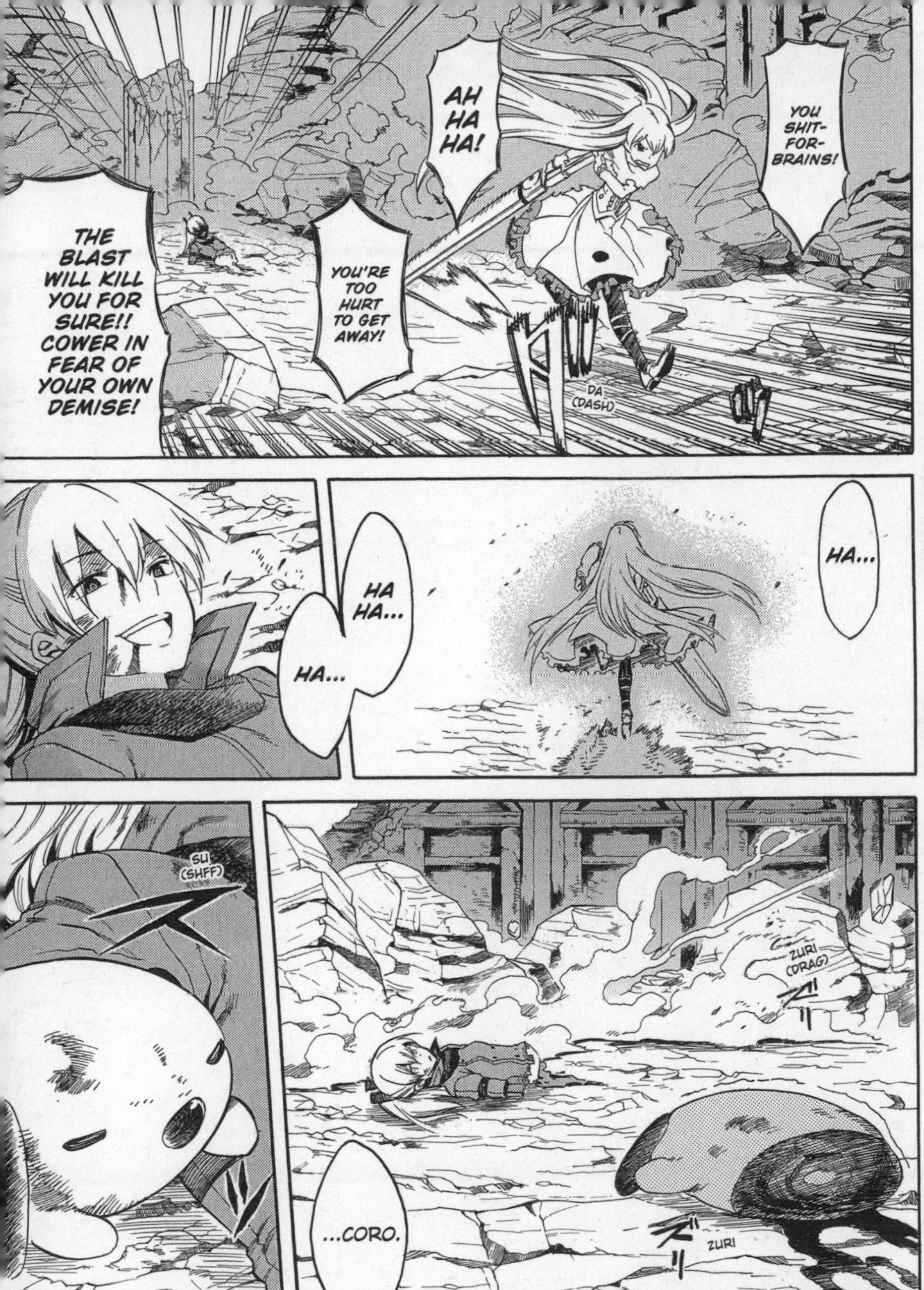
YOU SHIT-FOR-BRAINS!
AH HA HA!
YOU'RE TOO HURT TO GET AWAY!
THE BLAST WILL KILL YOU FOR SURE!! COWER IN FEAR OF YOUR OWN DEMISE!
DA (DASH)
HA...
HA HA...
HA...
ZURI (DRAG)
...CORO.
ZURI
SU (SHFF)

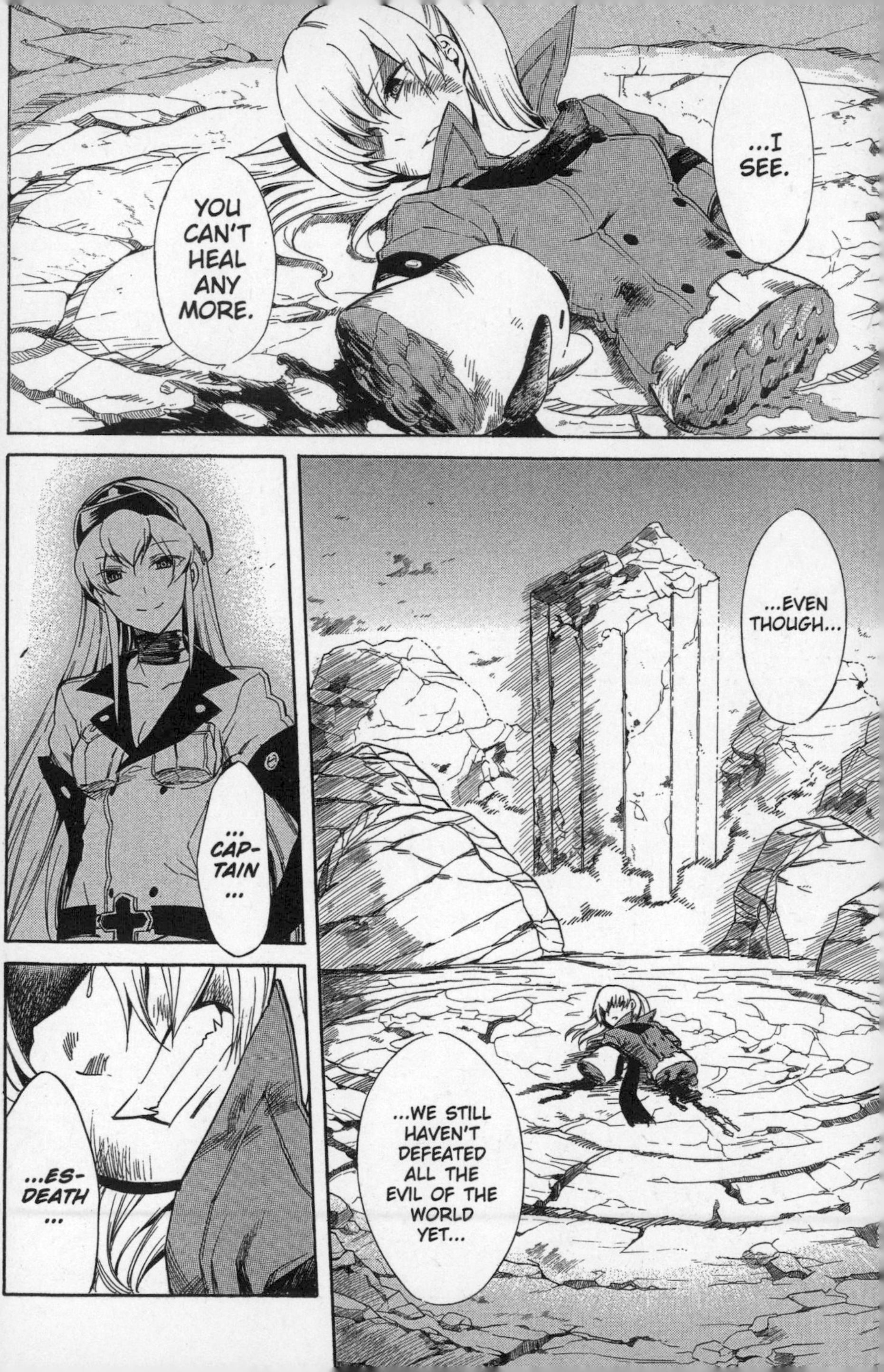
...I SEE.
YOU CAN'T HEAL ANY MORE.
...EVEN THOUGH...
...WE STILL HAVEN'T DEFEATED ALL THE EVIL OF THE WORLD YET...
... CAP-TAIN ...
...ES-DEATH ...

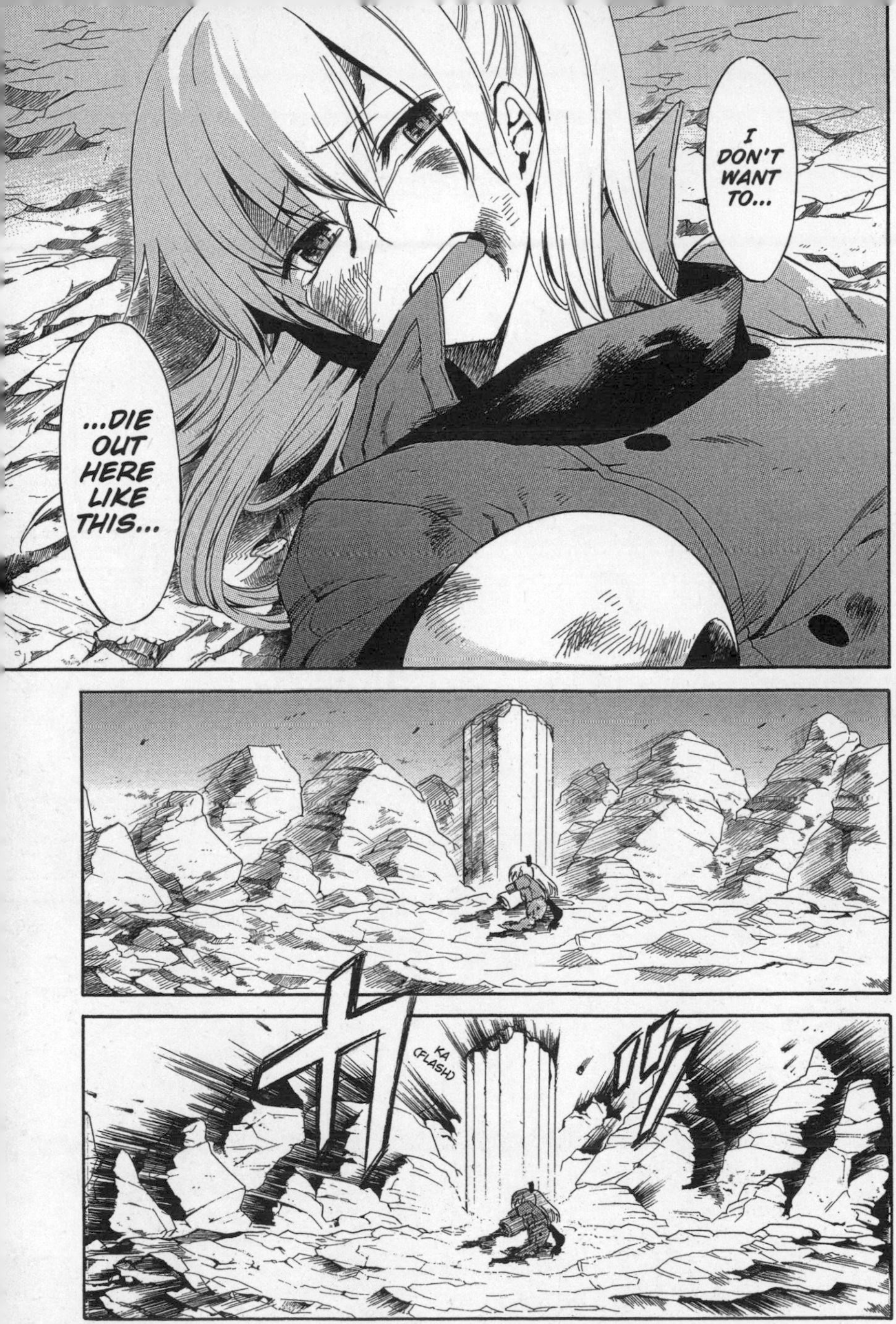
I DON'T WANT TO...
...DIE OUT HERE LIKE THIS...
KA (FLASH)

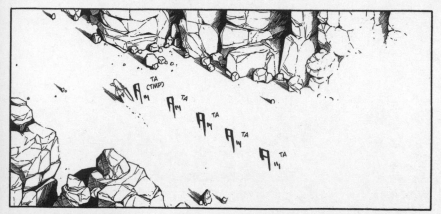

TA
(TMP)

TA

TA

TA

TA

UGH!

DOSA
(THUD)

GOTO
(CLACK)

GA
(TRIP)

SHIT
...

MY
LEG...

YOU'VE
GOT
TO BE
KIDDING
ME...!

I SWEAR
I'M GOING
TO SURVIVE
AND BE
ONE OF THE
WINNERS!!

GU
(STRAIN)

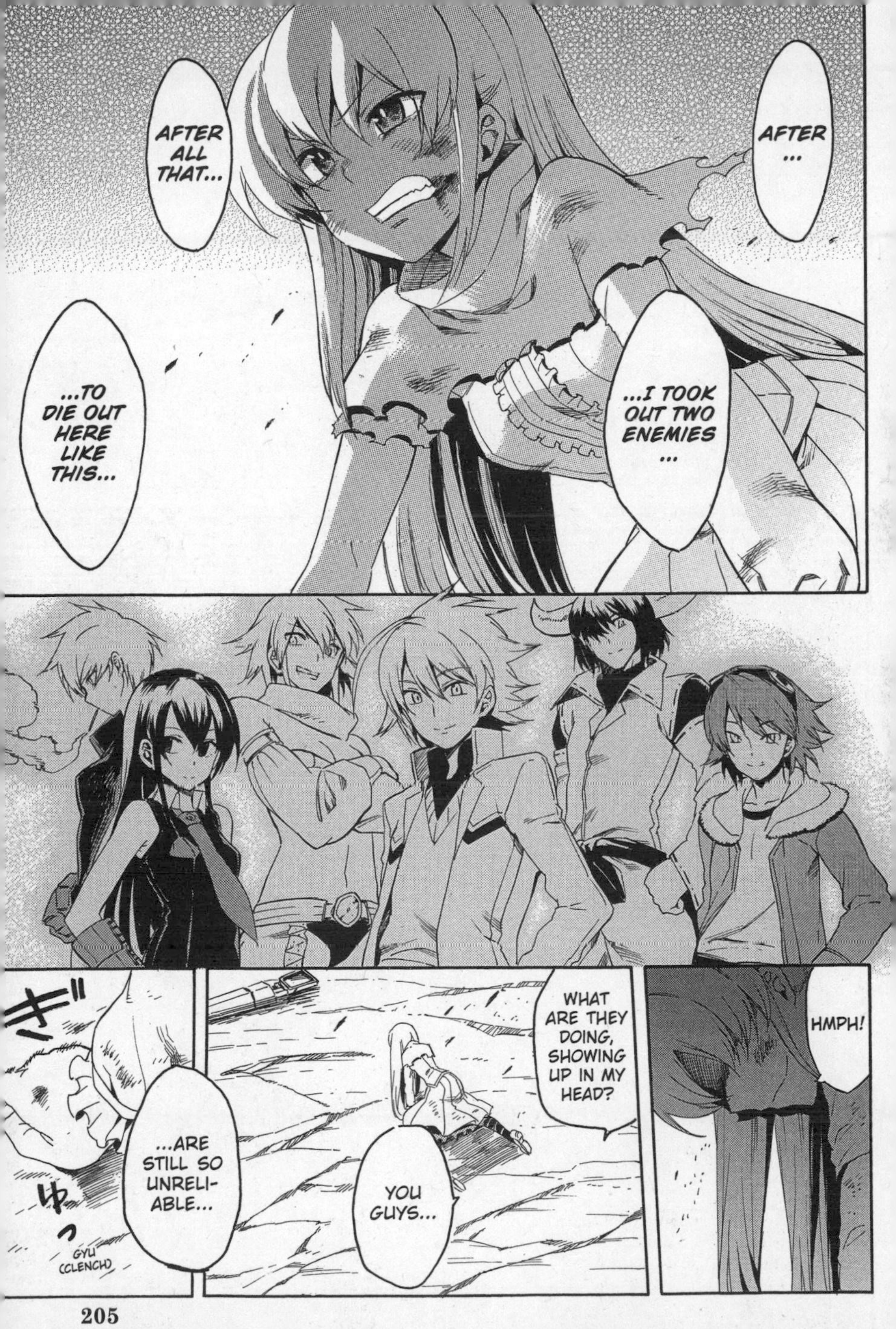
AFTER...
AFTER ALL THAT...
...I TOOK OUT TWO ENEMIES...
...TO DIE OUT HERE LIKE THIS...
HMPH!
WHAT ARE THEY DOING, SHOWING UP IN MY HEAD?
YOU GUYS...
...ARE STILL SO UNRELI-ABLE...
GYU (CLENCH)

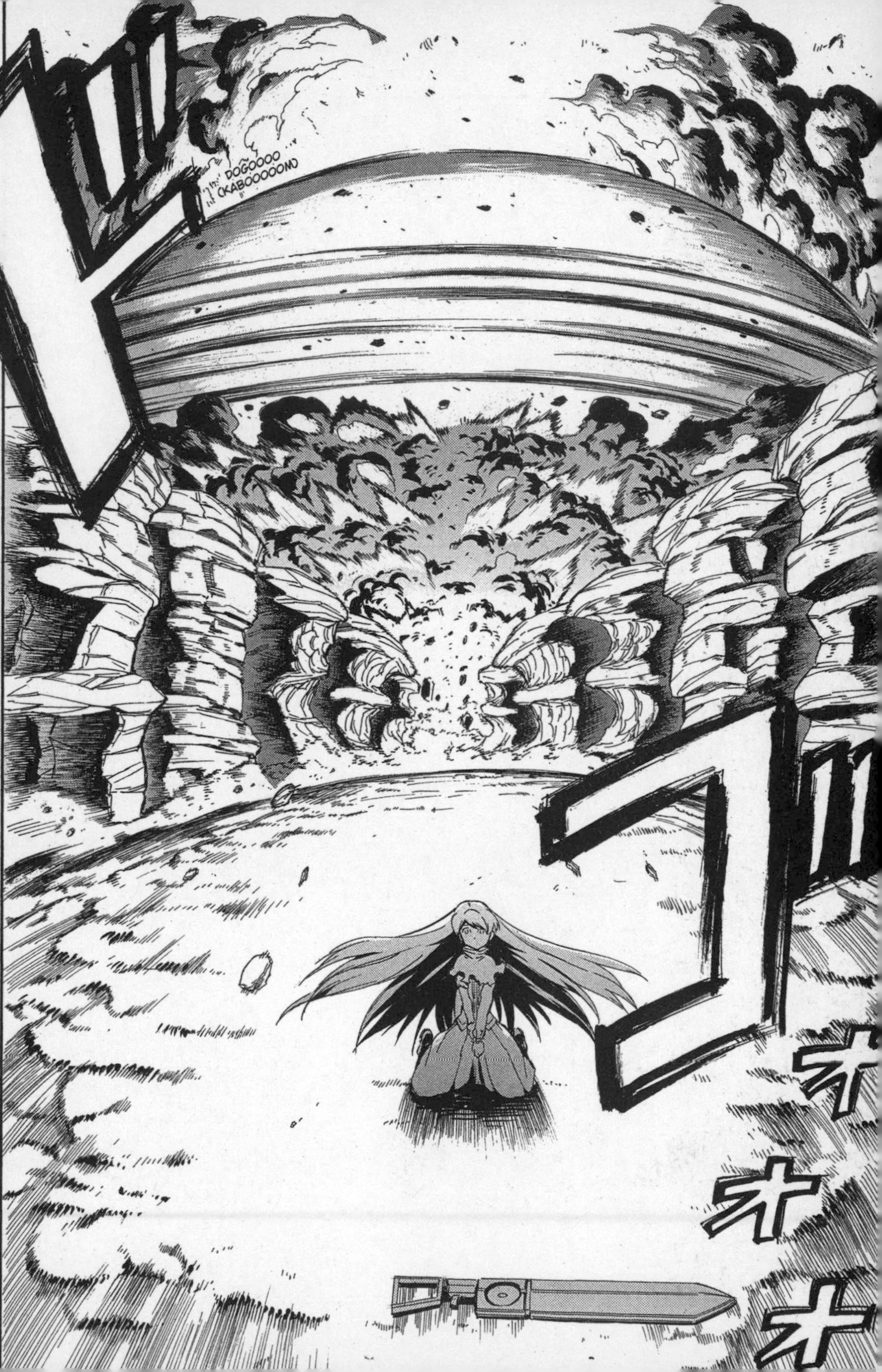
DOGOOOO
(KABOOOOOOM)

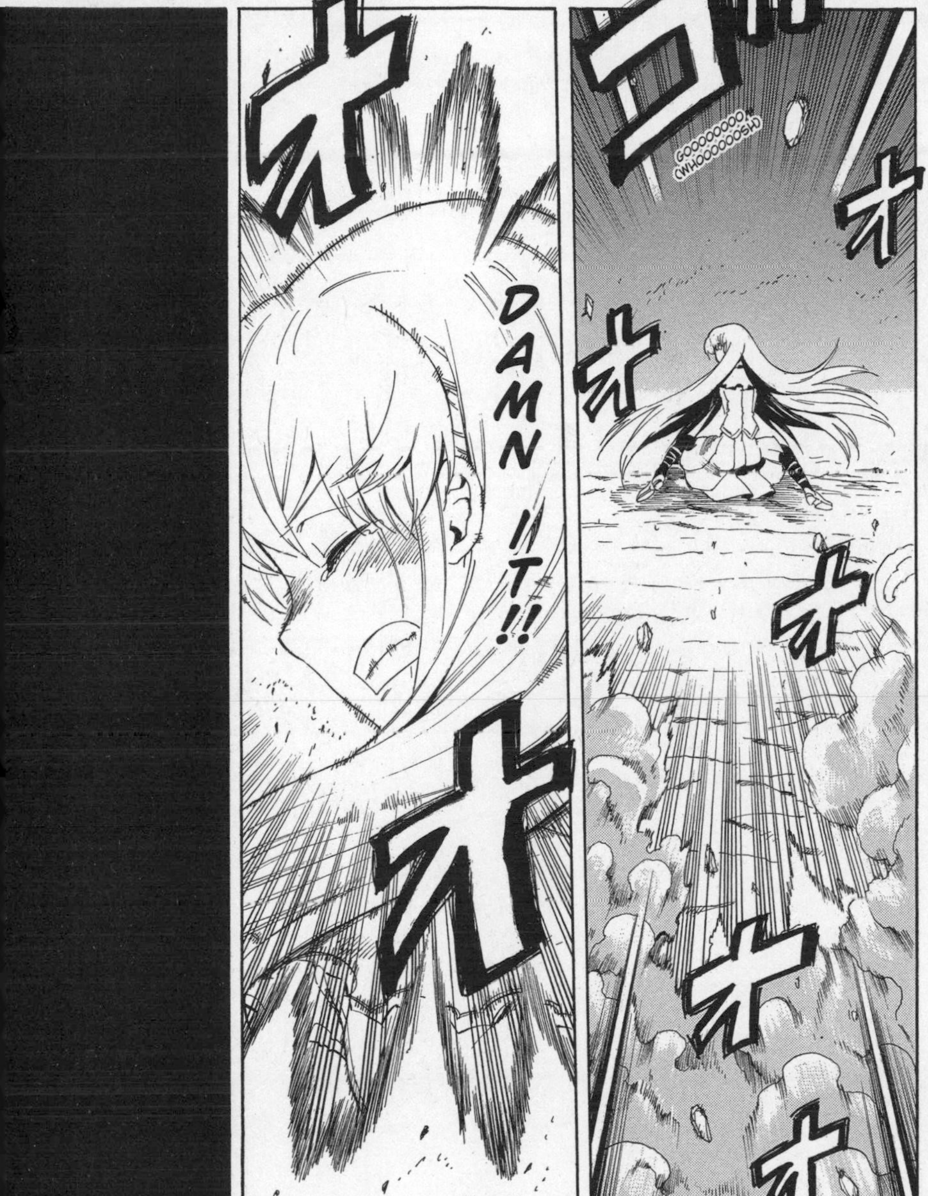
ゴッ
GOOOOOOOOO (WHOOOOOOSH)
DAMN IT!!

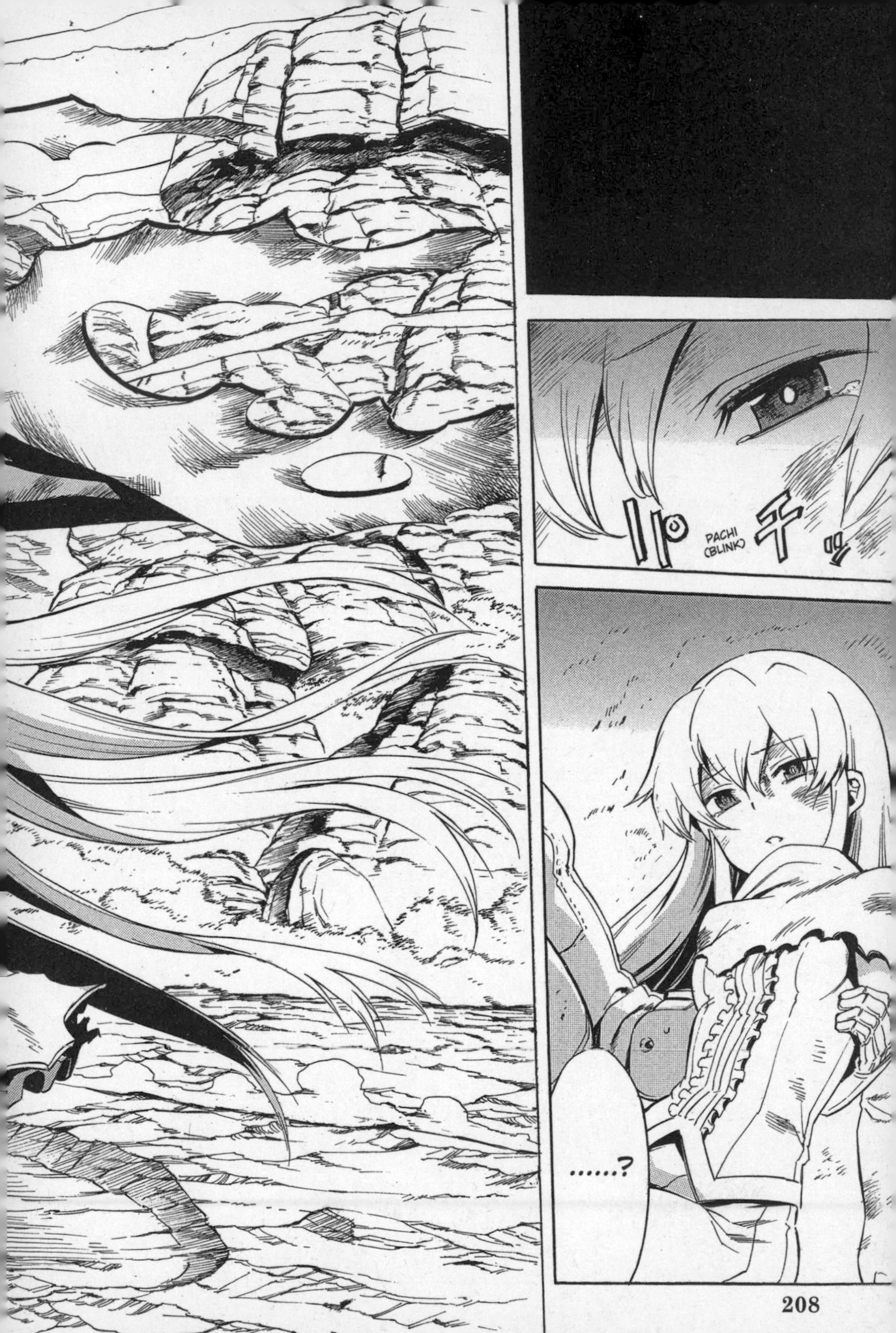
パチッ
PACHI
(BLINK)
......?

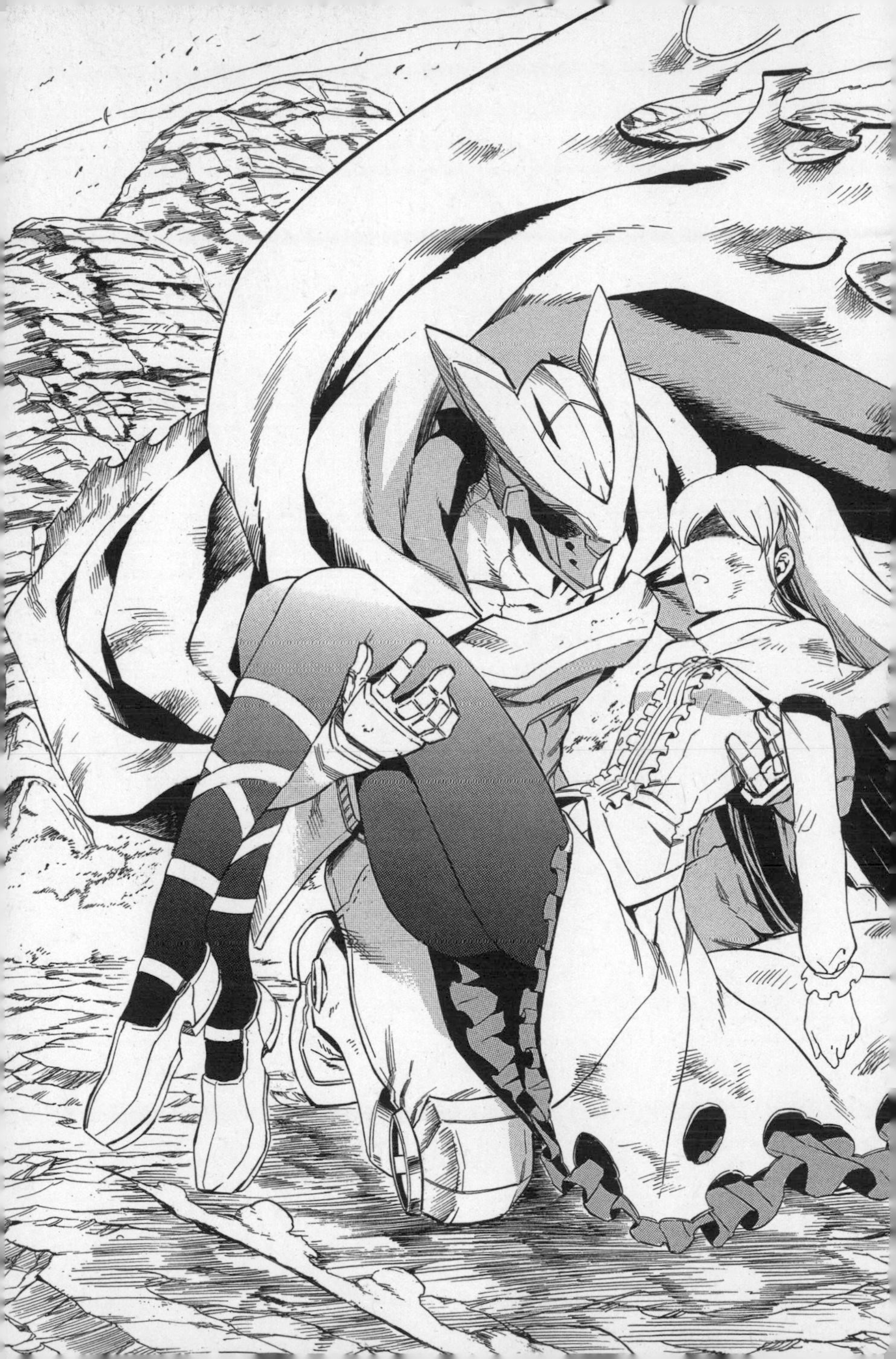

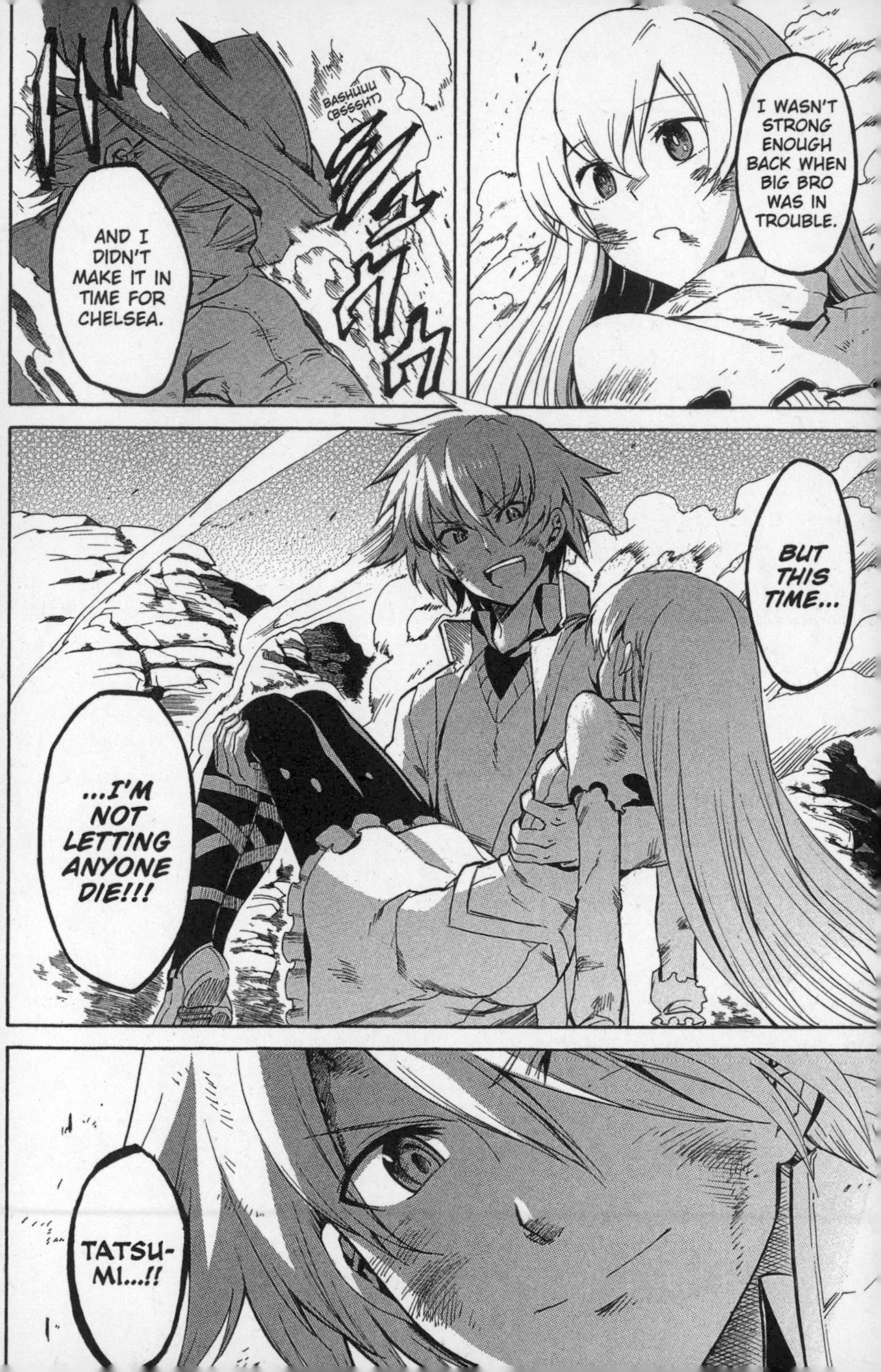
I WASN'T STRONG ENOUGH BACK WHEN BIG BRO WAS IN TROUBLE.
BASHUUU (BSSSHT)
AND I DIDN'T MAKE IT IN TIME FOR CHELSEA.
BUT THIS TIME...
...I'M NOT LETTING ANYONE DIE!!!
TATSU-MI...!!

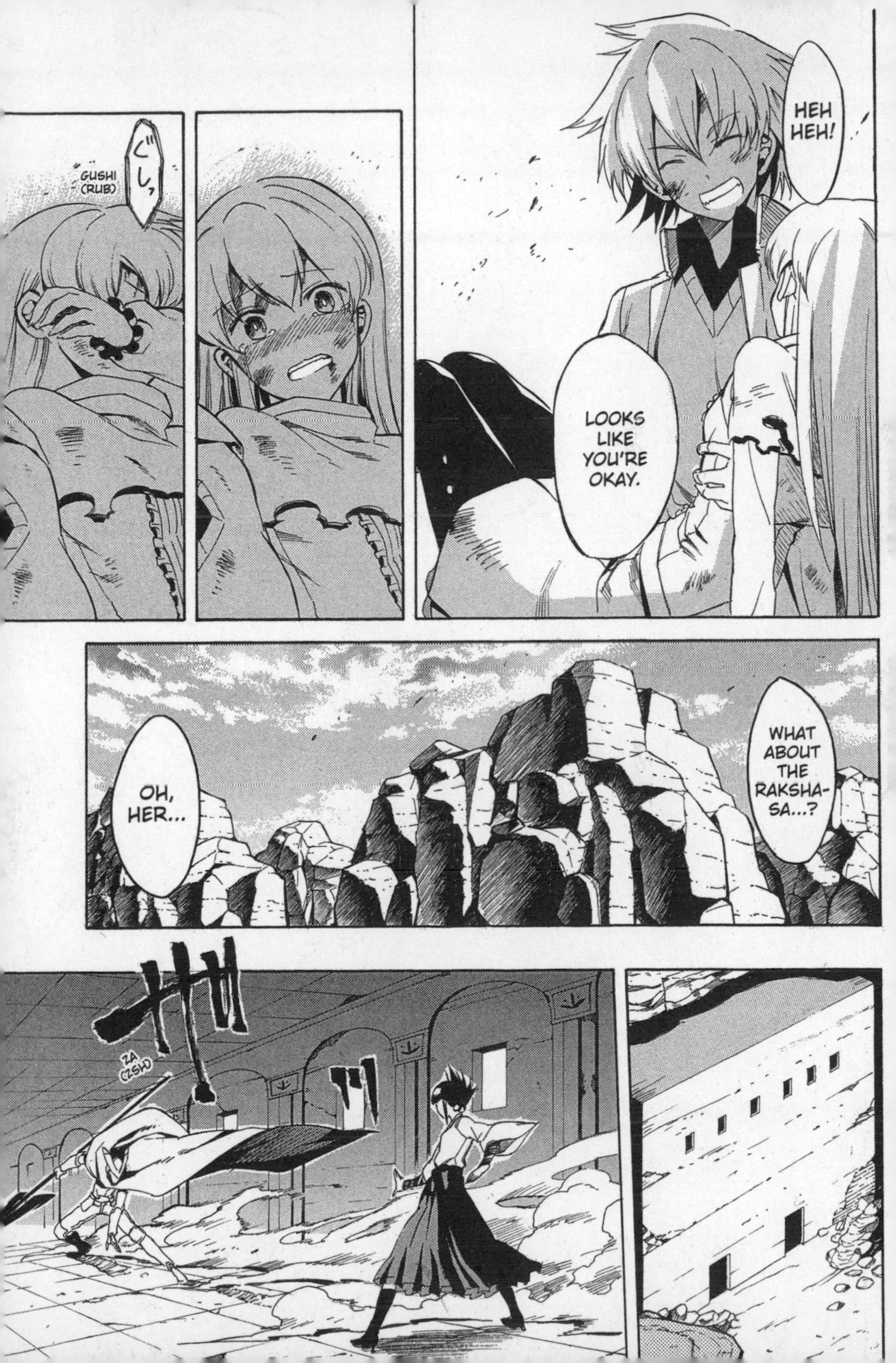
HEH HEH!
LOOKS LIKE YOU'RE OKAY.
ぐしっ
GUSHI (RUB)
WHAT ABOUT THE RAKSHA-SA...?
OH, HER...
ZA (ZSH)

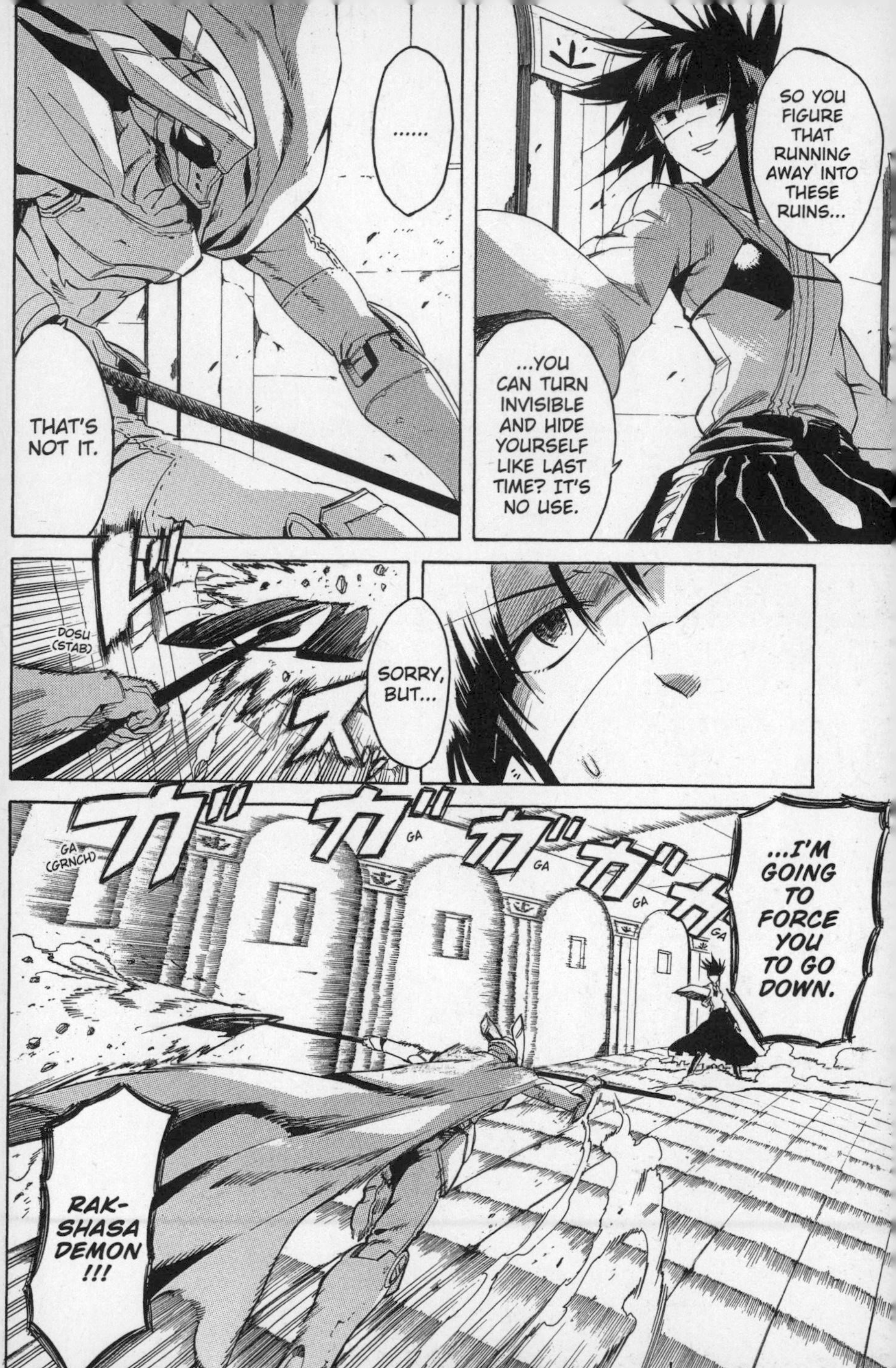
SO YOU FIGURE THAT RUNNING AWAY INTO THESE RUINS...
...YOU CAN TURN INVISIBLE AND HIDE YOURSELF LIKE LAST TIME? IT'S NO USE.
......
THAT'S NOT IT.
SORRY, BUT...
DOSU (STAB)
...I'M GOING TO FORCE YOU TO GO DOWN.
GA (GRNCH)
GA
GA
GA
GA
RAK-SHASA DEMON !!!

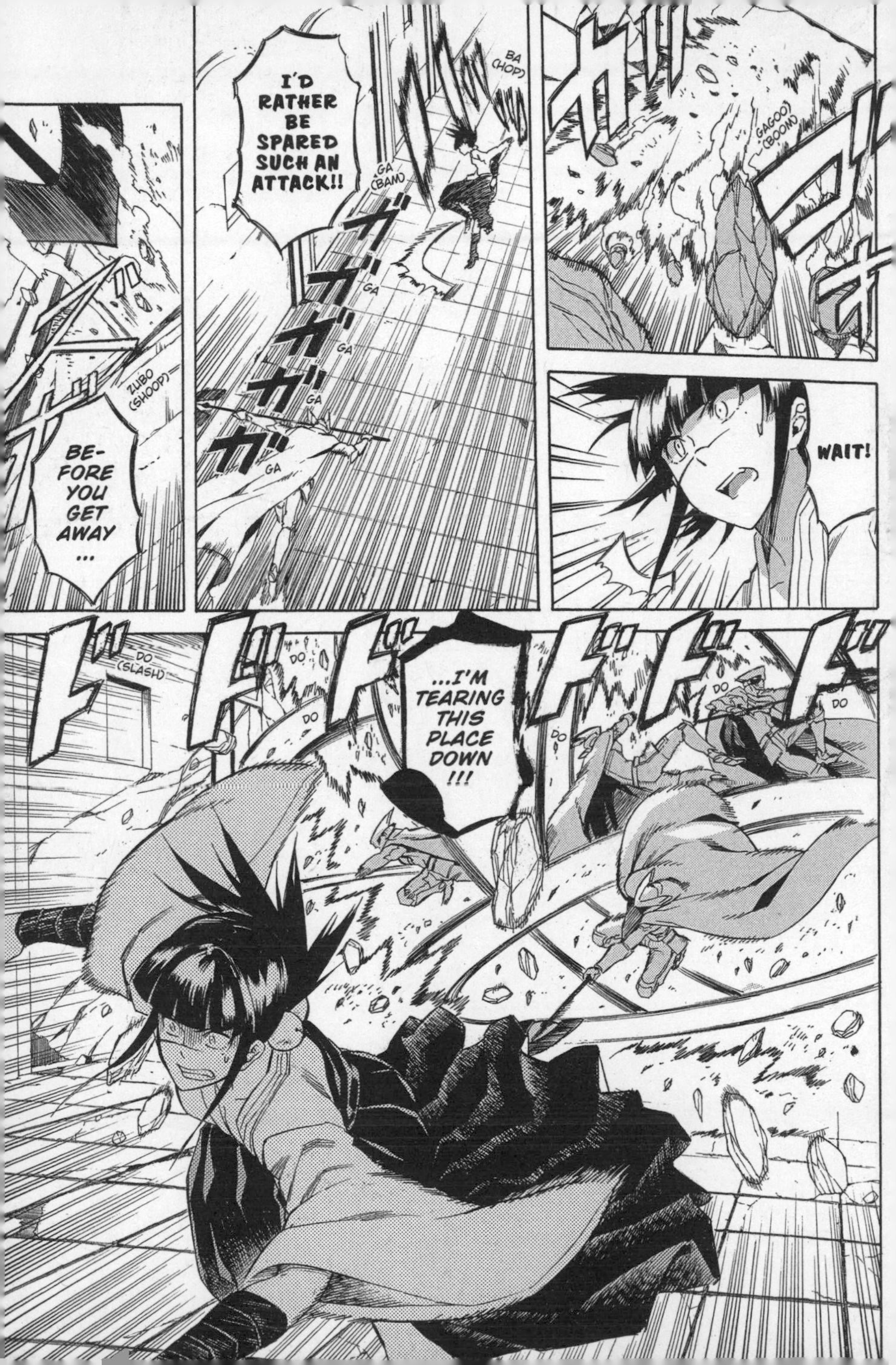
GAGOO (BOOM)
BA (HOP)
I'D RATHER BE SPARED SUCH AN ATTACK!!
GA (BAM)
GA
GA
GA
GA
ZUBO (SHOOP)
BE-FORE YOU GET AWAY ...
WAIT!
DO
DO
DO
DO
DO (SLASH)
DO
...I'M TEARING THIS PLACE DOWN!!!

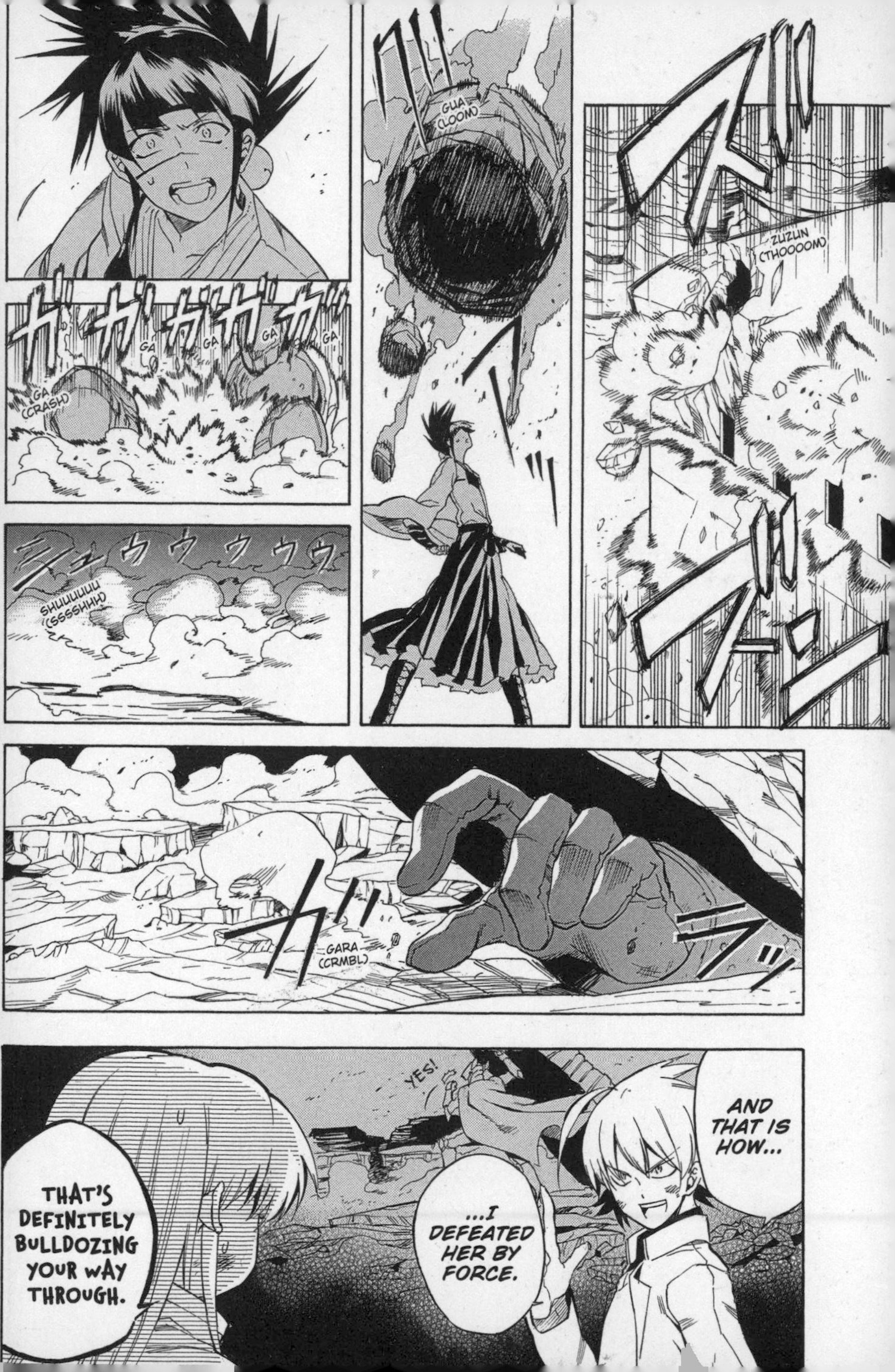
GUA (LOOM)
ZUZUN (THOOOOM)
GA GA GA GA
GA (CRASH)
SHUUUUUU (SSSSSHHH)
GARA (CRMBL)
YES!
AND THAT IS HOW...
...I DEFEATED HER BY FORCE.
THAT'S DEFINITELY BULLDOZING YOUR WAY THROUGH.

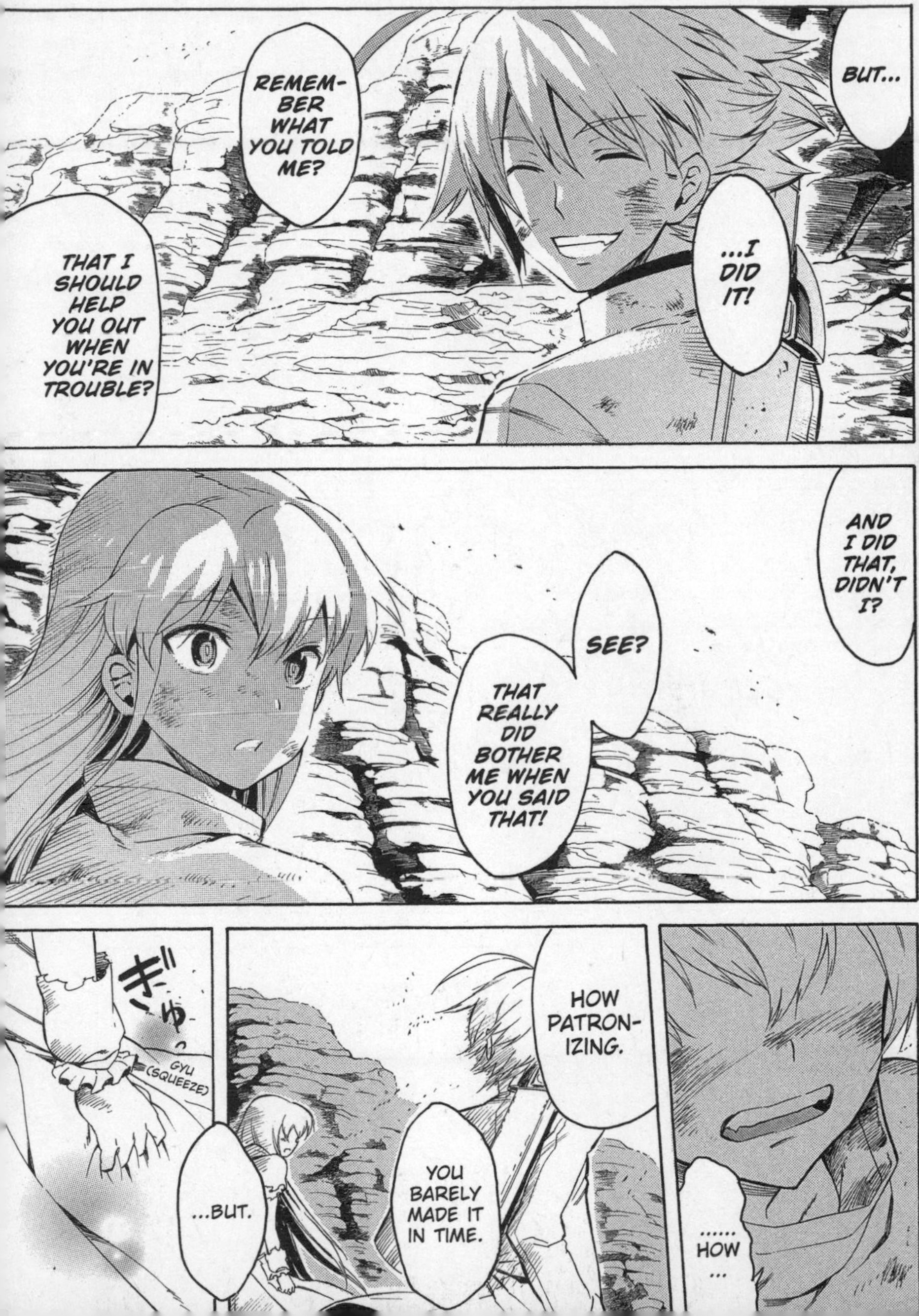
BUT...
...I DID IT!
REMEMBER WHAT YOU TOLD ME?
THAT I SHOULD HELP YOU OUT WHEN YOU'RE IN TROUBLE?
AND I DID THAT, DIDN'T I?
SEE?
THAT REALLY DID BOTHER ME WHEN YOU SAID THAT!
HOW PATRONIZING.
......HOW...
YOU BARELY MADE IT IN TIME.
...BUT.
ぎゅっ
GYU (SQUEEZE)

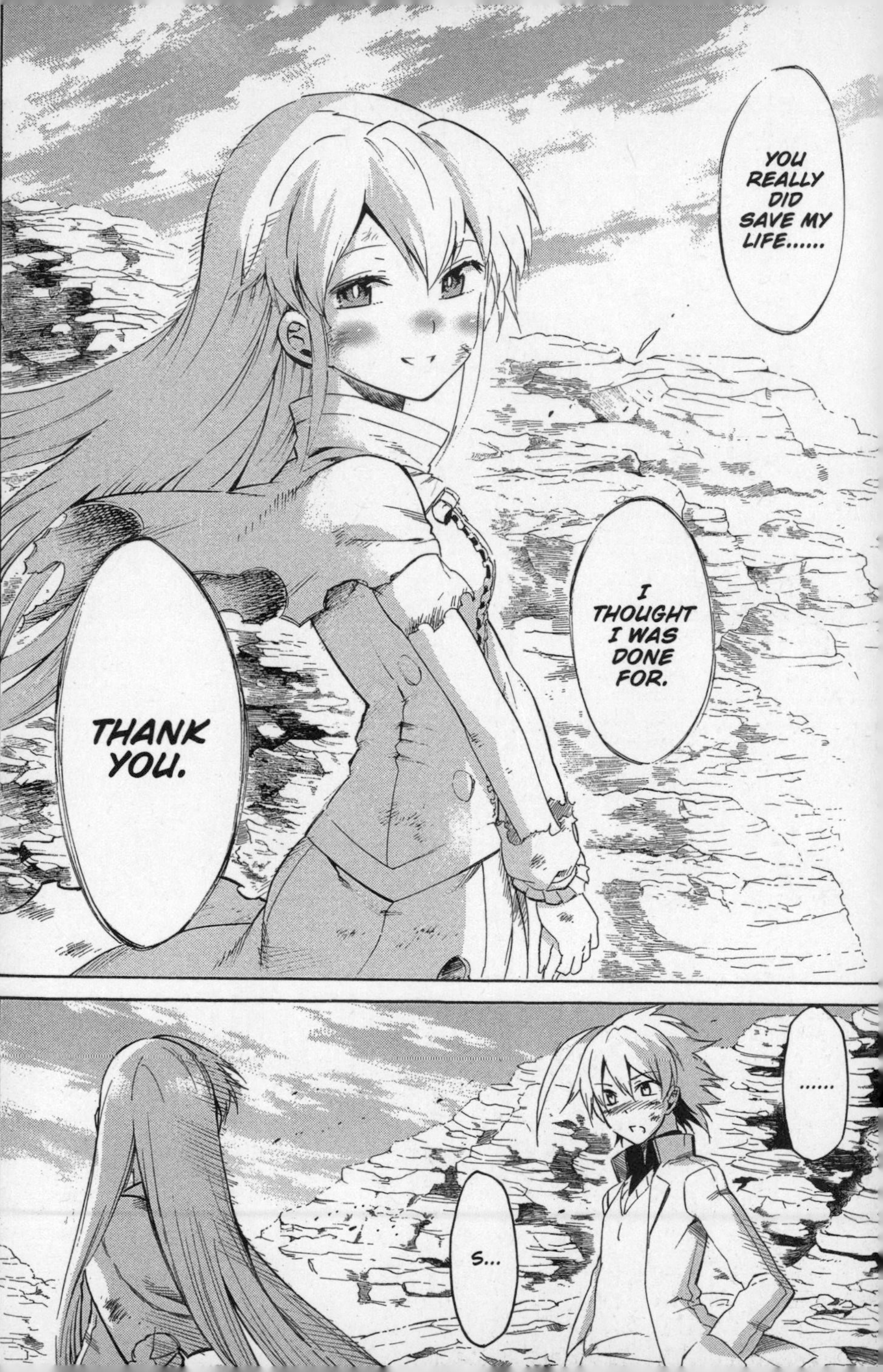
YOU REALLY DID SAVE MY LIFE......
I THOUGHT I WAS DONE FOR.
THANK YOU.
......
S...

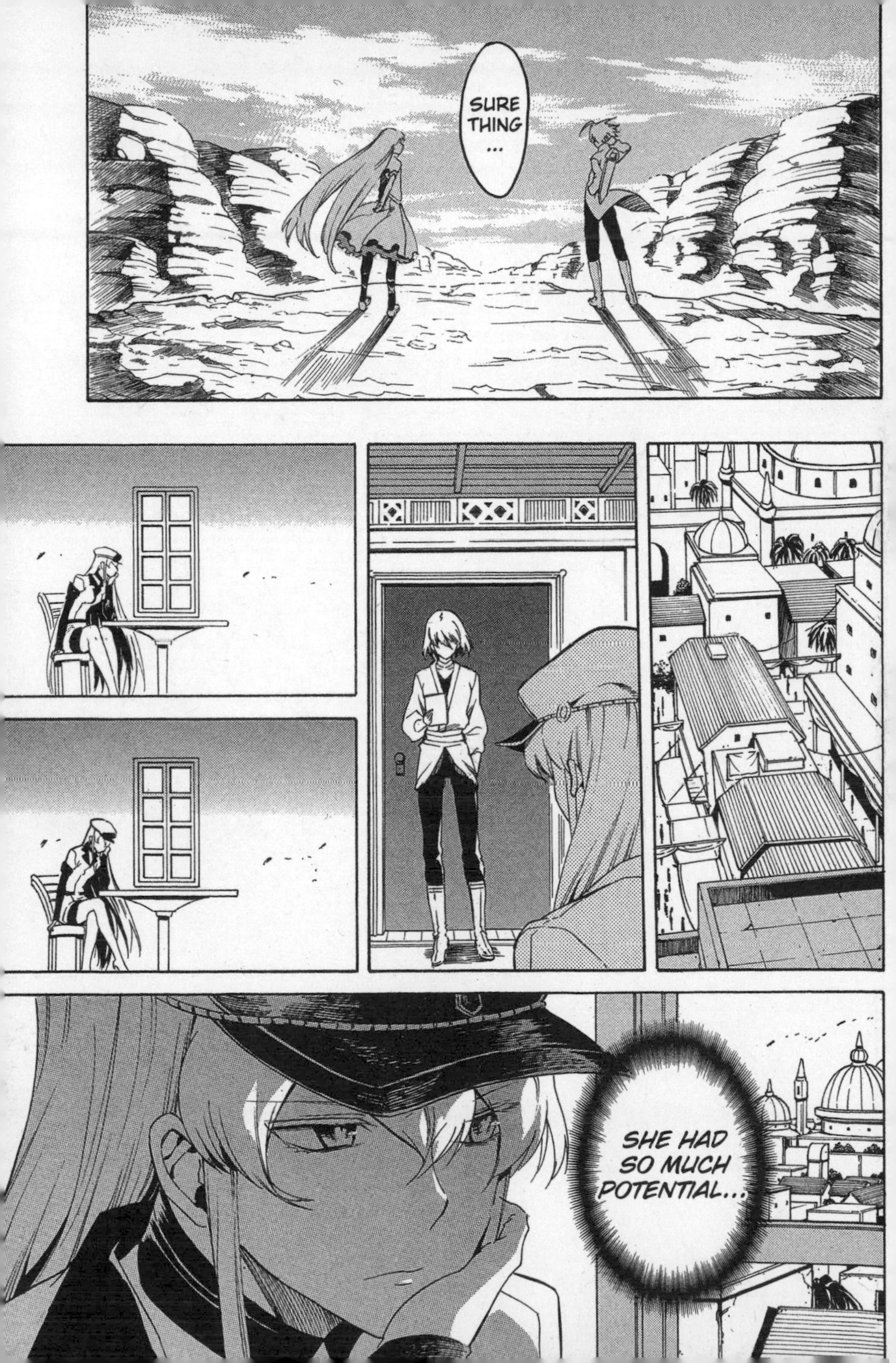
SURE THING ...
SHE HAD SO MUCH POTENTIAL...

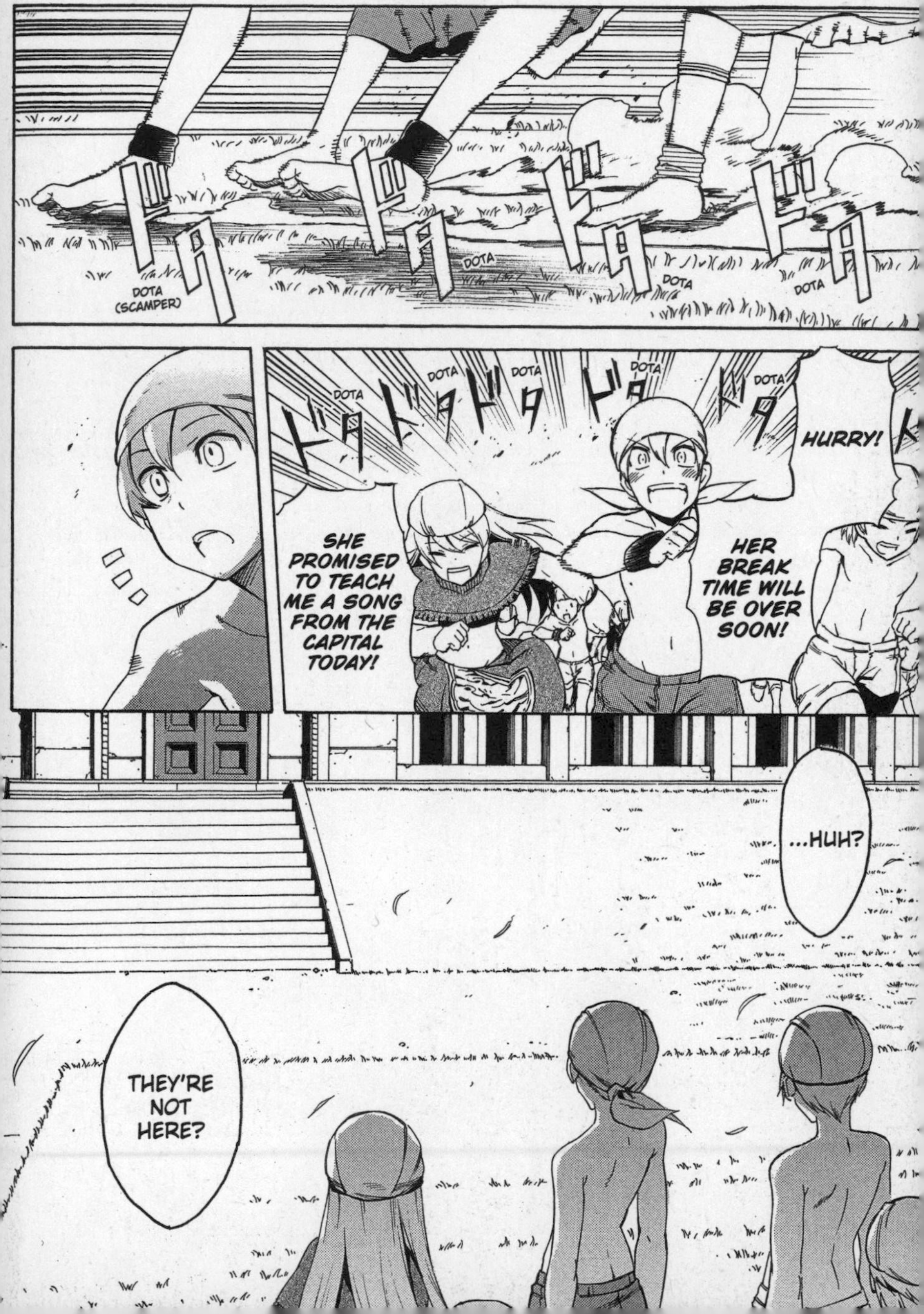

DOTA
DOTA
DOTA
DOTA (SCAMPER)
HURRY!
DOTA
DOTA
DOTA
DOTA
HER BREAK TIME WILL BE OVER SOON!
SHE PROMISED TO TEACH ME A SONG FROM THE CAPITAL TODAY!
...HUH?
THEY'RE NOT HERE?

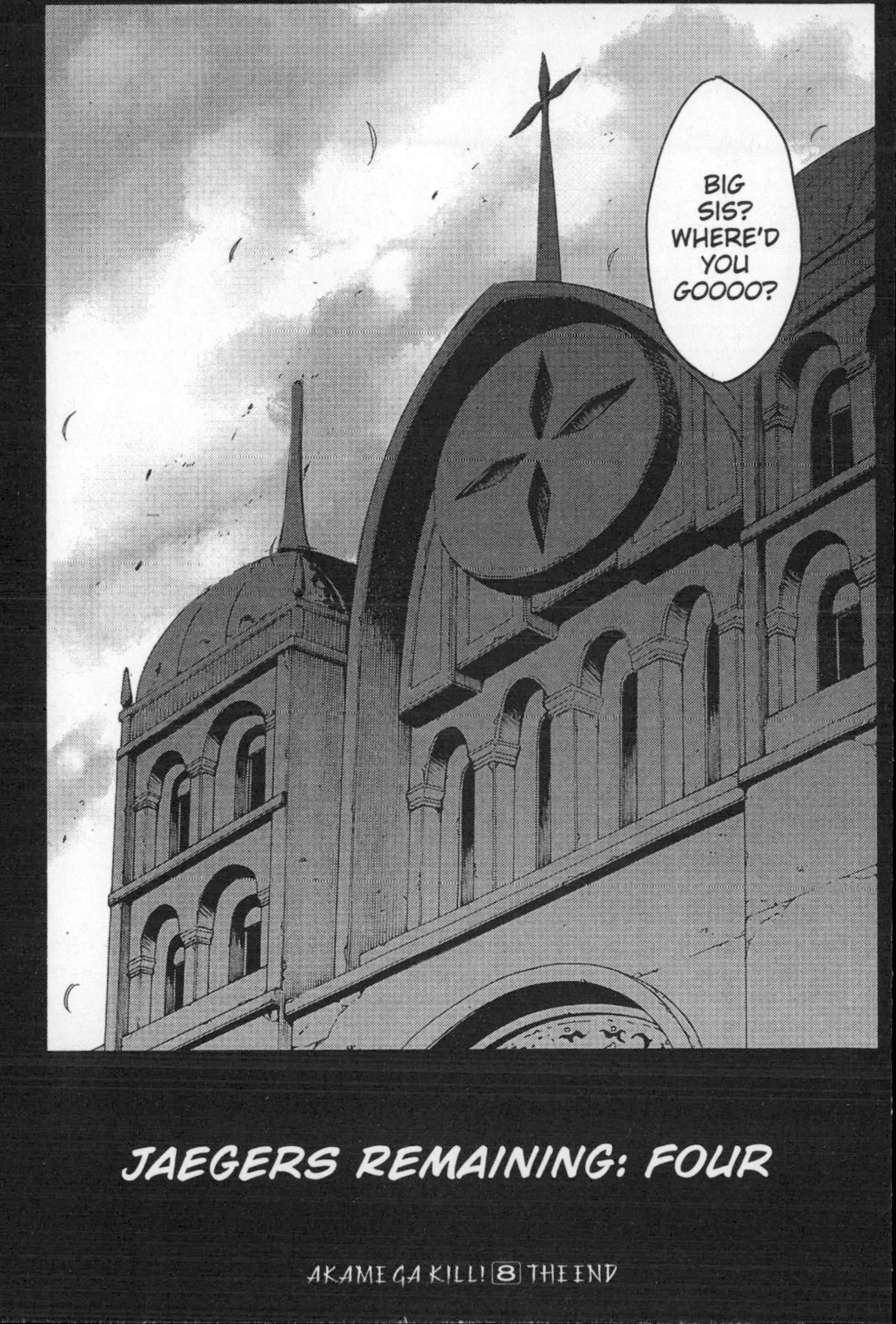
BIG SIS? WHERE'D YOU GOOOO?

JAEGERS REMAINING: FOUR

AKAME GA KILL! 8 THE END

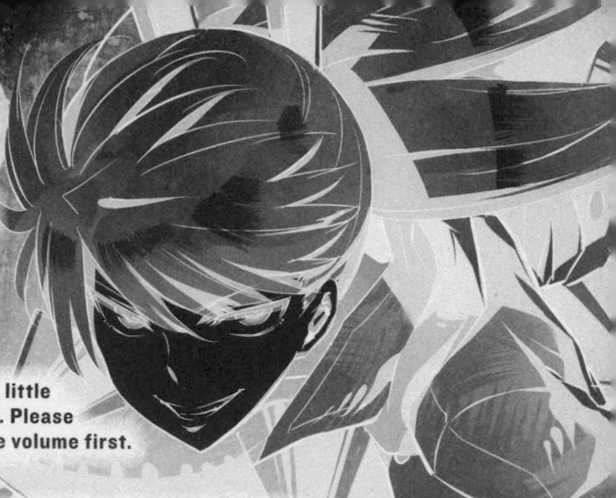

# TAKAHIRO's POSTSCRIPT

Thank you for purchasing this volume.
This is Takahiro from Minato Soft.
I'd like to take this opportunity to reveal a little more about the characters from Volume 8. Please read below after you've finished the entire volume first.

### ◆ Judgment of the Ten Kings

This time we got to see all the different forms it takes. In numerical order it's: iron ball, small missile, sword, winch, drill, large missile, cannon, land-and-sea torpedo, detector, and explosive. As Tatsumi indicated when he mentioned having never seen such weaponry before, a number of them are technology beyond their world's current capabilities. Stylish would be mad. As we see with form #8, she even has weapons that can be used underwater.

### ◆The Temple of the Imperial Fist's Four Rakshasas

The Temple of the Imperial Fist is the empire's greatest Shaolin kung fu establishment and continues to receive a number of benefits from the Empire, including generous contributions. In return for this financing, a portion of its more outstanding practitioners are loaned out to the Empire. They help out with the Empire's underhanded work of every kind. They're burdened with the task of gathering the teigu scattered throughout the land after the civil war five hundred years ago, and even though they don't possess teigu of their own, their skills and power enable them to challenge teigu users all the same. In fact, it's been reported that they've defeated a number of teigu users and confiscated their teigu. The Temple of the Imperial Fist as a whole has become so widespread, that the strength of its practitioners has become a touch watered down. However, those chosen to be the Four Rakshasas are given the most rigorous in religious austerities and have been bestowed with ancient strengths. They are the Minister of State's precious pawns.

**[Shuten]**
He believes that the living world is hell and that by killing his opponents he is liberating them from it. So he truly believes he is doing good work.

**[Ibara]**
He likes finding the good points about those he fights and derives pleasure by then killing the very person he's developed feelings for. Of all Four Rakshasas, he's the strongest and fought a fierce fight against Akame.

**[Mez]**
Full of spunk and vigor, she'll attack in an innocent and childlike way. She kills because it's her job, not to be cruel.

**[Suzuka]**
She enjoys taking attacks from the enemies she's battling. That's why she has to many wounds all over her body. In a word, she's a super masochist.

And that's all. Thank you very much for reading all the way up to the end.
And I hope to see you again in Volume 9.

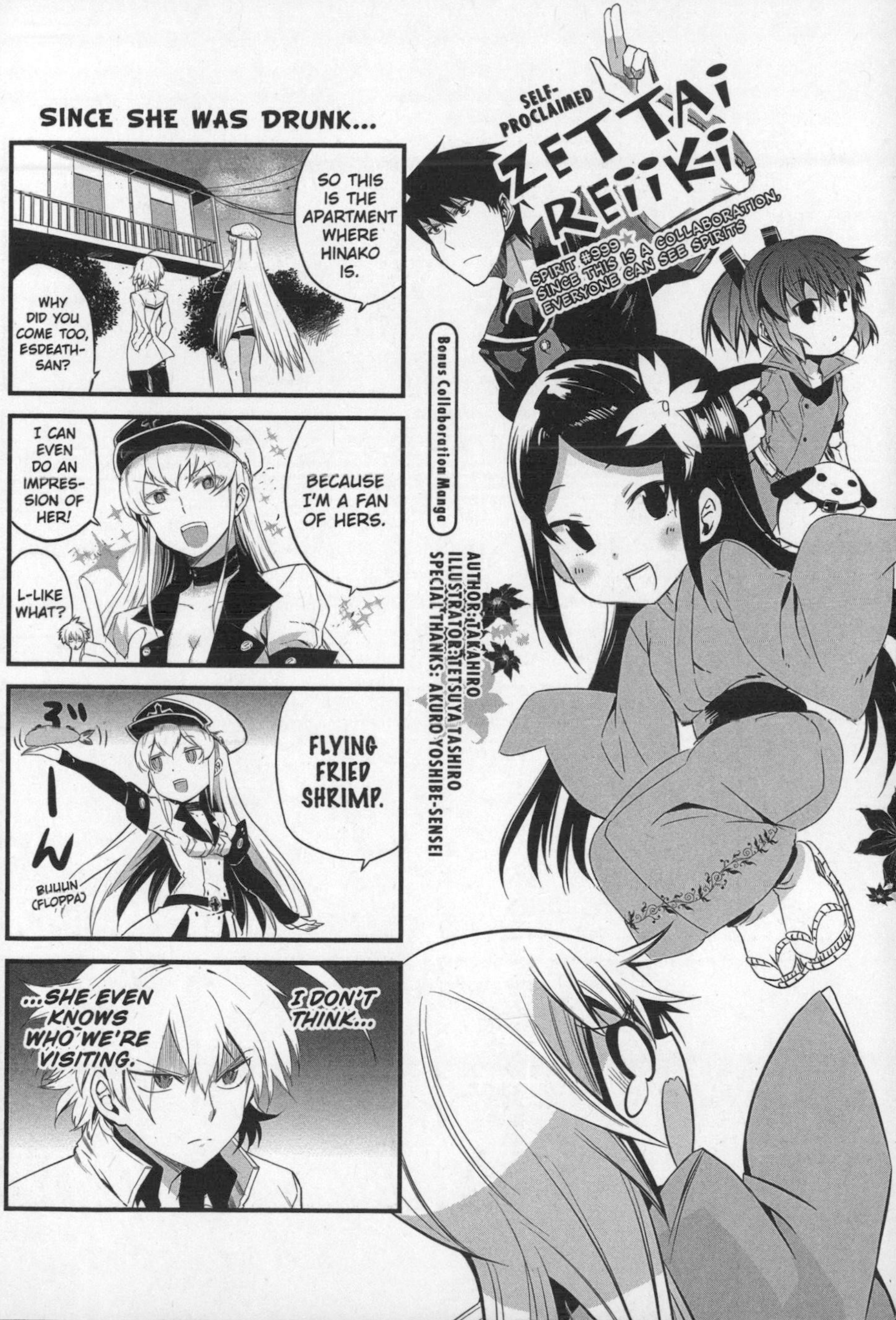
SELF-PROCLAIMED
ZETTAI REIIKI
SPIRIT #999 SINCE THIS IS A COLLABORATION, EVERYONE CAN SEE SPIRITS
Bonus Collaboration Manga
AUTHOR: TAKAHIRO
ILLUSTRATOR: TETSUYA TASHIRO
SPECIAL THANKS: AKURO YOSHIBE-SENSEI
SINCE SHE WAS DRUNK...
SO THIS IS THE APARTMENT WHERE HINAKO IS.
WHY DID YOU COME TOO, ESDEATH-SAN?
BECAUSE I'M A FAN OF HERS.
I CAN EVEN DO AN IMPRESSION OF HER!
L-LIKE WHAT?
FLYING FRIED SHRIMP.
BUUUN (FLOPPA)
I DON'T THINK...
...SHE EVEN KNOWS WHO WE'RE VISITING.

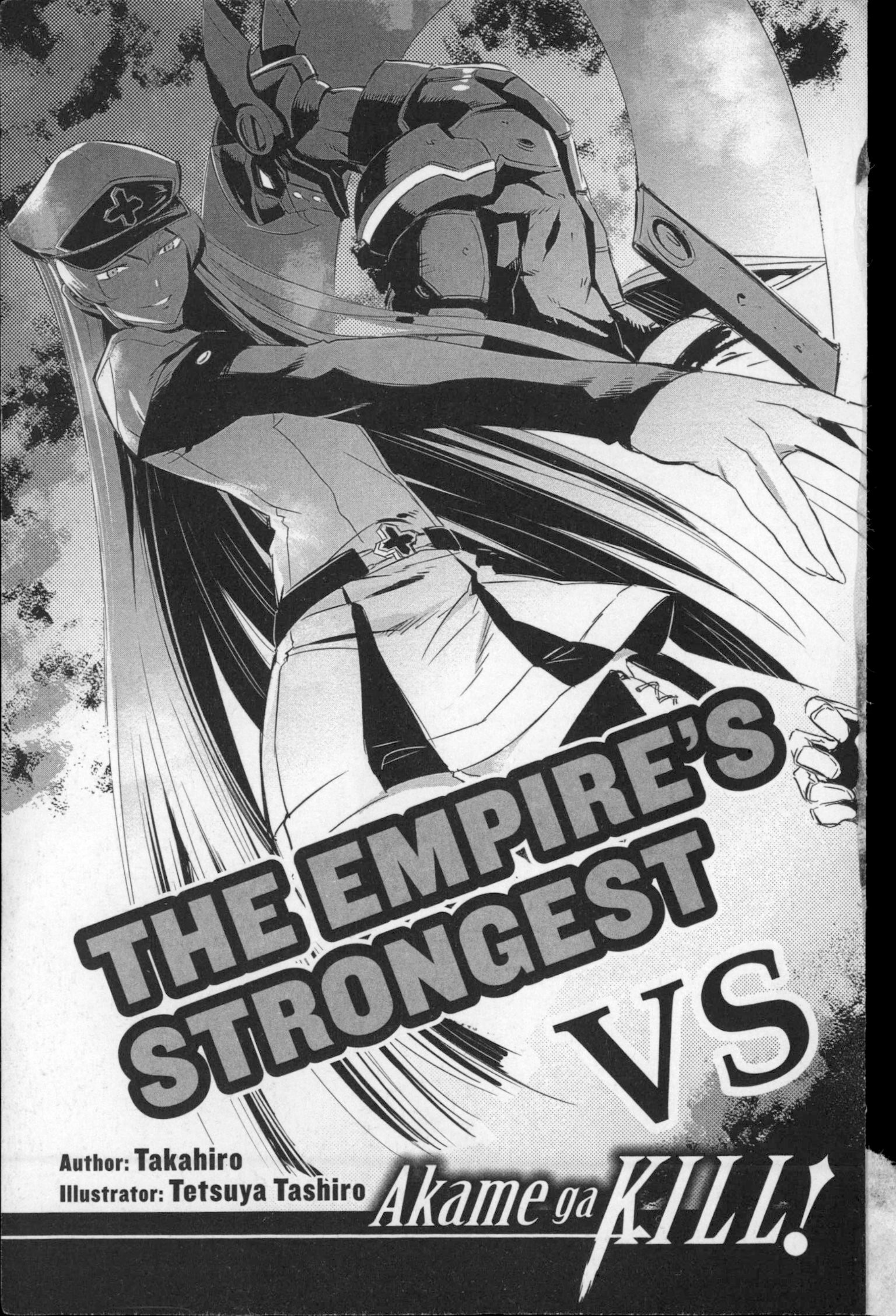
THE EMPIRE'S STRONGEST
VS
Author: Takahiro
Illustrator: Tetsuya Tashiro
Akame ga KILL!

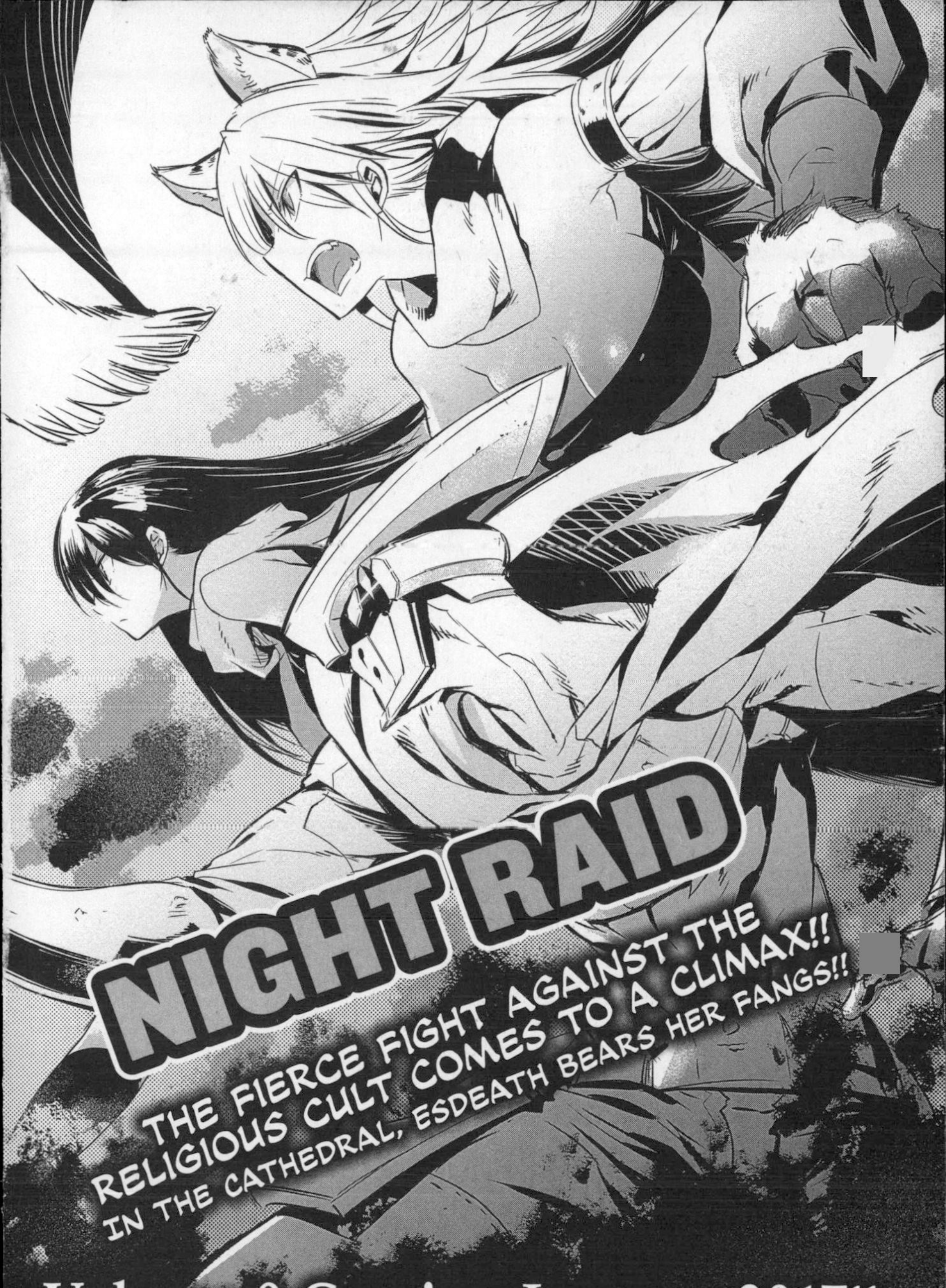
NIGHT RAID
THE FIERCE FIGHT AGAINST THE
RELIGIOUS CULT COMES TO A CLIMAX!!
IN THE CATHEDRAL, ESDEATH BEARS HER FANGS!!

Volume 9 Coming January 2017!!

# AKAME GA KILL 8

## STAFF

ITOU-SAN
IMAI-SAN
KANO-SAN
KITA-SAN
YAMAMOTO-SAN

THANK YOU
ALWAYS!

PEKOO
(BOW)

## ORIGINAL WRITER

TAKAHIRO-SAN

## EDITOR

KOIZUMI-SAN

SEE YA!

COME ON!
WE'RE
GOING,
CORO!

WE'RE ALREADY AT VOLUME 8! AND I'M STILL
ENJOYING MYSELF AS MUCH AS EVER.
I TRIED WRITING MY AFTERWORD DIGITALLY, BUT
SINCE I'M STILL LEARNING HOW TO USE IT, I CAN'T
YET USE IT FOR MY WORK IN THE ACTUAL BOOK.
I'M GOING TO KEEP TRYING MY HARDEST, SO
THANK YOU FOR ALL YOUR SUPPORT HEREAFTER.

| NAME | | | HP | MP | | | HIGH OUTPUT |
|------|---|---|-----|-----|---|---|---|
| MINE | | FIGHT | 22/500 | 28 | | LIMIT | BLAST |
| | | TEIGU | HIGH OUTPUT | | | | BLADE |
| | | | BLAST | | | | |
| | | | BLADE | | | | |

## THIS IS ALSO PURE LOVE

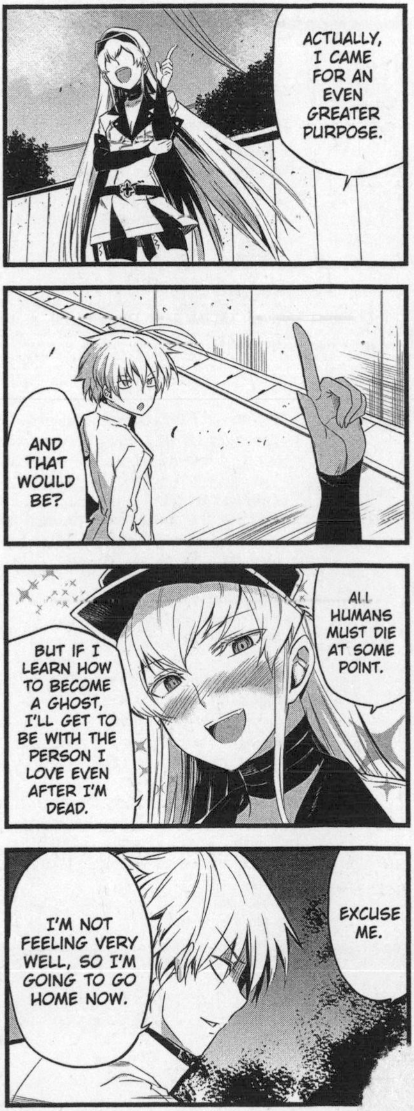
ACTUALLY, I CAME FOR AN EVEN GREATER PURPOSE.
AND THAT WOULD BE?
ALL HUMANS MUST DIE AT SOME POINT.
BUT IF I LEARN HOW TO BECOME A GHOST, I'LL GET TO BE WITH THE PERSON I LOVE EVEN AFTER I'M DEAD.
EXCUSE ME.
I'M NOT FEELING VERY WELL, SO I'M GOING TO GO HOME NOW.

## I LET MYSELF INTO YOUR ROOM

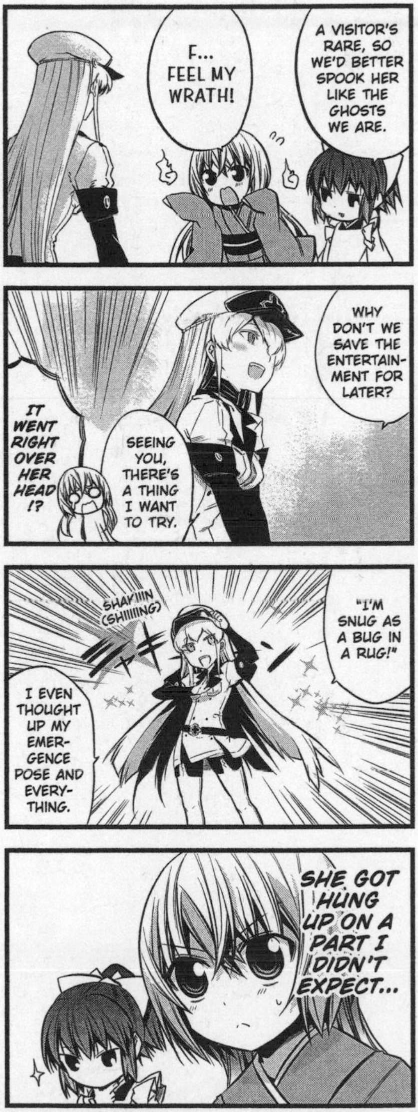
A VISITOR'S RARE, SO WE'D BETTER SPOOK HER LIKE THE GHOSTS WE ARE.
F... FEEL MY WRATH!
WHY DON'T WE SAVE THE ENTERTAINMENT FOR LATER?
SEEING YOU, THERE'S A THING I WANT TO TRY.
IT WENT RIGHT OVER HER HEAD!?
"I'M SNUG AS A BUG IN A RUG!"
I EVEN THOUGHT UP MY EMERGENCE POSE AND EVERYTHING.
SHE GOT HUNG UP ON A PART I DIDN'T EXPECT...

CHARACTERS FROM ZETTAI☆REIIKI: AKURO YOSHIBE-SENSEI

# AKAME GA KILL! 8

WITHDRAWN

**Takahiro**
**Tetsuya Tashiro**

**Translation: Christine Dashiell**
**Lettering: Erin Hickman**

AKAME GA KILL! Vol. 8
© 2013 Takahiro, Tetsuya Tashiro / SQUARE ENIX CO., LTD. First published in Japan in 2013 by SQUARE ENIX CO., LTD. English translation rights arranged with SQUARE ENIX CO., LTD. and Yen Press, LLC through Tuttle-Mori Agency, Inc., Tokyo.

English translation © 2016 by SQUARE ENIX CO., LTD.

Yen Press
1290 Avenue of the Americas
New York, NY 10104

Visit us at yenpress.com
facebook.com/yenpress
twitter.com/yenpress
yenpress.tumblr.com
instagram.com/yenpress

First Yen Press Edition: October 2016

Yen Press is an imprint of Yen Press, LLC.
The Yen Press name and logo are trademarks of Yen Press, LLC.

Library of Congress Control Number: 2015373812

ISBNs: 978-0-316-34011-3 (paperback)
       978-0-316-30594-5 (ebook)

10 9 8 7 6 5 4 3 2 1

BVG

Printed in the United States of America